THE
BEST
OF
Gourmet

THE BEST OF *Gourmet*

1993 EDITION

FROM THE EDITORS OF GOURMET

CONDÉ NAST BOOKS • RANDOM HOUSE, NEW YORK

Copyright © 1993 Condé Nast Publications, Inc.
All rights reserved under International and Pan-American
Copyright Conventions. Published in the United States by
Random House, Inc., New York, and simultaneously in Canada
by Random House of Canada Limited, Toronto.

LIBRARY OF CONGRESS
CATALOGING-IN-PUBLICATION DATA

(Revised for vol. 8)
Main entry under title:

The Best of Gourmet
  Includes Indexes
  1. Cookery, International. I. Gourmet.

TX723.B4686   1993   641.5945—dc20   92-36723
ISBN 0-679-42364-8 (v. 8)
ISSN 1046-1760
Most of the recipes in this work were published previously in
Gourmet Magazine.

Manufactured in the United States of America

98765432   24689753   23456789
First Edition

Grateful acknowledgment is made to Zanne Early Zakroff for
permission to reprint the following recipes previously published in
Gourmet Magazine:

"Asparagus Lasagne" (page 157); "Caviar Pancakes" (page
154); "Buttermilk Pancakes" (page 155); "Crab Salad" (page
195). Copyright ©—1992 by Zanne Early Zakroff. Reprinted by
permission of the author.

The following photographers have generously given their
permission to use the photographs listed below. With the
exception of Mr. Hanson's photograph, these photographs have
been published previously in *Gourmet* Magazine:

Robert Emmett Bright: "Tivoli" (page 274) Copyright © 1992.
Reprinted by permission of the photographer.

Ray Hanson: "Painter in Venice" (Table of Contents).
Copyright © 1992. Printed by permission of the photographer.

Ronny Jaques: "Sigurtà Park near Verona" (page 254) "Camogli
near Portofino" (page 266) "Positano" (page 282) Copyright ©
1982, 1991, and 1991. Reprinted by permission of the
photographer.

For Condé Nast Books

Jill Cohen, Vice President
Ellen Maria Bruzelius, Direct Marketing Manager
Kristine Smith-Cunningham, Advertising Promotion Manager
Mary Ellen Kelly, Fulfillment Manager
Lisa Faith Phillips, Direct Marketing Associate
Diane Pesce, Composition Production Manager
Serafino J. Cambareri, Quality Control Manager

For *Gourmet* Books

Diane Keitt, Editor
Judith Tropea, Associate Editor

For *Gourmet* Magazine

Gail Zweigenthal, Editor-in-Chief
Zanne Early Zakroff, Executive Food Editor
Kemp Miles Minifie, Senior Food Editor
Alexis M. Touchet, Associate Food Editor
Leslie Glover Pendleton, Food Editor
Amy Mastrangelo, Food Editor
Kathleen Nilon Atencio, Food Editor
Elizabeth S. Imperatore, Food Editor

Romulo A. Yanes, Photographer
Marjorie H. Webb, Stylist
Nancy Purdum, Stylist

Produced in association with **Media Projects Incorporated**

Carter Smith, Executive Editor
Anne Wright, Project Editor
Martina D'Alton, Associate Project Editor
Marilyn Flaig, Indexer
Michael Shroyer, Art/Production Director

The text of this book was set in Times Roman by the Composition
Department of Condé Nast Publications, Inc. and U. S.
Lithograph Typographers. The four-color separations were done
by The Color Company, Seiple Lithographers, and Applied
Graphic Technologies. The book was printed and bound at R. R.
Donnelley and Sons. Stock is Citation Web Gloss, Westvāco.

Front Jacket: "Chocolate Raspberry Cake" (page 216).

Back Jacket: "Lunch on the Lawn" (page 37).

Frontispiece: "Marinated Lobster Salad with Corn and
Tomatoes" (page 195).

ACKNOWLEDGMENTS

The Best of Gourmet, 1993 Edition is the compilation of shared ideas and skills, and the editors of *Gourmet* Books would like to thank the colleagues and freelancers who were so helpful in its creation.

This year, we turned to *Gourmet*'s Food Department to provide a sampler of regional foods of Italy for our Cuisines of the World section. Under the direction of Zanne Early Zakroff, three authentic menus were developed by Leslie Glover Pendleton (A Northern Buffet *alla Rustica*), Alexis M. Touchet (Dinner *alla Romana*), and Kathleen Nilon Atencio (Southern Sunday Lunch *in Famiglia*). All menus were photographed by Romulo Yanes and styled by Marjorie Webb and Nancy Purdum. Food stylists were Alexis M. Touchet, who styled her own menu, and Amy Mastrangelo. *Gourmet*'s Wine Editor, Gerald Asher, selected the wines for each menu; and *Gourmet* editor Lorraine Alexander, along with Anthony Russell, translated into Italian all menu and recipe titles throughout the section. Vivid line drawings by Agni Saucier and regional photography by Ronny Jaques, Robert Emmett Bright, and Ray Hanson transport us to Italy in spirit. We would also like to thank Steve Jenkins of Dean & DeLuca Inc., who graciously answered our questions about Italian cheese.

Georgia Chan Downard created and styled the outstanding Chocolate Raspberry Cake that appears on the front jacket. She also developed twenty-four delicious dinner party dishes from the freezer for this year's Addendum. Lovely line drawings by Lauren Jarrett complement this section.

We are also indebted to the many artists who provided the line drawings that appear throughout the book. They are Carla Borea, Beverly Charlton, Barbara Fiore, Kathy Foley Grimm, Vicky Harrison, Susie Howard, Lauren Jarrett, Zoe Elizabeth Mavridis, Jeanne Meinke, Agni Saucier, Jim Saucier, and Bebe Vann.

Michael Shroyer has been the designer for *The Best of Gourmet* for eight years and we would like to thank him for his continued hard work. Also, thank you to Elaine Richard for her care and attention to detail as she proofread the manuscript, and to Rebecca Ynocencio and Toni Rachiele, who answered our many editorial queries.

CONTENTS

INTRODUCTION 9

PART ONE: THE MENU COLLECTION 11

INTRODUCTION

The little pleasures in our lives make a significant difference. Whether it's a favorite restaurant where everyone knows our name, an old suit that fits perfectly, or simply the smile of a close friend, these dependable comforts make us feel good. And, either consciously or unconsciously, we grow to rely on them.

Over the years, our readers have come to count on *Gourmet* magazine and, consequently, on our annual collection of recipes. *The Best of Gourmet, 1993 Edition*, includes all the exciting menus that appeared in our columns during 1992. I particularly love our Enchanted Forest Birthday Parties (page 25), where inspired food creations and thematic settings capture a bit of magic that will please young and old alike. Chutney-Glazed Cornish Hens with Hazelnut and Dried-Fruit Stuffing and a very light Orange Chiffon Cake will dazzle your adult guests; while Individual Cheese and Pepperoni Pizzas and an Enchanted Forest Cake that looks just like the house Hansel and Gretel visited will surely thrill the little ones. When a simpler menu is desired, perhaps you'll enjoy our refreshing Dinner on the Veranda featuring Veal Scallops with Lemon and Artichokes, or our delightful Brunch on Christmas Day with Scalloped Potato, Cheddar, and Chive Pie....

All our menus are accompanied by full-color photographs that provide wonderful table setting ideas. And, of course, when you are looking for that perfect single dish, over 400 recipes of every description await in the Recipe Compendium.

In 1992, after celebrating our 50th anniversary here at *Gourmet*, we decided to surprise our readers with two new columns. Take an indulgent food passion and transform it into a recipe that dreams are made of, and you have Forbidden Pleasures, created by Zanne Early Zakroff, our executive food editor. Caviar Pan-cakes, Asparagus Lasagne, and Crab Salad are just a few of her sinfully good creations. On a more practical note, our food editors present Twice as Good, a column that gives you two meals for the work of one. For example, the planned leftovers from a Sunday dinner's Garlic-and-Soy-Marinated Pork Roast with Shiitake Mushroom Gravy can be prepared with additional mixed vegetables for a quick Thursday night repast of Pork Chow Mein. You'll find our favorite recipes from both of these brand-new columns in this volume.

But the best of the past year is not all this collection has to offer. It also includes two original sections, each filled with all-new recipes. This year Cuisines of the World takes you to Italy. Here we offer practical information on some of the essentials of the Italian kitchen—pasta, polenta, olive oil, and cheese. Then, three exceptional regional menus—A Northern Buffet *alla Rustica*, a Dinner *alla Romana*, and a Southern Sunday Lunch *in Famiglia*—highlight these basics and give you a real taste of this glorious country. Over 30 pages of helpful information, menus, and breathtaking photography of the country and its food begin on page 253.

This year's addendum, Dinner Party Dishes from the Freezer (page 289), offers a helping hand to all of us who enjoy entertaining but sometimes have difficulty finding the time. Our 24 make-ahead-and-freeze recipes can easily be mixed and matched to create a variety of delicious menus. We promise, no one will ever guess that *anything* was made weeks before.

As you can see, *The Best of Gourmet*, now in its eighth edition, is one annual that constantly gives you more. Personally, I would hate to be without it, and I think you'll feel the same way.

Gail Zweigenthal
Editor-in-Chief

THE MENU COLLECTION

*I*t's always time to entertain. After all, inviting family and friends to your home is one of life's pleasures. Before hosting your next dinner party, peruse The Menu Collection at your leisure, and let these 70 pages of spectacular photographs inspire you. Beautiful décor, sensational table settings, and, of course, wonderful meals are now at your fingertips. Twenty-four creative menus from the 1992 columns, *Gourmet*'s Menus and Cuisine Courante, await. And what an assortment there is—casual or elegant, alfresco or by the hearth, for two or for twenty—all are gathered here to stimulate you with year-round entertaining ideas.

Gourmet is particularly conscious of time, or the lack of it. To accommodate the needs of today's host, we have created additional make-ahead fare, as well as some shorter menus, that will allow you to spend more time with your guests. For example, on a chilly winter night we suggest our Hearty One-Pot Dinner of warming Cassoulet (White Bean Casserole with Pork, Lamb, and Duck), a Mixed Green Salad of *arugula* and *frisée* lettuce, and a tempting Gingerbread Roll with Lemon Cream Filling. This simple meal can be prepared ahead—it will surely delight your guests, and allow you to enjoy their company. Or, on a sunny afternoon let *Gourmet* show you how the grill can be your best friend as you enjoy our Lunch on the Lawn. Flavorful Bruschetta with Arugula, Smoked Mozzarella, and Tomatoes; tender Grilled Porterhouse Steaks with Olive and Caper Spread; and Mixed Grilled Vegetables can *all* be cooked outdoors. And for dessert, both the refreshing Cappuccino Gelato and the delicious Chocolate Nut Cookies can be made days before the party.

But while time is usually short, there are also those inspired occasions when a bit more preparation is well worth the effort. Our Enchanted Forest Birthday Parties, designed for young and old alike, let your imagination soar. Decorated with cinnamon/nutmeg party favors and assorted toy woodland animals, this fanciful celebration boasts inventive dishes such as Potato Nests with Sautéed Shiitake Mushrooms for the adults, and a chocolate "forest cabin" cake for the children.

Of course, you will also find all the wonderfully elegant holiday meals that you have come to expect from *Gourmet*. If it's your turn to host Thanksgiving dinner, try our updated menu of autumn classics that will surely make your mother proud. Sweet potatoes appear in a creamy soup with buttered pecans, followed by the star of the day—golden roast turkey accompanied by sophisticated herbed oyster stuffing and giblet gravy. Then, indulge your guests with *two* American favorites—Brandied Pumpkin Pie and Sour Cream Apple Pie—both topped with a dash of fresh Ginger Whipped Cream.

Christmas is also celebrated with style. This year, two festive menus give you the option of hosting a formal gathering or a more casual affair. For a traditional celebration, impress your guests with a fancy Three-Onion, Sun-Dried Tomato, and Olive Tart, succulent Roast Prime Ribs of Beef with Shiitake Pan Gravy, and, for dessert, a merry frozen cranberry soufflé! If you're having a more informal gathering our Brunch on Christmas Day will be sure to please with Cranberry Apple Cocktails followed by Scalloped Potato, Cheddar, and Chive Pie.

Gerald Asher, *Gourmet*'s wine editor, has recommended complementary beverage selections for each of our menus. His attentive choices include everything from robust Samuel Adams Winter Lager for our hearty New England Fireside Dinner to Cossart Special Ten-Year-Old Madeira to honor the scholar at our Graduation Dinner. These expert suggestions take the worry out of choosing the perfect libation for any meal.

Unique ideas and fine details abound in this collection. We hope the following pages will intrigue you and inspire you to be your creative best. The next time you entertain, bring a little bit of *Gourmet* into your home.

A QUINCENTENNIAL
CELEBRATION
1492–1992

Wild Rice and Spiced Shrimp Salad, p. 208

---

*Herb-Roasted Pork Loin
with Bourbon Gravy, p. 128*

Savory Corn Bread Pudding, p. 128

Sautéed Green Beans, p. 169

McDowell Valley Vineyards Le Trésor '87

---

*Chocolate-Frosted Devil's Food Cake
with Pecan and Coconut Filling, p. 214*

Heitz Cellar Angelica '74

Herb-Roasted Pork Loin with Bourbon Gravy;
Savory Corn Bread Pudding; Sautéed Green Beans

Chocolate-Frosted Devil's Food Cake
with Pecan and Coconut Filling

15

Cassoulet; Mixed Green Salad;
French Bread

HEARTY
ONE-POT DINNERS

Cassoulet, p. 170

Mixed Green Salad, p. 199

French Bread

Gigondas '89

---

*Gingerbread Roll with
Lemon Cream Filling, p. 218*

◆

Brazilian-Style Black Bean Stew, p. 168

*Boston Lettuce, Orange, and Onion Salad
with Citrus Chili Vinaigrette, p. 198*

Cuvaison Napa Valley Merlot '89

Caramelized Pineapple and Frangipane Tart, p. 235

◆

VALENTINE'S DAY
DINNER FOR TWO

Waffled Sweet-Potato Chips, p. 184

Bollinger '85

---

*Artichoke Heart and
Brin d'Amour Ravioli
with Three-Pepper Sauce,* p. 159

Seaview South Australian Sémillon/Chardonnay '89

Rack of Lamb with Cumin and Thyme, p. 135

*Hearts of Fennel
with Lemon and Coriander,* p. 176

Potatoes Parisienne, p. 180

Palmer Vineyards Long Island Cabernet Franc '89

Individual Chocolate Soufflés, p. 236

Cyprus Commandaria

Rack of Lamb with
Cumin and Thyme;
Hearts of Fennel with
Lemon and Coriander;
Potatoes Parisienne

Waffled Sweet-Potato Chips

Artichoke Heart and
Brin d'Amour Ravioli
with Three-Pepper Sauce

AN HORS D'OEUVRE BUFFET FOR THE OLYMPICS

Asian Spring Rolls, p. 87

Chicken Wings Africana, p. 88

Pirozhki, p. 94

Pissaladières, p. 92

*Spanish-Style Garlic Shrimp
with Ham and Bell Peppers, p. 96*

*South American-Style
Jícama and Orange Salad, p. 90*

Apple Raisin Strudels, p. 243

Kenwood Sonoma County Sauvignon Blanc '90

Heineken lager

Clausthaler non-alcoholic malt beverage

Asian Spring Rolls; Chicken Wings Africana;
Pirozhki; South American-Style
Jícama and Orange Salad; Pissaladière

For the Adults

ENCHANTED FOREST
BIRTHDAY PARTIES

FOR THE ADULTS

*Chutney-Glazed Cornish Hens
with Hazelnut and
Dried-Fruit Stuffing, p. 142*

*Potato Nests
with Sautéed Shiitake Mushrooms, p. 184*

Lemon-Buttered Broccoli Spears, p. 172

Sancerre Rouge '89

Orange Chiffon Cake, p. 220

Muscat of Samos

FOR THE CHILDREN

Basket of Crudités

*Individual Cheese and
Pepperoni Pizzas, p. 101*

Trail Mix, p. 247

Apple Juice

Enchanted Forest Cake, p. 216

Chutney-Glazed Cornish Hens with Hazelnut and
Dried-Fruit Stuffing; Potato Nests with Sautéed
Shiitake Mushrooms; Lemon-Buttered Broccoli Spears

For the Children—Basket of Crudités;
Individual Cheese and Pepperoni Pizzas;
Trail Mix; Enchanted Forest Cake

Beet Flowers and Beet Greens Vinaigrette

CUISINE COURANTE

A NEW ENGLAND FIRESIDE DINNER

Corned Beef with
Horseradish Mustard Sauce, p. 122

Steamed Root Vegetables
and Cabbage with Dill, p. 189

Boiled Yukon Gold Potatoes

Beet Flowers and
Beet Greens Vinaigrette, p. 171

Samuel Adams Winter Lager

Maple Walnut Pie, p. 232

EASTER LUNCHEON

Asparagus Napoleons
with Oriental Black Bean Sauce, p. 166

Firestone Rosé of Cabernet Sauvignon '90

———————

Boneless Leg of Lamb
Stuffed with Swiss Chard and Feta, p. 134

Spiced Quinoa Timbales, p. 135

Honey-Glazed Baby Carrots, p. 173

Mesclun Salad, p. 199

Boutari Naoussa '88

———————

Frozen Strawberry Lemon Meringue Torte, p. 240

Asti Spumante

Boneless Leg of Lamb Stuffed with Swiss Chard and Feta;
Spiced Quinoa Timbales; Honey-Glazed Baby Carrots

Frozen Strawberry Lemon Meringue Torte

A SPRING BRUNCH

Lemon Gem Muffins with Cream Cheese, p. 103

Papaya in Cinnamon Syrup, p. 246

Ham and Egg Biscuit Pizzas, p. 153

Aquavit Bloody Marys, p. 248

Café au Lait, p. 252

Aquavit Bloody Marys; Lemon Gem Muffins;
Ham and Egg Biscuit Pizzas; Papaya in Cinnamon Syrup

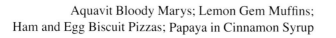

Bruschetta with Arugula,
Smoked Mozzarella, and Tomatoes

LUNCH
ON THE LAWN

Bruschetta with Arugula,
Smoked Mozzarella, and Tomatoes, p. 103

Lemonade

Grilled Porterhouse Steaks
with Olive and Caper Spread, p. 122

Mixed Grilled Vegetables, p. 188

Arborio Rice Salad
with Cucumber and Mint, p. 206

Grand Cru Vineyards
Sonoma County Cabernet Sauvignon '88

Cappuccino Gelato, p. 238

Chocolate Nut Cookies, p. 226

Grilled Porterhouse Steaks with Olive and Caper Spread; Arborio Rice Salad with Cucumber and Mint; Mixed Grilled Vegetables

Asparagus and Dill Avgolemono Soup

A SPRING DINNER

Asparagus and Dill Avgolemono Soup, p. 105

Chicken Breasts with Scallions,
Shiitake Mushrooms, and Tomatoes, p. 140

Herbed Farfalle, p. 156

Pea and Watercress Purée, p. 179

Stag's Leap Wine Cellars
Napa Valley Sauvignon Blanc '90

Orange Poppy-Seed Cake with Berries
and Crème Fraîche, p. 221

Freemark Abbey Edelwein Gold '91

Chicken Breasts with Scallions, Shiitake Mushrooms,
and Tomatoes; Herbed Farfalle; Pea and Watercress Purée

A BRIDAL

LUNCHEON

Champagne Punch, p. 248

———————

Lobster and Mango Cocktail, p. 117

———————

**Curried Smoked Chicken
and Wild Rice Salad**, p. 194

Mixed Vegetables Vinaigrette, p. 188

Reichsgraf von Kesselstatt Kaseler Nies'chen Kabinett '89

———————

Apricot Berry Trifle, p. 244

Candied Ginger Shortbread Hearts, p. 228

———————

Dr. Bürklin-Wolf Wachenheimer Gerümpel Auslese '89

Lobster and Mango Cocktail

Curried Smoked Chicken and Wild Rice Salad;
Mixed Vegetables Vinaigrette

A GRADUATION DINNER

Mumm Cuvée Napa Winery Lake '88 Brut

Red-Leaf Lettuce, Radish,
and Pine Nut Salad, p. 199

Roasted Loin of Veal with
Garlic, Shallots, and Mustard Gravy, p. 124

Paprika Potato Rosettes, p. 181

Sugar Snap Peas with Lemon Butter, p. 187

Château Figeac Premier Grand Cru Saint-Émilion '70

Bittersweet Chocolate Pecan Bourbon Cake, p. 214

Cossart Special Ten-Year-Old Madeira

Roasted Loin of Veal with Garlic, Shallots, and Mustard Gravy;
Paprika Potato Rosettes; Sugar Snap Peas with Lemon Butter

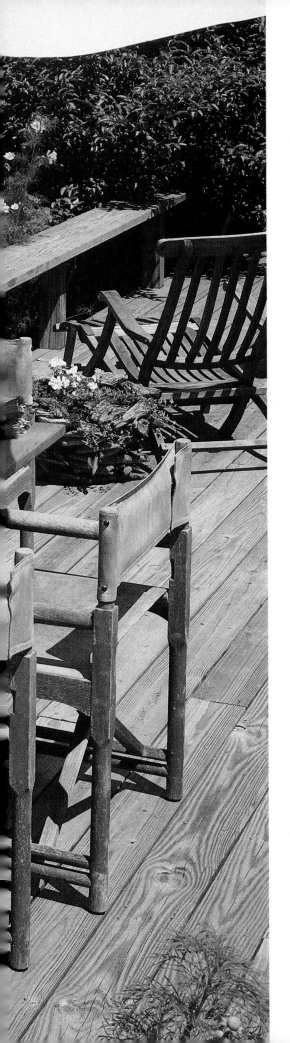

FOURTH OF JULY
PICNIC BY THE SEA

Chilled Tomato Basil Soup, p. 110

Garlic Baguette Toasts, p. 104

———————

Grilled Seafood Salad Niçoise, p. 196

*Greenwood Ridge
Johannisberg Riesling '91*

———————

Summer Berry Mint Cream Tart, p. 234

Chilled Tomato Basil Soup

Grilled Seafood Salad Niçoise

Summer Berry Mint Cream Tart

CUISINE COURANTE

A BASTILLE DAY COCKTAIL PARTY

*Cornmeal and Shallot Madeleines
with Crème Fraîche and Caviar, p. 89*

Quail Eggs with Olive Paste, p. 95

Savory Cheese Galette, p. 88

Crab Salad with Hearts of Palm, p. 90

Brandade de Morue Canapés, p. 98

Monégasque-Style Onions, p. 92

Charles Heidsieck Brut Reserve Champagne

Lillet au Citron, p. 248

Pernod and Water, p. 249

''Two-Dollar Cocktail'', p. 249

Cornmeal and Shallot Madeleines with Crème Fraîche and Caviar;
Lillet au Citron; Quail Eggs with Olive Paste ;
Savory Cheese Galette; ''Two-Dollar Cocktail'';
Pernod and Water; Crab Salad with Hearts of Palm

DINNER BY THE BAY

*Melon with Prosciutto
and Parmesan Curls,* p. 91

Arneis dei Roeri, Cantina Vietti '90

———————

*White Bean, Pasta, and Grilled Duck Salad
with Orange Cumin Vinaigrette,* p. 192

Herbed Pita Toasts, p. 104

Bianco di Valguarnera Duca di Salaparuta '88

———————

Key Lime Cheesecake, p. 220

White Bean, Pasta, and Grilled Duck Salad with
Orange Cumin Vinaigrette; Herbed Pita Toasts

Key Lime Cheesecake

Tomato, Arugula, and Ricotta Salata Salad

DINNER FROM
A COOL KITCHEN

Tomato, Arugula, and Ricotta Salata Salad, p. 197

*Cold Poached Chicken Breasts
with Tuna Basil Sauce,* p. 140

*Minted Green Beans
with Red Onion,* p. 169

Assorted Breads

White Oak Sonoma County Chardonnay '90

Toasted Almond Mocha Ice-Cream Tart, p. 238

Cold Poached Chicken Breasts with Tuna Basil Sauce;
Minted Green Beans with Red Onion; Assorted Breads

DINNER ON
THE VERANDA

Cascinetta Moscato d'Asti '91

———————

Spinach and Oyster Bisque, p. 109

———————

Veal Scallops with Lemon and Artichokes, p. 124

Roasted Potatoes and Cauliflower with Chives, p. 181

Baked Herbed Tomatoes, p. 190

Chicory and Carrot Salad, p. 198

Antinori Santa Cristina '90

———————

Black Bottom Butterscotch Cream Pie, p. 230

Spinach and Oyster Bisque

Black Bottom Butterscotch Cream Pie

Veal Scallops with Lemon and Artichokes; Roasted Potatoes
and Cauliflower with Chives; Baked Herbed Tomatoes

A LABOR DAY PICNIC
RAIN OR SHINE

Cumin Tortilla Crisps, p. 97

*Picadillo Empanadas with
Cornmeal Crust*, p. 120

Oven-Fried Chipotle Chili Chicken, p. 141

*Cucumber, Radish, and Tomato Salad
with Citrus Dressing*, p. 203

Pecan Coconut Tart, p. 235

"Damn the Weather" Cocktails, p. 248

Tequila Sunrises, p. 249

"Damn the Weather" Cocktails; Tequila Sunrises; Cumin Tortilla Crisps;
Picadillo Empanadas with Cornmeal Crust; Oven-Fried Chipotle Chili Chicken;
Cucumber, Radish, and Tomato Salad with Citrus Dressing

AN ELEGANT
FALL DINNER

Garlic Potato Purée with
Shiitake Ragout and
Potato Crisps, p. 183

Château Léoville-Barton Saint-Julien '87

———————

Five-Spice Roasted Guinea Hens, p. 143

Steamed Broccoli Rabe, p. 143

Lemon Barley Spring Rolls, p. 160

Château Ducru-Beaucaillou Saint-Julien '79

———————

Pistachio Praline Dacquoise, p. 222

Château Doisy-Védrines Sauternes '83

Five-Spice Roasted Guinea Hen;
Steamed Broccoli Rabe; Lemon Barley Spring Rolls

Pistachio Praline Dacquoise

Babas au Calvados with Glazed Apple Rings

CUISINE COURANTE

A SUNDAY
BISTRO SUPPER

Frisée Salad with
Goat Cheese Croques-Monsieurs, p. 198

Braised Lamb Shanks with
Tomatoes and Rosemary, p. 136

White Bean and
Watercress Gratin, p. 170

Guenoc North Coast Petite Sirah '89

Babas au Calvados with
Glazed Apple Rings, p. 242

Braised Lamb Shanks with Tomatoes and
Rosemary; White Bean and Watercress Gratin

THANKSGIVING
DINNER

Sweet Potato Soup with Buttered Pecans, p. 109

---

*Roast Turkey with Herbed Oyster Stuffing
and Giblet Gravy*, p. 144

Potato, Chestnut, and Celery Root Purée, p. 182

Diced Carrots and Turnips, p. 173

Lemon Rosemary Green Beans, p. 169

Jellied Apple Cranberry Sauce, p. 210

Bouchaine Carneros-Napa Valley Pinot Noir '88

Brandied Pumpkin Pie, p. 232   *Sour Cream Apple Pie*, p. 229

Ginger Whipped Cream, p. 230

Henry Winery Umpqua Valley Select Cluster White Riesling '87

Sweet Potato Soup with Buttered Pecans

Roast Turkey with Herbed Oyster Stuffing and
Giblet Gravy; Jellied Apple Cranberry Sauce;
Diced Carrots and Turnips; Lemon Rosemary
Green Beans; Potato, Chestnut, and Celery Root Purée

Goat Cheese and Pistachio Spread

CUISINE COURANTE

ELECTION NIGHT
POTLUCK SUPPER

Goat Cheese and Pistachio Spread, p. 100

---

*Layered Vegetable Salad with
Caper and Thyme Dressing, p. 204*

*Pork Fricassee with
Mushrooms and Carrots, p. 130*

Paprika Rice, p. 130

Château Ste. Michelle Columbia Valley Johannisberg Riesling '91

---

*Chocolate Buttermilk Layer Cake
with Chocolate Pudding Frosting, p. 213*

Layered Vegetable Salad with Caper and Thyme Dressing;
Pork Fricassee with Mushrooms and Carrots; Paprika Rice

CHRISTMAS DINNER

*Three-Onion, Sun-Dried Tomato,
and Olive Tart*, p. 93

Iron Horse Brut '88

---

*Roast Prime Ribs of Beef
with Shiitake Pan Gravy*, p. 122

Dried-Corn Puddings, p. 123

Broccoli with Lemon and Red Pepper Flakes, p. 172

*Watercress, Bell Pepper,
and Daikon Radish Salad*, p. 200

Plam Vineyards Napa Valley Cabernet Sauvignon '88

Walnut Spice Cake with Lemon Glaze, p. 224

*Frozen Cranberry Soufflé
with Spun Sugar Cranberry Wreath*, p. 237

Robert Mondavi Sauvignon Blanc Botrytis '85

Roast Prime Ribs of Beef with Shiitake Pan Gravy;
Dried-Corn Puddings; Broccoli with Lemon and Red Pepper Flakes

Walnut Spice Cake with Lemon Glaze;
Frozen Cranberry Soufflé
with Spun Sugar Cranberry Wreath

BRUNCH ON
CHRISTMAS DAY

*Scalloped Potato, Cheddar,
and Chive Pie*, p. 182

*Baked Irish Bacon
with Kumquat Glaze*, p. 131

*Red and Green Endive
and Walnut Salad*, p. 198

Cranberry Apple Cocktails, p. 250

*Winter Fruit Compote
with Ginger*, p. 247

Red and Green Endive and Walnut Salad;
Scalloped Potato, Cheddar, and Chive Pie;
Baked Irish Bacon with Kumquat Glaze;
Cranberry Apple Cocktails

A RECIPE COMPENDIUM

$\mathcal{I}$n keeping with tradition, Part Two of *The Best of Gourmet*, A Recipe Compendium, is a collection of the best recipes that appeared in *Gourmet* magazine during the previous year. Gathered here are all the recipes from *Gourmet*'s Menus and Cuisine Courante columns that are pictured in Part One, The Menu Collection, as well as selections from the magazine's other food columns—Gastronomie Sans Argent, In Short Order, and The Last Touch. During 1992 *two* new columns were introduced to *Gourmet* and now we have the pleasure of including sample dishes from both Forbidden Pleasures and Twice as Good.

These new additions to the magazine satisfy the indulgent and practical sides in all of us. Forbidden Pleasures gratifies the small bouts of excess and self-indulgence we all enjoy from time to time. The recipes from this column throw caution to the wind and encourage us to revel in the delight of a favorite food. Sumptuous Caviar Pancakes topped with sour cream and drizzled with brown butter and rich Asparagus Lasagne made with goat cheese and heavy cream are just two of the treats you can enjoy for an occasional splurge. On the other hand, Twice as Good answers to the call of economy and efficiency, along with the love of good food. Here, with only a bit of extra effort, two dishes can be made from the work of one. Poached Salmon with Green Peppercorn, Ginger, and Orange Sauce, for example, can be transformed into tasty Salmon Cakes a few days later. All it takes is some left-over salmon and a few additional ingredients, and dinner number-two is served!

When fruit and vegetables appear at your local farm stand or supermarket, it's always wise to stock up on the freshest bounty available. Gastronomie Sans Argent offers inexpensive ways to create a variety of exceptional dishes with the best the season has to offer. This spring, when juicy grapefruits are at their peak, look beyond breakfast to enjoy this refreshing fruit. Fish Fillets with Grapefruit Tarragon Beurre Blanc or Roast Pork Loin with Grapefruit makes an innovative entrée. For dessert, the tart citrus delightfully complements sweet partners in Grapefruit and Coconut Angel Pie; Gingered Grapefruit Sorbet; and Grapefruit and Banana Rum Gratins. And, in the summer those extra ears of fresh corn-on-the-cob take pride of place in an intriguing array of recipes—Grilled Corn and Shrimp Salad; Corn Chowder with Roasted Jalapeño and Parsley Purée; Fresh Corn, Cheddar, and Scallion Corn Bread; and Corn and Bacon Pancakes, to name a few.

Certain foods are associated with a particular season even if they are available year-round. Hearty sausage is a natural pleaser in the cold winter months, when its warming qualities enhance robust dishes such as Braised Sausage with Olives and Potatoes; Pasta with Kielbasa and Broccoli Rabe; Sausage and Feta Phyllo Triangles; Split-Pea Soup with Chorizo; and Sausage and Eggplant Kebabs with Hot Chili Sauce. During the hot and humid summer months keep a cool kitchen by cooking marinated meats out on the grill. Grilled Beef Blade Steaks and Bell Peppers with Spicy Orange Marinade; Barbecued Chili-Marinated Pork Spareribs; Grilled Apple- and Herb-Marinated Pork Chops and Potatoes; and Grilled Lamb Chops with Yogurt and Mint Marinade offer you plenty of choice for a memorable barbecue.

When you are pressed for time (and who isn't these days?) you can choose from the eclectic collection of

Lemon Gem Muffins; Ham and Egg Biscuit Pizzas;
Aquavit Bloody Marys; Papaya in Cinnamon Syrup

recipes culled from In Short Order. This column offers dishes for two that can be prepared in 45 minutes or less and mixed and matched as you please. The next time a friend stops in on a rainy afternoon, instead of braving the storm to find a restaurant, turn to a well-stocked kitchen and prepare Hot Open-Faced Ham, Swiss Cheese, and Mushroom Sandwiches; or Baked Orzo with Cheddar and Pepperoni; or maybe Bacon, Avocado, and Cheese Omelets with Tomato Salsa. If you are expecting a guest for a weeknight dinner, perhaps Warm Scallop, Black Bean, and Bell Pepper Salad or Grilled Chicken Breast with Arugula and Olive Thyme Vinaigrette will fit the bill—especially when followed by Coconut Snowballs with Mocha Sauce or Nectarine Almond Cobbler.

In Short Order recipes can also suit the most elegant occasions. Sautéed Filets Mignons with Peppered Cuminseed Crusts will impress any guest, particularly if accompanied by Spinach and Endive Salad with Blue Cheese Dressing. Fresh Strawberries with Zabaglione makes a perfect light finale to this inspired menu. Use our 45-Minute Index at the back of the book to help you find all these quick dishes easily.

And for the times when you need a little something to complete a near-perfect meal, The Last Touch provides thematic recipes that have *Gourmet* style. Begin a lovely warm-weather party with summer hors d'oeuvres, including Mustard-Ginger Shrimp Canapés; Cherry Tomatoes with Roasted Garlic Filling; Scallop Puffs; and Hoisin and Honey Pork Riblets. Or perhaps you want to complete a meal on a simple, sweet note with one or more of our delicious bar cookies—Triple-Chocolate Fudge Brownies; Peanut Butter Coconut Bars; or Apple Date-Nut Bars. You'll even find various quick mayonnaise sauces that will add a special touch to sandwiches, meats, salads, and vegetables—Curry Mayonnaise; Jalapeño Garlic Sauce; Tahini Mint Sauce; Spinach Herb Sauce; Lemon-Pepper Dill Sauce, and more.

Whether it's an hors d'oeuvre or a dessert, an elaborate entrée or a quick sandwich, a caloric indulgence or a healthful salad, you'll find it all in The Recipe Compendium. Take your time and flip through this organized collection of *Gourmet*'s best offerings. Whatever the occasion, whoever the guest, The Recipe Compendium has a dish to suit your needs.

HORS D'OEUVRES, CANAPÉS, DIPS AND SPREADS

HORS D'OEUVRES

Asian Spring Rolls

For the spring rolls

2 ounces cellophane (bean-thread) noodles*,
soaked in boiling-hot water to cover for
20 minutes, drained well, and chopped
6 dried *shiitake* mushrooms*, soaked in hot
water to cover for 20 minutes, rinsed,
squeezed dry, the stems discarded, and the
caps sliced thin
¾ pound lean ground pork
3 garlic cloves, minced
3 large shallots, minced
1 tablespoon minced peeled fresh gingerroot
1 large carrot, shredded
⅓ cup chopped fresh coriander
⅓ cup chopped fresh mint leaves
1 cup chopped mung bean sprouts*
2 tablespoons soy sauce
1½ teaspoons salt
1 teaspoon sugar
20 spring-roll wrappers*
an egg wash made by beating 1 large egg
with 1 teaspoon water
vegetable oil for deep-frying

For the dipping sauce

¼ cup soy sauce
¼ cup fresh lime juice
2 tablespoons water
2 garlic cloves, minced and mashed to a paste
with ½ teaspoon salt
2 tablespoons sugar
a 2-inch fresh red or green chili, seeded and
minced (wear rubber gloves), or
¼ teaspoon dried hot red pepper flakes,
or to taste

scallion brushes (page 88) for garnish

*available at Asian markets, some specialty
foods shops, and many supermarkets

Make the spring rolls: In a large bowl combine well the noodles, the mushrooms, the pork, the garlic, the shallots, the gingerroot, the carrot, the coriander, the mint, the sprouts, the soy sauce, the salt, and the sugar. Put 1 spring-roll wrapper on a work surface, keeping the remaining wrappers covered with plastic wrap, cut it in half diagonally, and arrange one half with the longest side facing you. Spread a rounded tablespoon of the filling down the long side, leaving a 2-inch border at each end, and brush the edges with some of the egg wash. Fold the corners of the long side over the filling and, rolling away from you, roll up the filling in the wrapper, sealing the roll, using some of the remaining egg wash if necessary. Make more spring rolls with the remaining filling, wrappers, and egg wash in the same manner, transferring them as they are made to a wax-paper–lined baking sheet and keeping them covered with plastic wrap. In a deep fryer heat 1¼ inches of the oil to 375° F. on a deep-fat thermometer and in it fry the spring rolls in batches, turning them, for 2 to 3 minutes, or until they are golden, transferring them as they are fried with a slotted spoon to paper towels to drain. *The spring rolls may be made 5 days in advance, cooled completely, and kept frozen in plastic freezer bags. Reheat the rolls, unthawed, on a rack set in a shallow baking pan in a preheated 450° F. oven for 10 minutes.*

Make the dipping sauce: In a small bowl stir together the soy sauce, the lime juice, the water, the garlic paste, the sugar, and the chili.

Cut the rolls diagonally into 1-inch-thick slices, arrange the slices on a platter with the sauce, and garnish the platter with the scallion brushes. Makes 40 rolls.

PHOTO ON PAGE 22

To Make Scallion Brushes

Trim the roots and the green parts from scallions, leaving about 2½ inches of stalk. Make crisscross cuts about ½ inch deep at both ends of each stalk and spread the fringed ends gently. Put the scallions in a bowl of ice and cold water and chill them for 2 hours, or until the fringed ends have curled. Drain the scallions well.

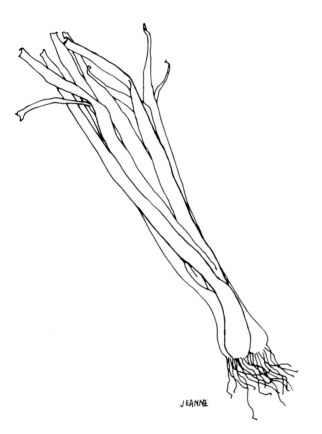

JEANNE

Savory Cheese Galette

For the filling
1 pound Roquefort or Camembert, softened and the rind discarded
¼ cup heavy cream
¼ cup dry white wine
1 large egg yolk
2 tablespoons all-purpose flour

3 cups all-purpose flour
2 tablespoons sugar
¼ teaspoon salt
1½ sticks (¾ cup) cold unsalted butter, cut into bits
2 large eggs, beaten lightly

¼ cup sliced almonds, preferably blanched, toasted lightly
an egg wash made by beating 1 large egg yolk with 1 tablespoon water
red grapes as an accompaniment

Make the filling: In a food processor blend together the Roquefort, cut into pieces, the cream, the wine, the egg yolk, the flour, and salt and pepper to taste until the filling is smooth.

In a bowl combine the flour, the sugar, and the salt, add the butter, and blend the mixture until it resembles coarse meal. Stir in the eggs and on a lightly floured surface knead the dough lightly for several seconds, or until it is combined. Divide the dough in half, form each half into a ball, and chill the dough, wrapped in plastic wrap, for 1 hour.

On the lightly floured surface roll out each ball of dough into a 10-inch round. Press 1 of the dough rounds into the bottom and ¾ inch up the side of a buttered 9-inch round cake pan, spread the filling evenly over the bottom of the dough with a narrow metal spatula, and sprinkle it with the almonds. Using the tip of the spatula, cleaned, fold the edge of the dough over the filling. Arrange the remaining dough round on top of the filling and with the spatula press the edge of the top round between the bottom round and the side of the pan, enclosing the filling and sealing the *galette*. Score the top in a diamond pattern with a fork, brush the dough with the egg wash, and chill the *galette* for at least 30 minutes and up to 8 hours. Bake the *galette* in the middle of a preheated 400° F. oven for 50 to 55 minutes, or until it is golden brown, and let it cool in the pan on a rack for 10 minutes. Run a thin knife around the edge of the *galette*, turn the *galette* out carefully onto a plate, and invert it onto the rack. Let the *galette* cool completely and serve it, cut into thin wedges, with the grapes.

PHOTO ON PAGE 53

Chicken Wings Africana

For the chicken wings
4 garlic cloves
2 shallots
1½ teaspoons salt
1 tablespoon Chinese five-spice powder (available at Asian markets and most supermarkets)
2 teaspoons paprika

1 teaspoon dried rosemary, crumbled
½ teaspoon cayenne, or to taste
2 tablespoons vegetable oil
4 pounds chicken wings (about 20 to 24), the
   tips cut off and reserved for another use
For the sauce
⅓ cup natural-style peanut butter
¼ cup well-stirred canned cream of coconut
2 garlic cloves, chopped
¼ cup water
¼ cup chopped red bell pepper
⅛ teaspoon dried hot red pepper flakes,
   or to taste
1 teaspoon soy sauce

coriander sprigs for garnish if desired

Prepare the chicken wings: Mince and mash the garlic and the shallots to a paste with the salt and in a large bowl stir the paste together well with the five-spice powder, the paprika, the rosemary, the cayenne, and the oil. Add the chicken wings, stirring to coat them well with the marinade, and let them marinate, covered and chilled, for 4 hours or overnight. Arrange the wings, skin sides up, on the rack of a foil-lined large broiler pan and bake them in the upper third of a preheated 425° F. oven for 25 to 30 minutes, or until they are golden brown. *The wings may be prepared 1 day in advance, kept covered and chilled, and reheated.*

Make the sauce: In a blender blend together the peanut butter, the cream of coconut, the garlic, the water, the bell pepper, the red pepper flakes, and the soy sauce until the mixture is smooth and season the sauce with salt to taste.

Transfer the sauce to a serving bowl set on a platter, arrange the wings around the bowl, and garnish the platter with the coriander. Makes 20 to 24 wings.

PHOTO ON PAGE 23

Cumin Coconut Chips

1 coconut without any cracks and
   containing liquid
2 teaspoons fresh lime juice
¾ teaspoon ground cumin
caynne to taste

With an ice pick or a skewer test the 3 eyes of the coconut to find the weakest one and pierce it to make a hole. Drain the liquid into a bowl and reserve it for another use. Bake the coconut in a preheated 400° F. oven for 15 minutes, break it with a hammer on a work surface, and with the point of a strong small knife lever the flesh out of the shell carefully. With a vegetable peeler peel thin 1-inch-long slices of the coconut.

In a bowl toss the coconut slices with the lime juice, the cumin, the cayenne, and salt to taste until they are coated well and bake them in a jelly-roll pan in the middle of a preheated 350° F. oven, stirring occasionally, for 12 to 15 minutes, or until they are golden. Makes about 2 cups.

Cornmeal and Shallot Madeleines with Crème Fraîche and Caviar

⅓ cup minced shallot
2 tablespoons cold unsalted butter
⅓ cup yellow cornmeal
⅓ cup all-purpose flour
¾ teaspoon double-acting baking powder
1 large egg, beaten lightly
¼ cup *crème fraîche* plus additional
   as a topping
3 tablespoons water
about 2 ounces caviar

In a skillet cook the shallot in 1 tablespoon of the butter over moderately low heat, stirring, until it is softened and let the mixture cool completely. In a bowl stir together the cornmeal, the flour, the baking powder, and the shallot mixture, add the remaining 1 tablespoon butter, cut into bits, and blend the mixture until it resembles fine meal. Stir in the egg, ¼ cup of the *crème fraîche*, the water, and salt and pepper to taste and stir the batter until it is combined well.

On a baking sheet heat 16 well-buttered 2⅔- by 1¾-inch *madeleine* tins (about 2 tablespoons capacity) in the middle of a preheated 400° F. oven for 2 minutes, remove the tins from the oven, and into each tin spoon a heaping 1½ teaspoons of the batter. Bake the *madeleines* on the baking sheet in the middle of the 400° F. oven for 6 to 8 minutes, or until a tester inserted in the centers comes out clean, turn them out onto racks, and let them cool completely. *The* madeleines *may be made 3 days in advance and kept chilled in an airtight container.* Top the *madeleines* with the additional *crème fraîche* and the caviar. Makes 16 hors d'oeuvres.

PHOTO ON PAGES 52 AND 53

Crab Salad with Hearts of Palm

⅔ cup mayonnaise
¼ cup bottled chili sauce
¼ cup thinly sliced scallion
1 tablespoon finely chopped fresh
    parsley leaves
¼ cup minced green bell pepper
1 tablespoon fresh lemon juice
1 teaspoon drained bottled horseradish
a dash of Worcestershire sauce
½ cup chopped drained canned hearts of palm
1 pound lump crab meat, picked over
watercress, coarse stems discarded and the
    leaves washed well and spun dry, for
    lining the platter
seedless cucumber slices as an accompaniment
toasted *pita* wedges as an accompaniment

In a bowl whisk together the mayonnaise, the chili sauce, the scallion, the parsley, the bell pepper, the lemon juice, the horseradish, the Worcestershire sauce, and salt and pepper to taste, fold in the hearts of palm and the crab meat, and combine the mixture gently but thoroughly. *The crab salad may be made 1 day in advance and kept covered and chilled.* Makes about 4 cups.

Transfer the crab salad to a platter lined with the watercress and serve it with the cucumber slices and the *pita* wedges.

PHOTO ON PAGE 53

Cucumber Mint Tea Sandwiches

¼ cup loosely packed fresh mint leaves,
    rinsed, spun dry, and chopped fine
2 tablespoons unsalted butter, softened
2 tablespoons cream cheese
6 slices of whole-wheat bread
a 3-inch length of seedless cucumber, cut into
    thin slices

In a small bowl combine the mint, the butter, and the cream cheese and stir the mixture until it is combined well. Spread the bread slices with the butter mixture, top 3 of them with the cucumber, distributing the cucumber evenly and seasoning it with salt, and top the cucumber with the remaining bread slices. Cut off and discard the crusts and cut each sandwich diagonally into quarters. Makes 12 tea sandwiches.

Deviled Eggs with Sun-Dried Tomato

6 hard-boiled large eggs
4 ounces sun-dried tomatoes packed in oil,
    drained, reserving 2 tomatoes whole for
    garnish, and the remaining tomatoes
    minced
¼ cup mayonnaise
3 tablespoons sour cream
½ teaspoon white-wine vinegar
finely chopped fresh parsley leaves for
    garnish if desired

Halve the eggs lengthwise, force the yolks through a sieve into a bowl, and stir in the minced tomatoes, the mayonnaise, the sour cream, the vinegar, and salt and pepper to taste. Transfer the filling to a pastry bag fitted with a ½-inch decorative tip and pipe it into the egg-white halves, mounding it. Garnish the stuffed eggs with the 2 reserved sun-dried tomatoes, cut into julienne strips, and the parsley. Makes 12 deviled eggs.

Spiced English Muffin Toasts

8 English muffins (not split), cut in
    ¼-inch slices
¾ stick (6 tablespoons) unsalted butter, melted
¾ teaspoon aniseed, ground in a spice grinder
2 teaspoons cinnamon
½ teaspoon ground allspice
2 tablespoons sugar
⅛ teaspoon salt

Brush a large baking sheet with some of the butter, arrange the muffin slices in one layer, touching, on the sheet, and brush them with the remaining butter. Bake the muffin slices in the upper third of a preheated 375° F. oven for 15 to 20 minutes, or until they are pale golden. In a small bowl combine well the aniseed, the cinnamon, the allspice, the sugar, and the salt, sprinkle the mixture over the toasts, and bake the toasts for 4 minutes more, or until they are crisp and golden brown. Makes about 76 toasts.

South American–Style Jícama and Orange Salad

⅓ cup fresh lime juice
1½ teaspoons salt, or to taste
1 teaspoon chili powder, or to taste
⅛ teaspoon cayenne, or to taste

1 pound *jícama* (available at specialty produce
markets and many supermarkets), peeled
and cut into ⅓-inch-thick sticks
4 navel oranges, rind and pith cut free with a
serrated knife and the sections cut away
from the membranes
2 scallions, minced

In a bowl whisk together the juice, the salt, the chili
powder, and the cayenne and add the *jícama*, tossing it
to coat it well with the dressing. Arrange the oranges
decoratively around the edge of a platter and mound the
jícama with a slotted spoon in the center. Drizzle the
dressing remaining in the bowl over the oranges and
sprinkle the scallions over the salad. Serves 8.

PHOTO ON PAGE 23

Curried Macaroni Crisps

2 cups elbow macaroni
vegetable oil for deep-frying
2 teaspoons curry powder
1 teaspoon salt
¼ teaspoon cayenne
2 teaspoons Oriental sesame oil

In a large saucepan of boiling salted water cook the
macaroni until it is tender and drain it very well (do not
rinse it). Spread the macaroni out in a well-oiled jelly-
roll pan and let it cool, tossing it to coat it with the oil in
the pan. In a kettle fry the macaroni in batches in 1 inch
of 350° F. vegetable oil for 2 minutes, or until it is pale
golden, and transfer it with a slotted spoon to paper
towels to drain. In a small bowl combine well the curry
powder, the salt, and the cayenne. In a bowl toss the
macaroni with the sesame oil, add the curry mixture,
and toss the mixture well. Makes about 3 cups.

Melon with Prosciutto and Parmesan Curls

sixteen ½-inch-thick wedges of peeled
cantaloupe (about 1½ melons)
16 thin slices of prosciutto (½ to ⅔ pound)
fresh lemon juice for sprinkling the melon
olive oil for drizzling the prosciutto if desired
freshly ground black pepper to taste
about ¼ pound Parmesan, shaved into curls
with a vegetable peeler
lemon slices for garnish

On each of 8 plates arrange 2 of the melon wedges
and 2 slices of the prosciutto, sprinkle the melon with
the lemon juice, and drizzle the prosciutto with the oil.
Season the dishes with the pepper, add the Parmesan
curls, and garnish each serving with a lemon slice.
Serves 8.

Stuffed Mushrooms with Sun-Dried Tomato

24 mushrooms (about 2½ pounds), the stems
removed and chopped fine, reserving
1 cup, and the caps left whole
12 ounces sun-dried tomatoes packed in oil,
drained, reserving 4 tablespoons of the oil,
and the tomatoes minced
⅓ cup finely chopped shallot
1 teaspoon finely chopped garlic
a pinch of dried thyme, crumbled
3 tablespoons heavy cream
freshly grated Parmesan for sprinkling the
mushrooms

Brush the mushroom caps with some of the reserved
tomato oil and arrange them, stemmed sides down, on
the rack of a broiler pan. Broil the mushroom caps under
a preheated broiler about 6 inches from the heat for 2
minutes, or until they are barely softened, and arrange
them, stemmed sides up, in one layer on a baking sheet.
In a large skillet cook the shallot and the garlic in the remaining reserved oil over moderately low heat, stirring
occasionally, until they are softened, stir in the reserved
mushroom stems, the tomatoes, the thyme, and salt and
pepper to taste, and cook the mixture, stirring occasionally, for 5 to 10 minutes, or until the liquid has evaporated and the mixture is thick. Stir in the cream and salt and
pepper to taste, divide the mixture among the mushroom caps, and sprinkle it with the Parmesan. Bake the
stuffed mushrooms in the middle of a preheated 350° F.
oven for 12 to 18 minutes, or until the filling is heated
through. Makes 24 hors d'oeuvres.

Monégasque-Style Onions

½ pound small white onions, blanched in
    boiling water for 30 seconds, plunged into a
    bowl of ice and cold water, and peeled
¼ cup olive oil
1 tomato, peeled, seeded, and chopped fine
½ cup white-wine vinegar
⅓ cup dried currants
2 thyme sprigs
1 tablespoon finely chopped fresh
    parsley leaves
about 2 cups water
1 garlic clove, minced and mashed to a
    paste with a pinch of salt
2 tablespoons sugar
toast points as an accompaniment

In a large saucepan sauté the onions in the oil over
moderately high heat, stirring, until they are browned,
add the tomato, the vinegar, the currants, the thyme, the
parsley, 1 cup of the water, the garlic paste, the sugar,
and salt and pepper to taste, and bring the mixture to a
boil. Simmer the mixture, adding more water, ½ cup at
a time, as the liquid evaporates, for 50 minutes, or until
the onions are tender. Cook the mixture over high heat,
stirring, until the liquid is reduced to a glaze and let it
cool. *The onion mixture may be made 1 day in advance
and kept covered and chilled.* Makes 1½ cups. Transfer
the mixture to a serving dish and serve it with the toast.

Herbed Vidalia Onion Tea Sandwiches

⅓ cup mayonnaise
½ cup minced fresh parsley leaves
2 tablespoons minced fresh tarragon leaves
fresh lemon juice to taste
Tabasco to taste
12 very thin slices of homemade-type
    white bread
1 Vidalia onion (available in the spring at
    specialty produce markets and some
    supermarkets), sliced very thin

In a small bowl stir together the mayonnaise, ¼ cup of
the parsley, the tarragon, the lemon juice, the Tabasco,
and salt and pepper to taste. Spread one side of the bread
slices with the mayonnaise, arrange the onion slices
evenly on half the bread slices, and top them with the
remaining bread slices. Press the sandwiches together

gently, trim the crusts, and cut the sandwiches into
quarters. Put the remaining ¼ cup parsley in a shallow
bowl and dip the edges of the sandwich quarters in the
parsley. Makes 24 tea sandwiches.

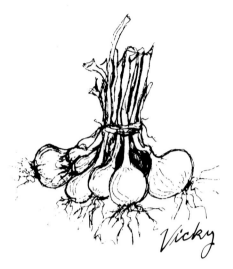

Pissaladières
(Onion, Anchovy, and Olive Tarts)

2 pounds onions, sliced
¼ teaspoon dried rosemary, crumbled
¼ teaspoon dried thyme, crumbled
2 tablespoons unsalted butter
1 tablespoon vegetable oil
1 teaspoon sugar
a 17¼-ounce package frozen puff pastry
    (2 sheets), thawed
an egg wash made by beating 1 large egg
    with 1 teaspoon water
6 tablespoons freshly grated Parmesan
a 2-ounce can flat anchovy fillets, drained and
    cut lengthwise into thin strips
about 28 Niçoise or other brine-cured black
    olives, pitted if desired

In a heavy kettle cook the onions with the rosemary,
the thyme, and salt and pepper to taste in the butter and
the oil, covered, over moderately low heat, stirring occasionally, for 20 to 30 minutes, or until they are soft
but not golden, add the sugar, and cook the mixture, uncovered, stirring, for 5 to 10 minutes, or until the excess
liquid is evaporated. Transfer the onion mixture to a
fine sieve and let it drain for 10 minutes. *The onion mixture may be made 1 day in advance and kept covered
and chilled.*

Roll each sheet of puff pastry lightly on a floured surface into an 11- by 10-inch rectangle and transfer the

rectangles to a baking sheet. Brush a 1-inch border around the edges of each rectangle with some of the egg wash and fold in the edges on all sides to form a ½-inch border, mitering the corners if desired. Brush the folded borders with the remaining egg wash and with the back of a knife score them in a crosshatch pattern. Sprinkle 4 tablespoons of the Parmesan evenly over the rectangles, divide the onion mixture between them, spreading it evenly, and arrange the anchovy strips and the olives decoratively on top. Sprinkle the remaining 2 tablespoons Parmesan evenly over the tarts and bake the tarts in the upper third of a preheated 400° F. oven for 15 to 20 minutes, or until the pastry is puffed and golden. *The tarts may be made 1 day in advance, kept covered loosely at room temperature, and reheated.* Makes 2 tarts.

PHOTO ON PAGE 23

Three-Onion, Sun-Dried Tomato, and Olive Tart

a ¼-ounce package (about 2½ teaspoons)
    active dry yeast
a pinch of sugar
¼ cup plus ⅔ cup lukewarm water
2¾ to 3 cups all-purpose flour
1 teaspoon salt
2 tablespoons olive oil
1 pound white or yellow onions, chopped fine
½ cup sour cream
2 large eggs
1 cup thinly sliced red onion
⅓ cup thinly sliced scallion greens
¼ cup minced drained sun-dried tomatoes
    packed in oil
⅓ cup minced Kalamata olives

In a small bowl proof the yeast with the sugar in ¼ cup of the water for 5 minutes, or until the mixture is foamy. In a large bowl stir together 2¾ cups of the flour, the salt, 1 tablespoon of the oil, the remaining ⅔ cup water, and the yeast mixture until the mixture forms a dough and knead the dough on a lightly floured surface, kneading in enough of the remaining ¼ cup flour to form a soft dough. Knead the dough for 8 to 10 minutes more, or until it is smooth and elastic, and form it into a ball. Transfer the dough to a lightly oiled bowl, turning it to coat it well, and let it rise, covered loosely, in a warm place for 1½ hours, or until it is double in bulk.

In a skillet cook the white onions in the remaining 1 tablespoon oil over moderate heat, stirring occasionally, until they are softened and golden and let them cool. In a bowl whisk together the sour cream and the eggs and stir in the white onions and salt and pepper to taste.

Punch down the dough and roll it into a 17- by 13-inch rectangle on a lightly floured surface. Transfer the rectangle to a large baking sheet, with your fingers form a ¼-inch rim around the edges of the rectangle, and spread the sour-cream mixture evenly over the dough. Scatter the red onion and the scallion greens over half the dough and scatter the sun-dried tomatoes and the olives over the remaining half. Bake the tart in the middle of a preheated 350° F. oven for 25 minutes, transfer it to a rack, and let it cool for 10 minutes. Cut the tart into 2-inch-wide diamonds. Makes about 24 diamonds.

Parsnip Shoestring Crisps

2 pounds parsnips, scrubbed
vegetable oil for deep-frying
1 tablespoon celery salt
1½ teaspoons dried dill, crumbled
¼ teaspoon pepper

In a food processor fitted with the fine julienne disk cut the parsnips lengthwise into strips. In a kettle fry the parsnips, a handful at a time, in 1½ inches of 375° F. oil for 1 minute, or until they are golden brown, and transfer them with a slotted spoon to paper towels to drain. In a small bowl combine well the celery salt, the dill, and the pepper and sprinkle the mixture over the parsnip crisps. Makes about ¾ pound.

Herbed Cheddar Pita Crisps

six 7-inch *pita* pockets, cut into 1½-inch
    pieces and separated
1 teaspoon dried sage, crumbled
1 teaspoon dried thyme, crumbled
½ teaspoon salt
½ teaspoon pepper
1½ cups grated sharp Cheddar (about 6 ounces)

Arrange the *pita* pieces close together, rough sides up, on 2 large baking sheets. In a small bowl combine well the sage, the thyme, the salt, and the pepper, sprinkle the mixture over the *pita* pieces, and scatter the Cheddar on top. Bake the crisps in a preheated 375° F. oven for 12 to 15 minutes, or until they are golden. Makes about ¾ pound.

Pirozhki
(Russian Potato-and-Cabbage Turnovers)

For the dough
2⅔ cups all-purpose flour
½ teaspoon double-acting baking powder
½ teaspoon salt
1½ sticks (¾ cup) cold unsalted butter,
  cut into bits
2 large egg yolks
½ cup sour cream
1 tablespoon cold water if necessary

For the filling
¾ pound russet (baking) potatoes
2 tablespoons unsalted butter
1 onion, chopped fine
¾ teaspoon caraway seeds
1 tablespoon vegetable oil
3 cups chopped cabbage
3 tablespoons sour cream
2 tablespoons water if necessary
3 tablespoons finely chopped fresh dill

an egg wash made by beating 1 large egg
  with 1 teaspoon water

Make the dough: In a food processor blend together the flour, the baking powder, the salt, and the butter until the mixture resembles meal. In a bowl whisk together the egg yolks and the sour cream, add the sour cream mixture to the flour mixture, and blend the mixture until it just forms a dough, adding the water if the dough seems dry. Divide the dough into fourths, form each fourth into a flattened round, and chill the dough, each round wrapped in wax paper, for 1 hour or overnight.

Make the filling: Peel the potatoes, cut them into ¾-inch pieces, and in a steamer set over boiling water steam them, covered, for 12 to 15 minutes, or until they are very tender. Force the potatoes through a ricer or food mill into a bowl and stir in 1 tablespoon of the butter. In a heavy saucepan cook the onion and the caraway seeds in the remaining 1 tablespoon butter and the oil over moderate heat, stirring, until the onion is golden, add the cabbage, and cook the mixture, stirring, for 5 minutes. Cook the mixture, covered, over moderately low heat, stirring occasionally, for 5 minutes more and stir it into the potato mixture with the sour cream, the water if the mixture is too thick, the dill, and salt and pepper to taste. *The filling may be made 1 day in advance and kept covered and chilled.*

On a lightly floured surface roll out 1 piece of the dough ⅛ inch thick, keeping the remaining pieces of dough wrapped and chilled, and with a 3-inch cutter cut out rounds. Brush each round with some of the egg wash, put 2 level teaspoons of the filling on one half of each round, and fold the dough over the filling to form a half-moon, pressing the edges together firmly to seal them and crimping them with a fork. Gather the scraps of dough, reroll them, and make more *pirozhki* with the remaining filling and dough and some of the remaining egg wash in the same manner. *The* pirozhki *may be made up to this point 5 days in advance and kept frozen in plastic freezer bags. The* pirozhki *need not be thawed before baking.*

Arrange the *pirozhki* on lightly greased baking sheets and brush the tops with the remaining egg wash. Bake the *pirozhki* in a preheated 350° F. oven for 25 to 30 minutes, or until they are golden, and serve them warm or at room temperature. Makes about 50 *pirozhki*.

PHOTO ON PAGE 23

Hoisin and Honey Pork Riblets

3½ pounds pork spareribs, halved crosswise
  and cut into individual ribs
⅓ cup honey
¼ cup soy sauce
1 large garlic clove, minced and mashed to a
  paste with ¼ teaspoon salt
⅓ cup hoisin sauce (available at specialty
  foods shops and many supermarkets)
½ teaspoon English-style dry mustard
¼ cup distilled white vinegar

In a kettle of boiling salted water simmer the ribs, covered, for 30 minutes and drain them well. In a large bowl whisk together the honey, the soy sauce, the garlic paste, the hoisin sauce, the mustard, the vinegar, and black pepper to taste, add the ribs, and toss the mixture well, coating the ribs thoroughly. Let the ribs marinate, chilled, for at least 1 hour or overnight.

Remove the ribs from the marinade, arrange them in one layer on the oiled rack of a foil-lined broiler pan, and broil them under a preheated broiler about 4 inches from the heat, basting them with the marinade, for 3 minutes. Turn the ribs and broil, basting them with the marinade, for 2 to 3 minutes more, or until they are browned well and glazed. Discard the marinade. Makes about 50 hors d'oeuvres.

Quail Eggs with Olive Paste

12 quail eggs (available at specialty foods
    shops) plus additional for garnish if desired
¼ cup bottled black olive paste such as
    tapenade or *olivada* (available at specialty
    foods shops and some supermarkets) for
    topping the eggs
24 drained bottled capers, patted dry
thyme branches for lining the platter plus
    24 sprigs for garnish if desired

In a saucepan cover the eggs with cold water, bring
the water just to a boil, and simmer the eggs for 5 minutes. Pour out the water, add cold water to the pan, and
let the eggs cool until they can be handled. Shell 12 of
the eggs carefully and halve them lengthwise, leaving
the additional eggs unshelled. Spoon a small dollop of
the olive paste onto each egg half, top the olive paste
with a caper, and arrange the egg halves on a platter
lined with the thyme branches and garnished with the
additional eggs. Garnish the egg halves with the thyme
sprigs. Makes 24 hors d'oeuvres.

PHOTO ON PAGE 53

Sausage and Feta Phyllo Triangles

¾ pound bulk fresh sausage
1 tablespoon vegetable oil
1 onion, chopped fine
10 ounces mushrooms, chopped fine and
    squeezed dry in a kitchen towel
½ pound Feta, rinsed, patted dry, and
    crumbled fine
½ cup drained bottled roasted red peppers,
    patted dry and chopped fine
½ teaspoon cinnamon
½ teaspoon freshly grated nutmeg
1⅓ cups fine fresh bread crumbs
⅓ cup minced fresh parsley leaves
3 large eggs, beaten lightly
20 *phyllo* sheets, cut lengthwise into 3-inch-
    wide strips, the strips stacked between
    2 sheets of wax paper and covered with
    a dampened kitchen towel
2 sticks (1 cup) unsalted butter, melted

In a large heavy skillet cook the sausage over moderate heat, stirring and breaking up the lumps, until it is
cooked through and transfer it with a slotted spoon to
paper towels to drain. Add the oil to the skillet, in the fat
cook the onion and the mushrooms, stirring occasionally, until the onion is softened, and in a bowl stir together
the sausage, the onion mixture, the Feta, the red peppers, the cinnamon, the nutmeg, the bread crumbs, the
parsley, the eggs, and salt and pepper to taste.

On a work surface arrange 1 strip of the *phyllo* with a
short side facing you, brush it lightly with some of the
butter, and put 1 heaping teaspoon of the filling about
1 inch from the bottom end of the strip. Fold the lower
right corner of the strip up over the filling, forming a triangle of the folded *phyllo*, continue to fold the filled triangle up the entire length of the strip, and brush the
triangle lightly with some of the butter. Form more triangles in the same manner with the remaining *phyllo*,
filling, and butter, transferring them to baking sheets as
they are formed. *The triangles may be made 1 week in
advance and kept frozen in airtight containers. Do not
thaw the triangles before baking.* Bake the triangles in
the middle of a preheated 350° F. oven for 20 to 25 minutes, or until they are golden. Makes about 80 triangles.

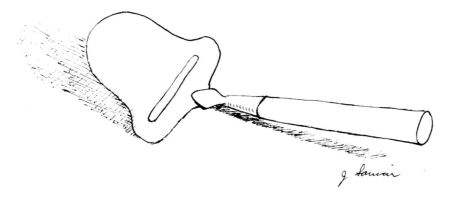

Scallop Puffs

½ pound sea scallops
¼ cup mayonnaise
¼ cup freshly grated Gruyère
½ teaspoon Dijon-style mustard
1 teaspoon fresh lemon juice
1 tablespoon finely chopped fresh
    parsley leaves
1 large egg white
8 slices of homemade-type white bread,
    toasted lightly, the crusts discarded, and
    each slice cut into 4 squares

In a saucepan combine the scallops with enough salted water to cover them completely, bring the water to a simmer, and poach the scallops for 5 minutes. Drain the scallops well and cut them into ½-inch pieces. In a bowl whisk together the mayonnaise, the Gruyère, the mustard, the lemon juice, the parsley, and salt and pepper to taste, add the scallops, and toss the mixture well. In a small bowl beat the egg white until it just holds stiff peaks and fold it into the scallop mixture gently but thoroughly. Top each bread square with a heaping teaspoon of the scallop mixture, arrange the puffs about ½ inch apart on baking sheets, and broil them under a preheated broiler about 6 inches from the heat for 1 to 2 minutes, or until the toppings are bubbling and lightly golden (do not allow the edges of the toasts to burn). Makes 32 hors d'oeuvres.

*Spanish-Style Garlic Shrimp
with Ham and Bell Pepper*

2 pounds large shrimp (about 28), shelled,
    leaving the tail and the first joint of the
    shell intact, and deveined
1½ teaspoons salt
8 garlic cloves, sliced thin lengthwise
½ cup olive oil
¼ pound thick-sliced cooked ham, chopped
¼ teaspoon dried hot red pepper flakes
1 red bell pepper, chopped
⅓ cup Oloroso Sherry
minced fresh parsley leaves for garnish
    if desired
slices of crusty bread as an accompaniment

Rinse the shrimp and pat them dry. Sprinkle the shrimp on both sides with the salt and let them stand between layers of paper towel for 10 minutes. In a large heavy skillet cook the garlic in the oil over moderate heat, stirring, until it is golden and transfer it with a slotted spoon to a small bowl. Add the ham and the red pepper flakes to the skillet and cook the mixture, stirring, for 3 to 5 minutes, or until the ham deepens in color. Add the bell pepper and cook the mixture, stirring, until the bell pepper is softened. Add the shrimp and sauté the mixture over moderately high heat, turning the shrimp, for 3 minutes. Add the Sherry and the garlic and simmer the mixture, stirring and turning the shrimp occasionally, until the shrimp are just cooked through. Transfer the shrimp mixture to a heated serving dish, sprinkle it with the parsley, and serve it with the bread. Serves 8 as an hors d'oeuvre.

Stilton, Bacon, and Scallion Puffs

½ cup water
½ stick (¼ cup) unsalted butter,
    cut into bits
½ cup all-purpose flour
2 large eggs
¼ pound Stilton, crumbled
    (about 1 cup)
4 slices of bacon, cooked crisp and
    crumbled fine
3 tablespoons minced scallion

In a small heavy saucepan combine the water, the butter, and a pinch of salt and bring the mixture to a boil over high heat. Reduce the heat to moderate, add the flour all at once, and with a wooden spoon beat the mixture until it pulls away from the sides of the pan and forms a ball. Remove the pan from the heat, add the eggs, 1 at a time, beating well after each addition, and stir in the Stilton, the bacon, the scallion, and salt and pepper to taste. Drop rounded teaspoons of the batter 2 inches apart onto lightly buttered baking sheets and bake the puffs in the middle of a preheated 425° F. oven for 15 to 20 minutes, or until they are crisp and golden. Makes about 36 hors d'oeuvres.

Cherry Tomatoes with Roasted Garlic Filling

a 6-ounce head of garlic, outer husk
    removed and ¼ inch trimmed from the
    stem end
1 tablespoon olive oil
1 pint cherry tomatoes (about 30)
6 ounces cream cheese, softened
1 teaspoon fresh lemon juice,
    or to taste
fresh basil leaves, shredded, for garnish

In a foil-lined baking dish drizzle the garlic with the oil, bake it, covered loosely with foil, in the middle of a preheated 325° F. oven for 1¼ hours, or until the pulp is very soft, and let it cool until it can be easily handled. Squeeze the pulp from the cloves into a bowl and let it cool. Mash the pulp until it is smooth (there should be about ¼ cup purée).

Using a serrated knife, on a work surface cut a thin slice from the bottom of each tomato so that it stands upright. Cut off a thin slice from each stem end, and with a small melon-ball cutter scoop out the flesh and seeds carefully, forming tomato shells. Sprinkle the insides of the tomato shells with salt, invert the tomatoes on racks set over paper towels, and let them drain for 30 minutes.

In a bowl whisk together the cream cheese, the lemon juice, the garlic purée, and salt and pepper to taste until the filling is smooth. Using a pastry bag fitted with a small star tip, pipe the filling into the tomato shells. Garnish the filled shells with the basil. Makes about 30 hors d'oeuvres.

Chili Jack Tortilla Chips

16 corn tortillas
vegetable oil for brushing the tortillas
1 tablespoon chili powder
1 teaspoon salt
½ teaspoon dried orégano, crumbled
1½ cups grated Monterey Jack
    (about 6 ounces)

Brush the tortillas lightly on one side with the oil. In a small bowl combine well the chili powder, the salt, and the orégano, sprinkle the mixture over the tortillas, and scatter the Monterey Jack on top. Cut each tortilla into fourths with a pizza wheel or sharp knife, arrange the wedges on 2 large baking sheets, and bake them in a preheated 400° F. oven for 12 to 15 minutes, or until they are golden and crisp. Makes about ½ pound.

Cumin Tortilla Crisps

12 corn tortillas, halved and cut crosswise into
    very thin strips
2 tablespoons olive oil
1 tablespoon ground cumin
coarse salt for sprinkling the crisps

Arrange the tortilla strips in one layer on 2 jelly-roll pans, cover them with a kitchen towel, and let them stand for 1 hour. In a small bowl stir together the oil, the cumin, and salt and pepper to taste, drizzle the mixture over the strips, and toss the strips to coat them with it. Bake the strips in a preheated 425° F. oven, shaking the pans occasionally and switching the pans once, for 8 to 10 minutes, or until they are golden and crisp. Transfer the crisps to paper towels to drain and sprinkle them with the salt. *The tortilla crisps may be made 1 day in advance and kept in an airtight container.*

PHOTO ON PAGE 65

Middle Eastern Lamb-Stuffed Zucchini
with Yogurt Sauce

four 6-ounce straight zucchini,
  scrubbed
1 tablespoon olive oil
½ pound ground lamb
1 teaspoon allspice
1 teaspoon dried mint,
  crumbled
1 cup chopped onion
1 garlic clove, minced
2 tablespoons pine nuts,
  toasted lightly
1 cup plain yogurt
2 tablespoons cornstarch, dissolved in
  2 tablespoons cold water
1 tablespoon sesame seeds,
  toasted lightly

Cut off and reserve the stem ends of the zucchini and with a zucchini corer hollow out the zucchini, being careful not to pierce the skins and leaving ¼-inch-thick shells. Chop the zucchini flesh and reserve it.

In a heavy skillet heat the oil over moderately high heat until it is hot but not smoking and in it sauté the lamb with the allspice, the mint, and salt and pepper to taste, stirring, until it is no longer pink. Transfer the lamb with a slotted spoon to a sieve to drain, pour off all but 1 tablespoon of the fat from the skillet, and in the skillet sauté the onion, stirring, until it is softened. Stir in the garlic, the reserved zucchini flesh, and salt and pepper to taste and sauté the mixture until it is golden. Remove the skillet from the heat, stir in the lamb mixture, the pine nuts, and 2 tablespoons of the yogurt, and let the filling cool. Stuff the zucchini with the filling and put the reserved stem ends back in place over the cut ends, securing them with wooden picks. Arrange the zucchini on a steamer rack set over simmering water, steam them, covered, for 20 to 25 minutes, or until they are tender, and let them cool slightly.

In the top of a double-boiler set over simmering water whisk together the remaining yogurt and the cornstarch mixture, stirred, cook the sauce, stirring, for 5 minutes, or until it is thickened, and let it cool slightly.

Cut the zucchini crosswise into 1-inch rounds, arrange the rounds on a platter, and spoon a dollop of the sauce onto each round. Sprinkle the zucchini rounds with the sesame seeds and serve them at room temperature. Makes about 24 hors d'oeuvres.

CANAPÉS

Brandade de Morue Canapés
(Roasted Potato Slices with Salt Cod
Purée and Roasted Red Pepper)

For the brandade de morue
½ pound thick-cut skinless boneless salt cod
½ cup finely chopped onion
⅓ cup plus 2 tablespoons olive oil
1 garlic clove
½ cup heavy cream plus, if desired,
  2 tablespoons for thinning the *brandade*
2 teaspoons fresh lemon juice,
  or to taste

3 russet (baking) potatoes (about 1½ pounds)
¼ cup olive oil
1 red bell pepper, roasted (procedure on
  page 196), or 1 drained bottled roasted
  red pepper, chopped fine and patted dry

Make the *brandade de morue*: In a ceramic or glass bowl let the salt cod soak in cold water to cover, changing the water several times, for 24 hours and drain it. In a kettle poach the cod in simmering water to cover for 25 minutes, or until it flakes easily when tested with a fork, drain it in a colander, and refresh it under cold water. Pat the cod dry and break it into pieces. In a skillet cook the onion in 2 tablespoons of the oil over moderately low heat, stirring, until it is soft and let it cool. In a food processor purée the onion mixture, the garlic, and the cod until the mixture is smooth, with the motor running add the remaining ⅓ cup oil in a stream, ½ cup of the cream, the lemon juice, and salt and pepper to taste, and purée the mixture until it is smooth. *The* brandade de morue *may be made 2 days in advance and kept covered and chilled*. If desired, thin the *brandade* with the remaining 2 tablespoons cream.

On oiled baking sheets arrange the potatoes, cut crosswise into ¼-inch-thick slices, without touching, drizzle them with the oil, and roast them in a preheated 400° F. oven, turning them once, for 30 to 40 minutes, or until they are tender, slightly crisp around the edges, and pale golden. Transfer the potatoes to paper towels to drain. Arrange the potato slices on a platter, top each slice with a dollop of the *brandade*, and top the *brandade* with the roasted red pepper. Makes about 60 hors d'oeuvres.

Mustard-Ginger Shrimp Canapés

1 cup cider vinegar
¾ cup vegetable oil
2 tablespoons sugar
1 tablespoon Worcestershire sauce
1 teaspoon Tabasco
2 teaspoons English-style dry mustard
4½ teaspoons minced peeled fresh gingerroot
2 pounds medium shrimp (about 50), shelled
    and, if desired, deveined
1 cup julienne strips of assorted red, yellow,
    and green bell peppers
¼ cup finely chopped fresh coriander plus
    sprigs for garnish
dried hot red pepper flakes to taste
pita pockets, cut into about 50 wedges and
    toasted lightly

In a saucepan whisk together the vinegar, the oil, the sugar, the Worcestershire sauce, the Tabasco, the mustard, the gingerroot, and salt and black pepper to taste, bring the mixture to a boil, and simmer it, stirring occasionally, for 5 minutes. Add the shrimp and simmer them, stirring occasionally, for 3 minutes, or until they are cooked through. Transfer the mixture to a heatproof bowl, add the bell peppers, tossing the mixture well, and chill the mixture, covered, for 2 hours. Drain the mixture, discarding the liquid, and stir in the chopped coriander, the red pepper flakes, and salt and black pepper to taste. Arrange a shrimp and several pepper strips on each *pita* wedge and garnish them with the coriander sprigs. Makes 50 hors d'oeuvres.

DIPS AND SPREADS

Sun-Dried Tomato, Coriander,
and Roasted Red Pepper Dip

two 7-ounce jars roasted red peppers,
    drained
3 ounces sun-dried tomatoes (not packed in
    oil, about 30), soaked in hot water for
    5 minutes and drained well, reserving
    3 tablespoons of the soaking liquid
2 garlic cloves, chopped fine
1½ teaspoons ground cumin
1 to 2 bottled pickled *jalapeño* chilies,
    seeded and minced
    (wear rubber gloves)
1 teaspoon fresh lemon juice
¼ cup chopped fresh coriander
¼ cup chopped scallion
4 ounces cream cheese, cut into bits
    and softened
tortilla chips as an accompaniment

In a food processor purée the red peppers, the tomatoes, the garlic, the cumin, the *jalapeños*, the lemon juice, the coriander, and the scallion until the mixture is smooth, add the cream cheese and salt to taste, and purée the mixture, adding enough of the reserved tomato-soaking liquid to thin the dip to the desired consistency and scraping down the side of the bowl occasionally, until it is smooth. Transfer the dip to a serving bowl and serve it with the tortilla chips. Makes about 2⅓ cups.

Tuna Horseradish Dip with Pita Triangles

a 6½-ounce can tuna packed in oil,
    drained well
3 tablespoons plain yogurt
2 tablespoons mayonnaise
2 tablespoons finely chopped onion
1½ teaspoons drained bottled horseradish,
    or to taste
2 teaspoons finely chopped fresh
    parsley leaves
cayenne to taste for sprinkling the dip
    if desired
lightly toasted *pita* triangles

In a food processor purée the tuna, the yogurt, the mayonnaise, the onion, the horseradish, the parsley, and salt and pepper to taste until the mixture is smooth. Transfer the dip to a serving bowl, sprinkle it with the cayenne, and serve it with the *pita* triangles. Makes about 1 cup, serving 2 as an hors d'oeuvre.

Goat Cheese and Pistachio Spread

three 3.5-ounce logs of mild soft goat cheese
    such as Montrachet
1 stick (½ cup) unsalted butter,
    softened
1 large garlic clove, minced and mashed to a
    paste with 1 teaspoon salt
¼ cup chopped pistachio nuts, toasted lightly
    and cooled

¼ cup thinly sliced chives plus chive blades
    for garnish
1 loaf of French bread, cut into ¼-inch-thick
    slices and toasted lightly

In a bowl with an electric mixer beat together the goat cheese, the butter, the garlic paste, the pistachio nuts, the sliced chives, and salt and pepper to taste until the mixture is combined well, spoon the spread into a serving dish, and chill it, its surface covered with plastic wrap, overnight. *The spread may be made 2 days in advance and kept covered and chilled.* Garnish the spread with the chive blades and serve it with the toasts. Makes about 1 cup.

PHOTO ON PAGE 76

Sherried Stilton and
Green Peppercorn Spread

¾ pound Stilton, crumbled and softened
6 ounces cream cheese, softened
2 to 3 tablespoons drained green peppercorns
    packed in brine
¼ cup medium-dry Sherry, or to taste

In a food processor blend the Stilton, the cream cheese, the peppercorns to taste, the Sherry, and salt and pepper to taste until the mixture is smooth and transfer the spread to crocks or ramekins. The spread keeps, covered and chilled, for 1 week. Serve the spread with crackers. Makes about 2½ cups.

BREADS

YEAST BREADS

Individual Cheese and Pepperoni Pizzas

For the dough
a ¼-ounce package active dry yeast
½ teaspoon sugar
⅔ cup lukewarm water
2 tablespoons olive oil
2 to 2¼ cups unbleached all-purpose flour
½ teaspoon salt

cornmeal for sprinkling the baking sheets
⅓ cup tomato sauce
½ pound whole-milk mozzarella, grated
freshly grated Parmesan for sprinkling the pizzas
36 thin slices of pepperoni
2 teaspoons olive oil

Make the dough: In the bowl of an electric mixer proof the yeast with the sugar in ⅓ cup of the water for 5 minutes, or until the mixture is foamy, stir in the remaining ⅓ cup water, the oil, 2 cups of the flour, and the salt, and blend the mixture until it forms a dough. Fit the mixer with the dough hook and knead the dough, incorporating as much of the remaining ¼ cup flour as necessary to prevent the dough from sticking, for 3 minutes, or until it is smooth and elastic. Transfer the dough to an oiled bowl and turn it to coat it with the oil. Let the dough rise, covered with plastic wrap, in a warm place for 1 hour, or until it is double in bulk, and punch it down.

Divide the dough into 6 pieces and on a floured surface roll out each piece into a 6-inch round. Transfer the rounds to baking sheets (preferably black steel) oiled and sprinkled with the cornmeal, and spread each of the rounds with a scant 1 tablespoon of the tomato sauce. Sprinkle the rounds evenly with the mozzarella and the Parmesan and top them with the pepperoni. Add salt and pepper to taste and drizzle the rounds with the oil. Bake them on the bottom rack of a preheated 500° F.

electric oven or on the floor of a preheated 500° F. gas oven for 10 minutes, or until the crusts are golden brown. Cool them slightly before serving. Serves 6.

PHOTO ON PAGE 27

Salami Rosemary Bread

two ¼-ounce packages active dry yeast
2 cups warm water
2 teaspoons table salt
5 to 6 cups bread flour
½ pound pork salami, chopped fine
2 teaspoons dried rosemary, crumbled
a glaze made by beating 1 large egg white
    with 1 tablespoon water
coarse salt for sprinkling the bread

In a bowl proof the yeast in 1 cup of the water for 5 minutes, or until the mixture is foamy, and in another bowl dissolve the table salt in the remaining 1 cup water. In a large bowl stir together the yeast mixture, the salt water, and 4 cups of the flour until a dough is formed, turn the dough out onto a floured surface, and knead in the salami, the rosemary, and enough of the remaining 2 cups flour to form a slightly sticky dough. Knead the dough for 10 minutes, form it into a ball, and transfer it to a lightly oiled bowl, turning it to coat it with the oil.

Let the dough rise, covered with plastic wrap, in a warm place for 1 hour, or until it is double in bulk, knead it for 30 seconds, and form it into a 16-inch-long loaf. Transfer the loaf to a lightly oiled baking sheet and let it rise, uncovered, in a warm place for 1 hour, or until it is double in bulk. Make four ¼-inch-deep slashes in the top of the loaf and brush the loaf with the glaze. Sprinkle the loaf with the coarse salt and bake it in the middle of a preheated 425° F. oven for 15 minutes. Reduce the temperature to 350° F. and bake the loaf for 30 minutes more, or until it sounds hollow when the bottom is tapped. Transfer the loaf to a rack and let it cool. Makes 1 loaf.

QUICK BREADS

Fresh Corn, Cheddar, and Scallion Corn Bread

1½ cups yellow cornmeal
½ cup all-purpose flour
1 tablespoon sugar
2 teaspoons double-acting baking powder
1 teaspoon baking soda
1 teaspoon salt
2 large eggs
1½ cups buttermilk
1 cup fresh corn kernels including the pulp
  scraped from the cobs (cut from about
  2 ears of corn)
1½ cups grated sharp Cheddar
3 scallions, sliced thin

Grease a jelly-roll pan, 15½ by 10½ by 1 inches. Into a bowl sift together the cornmeal, the flour, the sugar, the baking powder, the baking soda, and the salt. In a small bowl beat together the eggs and the buttermilk. To the cornmeal mixture add the buttermilk mixture, the corn, the Cheddar, and the scallions, stir the batter until it is just combined, and pour it into the pan, spreading it evenly. Bake the corn bread in the middle of a preheated 425° F. oven for 8 to 10 minutes, or until a tester comes out clean.

Chocolate-Chip Oatmeal Muffins

1 cup all-purpose flour
¼ cup sugar
1 teaspoon double-acting baking powder
¼ teaspoon salt
1 large egg
½ stick (¼ cup) unsalted butter, melted and
  cooled
¼ cup milk
⅓ cup rolled oats, toasted lightly
⅓ cup walnuts, chopped and toasted lightly
⅓ cup semisweet chocolate chips

In a bowl whisk together the flour, the sugar, the baking powder, and the salt. In another bowl whisk together the egg, the butter, and the milk, stir the egg mixture into the flour mixture until the mixtures are just combined, and stir in the oats, the walnuts, and the chocolate chips. Divide the batter among 6 paper-lined ½-cup muffin tins and bake the muffins in the middle of a preheated 400° F. oven for 15 to 20 minutes, or until a tester comes out clean. Transfer the muffins to a rack, let them cool, and serve them warm. Makes 6 muffins.

Coconut and Pineapple Upside-Down Muffins

6 heaping teaspoons pineapple preserves
¼ cup firmly packed brown sugar
¼ cup vegetable oil
1 large egg white
½ cup milk
1 cup all-purpose flour
1½ teaspoons double-acting baking powder
½ teaspoon cinnamon
¼ teaspoon salt
¾ cup sweetened flaked coconut,
  toasted lightly

Drop 1 heaping teaspoon of the preserves into each of 6 well-buttered ⅓- to ½-cup muffin tins. In a bowl whisk together the brown sugar, the oil, and the egg white until the mixture is smooth and whisk in the milk. In another bowl whisk together the flour, the baking powder, the cinnamon, the salt, and the coconut, add the milk mixture, and stir the batter until it is just combined. Divide the batter among the tins and bake the muffins in the middle of a preheated 400° F. oven for 20 minutes, or until a tester comes out clean. Let the muffins cool for 3 minutes, run a knife around each muffin, and lift each muffin out with a fork, inverting it onto a rack. Makes 6 muffins.

Date and Oatmeal Yogurt Muffins

¾ cup all-purpose flour
¾ cup old-fashioned rolled oats
¼ cup firmly packed dark brown sugar
1½ teaspoons double-acting baking powder
½ teaspoon salt
⅛ teaspoon cinnamon
⅓ cup chopped pitted dried dates
⅓ cup walnuts, toasted lightly and
  chopped fine
½ cup plain yogurt
¼ cup milk
2 tablespoons unsalted butter, melted
  and cooled
1 large egg, beaten lightly

In a bowl stir together the flour, the oats, the brown sugar, the baking powder, the salt, the cinnamon, the dates, and the walnuts and in another bowl whisk together the yogurt, the milk, the butter, and the egg. Stir the yogurt mixture into the flour mixture and stir the batter until it is just combined. Divide the batter among 6 paper-lined ½-cup muffin tins and bake the muffins in the middle of a preheated 400° F. oven for 30 minutes. Makes 6 muffins.

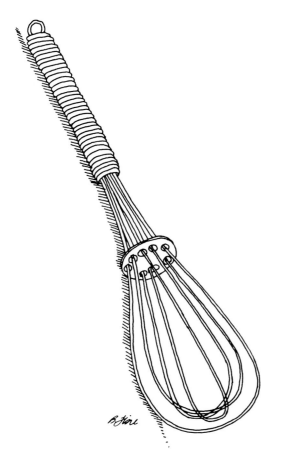

Lemon Gem Muffins with Cream Cheese

2 cups all-purpose flour
1 teaspoon baking soda
½ teaspoon salt
⅓ cup sugar
2 large eggs
½ cup fresh lemon juice
1 stick (½ cup) unsalted butter, melted and cooled
1 teaspoon vanilla
cream cheese as an accompaniment
papaya in cinnamon syrup (page 246) as an accompaniment

In a bowl whisk together the flour, the baking soda, the salt, and the sugar. In another bowl whisk together the eggs, the lemon juice, the butter, and the vanilla, add the egg mixture to the flour mixture, and stir the batter until it is just combined. Divide the batter among 24 buttered ⅛-cup muffin tins and bake the muffins in the upper third of a preheated 400° F. oven for 10 to 12 minutes, or until a tester comes out clean. Turn the muffins out onto a rack, let them cool, and serve them with the cream cheese and the papaya in cinnamon syrup. Makes 24 small muffins.

PHOTO ON PAGE 35

TOASTS

Bruschetta with Arugula, Smoked Mozzarella, and Tomatoes

1 large bunch of *arugula* (about ¼ pound), coarse stems discarded and the leaves washed well and spun dry
½ pound smoked mozzarella, chopped fine
2 tomatoes (½ pound total), seeded and chopped fine
12 diagonally cut ½-inch-thick slices of Italian bread (about 1½ loaves)
2 garlic cloves, halved
¼ cup extra-virgin olive oil

Chop the *arugula* fine and in a bowl stir it together with the mozzarella, the tomatoes, and salt and pepper to taste. Grill the bread on a rack set 4 inches over glowing coals, turning it once, until it is golden. (Alternatively, the bread may be toasted on a rack in a preheated broiler about 4 inches from the heat, turning it once.) Rub the toasts with the garlic on one side, and brush the same side with half the oil. Spoon the *arugula* mixture onto the oiled sides of the toasts and drizzle the remaining 2 tablespoons oil over it. Serves 6.

PHOTO ON PAGE 36

Garlic Baguette Toasts

1 large garlic clove, minced or forced through
    a garlic press
¼ cup olive oil
a French *baguette*, cut lengthwise into 6 long
    wedges
coarse salt to taste

In a small skillet cook the garlic in the oil over moderate heat, stirring, until it begins to turn golden, brush the bread wedges with the oil, and on a baking sheet bake them in the middle of a preheated 375° F. oven for 10 minutes, or until they are golden. Sprinkle the toasts with the salt and break them in half. Makes 12 toasts.

Garlic Rosemary Bagel Crisps

4 bagels (about 1 pound), cut into very thin
    slices with a serrated knife
1½ teaspoons dried rosemary, crumbled
4 large garlic cloves, minced with
    ¼ teaspoon salt
½ cup olive oil
1 tablespoon coarse salt

Arrange the bagel slices in one layer on 2 large baking sheets. In a blender purée the rosemary and the garlic mixture with the oil until the mixture is smooth. Brush the slices with the mixture, sprinkle them with the salt, and bake them in a preheated 350° F. oven for 15 to 18 minutes, or until they are golden. Makes about 1 pound.

Herbed Pita Toasts

1¼ sticks (10 tablespoons) unsalted butter,
    softened
2 tablespoons minced fresh parsley leaves
1 large garlic clove, minced and
    mashed to a paste with a pinch
    of salt
1 teaspoon fresh lemon juice
8 mini *pita* pockets, halved horizontally

In a bowl cream together the butter, the parsley, the garlic paste, the lemon juice, and salt and pepper to taste and let the mixture stand, covered, for 1 hour. *The garlic butter may be made 8 hours in advance and kept covered and chilled.* Spread each *pita* half with some of the butter mixture, arrange the *pita* halves in one layer on baking sheets, and bake them in batches in the upper third of a preheated 400° F. oven for 5 to 8 minutes, or until they are browned lightly and crisp. Makes 16 pita toasts.

PHOTO ON PAGE 56

SOUPS

Asparagus and Dill Avgolemono Soup

1⅓ cups finely chopped white part of leek,
    washed well and drained
1⅓ cups finely chopped onion
1 cup thinly sliced celery
2 tablespoons unsalted butter
3 pounds asparagus, trimmed and
    cut into 1-inch pieces,
    reserving about 30 tips
    for garnish
4 cups chicken broth
2 cups water
3 large eggs
¼ cup fresh lemon juice plus additional to
    taste if desired
3 tablespoons minced fresh dill
dill sprigs for garnish

In a large heavy saucepan cook the leek, the onion, and the celery with salt and pepper to taste in the butter over moderate heat, stirring, until the vegetables are softened, add the asparagus pieces, the broth, and the water, and simmer the mixture, covered, for 10 to 15 minutes, or until the asparagus is tender. Purée the soup in batches in a blender or food processor until it is smooth, transferring it as it is puréed to another large heavy saucepan, and let it cool to lukewarm.

In a saucepan of boiling water cook the reserved asparagus tips for 3 to 4 minutes, or until they are tender, and transfer them with a slotted spoon to a bowl of ice and cold water to stop the cooking. Drain the asparagus tips and reserve them.

In a heatproof bowl whisk together the eggs and ¼ cup of the lemon juice, add 1 cup of the lukewarm soup in a stream, whisking, and whisk the egg mixture into the remaining soup. Cook the soup over moderately low heat, whisking and being careful not to let it boil, until it is thickened slightly and registers 160° F. on a candy thermometer and whisk in the minced dill, the additional lemon juice, and salt and pepper to taste. *The soup may be prepared up to this point 1 day in advance and kept covered and chilled. To reheat the soup, cook it over low heat, stirring, until it is hot, being careful not to let it boil.* Serve the soup either hot or chilled, garnished with the reserved asparagus tips and the dill sprigs. Makes about 9 cups, serving 6 to 8.

PHOTO ON PAGE 40

Avgolemono Soup with Spinach
(Rice, Lemon, Egg, and Spinach Soup)

2 cups chicken broth
1 cup water
⅓ cup long-grain rice
5 cups packed spinach leaves, washed well
    and chopped fine
2 large eggs
3 tablespoons fresh lemon juice

In a saucepan combine the broth and the water and bring the liquid to a boil. Add the rice and simmer the mixture, covered, for 20 minutes. Add the spinach and simmer the mixture, uncovered, for 2 minutes. In a small bowl whisk together the eggs and the lemon juice, whisk in 1 cup of the hot broth mixture, and whisk the egg mixture into the pan. Heat the soup over low heat, stirring, until it is very hot and thickened, but do not let it boil. Makes about 3½ cups, serving 2.

Cauliflower Soup with Toasted Cumin and Lime

½ teaspoon cuminseed
1 onion, chopped fine
1 tablespoon unsalted butter
2½ cups chopped cauliflower
1 cup chicken broth
1 cup water
¼ cup half-and-half
2 teaspoons fresh lime juice, or to taste

In a dry small skillet cook the cuminseed over moderate heat, stirring, for 3 to 4 minutes, or until it is fragrant and several shades darker, being careful not to let it burn, and transfer it to a sheet of wax paper. Let the cuminseed cool, fold the wax paper over it, and with a rolling pin crush it to a coarse powder.

In a heavy saucepan cook the onion in the butter over moderately low heat, stirring, until it is softened. Add the cauliflower, the broth, and the water and simmer the mixture, covered, for 20 minutes, or until the cauliflower is tender. In a blender or food processor purée the mixture in batches, return it to the pan, and stir in the half-and-half, the lime juice, and salt and pepper to taste. Heat the soup over low heat, stirring, until it is hot, but do not let it boil, ladle it into bowls, and sprinkle it with the cuminseed powder to taste. Makes about 3 cups, serving 2.

Clam Chowder

1 slice of lean bacon, chopped
1 small onion, chopped fine
1 rib of celery, chopped fine
1 tablespoon unsalted butter
1½ cups milk
a 10-ounce can whole baby clams including
    the liquor or two 6½-ounce cans minced
    clams including the liquor
½ pound potatoes
¼ cup chopped scallion greens

In a heavy saucepan cook the bacon, the onion, and the celery in the butter over moderately low heat, stirring, until the celery is softened, add the milk, the clams with the liquor, and the potatoes, peeled and cut into ½-inch pieces, and simmer the chowder, stirring occasionally, for 15 minutes, or until the potatoes are very tender. Stir in the scallion greens and salt and pepper to taste. Makes about 4 cups, serving 2.

Corn Chowder with Roasted Jalapeño and Parsley Purée

For the purée
5 fresh *jalapeño* chilies
¼ cup olive oil
1½ tablespoons fresh lime juice
1 tablespoon water
1 garlic clove, minced
1 cup packed fresh parsley leaves
For the chowder
1 onion, chopped fine
2 ribs of celery,
    chopped fine
2 tablespoons vegetable oil
2 cups chicken broth
2½ cups water
1½ pounds boiling potatoes
½ pound ham steak if desired, cut into
    ⅜-inch cubes
4 cups fresh corn kernels including the
    pulp scraped from the cobs (cut from
    about 6 ears of corn)
2 teaspoons fresh thyme leaves,
    minced

Make the purée: Broil the *jalapeños* on the rack of a broiler pan under a preheated broiler about 2 inches from the heat, turning them every 5 minutes, for 15 to 20 minutes, or until the skins are blistered and charred. Transfer the *jalapeños* to a bowl and let them stand, covered tightly, until they are cool enough to handle. Wearing rubber gloves, peel the *jalapeños*, cut off the tops, and discard all but 1 teaspoon of the seeds. In a blender purée the *jalapeños* with the seeds, the oil, the lime juice, the water, the garlic, the parsley, and salt to taste. *The purée may be made 3 days in advance and kept covered and chilled.*

Make the chowder: In a kettle cook the onion and the celery in the oil over moderate heat, stirring, until the celery is softened, add the broth, the water, the potatoes, peeled and cut into ⅜-inch cubes, and the ham, and simmer the mixture for 10 minutes. Stir in the corn and the thyme and simmer the chowder for 5 minutes, or until the potatoes are tender. In a blender or food processor purée 2 cups of the chowder and stir the purée into the remaining chowder.

Serve the chowder with a small dollop of the *jalapeño* and parsley purée swirled into it. Makes about 8 cups, serving 4 to 6.

Cold Garlic Potato Soup

¾ cup finely chopped white part of leek,
  washed well and drained
4 large garlic cloves, chopped coarse
1 tablespoon olive oil
a ½-pound russet (baking) potato
2½ cups chicken broth
3 tablespoons heavy cream
1½ tablespoons minced fresh chives

In a heavy saucepan cook the leek and the garlic with salt and pepper to taste in the oil over moderately low heat, stirring, until the leek just begins to soften, add the potato, peeled and cut into 1-inch pieces, and the broth, and simmer the mixture, covered, for 10 to 15 minutes, or until the potato is very tender. In a blender purée the mixture in batches, transferring the soup as it is puréed to a metal bowl set in a larger bowl of ice and cold water. Let the soup cool, stirring occasionally, for 15 minutes, or until it is cold, stir in the cream, the chives, and salt and pepper to taste, and divide the soup between 2 bowls. Makes about 3½ cups, serving 2.

Cold Honeydew and Mint Soup in Cantaloupe

½ large honeydew melon, cut into
  1-inch pieces
1 cup loosely packed fresh mint leaves,
  rinsed and spun dry, plus, if desired,
  6 mint sprigs for garnish
3 tablespoons fresh lime juice
1 to 2 tablespoons sugar
3 cantaloupes, halved and trimmed
  decoratively

In a blender in batches or in a food processor purée the honeydew, the mint leaves, the lime juice, the sugar to taste, and a pinch of salt until the mixture is smooth,

transfer the soup to a bowl, and chill it, covered, for at least 1 hour or overnight. *The soup may be made 2 days in advance and kept covered and chilled.* Arrange the cantaloupe halves on each of 6 small plates, ladle the soup into them, and garnish each serving with a mint sprig. Makes about 6 cups, serving 6.

Leek and Stilton Soup with Port

1 cup finely chopped white and pale green
  part of leek, washed well and drained
1 large garlic clove, minced
½ cup finely chopped celery
½ cup finely chopped carrot
1 bay leaf
½ teaspoon dried thyme, crumbled
2 tablespoons unsalted butter
2 russet (baking) potatoes (about 1 pound)
3 cups chicken broth
1 cup half-and-half
6 ounces Stilton, crumbled (about 1½ cups)
3 tablespoons Tawny Port, or to taste
minced fresh chives for garnish if desired

In a large saucepan cook the leek, the garlic, the celery, and the carrot with the bay leaf and the thyme in the butter over moderate heat, stirring, for 5 minutes, or until the vegetables are softened. Add the potatoes, peeled and sliced thin, and the broth and simmer the mixture, covered, for 15 minutes, or until the potatoes are very tender. Discard the bay leaf and in a blender purée the soup in batches. Transfer the purée to the cleaned pan and stir in the half-and-half. Heat the soup over low heat, whisk in the Stilton, whisking until the cheese is melted and the soup is smooth, and whisk in the Port and salt and pepper to taste. (Do not let the soup boil.) Serve the soup garnished with the chives. Makes about 6 cups, serving 6.

Vicky

Lentil Soup

1 carrot, halved lengthwise and sliced
   thin crosswise
1 small onion, sliced thin
1 garlic clove, minced
1 small bay leaf
1 tablespoon olive oil
2½ cups chicken broth
½ cup lentils, picked over and rinsed
⅓ cup chopped smoked ham
½ cup finely chopped drained bottled roasted
   red peppers
3 tablespoons minced fresh parsley leaves
1 teaspoon balsamic vinegar, or to taste

In a heavy saucepan cook the carrot, the onion, the garlic, and the bay leaf in the oil over moderate heat, stirring occasionally, until the vegetables are softened. Stir in the broth and the lentils and simmer the mixture, covered partially, stirring occasionally, for 25 minutes. Stir in the ham, the roasted peppers, 2 tablespoons of the parsley, the vinegar, and salt and pepper to taste and cook the soup for 1 minute. Discard the bay leaf, divide the soup between 2 bowls, and garnish it with the remaining 1 tablespoon parsley. Serves 2.

Cold Minted Pea and Buttermilk Soup

a 10-ounce package frozen peas
⅔ cup chicken broth
2 tablespoons chopped fresh mint leaves
1 cup buttermilk

In a small saucepan simmer the peas in the broth, covered, for 10 minutes. Transfer the mixture to a blender, add the mint and the buttermilk, and purée the mixture until it is smooth. Transfer the soup to a bowl set in a larger bowl of ice and cold water and chill it, stirring occasionally, for 10 minutes, or until it is cold. Makes about 2½ cups, serving 2.

Split-Pea Soup with Chorizo

1½ pounds cured *chorizo* (spicy pork sausage,
   available at Hispanic markets and many
   supermarkets), sliced thin
1 onion, chopped
1 rib of celery, chopped fine
2 garlic cloves, minced

1 pound split peas, picked over
4 cups chicken broth
4 cups water
½ teaspoon dried thyme, crumbled
1 bay leaf
3 carrots, halved lengthwise and sliced
   thin crosswise
croutons as an accompaniment

In a heavy kettle brown the *chorizo* over moderate heat, stirring, transfer it with a slotted spoon to paper towels to drain, and pour off all but 1 tablespoon of the fat. In the fat remaining in the kettle cook the onion, the celery, and the garlic over moderately low heat, stirring, until the celery is softened, add the split peas, the broth, the water, the thyme, and the bay leaf, and simmer the mixture, covered, stirring occasionally, for 1¼ hours. Stir in the carrots and simmer the soup, covered, for 30 to 35 minutes, or until the carrots are tender. Discard the bay leaf, season the soup with salt and pepper, and serve it with the croutons. Makes about 10 cups, serving 4 to 6.

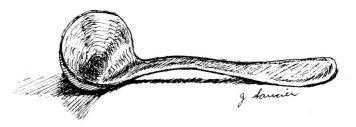

Potato and Leek Soup

the white and pale green part of 2 large leeks,
   split lengthwise, washed well, and chopped
1 tablespoon unsalted butter
1½ cups water
1 cup chicken broth

1 pound boiling potatoes
2 tablespoons minced fresh parsley leaves

In a large heavy saucepan cook the leeks in the butter with salt and pepper to taste, covered, over moderately low heat, stirring occasionally, for 8 to 10 minutes, or until they are softened but not browned. Add the water, the broth, and the potatoes, peeled and cut into ½-inch dice, and simmer the mixture, covered, for 20 minutes, or until the potatoes are tender. In a blender purée 1 cup of the soup, stir the purée into the remaining soup with the parsley, and season the soup with salt and pepper. Makes about 4 cups, serving 2 generously.

Sweet Potato Soup with Buttered Pecans

For the soup
¾ cup finely chopped onion
1 cup finely chopped leek, washed well
    and drained
2 large garlic cloves, minced
3 large carrots, sliced thin (about 1½ cups)
1 bay leaf
3 tablespoons unsalted butter
2 pounds (about 3 large) sweet potatoes
a ½-pound russet (baking) potato
5 cups chicken broth plus additional for
    thinning the soup if desired
¾ cup dry white wine
1½ cups water
For the buttered pecans
¾ cup chopped pecans
2 tablespoons unsalted butter

crème fraîche or sour cream as an
    accompaniment

Make the soup: In a kettle cook the onion, the leek, the garlic, and the carrots with the bay leaf and salt and pepper to taste in the butter over moderate heat, stirring, until the vegetables are softened. Add the sweet potatoes, peeled, halved lengthwise, and sliced thin, the russet potato, peeled, halved lengthwise, and sliced thin, the broth, the wine, and the water, simmer the mixture, covered, for 15 to 20 minutes, or until the potatoes are very tender, and discard the bay leaf. In a blender purée the mixture in batches until it is very smooth, transferring it as it is puréed to a large saucepan, add the additional broth to thin the soup to the desired consis-

tency, and season the soup with salt and pepper. *The soup may be made 1 day in advance, kept covered and chilled, and reheated.*

Make the buttered pecans: In a skillet cook the pecans in the butter with salt to taste over moderate heat, stirring occasionally, for 10 minutes, or until they are golden brown, and transfer them to paper towels to drain. *The pecans may be made 2 days in advance and kept in an airtight container or a resealable plastic bag.*

Divide the soup among bowls and top each serving with a dollop of the *crème fraîche* and some of the buttered pecans. Makes about 11 cups, serving 8 to 10.

PHOTO ON PAGE 73

Spinach and Oyster Bisque

1½ pints shucked oysters including the liquor
1 large onion, chopped
3 tablespoons unsalted butter
1 tablespoon all-purpose flour
1 pound spinach, washed well and the
    coarse stems discarded
½ teaspoon dried tarragon, crumbled
1 cup heavy cream
½ teaspoon freshly grated lemon zest
¼ teaspoon sugar
freshly grated nutmeg to taste
oyster crackers as an accompaniment

Drain the oysters in a fine sieve set over a measuring cup, add enough water to the oyster liquor to measure 2½ cups, and reserve the liquid. Discard any shell fragments from the oysters, rinse the oysters briefly, and chop them into ½-inch pieces. In a kettle cook the onion in the butter over moderate heat, stirring occasionally, until it is pale golden, add the flour, and cook the *roux*, stirring, for 2 minutes. Whisk in the reserved oyster liquid and bring the mixture to a boil, whisking. Add the spinach, half the oysters, and the tarragon and simmer the mixture, stirring, for 2 minutes. In a blender purée the mixture in batches until it is smooth, transferring it as it is puréed to a bowl, and return it to the kettle. Add the cream and the remaining oysters and heat the bisque over moderate heat, stirring, until it is hot and the oysters are cooked, but do not let it boil. Stir in the zest, the sugar, and salt and pepper to taste and serve the bisque with the oyster crackers. Makes about 6½ cups, serving 4 to 6.

PHOTO ON PAGE 60

Chilled Tomato Basil Soup

2½ pounds (about 6) tomatoes,
  cored and cut
  into chunks
1 tablespoon cornstarch
½ cup beef broth
1 tablespoon fresh lemon juice
½ teaspoon sugar
10 whole fresh basil leaves plus
  ⅓ cup chopped fresh basil leaves
  for garnish
sour cream for garnish
extra-virgin olive oil for
  drizzling the soup
garlic *baguette* toasts (page 104) as
  an accompaniment

In a food processor purée the tomatoes and force the purée through a fine sieve into a saucepan, pressing hard on the solids. In a small bowl stir together the cornstarch and the broth and stir the mixture into the tomato purée. Bring the mixture to a boil, stirring, remove the pan from the heat, and stir in the lemon juice, the sugar, the whole basil leaves, and salt and pepper to taste. Let the soup cool and chill it, covered, for at least 8 hours. *The soup may be made 2 days in advance and kept covered and chilled.*

Discard the whole basil leaves, ladle the soup into 6 bowls, and garnish each serving with a dollop of the sour cream and some of the chopped basil. Drizzle the soup with the oil and serve it with the toasts. Makes about 6 cups, serving 6.

PHOTO ON PAGES 48 AND 49

Creamy Tofu, Scallop, Cucumber, and Dill Chowder

¾ cup chopped onion
1 tablespoon olive oil
1 teaspoon all-purpose flour
1 cup chicken broth
1 cup peeled, seeded, and chopped cucumber
¾ cup drained soft or silken tofu
2 teaspoons fresh lemon juice
½ pound bay scallops, rinsed well
2 tablespoons minced fresh dill

In a saucepan cook the onion in the oil over moderately low heat, stirring occasionally, until it is softened, add the flour, and cook the mixture, stirring, for 1 minute. Stir in the broth, bring the mixture to a boil, stirring, and add the cucumber. Bring the mixture to a simmer, transfer half the mixture to a blender, and purée it with the tofu and the lemon juice until the mixture is smooth. Bring the remaining broth mixture in the pan to a boil, add the scallops, and simmer them, stirring, for 3 minutes, or until they are just firm. Reduce the heat to moderately low, stir in the tofu mixture, the dill, and salt and pepper to taste, and heat the chowder, stirring, until it is hot, but do not let it boil. Makes about 3 cups, serving 2.

FISH AND SHELLFISH

FISH

Sautéed Catfish Fillets with Pecan Butter Sauce

all-purpose flour seasoned with salt and
   pepper for dredging the fish
1 large egg
3 tablespoons water
six 6- to 8-ounce catfish fillets
about ⅓ cup vegetable oil for sautéing the fish
¼ cup minced onion
1 garlic clove, minced
¾ stick (6 tablespoons) unsalted butter
½ cup pecans, toasted lightly and
   chopped fine
1 tablespoon fresh lemon juice plus
   6 lemon wedges for garnish
Tabasco to taste

Have ready in separate shallow dishes the flour, and the egg beaten with the water. Dredge each catfish fillet in the flour, shaking off the excess, dip it in the egg mixture, letting the excess drip off, and dredge it in the flour again, shaking off the excess. Transfer the fish as it is coated to a wax paper–lined baking sheet. In a large skillet heat 2 tablespoons of the oil over moderately high heat until it is hot but not smoking and in it sauté the fish in batches, adding the remaining oil as necessary, for 2 to 3 minutes on each side, or until it just flakes. Transfer the fish to paper towels to drain and keep it warm, covered.

In a skillet cook the onion and the garlic in the butter over moderately low heat, stirring, until they are softened, add the pecans, and cook the mixture over moderately high heat, swirling the skillet, until the butter is browned and the pecans are toasted well. Stir in the lemon juice, the Tabasco, and salt and pepper to taste. Divide the fish among 6 heated plates, spoon the butter sauce over it, and garnish each serving with a lemon wedge. Serves 6.

Flounder "Kiev"
(Flounder Rolls with Herbed Butter Filling)

¾ stick (6 tablespoons) unsalted butter, softened
1 garlic clove, minced and mashed to a paste
   with a pinch of salt
2 teaspoons minced fresh parsley leaves
1 teaspoon minced fresh thyme leaves
six ½-pound flounder fillets, halved lengthwise
all-purpose flour seasoned with salt and
   pepper for dredging the fish
2 large eggs, beaten lightly
¼ cup milk
about 2 cups fine dry bread crumbs
vegetable oil for frying the fish

In a bowl whisk together the butter, the garlic paste, the parsley, the thyme, and salt and pepper to taste. Using wax paper as a guide roll the butter mixture into a 6-inch-long log and chill it for 1 hour, or until it is firm. Cut the butter mixture into 1-inch pieces, cut each piece in half, and roll each half into a 1-inch-long log. Chill the logs for 30 minutes, or until they are firm.

On a work surface season the flounder fillet halves, skinned sides up, with salt and pepper, beginning with the narrow end roll up each fillet half around a butter log, and secure each roll, including the sides, with wooden picks to enclose the butter completely.

Have ready in separate shallow dishes the flour, the eggs beaten with the milk and salt and pepper to taste, and the bread crumbs. Dredge each roll in the flour, shaking off the excess, dip it in the egg mixture, letting the excess drip off, and dredge it in the bread crumbs, making sure the roll is coated completely and evenly. Transfer the fish rolls as they are coated to a wax paper–lined baking sheet and chill them, covered, for 1 hour.

In a kettle heat 1½ inches of the oil to 375° F. on a deep-fat thermometer, in it fry the rolls in batches, turning them carefully, for 7 minutes, or until the fish is cooked and the coating is crisp, and transfer them with a slotted spoon to paper towels to drain. Serves 6.

Baked Flounder Fillets
with Lemon-Pepper Vegetables

¼ cup dry white wine
3 tablespoons fresh lemon juice
2 tablespoons finely chopped fresh
  parsley leaves
¼ cup olive oil
½ teaspoon coarsely ground black pepper
1 onion, sliced thin
3 carrots, cut into 2-inch julienne strips
1 yellow squash, cut into 2-inch julienne
  strips
1 zucchini, cut into 2-inch julienne strips
six 6- to 8-ounce flounder fillets,
  halved lengthwise and seasoned
  with salt and pepper

In a bowl whisk together the wine, the lemon juice, the parsley, the oil, the pepper, and salt to taste and add the onion. In another bowl toss together the carrots, the squash, and the zucchini, add about ¼ cup of the liquid from the onion mixture, and toss the mixture well. Spread the onion mixture in the bottom of a greased glass baking dish, 15 by 10 by 2 inches. On a work surface arrange the flounder fillet halves, skinned sides up, beginning with the narrow end roll up each fillet half jelly-roll fashion, and secure each roll with a wooden pick. Arrange the fish rolls, seam sides down and not touching each other, on the onion mixture, put an oiled sheet of parchment or wax paper directly on them, and bake the mixture in the middle of a preheated 400° F. oven for 8 minutes. Spread the vegetable mixture around the rolls and bake the mixture, the fish covered directly with the parchment, for 7 to 12 minutes more, or until the fish just flakes. Transfer the vegetables to a heated platter, arrange the fish rolls on top of them, and spoon the juices over the top. Serves 6.

Baked Flounder Rolls
with Tomato, Bell Pepper, and Bacon

6 slices of lean bacon, chopped fine
¼ cup finely chopped shallot
⅔ cup minced green bell pepper
½ cup dry white wine
a 28-ounce can tomatoes including the juice,
  chopped
½ teaspoon dried basil,
  crumbled

six ½-pound flounder fillets, halved
  lengthwise and seasoned with salt
  and pepper
½ cup fine fresh bread crumbs
2 tablespoons finely chopped fresh
  parsley leaves
1 tablespoon olive oil

In a skillet cook the bacon over moderate heat until it is crisp, transfer it to paper towels to drain, and discard all but 2 tablespoons of the fat. In the fat remaining in the skillet cook the shallot and the bell pepper over moderately low heat, stirring, for 3 minutes, add the wine, and boil the mixture, scraping up the brown bits, for 1 minute. Add the tomatoes with the juice, the basil, and salt and pepper to taste and simmer the sauce, stirring occasionally, for 10 minutes, or until it is thickened.

On a work surface arrange the flounder fillet halves, skinned sides up, beginning with the narrow end roll up each fillet half jelly-roll fashion, and secure each roll with a wooden pick.

In an oiled flameproof baking pan, 15 by 10 by 2 inches, arrange the fish rolls, seam sides down and not touching each other, pour the sauce evenly over them, and bake the mixture in the middle of a preheated 400° F. oven for 10 minutes. In a bowl stir together the bread crumbs, the parsley, the bacon, and salt and pepper to taste and sprinkle the topping over the rolls. Drizzle the fish rolls with the oil and bake the mixture for 10 minutes, or until the fish just flakes. (For a crisper topping, the cooked mixture may be broiled under a preheated broiler about 4 inches from the heat for 1 to 2 minutes.) Transfer the fish rolls to a heated platter and spoon the sauce and topping over them. Serves 6.

Grilled Halibut with Creamy Guacamole Sauce

1 avocado (preferably California)
fresh lemon juice for rubbing the avocado
2 teaspoons fresh lime juice plus 2 lime slices,
  halved, for garnish if desired
2 tablespoons water plus, if desired,
  additional to thin the sauce
1½ tablespoons finely chopped scallion
⅛ teaspoon ground cumin
a pinch of cayenne, or to taste
2 tablespoons sour cream
two ½-pound halibut steaks, seasoned with
  salt and pepper

olive oil for brushing the fish
finely chopped seeded tomato for garnish

Halve the avocado and reserve one half, rubbed with the lemon juice. In a blender purée the remaining avocado half, peeled, the lime juice, 2 tablespoons of the water, the scallion, the cumin, the cayenne, the sour cream, and salt and pepper to taste, scraping down the sides of the blender, until the sauce is smooth. Transfer the sauce to a small bowl and stir in enough additional water to thin the sauce to the desired consistency.

Grill the halibut, brushed generously on both sides with the oil, in an oiled ridged grill pan or on an oiled rack set about 6 inches over glowing coals for 4 to 5 minutes on each side, or until it just flakes. Arrange the steaks on 2 plates, nap them with the sauce, and garnish each serving with the reserved avocado, peeled and sliced thin, fanning the slices, and the lime slices. Sprinkle the plates with the tomato. Serves 2.

Broiled Salmon Steaks with Horseradish Crust
two ¾-inch-thick salmon steaks
2 tablespoons unsalted butter, melted
¼ cup dry white wine
½ cup coarse dry bread crumbs

2 tablespoons well-drained bottled horseradish
1 scallion, minced

Arrange the salmon steaks in a buttered flameproof baking dish just large enough to hold them in one layer, brush them lightly with some of the butter, and season them with salt and pepper. Pour the wine around the steaks and broil the steaks under a preheated broiler about 4 inches from the heat for 4 to 5 minutes, or until they are almost cooked through. While the steaks are cooking, stir together well the remaining butter, the bread crumbs, the horseradish, and the scallion, pat the crumb mixture evenly on the steaks, and broil the steaks for 2 to 4 minutes more, or until they are just cooked through and the crumbs are golden. Serves 2.

Smoked Salmon Horseradish Mousse
¾ teaspoon unflavored gelatin
1 tablespoon cold water
¾ cup sour cream
2 ounces smoked salmon, chopped
    (about ⅓ cup), plus 6 ounces smoked
    salmon, sliced thin
1 tablespoon finely grated peeled fresh
    horseradish or drained bottled horseradish,
    or to taste
2 teaspoons minced fresh dill plus dill sprigs
    for garnish
pumpernickel toast points as an
    accompaniment if desired

In a small saucepan sprinkle the gelatin over the water and let it soften for 1 minute. Heat the mixture over low heat, stirring, until the gelatin is dissolved, add ¼ cup of the sour cream, and cook the mixture, whisking, until it is smooth. In a food processor purée the chopped salmon until it is very smooth. In a small bowl whisk together the gelatin mixture, the remaining ½ cup sour cream, the puréed salmon, the horseradish, the minced dill, and salt and pepper to taste and chill the mousse, covered, for 1 hour, or until it is firm. *The mousse may be made 2 days in advance and kept covered and chilled.*

Scoop oval-shaped mounds of the mousse onto each of 6 chilled plates, arrange the sliced salmon decoratively on the plates, and garnish each serving with a dill sprig. Serve the salmon with the toast points. Serves 6 as a first course.

The following recipe and its accompaniments have been designed to produce leftovers that can be used to make the Salmon Cakes below.

Poached Salmon with Green Peppercorn, Ginger, and Orange Sauce

2 cups water
1 cup dry white wine
4 slices of fresh gingerroot, flattened with the side of a knife
1 tablespoon black peppercorns, bruised
1 bay leaf
a 3½- to 4-pound salmon fillet
For the sauce
½ cup sour cream
¼ cup mayonnaise
2 teaspoons Dijon-style mustard
1½ tablespoons grated peeled fresh gingerroot
1 teaspoon freshly grated orange zest
2 tablespoons fresh orange juice
1½ tablespoons drained green peppercorns
½ teaspoon sugar
1 tablespoon white-wine vinegar

braised onion ribbons with celery and sliced baked potatoes with parsley butter (recipes follow) as accompaniments

In a small saucepan bring the water and the wine to a boil with the gingerroot, the black peppercorns, and the bay leaf and let the mixture stand, off the heat, for 5 minutes. In a large buttered baking dish arrange the salmon, skin side down, and sprinkle it with salt to taste. Add the wine mixture and poach the salmon, covered tightly with foil, in the middle of a 400° F. oven for 20 to 25 minutes, or until it just flakes and is cooked through. (If planning to make the salmon cakes, recipe below, flake enough of the poached salmon to measure 2 cups and reserve it, covered and chilled.)

Make the sauce while the salmon is poaching: In a bowl whisk together the sour cream, the mayonnaise, the mustard, the gingerroot, the zest, the juice, the green peppercorns, the sugar, the vinegar, and salt to taste and let the mixture stand at room temperature for 20 minutes to let the flavors develop.

Serve the salmon with the sauce, the onion ribbons, and the potatoes. Serves 6.

Braised Onion Ribbons with Celery

3½ pounds onions, halved lengthwise and cut crosswise into ½-inch-thick slices
¼ cup olive oil
7 celery ribs, cut diagonally into ½-inch-thick slices

In a large heavy skillet cook the onions in the oil, covered, over moderately low heat, stirring occasionally, for 45 minutes. Season the onions with salt and pepper and cook them, uncovered, over moderately high heat, stirring occasionally, for 30 minutes, or until they are tender and beginning to turn golden. Add the celery and cook the mixture, stirring, for 5 minutes, or until the celery is crisp-tender. (If planning to make the salmon cakes, recipe below, reserve 1½ cups of the mixture, chilled.) Serves 6.

Sliced Baked Potatoes with Parsley Butter

6 russet (baking) potatoes, plus
    2 additional potatoes if planning to make salmon cakes (recipe follows)
¾ stick (6 tablespoons) unsalted butter
2 tablespoons minced fresh parsley leaves

Prick the potatoes a few times with a fork and bake them in the middle of a preheated 400° F. oven for 1 hour. (If planning to make the salmon cakes, recipe follows, reserve the 2 additional baked potatoes, chilled.) In a small saucepan melt the butter and stir in the parsley and salt and pepper to taste. Cut the warm baked potatoes crosswise into ¼-inch-thick slices, arrange the slices, overlapping them, on plates, and drizzle each serving with some of the parsley butter. Serves 6.

Salmon Cakes

2 chilled baked potatoes (preceding recipe)
1½ cups braised onion ribbons with celery (recipe above), chopped
3 tablespoons mayonnaise
1 large egg
1 tablespoon white-wine Worcestershire sauce
½ teaspoon dried thyme, crumbled
2 tablespoons drained bottled capers
2 cups flaked poached salmon fillet (recipe above), or 1 pound drained canned salmon

all-purpose flour for dredging the salmon
   cakes
2 tablespoons unsalted butter
2 tablespoons olive oil
Bibb lettuce for lining the platter
lemon slices for garnish

Remove the skins from the potatoes, grate the potatoes coarse into a large bowl, and add the onion mixture.
In a small bowl whisk together well the mayonnaise, the
egg, the Worcestershire sauce, the thyme, the capers,
and salt and pepper to taste, add the mixture to the potato mixture, and stir the mixture until it is combined well.
Add the salmon and stir the mixture until the salmon is
just distributed evenly. Form ⅓-cup measures of the
mixture into patties and dredge the patties in the flour.
In a large skillet heat the butter and the oil over moderately high heat until the fat is hot but not smoking and in
the fat sauté the patties in batches for 3 minutes on each
side, or until they are golden brown. Line a platter with
the lettuce and serve the salmon cakes with the lemon.
Serves 6.

Steamed Scrod Fillets Chinese Style

½ cup thinly sliced scallion
¼ cup soy sauce
2 tablespoons rice-wine vinegar (available at
   Oriental markets) or white-wine vinegar
a 1½-inch piece of peeled fresh gingerroot,
   cut into very fine julienne strips
2 tablespoons vegetable oil

1 tablespoon Oriental sesame oil plus
   1 teaspoon for drizzling the fish
2 teaspoons sugar
2 garlic cloves, minced and mashed to a
   paste with a pinch of salt
¼ to ½ teaspoon dried hot red pepper flakes
six 6-ounce scrod fillets
cabbage or romaine leaves for lining the
   steamer if desired

In a bowl whisk together the scallion, the soy sauce,
the vinegar, the gingerroot, the vegetable oil, 1 tablespoon of the sesame oil, the sugar, the garlic paste, the
red pepper flakes, and salt and pepper to taste. In a shallow dish arrange the scrod fillets in one layer, pour the
soy sauce mixture over them, and let the fish marinate,
covered and chilled, for 30 minutes.

Put a bamboo steamer in a wok and add enough water
to the wok to allow the bottom rim of the steamer to sit in
the water but the tray to remain above it. (Alternatively,
arrange a steamer rack in a wide deep kettle and add water to the kettle to reach just below the steamer rack.)
Bring the water to a boil. Line the steamer with the cabbage or with a glass pie plate at least 1 inch smaller in
diameter than the steamer, arrange the fillets, folded
into thirds, skinned sides up and seam sides down, on
the cabbage, and pour the marinade evenly over them.
Steam the fish, covered, over the boiling water for 8 to
12 minutes, or until it just flakes, and with oven mitts
remove the steamer from the wok. Transfer the fillets
carefully to a heated platter and drizzle them with the remaining 1 teaspoon sesame oil. Serves 6.

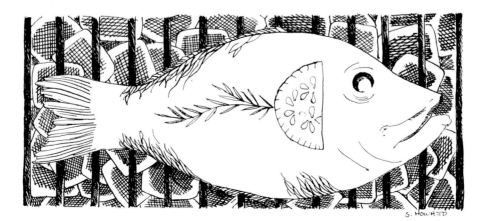

Fish Fillets with Grapefruit Tarragon Beurre Blanc
¼ cup minced shallot
four 6- to 8-ounce white fish fillets such as red
    snapper or scrod
¼ cup plus 2 tablespoons dry white wine
¼ cup plus 2 tablespoons bottled clam juice
⅔ cup fresh grapefruit juice
¼ cup heavy cream
¾ stick (6 tablespoons) cold unsalted butter,
    cut into bits
2 teaspoons minced fresh tarragon leaves or
    ¼ teaspoon dried, crumbled, or to taste
fresh grapefruit sections as an accompaniment

Sprinkle the shallot into a buttered shallow baking
dish just large enough to hold the fish fillets in one layer,
on the shallot arrange the fillets, skin sides down, and
pour the wine and the clam juice over them. Sprinkle the
fillets with salt and pepper to taste and bake them, covered with a buttered piece of wax paper, in the middle
of a preheated 425° F. oven for 10 to 12 minutes, or
until they are just cooked through. Transfer the fillets
with a slotted spatula to a large platter and keep them
warm, covered.

Strain the cooking liquid through a fine sieve into a
small saucepan, add the grapefruit juice, and boil the
mixture until it is reduced to about ⅔ cup. Add the
cream and boil the mixture until it is reduced by half.
Reduce the heat to low and whisk in the butter, 1 bit at a
time, lifting the pan from the heat occasionally to let the
mixture cool and adding each new bit of butter before
the previous one has melted completely. (The sauce
should not get hot enough to liquefy. It should be the
consistency of thin hollandaise.) Whisk in the tarragon
and salt and pepper to taste. With the slotted spatula
transfer each fillet, skin side down, to a plate. Pour one
fourth of the sauce over each fillet and arrange some of
the grapefruit sections around each plate. Serves 4.

Sautéed Red Snapper
with Creamed Fennel and Onion
1 small onion, sliced thin
1 fennel or anise bulb (about ¾ pound),
    trimmed and sliced thin
3 tablespoons unsalted butter
2 tablespoons medium-dry Sherry
¼ cup heavy cream
1 teaspoon balsamic vinegar

⅛ teaspoon fennel seeds, or to taste
about ¼ cup water
two ½-pound red snapper fillets seasoned on
    both sides with salt and pepper

In a skillet cook the onion and the sliced fennel in 2
tablespoons of the butter, covered, over moderate heat,
stirring occasionally, for 12 minutes, or until the fennel
is just tender. Stir in the Sherry and boil the mixture, uncovered, for 1 minute. Stir in the cream, the vinegar, the
fennel seeds, and salt and pepper to taste, cook the mixture over moderate heat, stirring, adding the water as
needed to thin the sauce if desired, for 30 seconds.
Transfer the mixture to a bowl and keep it warm.

In the skillet, cleaned, heat the remaining 1 tablespoon butter over moderately high heat until the foam
subsides and in it sauté the snapper, starting skin sides
down, for 3 minutes on each side, or until it just flakes.
Divide the onion and fennel mixture between 2 heated
plates and arrange a snapper fillet on each plate.
Serves 2.

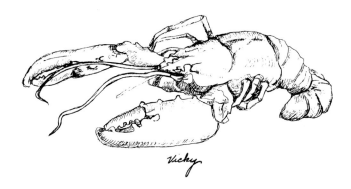

Vicky.

Broiled Swordfish with Watercress Yogurt Topping
½ cup plain yogurt
2 cups loosely packed watercress leaves,
    rinsed and spun dry
3 tablespoons mayonnaise
1 garlic clove, minced
two 1-inch-thick swordfish steaks
    (about 6 ounces each)

Let the yogurt drain in a fine sieve for 20 minutes. In a
food processor purée coarse the watercress with the yogurt, the mayonnaise, the garlic, and salt and pepper to
taste. Season the swordfish with salt and pepper, arrange it on the oiled rack of a broiler pan lined with foil,

and spread half the watercress topping on it. Broil the swordfish under a preheated broiler about 4 inches from the heat for 8 minutes. Turn the swordfish, spread it with the remaining topping, and broil it for 5 minutes more, or until it is cooked through. Serves 2.

Tuna and Sun-Dried Tomato Sandwiches

2 tablespoons mayonnaise
2 tablespoons plain yogurt
1 garlic clove, minced and mashed to a paste
    with ¼ teaspoon salt
3 tablespoons minced fresh basil leaves
1 to 2 teaspoons fresh lemon juice
a 6½-ounce can tuna packed in oil or water,
    drained and flaked
1 tablespoon finely chopped pitted Kalamata
    or other brine-cured black olives, or to taste
2 tablespoons minced drained sun-dried
    tomatoes packed in oil
2 scallions, chopped fine
two 5-inch lengths of Italian or French bread,
    halved horizontally and toasted or grilled
arugula or lettuce leaves

In a bowl whisk together the mayonnaise, the yogurt, the garlic paste, the basil, the lemon juice to taste, and salt and pepper to taste and stir in the tuna, the olives, the sun-dried tomatoes, and the scallions. Divide the tuna mixture between the bottom halves of the bread, top the sandwiches with the *arugula*, and cover them with the top halves of the bread, pressing them firmly. Makes 2 sandwiches.

SHELLFISH

Lobster and Mango Cocktail

⅓ cup mayonnaise
⅓ cup plain yogurt
2 tablespoons Cognac
1 tablespoon ketchup
1 tablespoon fresh lemon juice, or to taste
four 1½-pound live lobsters
3 firm-ripe mangoes
1 cup finely diced celery
4 whole Belgian endives plus 12 leaves
    for garnish

3 tablespoons minced fresh chives plus
    24 whole chives for garnish

In a small bowl whisk together the mayonnaise, the yogurt, the Cognac, the ketchup, the lemon juice, and salt and pepper to taste and chill the sauce, covered. Plunge the lobsters into a large kettle of boiling salted water and boil them, covered, for 10 minutes. Transfer the lobsters with tongs to a bowl and let them cool until they can be handled. Crack the shells, remove the meat, and cut it into ¾-inch pieces. Transfer the lobster meat to a large bowl and chill it, covered. *The lobster cocktail may be prepared up to this point 1 day in advance.*

Halve the mangoes by cutting just to the sides of each pit and using a ¾-inch melon-ball cutter scoop the flesh from the mango halves. (There should be about 2 cups.) To the lobster meat add the mango balls, the celery, the whole endives, trimmed and sliced thin crosswise, the minced chives, and the sauce and toss the mixture until it is combined. Divide the lobster mixture among 12 chilled small glasses and garnish each serving with 1 of the endive leaves and 2 of the whole chives. Serves 12.

PHOTO ON PAGE 44

Mussels with Shallots and Tarragon

24 mussels (preferably cultivated)
½ cup dry white wine
2 shallots, sliced thin
a 2½- by 1-inch strip of lemon zest
½ teaspoon fennel seeds
¼ teaspoon dried tarragon,
    crumbled
½ cup thinly sliced red onion
2 tablespoons extra-virgin olive oil

Scrub the mussels well in several changes of water, scrape off the beards, and rinse the mussels. In a 2-quart microwave-safe round glass casserole with a lid combine the wine, the shallots, the zest, the fennel seeds, and the tarragon and microwave the mixture, covered, at high power (100%) for 3 minutes. Stir in the mussels and microwave the mixture, covered, at high power, stirring once every minute and transferring any mussels that are wide open to a bowl and keeping them warm, for 2½ to 4 minutes. Discard any unopened mussels. Return the mussels to the casserole, sprinkle them with the onion, and drizzle them with the oil. Let the mussels stand for 1 minute. Serves 2.

Mussels and Zucchini Marinière

2 cups chopped onion
2 tablespoons unsalted butter
2 garlic cloves, minced
¾ cup dry white wine or vermouth
⅓ cup heavy cream
3 tablespoons fresh fine bread crumbs
2 zucchini, scrubbed, halved lengthwise, and
   cut into ⅛-inch-thick slices
2 pounds mussels, scrubbed and the beards
   pulled off
⅓ cup minced fresh parsley leaves
crusty bread as an accompaniment

In a kettle cook the onion in the butter over moderate heat, stirring occasionally, until it is softened, add the garlic, and cook the mixture for 1 minute. Stir in the wine, simmer the mixture for 2 minutes, and stir in the cream and the bread crumbs. Bring the cream mixture to a simmer, add the zucchini and the mussels, and steam the mixture, covered, for 3 minutes, or until the zucchini is crisp-tender and the mussels are opened. Discard any unopened mussels. Stir in the parsley and salt to taste, divide the mussel mixture between 2 soup plates, and serve it with the bread. Serves 2.

Fried Shrimp with Peanut Sauce

¼ cup creamy peanut butter
4 teaspoons soy sauce
4 teaspoons fresh lemon juice,
   or to taste
2 teaspoons firmly packed light
   brown sugar
1 large garlic clove, minced
⅓ cup plus 2 tablespoons water
cayenne to taste
2 tablespoons thinly sliced scallion greens
1 large egg
¾ pound small shrimp (about 32), shelled
all-purpose flour seasoned with salt
   and pepper
vegetable oil for deep-frying the shrimp

In a small heavy saucepan combine the peanut butter, the soy sauce, the lemon juice, the brown sugar, the garlic, ⅓ cup of the water, and the cayenne, bring the mixture just to a boil, whisking until it is smooth, and whisk in the scallion greens. Keep the sauce warm. In a small bowl whisk together the egg and the remaining 2 tablespoons water and add the shrimp. In a large plastic bag have ready the flour. Add the shrimp, drained well, to the flour, shake them to coat them with the flour, and in a sieve shake them to knock off the excess flour. In a deep skillet heat 1 inch of the oil until a deep-fat thermometer registers 375° F., in it fry the shrimp in 2 batches, stirring them once, for 1 minute, or until they are just cooked through, and transfer them with a slotted spoon to paper towels to drain. Serve the shrimp with the sauce. Serves 2.

MEAT

BEEF

Grilled Beef Blade Steaks and Bell Peppers
with Spicy Orange Marinade

six 1-inch-thick boneless beef blade steaks,
  pierced all over on both sides with a fork
2 large red bell peppers, quartered
the zest from 2 navel oranges, removed with
  a vegetable peeler
1 cup fresh orange juice
⅓ cup vegetable oil
2 garlic cloves
1 tablespoon soy sauce
1 teaspoon dried hot red pepper flakes
1 tablespoon cider vinegar
½ teaspoon salt

In a large shallow dish arrange the blade steaks in one
layer and add the bell peppers. In a blender blend
together the orange zest, the orange juice, the oil, the
garlic, the soy sauce, the red pepper flakes, the vinegar, and the salt until the marinade is smooth, pour the
marinade over the steaks and peppers, coating them
thoroughly, and let the mixture marinate, covered and
chilled, overnight.
  Grill the steaks and the bell peppers, the marinade
discarded, on an oiled rack set 5 to 6 inches over glowing coals for 8 minutes on each side for medium-rare
steaks, transfer them to a platter, and let the steaks stand
for 5 minutes. Serves 6.

Grilled Beer-Marinated Chuck Steak and Onions

12 ounces beer
  (not dark)
⅔ cup vegetable oil
2 tablespoons cider vinegar
1 tablespoon Worcestershire sauce
1 teaspoon salt
½ teaspoon freshly ground black pepper
six ½-inch-thick slices of yellow or red
  onion, secured horizontally with
  wooden picks, plus 1 tablespoon
  grated onion
3½ pounds 1-inch-thick boneless chuck steak,
  trimmed and pierced all over on both sides
  with a fork

In a large shallow dish whisk together the beer, the
oil, the vinegar, the Worcestershire sauce, the salt, the
pepper, and the grated onion and add the chuck steak
and the onion slices, coating them thoroughly with the
marinade. Let the mixture marinate, covered and
chilled, turning the steak once, overnight.
  Let the mixture stand at room temperature for 1 hour
and grill the steak with the onions, the marinade discarded, on an oiled rack set 5 to 6 inches over glowing
coals for 8 minutes on each side for medium-rare steak.
Transfer the steak to a carving board and the onions to a
platter, discarding the wooden picks. Let the steak stand
for 5 minutes and, holding a carving knife at a 45° angle,
cut the steak across the grain into thin slices. Transfer
the steak to the platter. Serves 6.

Cincinnati-Style Chili

3 onions, chopped
6 garlic cloves, minced
3 tablespoons vegetable oil
4 pounds ground beef chuck
⅓ cup chili powder
2 tablespoons sweet paprika
2 teaspoons ground cumin
1 teaspoon ground coriander
1 teaspoon ground allspice
1 teaspoon dried orégano, crumbled
½ teaspoon cayenne
½ teaspoon cinnamon
¼ teaspoon ground cloves
¼ teaspoon ground mace
1 bay leaf
3 cups water
a 16-ounce can tomato sauce
2 tablespoons wine vinegar
2 tablespoons molasses
spaghetti, kidney beans, chopped onion,
    grated Cheddar, and oyster crackers as
    traditional accompaniments if desired

In a large heavy kettle cook the onions and the garlic in the oil over moderate heat, stirring, until the onions are softened, add the beef, and cook the mixture, stirring and breaking up the lumps, until the beef is no longer pink. Add the chili powder, the paprika, the cumin, the coriander, the allspice, the orégano, the cayenne, the cinnamon, the cloves, and the mace and cook the mixture, stirring, for 1 minute. Add the bay leaf, the water, the tomato sauce, the vinegar, and the molasses and simmer the mixture, uncovered, stirring occasionally and adding more water if necessary to keep the beef barely covered, for 2 hours, or until it is thickened but soupy enough to be ladled. Discard the bay leaf and season the chili with salt and pepper. *The chili may be frozen or made 4 days in advance, cooled, uncovered, and kept covered and chilled.* Serve the chili as is or in the traditional Cincinnati ''five-way'' style: Ladle the chili over the spaghetti and top it with the beans, the onion, the Cheddar, and the oyster crackers. Makes about 8 cups, serving 6.

Texas-Style Chili

¼ pound bacon, chopped
3 medium onions, chopped
8 garlic cloves, minced
⅓ cup medium-hot pure chili powder*
1 tablespoon ground cumin
4 pounds boneless beef chuck, cut into
    ½-inch pieces
5 cups water
2 teaspoons dried orégano,
    crumbled
2 teaspoons salt, or to taste
1 tablespoon cornmeal

* available at some specialty foods shops and
    by mail order from Los Chileros de Nueva
    Mexico, Santa Fe, NM, Tel. (505) 471-6967
    or Adriana's Bazaar, New York City,
    Tel. (212) 877-5757

In a large heavy kettle cook the bacon over moderate heat, stirring, until it is crisp, add the onions and the garlic, and cook the mixture, stirring, until the onions are softened. Add the chili powder and the cumin and cook the mixture, stirring, for 30 seconds. Add the beef, the water, the orégano, and the salt and simmer the mixture, uncovered, adding more water if necessary to keep the beef barely covered, for 2 to 2½ hours, or until the beef is tender. Stir in the cornmeal and simmer the chili, stirring occasionally, for 5 minutes, or until it is thickened slightly. *The chili may be frozen or made 4 days in advance, cooled, uncovered, and kept covered and chilled.* Makes about 8 cups, serving 6.

Picadillo Empanadas with Cornmeal Crust

For the cornmeal dough
a ¼-ounce package (2½ teaspoons)
    active dry yeast
1½ tablespoons sugar
½ cup milk, heated to lukewarm
1 large whole egg, beaten lightly
1 large egg yolk, beaten lightly
⅓ cup sour cream
5 tablespoons unsalted butter, melted
    and cooled
2½ cups all-purpose flour
1¼ cups yellow cornmeal
¾ teaspoon salt
For the picadillo
1¼ cups finely chopped onion
2 teaspoons minced garlic

2 drained bottled pickled large *jalapeño*
  chilies, seeded and minced (wear
  rubber gloves), about 1½ tablespoons
2 teaspoons ground cumin
1 tablespoon chili powder
1 teaspoon dried orégano, crumbled
½ teaspoon cinnamon
a pinch of ground cloves
2 tablespoons vegetable oil
1 pound ground beef chuck
¼ cup tomato paste
a 28-ounce can plum tomatoes including
  the juice, chopped
⅓ cup raisins
½ cup plus 2 tablespoons finely chopped
  pimiento-stuffed green olives
  (about 4½ ounces)
dried hot red pepper flakes to taste

Make the cornmeal dough: In the large bowl of an electric mixer proof the yeast with the sugar in ¼ cup of the milk for 5 minutes, or until the mixture is foamy. Beat in the remaining ¼ cup milk, the whole egg, the egg yolk, the sour cream, and the butter, add 2 cups of the flour, the cornmeal, and the salt, and beat the mixture until it forms a dough. With the dough hook knead the dough, adding as much of the remaining ½ cup flour as necessary to keep the dough from sticking, for 4 minutes, or until it is smooth and elastic. Form the dough into a ball, transfer it to an oiled bowl, and turn it to coat it with the oil. Let the dough rise, covered with plastic wrap, in a warm place for 1½ hours and punch it down.

The dough may be made 1 day in advance and kept covered and chilled. Let the dough return to room temperature before proceeding with the recipe.

Make the *picadillo*: In a large heavy skillet cook the onion, the garlic, the *jalapeños*, the cumin, the chili powder, the orégano, the cinnamon, the cloves, and pepper to taste in the oil over moderately low heat, stirring, until the onion is softened, add the chuck, and cook the mixture over moderately high heat, stirring and breaking up any lumps, until the meat is no longer pink. Add the tomato paste, the tomatoes with the juice, the raisins, the olives, the red pepper flakes, and salt and pepper to taste, simmer the *picadillo*, stirring occasionally, for 10 to 15 minutes, or until it is thickened and most of the liquid is evaporated, and let it cool. *The* picadillo *may be made 1 day in advance and kept covered and chilled. Let the* picadillo *return to room temperature before proceeding with the recipe.*

Divide the dough into 12 pieces. Working with 1 piece of dough at a time and keeping the remaining pieces covered with plastic wrap, on a lightly floured surface roll out the dough ⅛ thick and with a 6-inch round cutter cut each piece into a round. Put about ⅓ cup of the *picadillo* onto the bottom two thirds of each round and fold the rounds in half, enclosing the filling. Seal the edges of the dough and crimp them decoratively. Transfer the *empanadas* with a spatula to a lightly oiled baking sheet and bake them in the middle of a preheated 450° F. oven for 10 to 15 minutes, or until they are golden. Transfer the *empanadas* to a rack and let them cool. Makes 12 *empanadas*.

PHOTO ON PAGE 64

Corned Beef with Horseradish Mustard Sauce

a 3-pound corned beef brisket
2 tablespoons bottled horseradish
2 tablespoons Dijon-style mustard

In a kettle combine the corned beef with enough cold water to cover it by 2 inches, bring the water just to a boil, skimming the froth, and simmer the corned beef, covered, for 3 hours, or until it is tender. (Do not let the cooking liquid boil.) Remove the kettle from the heat and let the corned beef stand in the cooking liquid for 20 minutes. In a small bowl stir together the horseradish and the mustard. Transfer the corned beef to a cutting board and with a sharp knife remove all but a very thin layer of fat. Cut the corned beef across the grain into ¼-inch-thick slices and serve it with the sauce. Serves 4 generously.

PHOTO ON PAGE 28

Sautéed Filets Mignons with Peppered Cuminseed Crusts

1 tablespoon freeze-dried green peppercorns, chopped coarse
1 teaspoon cuminseed, chopped coarse
coarse salt to taste
two 1½-inch-thick filets mignons (about ½ pound each), tied
1 tablespoon vegetable oil

In a small bowl combine well the peppercorns, the cuminseed, and the salt, pat the mixture onto both sides of each filet, and let the filets stand, uncovered, at room temperature for 15 minutes. In a heavy skillet, preferably cast iron, heat the oil over moderately high heat until it is hot but not smoking and in it sauté the filets for 1 minute on each side. Reduce the heat to moderately low and cook the filets for 5 minutes more on each side for medium-rare meat. Transfer the filets to plates, let them stand for 5 minutes, and discard the string. Serves 2.

Grilled Porterhouse Steaks with Olive and Caper Spread

1 cup green olives (such as Picholine or Calabrese), pitted
1 cup black olives (such as Niçoise or Kalamata), pitted
1 tablespoon drained bottled capers

two 2-inch-thick porterhouse steaks
olive oil for brushing the steaks
parsley sprigs for garnish if desired

In a food processor chop coarse the olives and the capers. *The olive and caper spread may be made 1 day in advance and kept covered and chilled.* Pat the steaks dry with paper towels, brush them with the oil, and season them with salt and pepper. Grill the steaks on a rack set 4 inches over glowing coals for 10 minutes on each side for rare to medium-rare meat. (Alternatively, the steaks may be broiled on the rack of a broiler pan under a preheated broiler about 4 inches from the heat for 10 minutes on each side.) Let the steaks stand, covered loosely with foil, for 8 minutes. Serve the steaks, sliced, with the olive and caper spread garnished with the parsley. Serves 6.

PHOTO ON PAGES 38 AND 39

Roast Prime Ribs of Beef with Shiitake Pan Gravy

a 4-rib standing rib roast (trimmed weight 10 to 10½ pounds)
1 tablespoon minced fresh rosemary leaves
1 teaspoon salt
½ stick (¼ cup) plus 1½ tablespoons unsalted butter, softened
1 onion, chopped
1 green bell pepper, chopped
1 ounce dried *shiitake* mushrooms
2 cups hot water
¼ pound fresh mushrooms, sliced
2½ cups canned beef broth
½ cup medium-dry Sherry
4 teaspoons arrowroot, dissolved in 2 tablespoons cold water
dried-corn puddings as an accompaniment (recipe follows)

Let the rib roast stand at room temperature for 1 hour. In a small bowl knead together the rosemary, the salt, and ½ stick of the butter and rub the meat with the mixture. In a roasting pan roast the meat, ribs side down, in a preheated 500° F. oven for 30 minutes, reduce the heat to 350° F., and roast the meat for 1¾ to 2 hours more, or until a meat thermometer inserted in a fleshy section registers 130° F. for medium-rare meat. Forty-five minutes before the roast is done add the onion and the bell pepper to the pan. During the last 40 minutes of roasting, in a bowl let the *shiitake* mushrooms soak in the water for 30 minutes, squeeze out the excess liquid, and reserve the soaking liquid in the bowl. Discard the stems and slice the caps thin. Strain the reserved liquid through a fine sieve into another bowl. Transfer the roast to a heated platter, discarding the strings, transfer the onion and the bell pepper to paper towels to drain, and reserve them for the *shiitake* pan gravy. Let the roast stand for 20 to 30 minutes before carving.

In a heavy skillet sauté the fresh mushrooms in the remaining 1½ tablespoons butter over moderately high heat, stirring, for 1 minute, add the *shiitake* mushrooms, and sauté the mixture, stirring, for 1 minute. Add the broth and the reserved mushroom liquid and boil the liquid until it is reduced to about 2½ cups. Skim all but 1 tablespoon of the fat from the pan juices in the roasting pan, add the reserved onion and bell pepper and the Sherry, and sauté the mixture over moderately high heat, scraping up the brown bits, for 1 minute. Boil the Sherry mixture until it is reduced by half, strain it through the fine sieve into the mushroom mixture, and bring the mixture to a boil. Stir the arrowroot mixture and add it to the gravy, stirring. Simmer the gravy, stirring, for 3 minutes, add salt and pepper to taste, and transfer the gravy to a heated sauceboat.

Serve the roast with the pan gravy and the dried-corn puddings. Serves 8 generously.

PHOTO ON PAGE 80

Dried-Corn Puddings

2 cups dried sweet corn (available by mail order from John Cope's Food Products, Inc., P.O. Box 419, Rheems, PA 17570-0419, Tel. 717-367-5142, and at some specialty foods shops)
2 teaspoons salt
4½ teaspoons sugar
3½ cups milk, scalded
1 tablespoon double-acting baking powder
4 large eggs, beaten lightly
1 cup thinly sliced scallion greens
⅔ cup thawed frozen corn kernels, patted dry
rosemary sprigs for garnish

In a blender grind the dried corn until it resembles coarse meal. In a bowl whisk together the ground corn, the salt, the sugar, and the milk and let the mixture stand at room temperature for 1 hour. Whisk in the baking

powder, the eggs, the scallion greens, the corn kernels, and pepper to taste, pour the batter into sixteen ½-cup metal charlotte molds coated with non-stick spray, and bake the puddings on a baking sheet in the middle of a preheated 375° F. oven for 20 to 25 minutes, or until a knife inserted in the centers comes out clean. (Alternatively, the pudding may be baked in a buttered 1½-quart shallow baking dish.) Let the puddings cool for 5 minutes, run a thin knife around the side of each pudding, and invert the puddings, 1 at a time, onto a spatula. Invert the puddings onto a platter and garnish them with the rosemary. Serves 8.

PHOTO ON PAGE 80

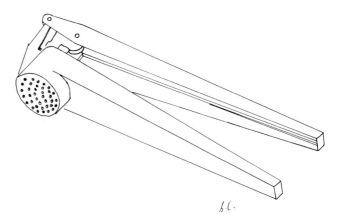

Barbecued Beef Rib Bones

18 meaty beef rib bones (cut from a rib roast), separated
⅓ cup soy sauce
2 large garlic cloves, forced through a garlic press or minced
3 tablespoons fresh lemon juice
¼ cup ketchup
1 tablespoon sugar
1 teaspoon freshly ground black pepper
¼ teaspoon salt

Divide the beef rib bones between 2 resealable plastic bags, in a bowl whisk together the soy sauce, the garlic, the lemon juice, the ketchup, the sugar, the pepper, and the salt, and divide the marinade between the bags, coating the ribs thoroughly. Seal the bags and let the ribs marinate, chilled, turning the bags occasionally, for at least 8 hours or overnight.

Grill the ribs, the marinade discarded, on an oiled rack set 5 to 6 inches over glowing coals for 8 minutes on each side for medium-rare meat. Serves 6.

VEAL

Veal Chops with Saga Blue Butter

¼ cup Saga Blue or other blue cheese
    (about 1 ounce)
1 teaspoon unsalted butter, softened
¾ teaspoon fresh lemon juice
1 teaspoon finely chopped fresh parsley leaves
1 tablespoon olive oil
two 1-inch-thick rib veal chops
    (about ½ pound each), frenched if desired

In a small bowl mash together the Saga Blue, the butter, the lemon juice, the parsley, and salt and pepper to taste until the mixture is smooth. Transfer the mixture to a sheet of wax paper, roll it into a log, and chill it for 15 minutes.

In a skillet, preferably cast-iron, heat the oil over moderately high heat until it is hot but not smoking, in it sauté the chops, patted dry and seasoned with salt and pepper, for 5 to 6 minutes on each side for barely pink meat, and top each chop with half the Saga Blue butter. Serves 2.

Roasted Loin of Veal with Garlic, Shallots, and Mustard Gravy

a 2- to 2½-pound boned veal loin (preferably
    naturally raised*), trimmed and tied loosely
    at 1-inch intervals with kitchen string
⅓ cup Dijon-style mustard
thin slices of fatback for covering the veal
    (about 6 ounces)
1 head of garlic, separated into cloves
    and peeled
12 shallots, peeled
½ cup dry white wine
3 teaspoons finely chopped fresh tarragon plus
    tarragon sprigs for garnish
¼ cup water

*naturally raised prepared veal loin is
    available by mail from Summerfield Farm,
    HC 4 Box 195A, Brightwood, VA 22715,
    Tel. (703) 948-3100

Season the veal with salt and pepper, spread the mustard over the top and sides, and cover the veal with the fatback. Arrange the veal, the garlic, and the shallots in a roasting pan just large enough to hold them, add the wine, and roast the veal in the middle of a preheated 325° F. oven, basting every 15 minutes, for 1 hour. Discard the fatback and roast the veal for 15 to 20 minutes more, or until it registers 150° F. on a meat thermometer. Transfer the veal to a cutting board and let it stand, covered loosely with foil, for 15 minutes. Transfer the garlic and the shallots with a slotted spoon to a bowl, toss them with 2 teaspoons of the chopped tarragon, and keep them warm, covered with foil.

While the veal is standing, skim the fat from the pan juices, add the water, and deglaze the pan over high heat, scraping up the brown bits, until the mixture is reduced by half. Strain the mixture through a fine sieve into a bowl and season the gravy with salt and pepper. Cut the veal into ½-inch-thick slices, arrange the slices on a platter, and scatter the garlic and the shallots around them. Nap the veal with some of the gravy, sprinkle it with the remaining 1 teaspoon chopped tarragon, and garnish the platter with the tarragon sprigs. Serve the remaining gravy separately. Serves 6.

PHOTO ON PAGE 47

Veal Scallops with Lemon and Artichokes

1½ pounds veal scallops, each about ⅛ inch thick
all-purpose flour seasoned with salt
    and pepper for dredging the veal
2 tablespoons olive oil
3 tablespoons unsalted butter
3 tablespoons fresh lemon juice
¾ cup chicken broth
a 6-ounce jar marinated artichoke hearts,
    drained, rinsed well, and cut lengthwise
    into ¼-inch-thick slices

Dredge the veal in the flour, shaking off the excess. In a large heavy skillet heat the oil and 2 tablespoons of the butter over moderately high heat until the foam subsides, in the fat sauté the veal in batches for 45 seconds on each side, or until it is golden, transferring it as it is cooked to a heated platter, and keep it warm. To the skillet add the lemon juice and the broth and simmer the mixture, stirring and scraping up the brown bits, for 2 minutes. Strain the mixture through a fine sieve into a small saucepan, add the artichokes, and simmer the sauce for 2 minutes. Remove the pan from the heat, swirl in the remaining 1 tablespoon butter, and season the sauce with salt and pepper. Divide the veal among 4 heated plates and nap it with the sauce. Serves 4.

PHOTO ON PAGE 62

Veal Scallops with Lemon and Capers

¼ cup all-purpose flour
½ teaspoon salt
four 3-ounce veal scallops,
  each about ⅛ inch thick
1 tablespoon olive oil
½ cup dry white wine
three ¼-inch lemon slices, halved
1 teaspoon drained bottled capers
1 tablespoon unsalted butter
1 teaspoon minced fresh parsley leaves

In a dish stir together the flour and the salt and in the flour mixture dredge the veal, shaking off the excess. In a non-stick skillet heat the oil over moderately high heat until it is hot but not smoking and in it sauté the veal for 1 minute, or until it is pale golden. Turn the veal and sauté it for 30 seconds more, or until it is pale golden and just springy to the touch. Transfer the veal to a platter and keep it warm, covered. Add to the skillet the wine, the lemon, and the capers and simmer the mixture for 1 minute. Swirl in the butter and the parsley and pour the sauce over the veal. Serves 2.

PORK

Broiled Spiced Pork Chops

¼ teaspoon salt
⅛ teaspoon cinnamon
⅛ teaspoon ground allspice
a pinch of ground cloves
two ½-inch-thick loin pork chops

In a small bowl stir together the salt, the cinnamon, the allspice, the cloves, and pepper to taste. Pat the pork chops dry with paper towels, rub the spice mixture on both sides of them, and chill the chops, covered, for 30 minutes. Broil the chops on the oiled rack of a broiler pan under a preheated broiler about 4 inches from the heat for 5 minutes on each side, or until they are cooked through. Serves 2.

Grilled Apple- and Herb-Marinated Pork Chops and Potatoes

six 1-inch-thick center-cut loin or shoulder
  pork chops
2 pounds small boiling potatoes, scrubbed
a 6-ounce can frozen apple juice concentrate,
  thawed
⅓ cup apple jelly
¼ cup vegetable oil
3 tablespoons cider vinegar
2 tablespoons Worcestershire sauce
2 tablespoons Dijon-style mustard
2 teaspoons dried rosemary, crumbled
1 teaspoon dried sage, crumbled
2 teaspoons salt
1 teaspoon freshly ground black pepper

Arrange the pork chops in one layer in a large shallow dish. In a kettle combine the potatoes with enough water to cover them by 1 inch, simmer them for 10 minutes, or until they are just tender, and drain them. In a blender blend together well the apple juice concentrate, the jelly, the oil, the vinegar, the Worcestershire sauce, the mustard, the rosemary, the sage, the salt, and the pepper. Halve the potatoes and in a bowl toss them gently with ¼ cup of the apple and herb marinade. Pour the remaining marinade over the chops, coating them thoroughly, and let the chops and the potatoes marinate separately, covered and chilled, overnight.

Grill the chops, the marinade discarded, on an oiled rack set 5 to 6 inches over glowing coals for 7 to 8 minutes on each side, or until they are just cooked through. Grill the potatoes, cut sides down, for 10 minutes, or until they are golden brown. Serves 6.

Sautéed Pork Chops with Sauerkraut

1 slice of lean bacon,
  chopped
1 small onion, sliced thin
¾ teaspoon caraway seeds
1½ cups sauerkraut (about ½ pound), rinsed
  and drained
½ cup apple juice
two 1-inch-thick loin pork chops
1 tablespoon vegetable oil
2 tablespoons finely chopped fresh dill

In a heavy saucepan cook the bacon over moderate heat, stirring, until it is crisp, add the onion and the caraway seeds, and cook the mixture, stirring, until the onion is golden. Add the sauerkraut and the apple juice and simmer the mixture, covered, for 20 minutes.

While the sauerkraut mixture is simmering, sprinkle both sides of the chops with salt, let the chops stand between layers of paper towel for 10 minutes, and season them with pepper. In a heavy skillet heat the oil over moderately high heat until it is hot but not smoking and in it sauté the chops for 5 to 6 minutes on each side, or until they are just cooked through. Stir 1 tablespoon of the dill into the sauerkraut mixture and transfer the mixture to a heated platter. Top the sauerkraut mixture with the chops and sprinkle the chops with the remaining 1 tablespoon dill. Serves 2.

The following recipe and its accompaniment have been designed to produce leftovers that can be used to make the Pork Chow Mein (recipe opposite).

Garlic- and Soy-Marinated Pork Roast with Shiitake Mushroom Gravy

a 4½- to 5-pound center-cut pork loin
  roast (may include a few ribs)
⅔ cup soy sauce
⅓ cup medium-dry Sherry
¼ cup firmly packed brown sugar
3 large garlic cloves, minced
3 onions, chopped coarse
1 tablespoon olive oil
⅔ cup water plus additional
  if necessary
For the gravy
½ pound fresh *shiitake* mushrooms, stems
  discarded and the caps sliced

1½ tablespoons olive oil
1 cup dry white wine
2 cups chicken broth
a *beurre manié* made by kneading together
  3 tablespoons softened unsalted
  butter and 3 tablespoons
  all-purpose flour

mixed vegetables with parsley and pine nuts
  (recipe follows) as an accompaniment

In a shallow dish just large enough to hold the pork roast whisk together the soy sauce, the Sherry, the brown sugar, the garlic, and salt and pepper to taste until the sugar is dissolved, add the pork, and let it marinate, covered and chilled, turning it several times, for at least 8 hours or overnight. Transfer the pork to a work surface and pat it dry, discarding the marinade. In a roasting pan toss the onions with the oil, add the pork, seasoned with salt and pepper, and pour ⅔ cup of the water over the onions. Roast the pork in the middle of a preheated 350° F. oven, stirring the onions occasionally and, if necessary, adding just enough of the additional water to prevent the onions from burning, for 2 to 2¼ hours, or until a meat thermometer registers 160° F. Transfer the pork to a cutting board, reserving the brown bits in the roasting pan, and let it stand, covered loosely with foil, for 10 minutes.

Make the gravy: In a large skillet cook the mushrooms with salt and pepper to taste in the oil over moderate heat, stirring, for 5 minutes, or until they are tender, and reserve them. To the roasting pan add the wine and deglaze the pan over moderately high heat, scraping up the brown bits. Boil the liquid until it is reduced almost completely and add the broth. Strain the deglazing mixture through a fine sieve into a saucepan, pressing hard on the solids, and bring it to a boil. Whisk in the *beurre manié*, a little at a time, whisking after each addition until the mixture is smooth, add the reserved mushrooms, and simmer the gravy, stirring occasionally, for 2 minutes. Stir in any juices that have accumulated on the cutting board and season the gravy with salt and pepper to taste.

Transfer the pork roast to a platter, spoon the mixed vegetables around it, and serve it with the gravy. (If planning to make the pork chow mein, recipe opposite, reserve enough pork, cut into thin strips, to measure 2 cups, and ¾ cup of the gravy, both covered and chilled.) Serves 4.

Pork Chow Mein

¼ cup soy sauce plus additional to taste
2 tablespoons Scotch
1½ teaspoons sugar
1 teaspoon salt
2 teaspoons cornstarch
⅔ cup chicken broth
1 tablespoon Oriental sesame oil*
  plus additional to taste
¾ cup *shiitake* mushroom gravy (reserved from
  the pork roast, recipe opposite)
½ pound thin dried Oriental wheat-flour
  noodles* or vermicelli
2 tablespoons peanut oil
1 tablespoon minced garlic
¼ teaspoon dried hot red pepper flakes,
  or to taste
3 cups coarsely shredded Napa cabbage
1 bunch of scallions (about 6), trimmed and
  cut crosswise into ½-inch-thick pieces
an 8-ounce can sliced water chestnuts,
  drained
2 cups thin strips of roast pork (reserved from
  the pork roast, recipe opposite)
3 cups mixed vegetables with parsley and pine
  nuts (reserved from preceding recipe)

*available at Asian markets, specialty foods
  shops, and some supermarkets

In a small bowl whisk together ¼ cup of the soy sauce, the Scotch, the sugar, the salt, and the cornstarch until the mixture is smooth and whisk in the broth, 1 tablespoon of the sesame oil, and the gravy. In a kettle of boiling salted water cook the noodles for 3 minutes, or until they are *al dente*, drain them in a colander, and rinse them under cold water. In a wok heat the peanut oil over high heat until it is hot, in it stir-fry the garlic and the red pepper flakes for 10 seconds, and add the cabbage, the scallions, and the water chestnuts. Stir-fry the mixture for 1 to 2 minutes, or until the cabbage is wilted, add the pork and the mixed vegetables, and stir-fry the mixture for 1 minute, or until it is heated through. Stir the soy sauce mixture, add it to the wok, and bring the liquid to a boil, stirring. Add the noodles, drained well, and cook the mixture, tossing it constantly, for 1 minute, or until it is heated through. Add the additional soy sauce, the additional sesame oil, and salt to taste and toss the chow mein well. Serves 4 to 6.

Mixed Vegetables with Parsley and Pine Nuts

1½ pounds broccoli, cut into flowerets and the
  stems reserved for another use
5 carrots, sliced thin on the diagonal
  (about 2 cups)
3 red bell peppers, cut into thin strips
  (about 2 cups)
2 tablespoons unsalted butter
  plus additional to taste
¼ cup minced fresh parsley leaves
3 tablespoons pine nuts, toasted lightly

In a large kettle of boiling water cook the broccoli and the carrots for 3 to 4 minutes, or until they are crisp-tender, and drain them well. In a large skillet cook the bell peppers in 2 tablespoons of the butter over moderate heat, stirring, for 3 to 5 minutes, or until they are just tender, add the broccoli and carrots, the parsley, the pine nuts, the additional butter, and salt and pepper to taste, and cook the mixture, stirring, until it is heated through. (If planning to make the pork chow mein, recipe follows, reserve 3 cups of the vegetables, covered and chilled.) Serves 4.

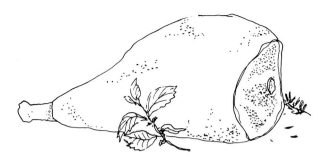

s. Charlton

Herb-Roasted Pork Loin with Bourbon Gravy

2 tablespoons vegetable oil
1 teaspoon dried thyme, crumbled
1 teaspoon dried orégano, crumbled
1 tablespoon caraway seeds
1 small onion, chopped fine
1 large garlic clove, minced
2 teaspoons coarse salt
a 4½-pound boneless pork loin, tied
1 tablespoon bourbon, or to taste
1 cup chicken broth
½ cup water
1 tablespoon unsalted butter
2 tablespoons all-purpose flour
½ cup chopped scallion greens
savory corn bread pudding as an
    accompaniment (recipe follows)

In a small bowl combine well the oil, the thyme, the orégano, the caraway seeds, the onion, the garlic, and the salt, rub the mixture onto the pork loin, and in a large roasting pan chill the pork, covered, overnight.

Roast the pork in the middle of a preheated 350° F. oven for 50 minutes to 1 hour, or until a meat thermometer registers 155° F., remove it from the oven, and transfer it to a cutting board. Let the pork stand, covered loosely with foil, for 10 minutes.

While the pork is standing, add the bourbon, the broth, and the water to the pan juices, boil the mixture for 1 minute, scraping up the brown bits, and strain it through a sieve into a bowl. In a heavy saucepan combine the butter and the flour, cook the *roux* over moderately low heat, whisking, for 3 minutes, and add the broth mixture in a stream, whisking. Bring the gravy to a boil, whisking, add the scallion greens, and simmer

the gravy for 1 minute. Discard the strings from the pork, cut the pork into ½-inch-thick slices, and serve it with the gravy and the savory corn bread pudding. Serves 10.

PHOTO ON PAGE 14

Savory Corn Bread Pudding
For the corn bread
1 cup all-purpose flour
1½ cups yellow cornmeal
1 tablespoon double-acting baking powder
1 teaspoon salt
1 cup milk
1 large egg
3 tablespoons unsalted butter, melted
    and cooled

4 large eggs
4 cups milk
½ teaspoon cayenne, or to taste
a 14-ounce can tomatoes, drained well
    and chopped
6 scallions, chopped fine

Make the corn bread: In a bowl stir together the flour, the cornmeal, the baking powder, and the salt. In a small bowl whisk together the milk, the egg, and the butter and stir the mixture into the cornmeal mixture, stirring until the batter is just combined. Pour the batter into a greased 8-inch-square baking pan and bake the corn bread in the middle of a preheated 425° F. oven for 20 to 25 minutes, or until a tester comes out clean. Let the corn bread cool in the pan for 5 minutes, invert it onto a rack, and let it cool completely. Crumble the corn bread coarse into 2 shallow baking pans and toast it in the middle of a preheated 325° F. oven, stirring occasionally, for 30 to 35 minutes, or until it is dried and deep golden. *The crumbled corn bread may be made 3 days in advance and kept in an airtight container.*

In a large bowl whisk together the eggs, the milk, the cayenne, and salt to taste, add the crumbled corn bread, the tomatoes, and the scallions, and combine the mixture well. Divide the corn bread mixture between 2 greased 9-inch round cake pans, let it stand for 15 minutes, and bake the pudding in the middle of a preheated 375° F. oven for 40 to 45 minutes, or until it is golden. Cut the pudding into wedges. Serves 10.

PHOTO ON PAGE 14

Roast Pork Loin with Grapefruit

2 onions, sliced
4 large garlic cloves, crushed
1 tablespoon vegetable oil
a 3½- to 4-pound boneless pork loin, tied
1 tablespoon coriander seeds, crushed
3 grapefruit
4½ tablespoons sugar
¾ cup dry white wine
1½ cups chicken broth
a *beurre manié* made by kneading together
    3 tablespoons softened unsalted butter
    and 3 tablespoons all-purpose flour

In a roasting pan toss the onions and the garlic with the oil, add the pork, and season it with salt and pepper. Rub the coriander seeds over the pork and roast it in the middle of a preheated 350° F. oven for 1 hour, or until a meat thermometer registers 155° F. to 160° F.

While the pork is roasting, remove 3 or 4 long strips of zest from 1 of the grapefruit with a vegetable peeler, scrape off as much of the white pith from the zest as possible, and cut enough of the zest into fine julienne strips to measure ¼ cup. Cut away the zest and pith from all 3 grapefruit with a serrated knife and, working over a bowl to catch the juice, cut the flesh into sections, reserving the juice. Transfer the grapefruit sections to a sieve and let them drain.

In a small heavy saucepan combine 3 tablespoons of the sugar, the zest strips, and ½ cup of the reserved juice. Bring the mixture to a boil, stirring until the sugar is dissolved, and boil it until it is thickened and turns a light caramel.

Transfer the pork to a cutting board and let it stand, covered loosely with foil, for 10 minutes. While the pork is standing, deglaze the roasting pan with the wine, boiling the mixture and scraping up the brown bits, until the wine is reduced almost completely and add the broth. Pour the deglazing mixture through a fine sieve into the pan containing the zest mixture, pressing hard on the solids, and bring the gravy to a boil, stirring. Add the *beurre manié*, a little at a time, whisking until the gravy is smooth, simmer the gravy, whisking occasionally, for 2 minutes, and whisk in any juices that have accumulated on the cutting board. Season the gravy with salt and pepper and keep it warm.

Arrange the grapefruit sections in a shallow baking pan or gratin dish just large enough to hold them in one layer, sprinkle them with the remaining 1½ tablespoons

sugar, and broil them under a preheated broiler about 2 to 3 inches from the heat for 3 to 5 minutes, or until they are just golden. Discard the string from the pork, cut the pork into ½-inch-thick slices, and serve it with the gravy and the grapefruit sections. Serves 6 to 8.

Red Pork and Bean Chili

6 ounces dried New Mexican red chilies*,
    stemmed and seeded (wear rubber gloves)
7 cups water
2 large onions, chopped
8 garlic cloves, minced
3 tablespoons vegetable oil
1 tablespoon ground cumin
4½ pounds boneless pork shoulder, trimmed
    of excess fat and cut into ½-inch pieces
a 28-ounce can tomatoes, drained and chopped
1 bay leaf
2 teaspoons salt
1 teaspoon dried orégano, or to taste, crumbled
a 19-ounce can (about 2 cups) kidney beans,
    rinsed and drained
sour cream as an accompaniment if desired

* available at some specialty foods shops and
    by mail order from Los Chileros de Nueva
    Mexico, Santa Fe, NM, (505) 471-6967 or
    Adriana's Bazaar, NY, (212) 877-5757

In a large saucepan simmer the chilies in 6 cups of the water for 20 minutes, in a blender purée the chilies with the liquid in batches, and force the purée through a fine sieve into a bowl, pressing hard on the solids before discarding them.

In a large heavy kettle cook the onions and the garlic in the oil over moderate heat, stirring, until the onion is softened, add the cumin, and cook the mixture, stirring, for 30 seconds. Add the pork, the chili purée, the tomatoes, the bay leaf, the salt, the orégano, and the remaining 1 cup water and simmer the mixture, uncovered, adding more water if necessary to keep the pork barely covered, for 2 hours, or until the pork is tender. Add the kidney beans, simmer the chili, stirring occasionally, for 5 minutes, or until the beans are heated through, and discard the bay leaf. *The chili may be frozen or made 4 days in advance, cooled, uncovered, and kept covered and chilled.* Serve the chili with the sour cream. Makes about 12 cups, serving 6 to 8.

New Mexican Pork and Green Chili Stew

2 medium onions, chopped
8 garlic cloves
3 tablespoons vegetable oil
4½ pounds boneless pork shoulder, trimmed
    of excess fat and cut into 1-inch pieces
5 pounds frozen roasted New Mexican green
    chilies*, thawed, peeled if necessary,
    seeded, and chopped (wear rubber gloves)
7 cups water
2 teaspoons salt
1½ pounds boiling potatoes

*available by mail order from Los Chileros
    de Nueva Mexico, Santa Fe, NM,
    Tel. (505) 471-6967

In a large heavy kettle cook the onions and 6 of the garlic cloves, minced, in the oil over moderate heat, stirring, until the onions are softened, add the pork, the chilies, the water, and the salt, and simmer the mixture, uncovered, adding more water if necessary to keep the pork barely covered, for 1½ hours. Stir in the potatoes, peeled and cut into 1-inch pieces, making sure they are covered by the cooking liquid, and simmer the mixture, stirring occasionally, for 30 minutes, or until the pork and the potatoes are tender. Stir in the remaining 2 garlic cloves, minced, and salt to taste and simmer the stew for 5 minutes. *The stew may be frozen or made 3 days in advance, cooled, uncovered, and kept covered and chilled.* Makes about 14 cups, serving 6 to 8.

Pork Fricassee with Mushrooms and Carrots

3 tablespoons vegetable oil
3½ pounds boneless pork shoulder, trimmed
    of excess fat and cut into 2-inch pieces
1 large onion, chopped
2 ribs of celery, chopped
1 bay leaf
4 cups chicken broth
4 cups water
8 large carrots, cut diagonally into
    1-inch-thick pieces
1 pound mushrooms, sliced thin
½ stick (¼ cup) unsalted butter
¼ cup all-purpose flour
1 cup heavy cream
1 tablespoon fresh lemon juice, or to taste

½ cup minced fresh parsley leaves
paprika rice (recipe follows) as an accompaniment

In a kettle heat the oil over moderately high heat until it is hot but not smoking and in it brown the pork, patted dry, in batches, transferring it as it is browned to a bowl. Pour off the fat from the kettle, return the pork to the kettle with the onion, the celery, the bay leaf, the broth, and the water, and simmer the mixture, uncovered, for 1½ hours, or until the pork is tender. Add the carrots, simmer the mixture, covered, for 15 minutes, or until the carrots are tender, and transfer the pork and the carrots with tongs to a bowl. Strain the mixture through a fine sieve into a bowl, return the cooking liquid to the kettle, and boil it until it is reduced to 3 cups.

In a large heavy skillet cook the mushrooms in the butter over moderate heat, stirring occasionally, until most of the liquid the mushrooms give off is evaporated, sprinkle the mixture with the flour, and cook it over moderately low heat, scraping up the brown bits, for 3 minutes. Stir in the cream, stirring until the mixture is combined well, add the mushroom mixture to the cooking liquid, and simmer the sauce, stirring, until it is thickened. Stir in the lemon juice, the pork, the carrots, and salt and pepper to taste. *The fricassee may be made 2 days in advance and kept covered and chilled.* Stir in the parsley and serve the fricassee over the paprika rice. Serves 8.

PHOTO ON PAGE 77

Paprika Rice

5 quarts water
2½ cups long-grain rice
2 teaspoons paprika

In a kettle bring the water to a boil, sprinkle in the rice and salt to taste, stirring until the water returns to a boil, and boil the rice for 10 minutes. Drain the rice in a large colander and rinse it. Set the colander over a large saucepan of boiling water and steam the rice, covered with a kitchen towel and the lid, for 15 minutes, or until it is fluffy and dry. *The rice may be made 2 days in advance and kept chilled in an airtight container. Reheat the rice in the colander set over a saucepan of boiling water.* Transfer the rice to a large bowl, sprinkle it with the paprika, and toss the mixture to coat the rice thoroughly. Makes about 7 cups, serving 8.

PHOTO ON PAGE 77

β. Charlton

½ cup vegetable oil
½ teaspoon ground cumin
⅛ teaspoon ground allspice

*available by mail from The Chile Shop,
    109 East Water Street, Santa Fe,
    NM 87501, Tel. (505) 983-6080

In a large kettle combine the spareribs with water to cover, bring the water to a boil, and simmer the spareribs, skimming the froth as necessary, for 50 minutes. Drain the spareribs well and pat them dry.

While the spareribs are simmering, in a blender purée the chilies, the water, the ketchup, the garlic, the vinegar, the brown sugar, the salt, the Tequila, the oil, the cumin, and the allspice. In a jelly-roll pan or on a tray coat the spareribs generously with some of the chili sauce, reserving the remaining sauce in a small bowl, covered and chilled, and let the spareribs marinate, covered with plastic wrap and chilled, for at least 8 hours or overnight.

Let the spareribs stand at room temperature for 1 hour and grill them on an oiled rack set 5 to 6 inches over glowing coals for 6 minutes on each side. In a small saucepan simmer the reserved sauce for 3 minutes and serve it with the ribs. Serves 6.

Baked Irish Bacon with Kumquat Glaze

1 cup preserved kumquats in syrup (available
    at specialty foods shops and some
    supermarkets)
1 tablespoon lemon juice, or to taste
2 tablespoons dry mustard
a 2-pound piece of Irish bacon (available at
    specialty foods shops) or Canadian bacon
fresh kumquats for garnish
parsley sprigs for garnish

In a food processor purée the preserved kumquats and the syrup with the lemon juice and the mustard. In a shallow baking pan pour the kumquat glaze over the bacon, bake the bacon in the middle of a preheated 350° F. oven, basting it several times with the glaze, for 30 minutes, and let it stand, covered loosely with foil, for 10 minutes before slicing. Transfer the bacon to a platter and garnish it with the fresh kumquats and the parsley. Serves 8.

PHOTO ON PAGE 83

Barbecued Chili-Marinated Pork Spareribs

2 racks of pork spareribs (about 6 pounds)
8 dried New Mexican red chilies*
    (about 2 ounces), the seeds and stems
    discarded and the chilies rinsed well
    (use rubber gloves)
¾ cup hot water
½ cup ketchup
2 garlic cloves
½ cup cider vinegar
3 tablespoons firmly packed brown sugar
2 teaspoons salt
3 tablespoons Tequila

Ham and Succotash Stew with Cheddar Biscuits

1 medium onion, chopped fine
2 garlic cloves, minced
1 tablespoon unsalted butter
¾ pound ham steak, cut into 1-inch pieces
   (about 2 cups)
1 carrot, cut on the diagonal into ½-inch slices
1 cup frozen corn
1 cup frozen baby lima beans
¾ cup chicken broth
¾ cup water
¼ teaspoon dried thyme,
   crumbled
¼ cup yellow cornmeal
¼ cup all-purpose flour
¾ teaspoon double-acting baking powder
¼ teaspoon salt
½ cup finely grated sharp Cheddar
¼ cup milk
a *beurre manié* made by kneading
   together 1 tablespoon softened
   unsalted butter and 2 tablespoons
   all-purpose flour

In a large saucepan cook the onion and the garlic in the butter over moderately low heat, stirring, until the onion is softened. Add the ham, the carrot, the corn, the lima beans, the broth, the water, and the thyme and simmer the stew, covered, for 10 to 12 minutes, or until the carrot is tender. While the stew is simmering, in a bowl whisk together the cornmeal, the flour, the baking powder, and the salt, add the Cheddar, and toss the mixture well. Stir in the milk until the dough is just combined.

Add the *beurre manié* to the stew, a little at a time, stirring until the sauce is thickened, and simmer the stew for 2 minutes. Transfer the stew to a buttered 1-quart shallow baking dish, drop the biscuit dough in 6 mounds on top of it, and bake the stew in the upper third of a preheated 425° F. oven for 15 minutes, or until the biscuits are golden. Serves 2.

*Hot Open-Faced Ham, Swiss Cheese,
and Mushroom Sandwiches*

1 tablespoon mayonnaise
2 teaspoons Dijon-style mustard
1 teaspoon finely chopped fresh dill
½ pound mushrooms, sliced thin
1 tablespoon olive oil
2 slices of rye bread, toasted
2 thin slices of cooked ham
2 thin slices of Swiss cheese
½ small red onion,
   sliced thin

In a small bowl whisk together the mayonnaise, the mustard, the dill, and salt and pepper to taste. In a skillet cook the mushrooms in the oil over moderately high heat, stirring occasionally, for 5 minutes, or until the liquid the mushrooms give off is evaporated, and remove the skillet from the heat. On a baking sheet spread one side of each slice of toast with half the mayonnaise mixture, top each toast with a slice of the ham, half the mushrooms, a slice of the Swiss cheese, half the onion, and salt and pepper to taste, and broil the sandwiches under a preheated broiler about 4 inches from the heat for 1 to 2 minutes, or until the cheese is melted and browned lightly. Serves 2.

Hoagies
(Italian-Style Meat and Cheese Sandwiches)

2 Italian sandwich rolls or one 9-inch loaf
   of Italian bread
2 tablespoons mayonnaise if desired
¾ cup finely shredded lettuce
½ small onion, sliced very thin
6 slices of hard salami
6 thin slices of *capicola* (seasoned smoked
   ham) or other cooked ham
4 thin slices of provolone
6 thin slices of tomato
3 tablespoons olive oil
1 tablespoon red-wine vinegar
½ teaspoon dried orégano,
   crumbled
2 bottled hot cherry peppers, or to taste,
   sliced thin

Halve the rolls horizontally, leaving an edge uncut to form a hinge, spread the mayonnaise on the cut sides of the rolls, and on the bottom halves of the rolls layer the lettuce, the onion, the salami, the *capicola*, the provolone, and the tomato. In a small bowl whisk together the oil, the vinegar, the orégano, the cherry peppers, and salt and pepper to taste, drizzle the dressing over the fillings, and cover the fillings with the top halves of the rolls. Cut each sandwich in half. Serves 2.

Sausage and Eggplant Kebabs
with Hot Chili Sauce

3 large garlic cloves, minced
2 teaspoons sugar
1 teaspoon anchovy paste
¼ cup fresh lime juice
two 2-inch *jalapeño* chilies, minced,
    including the seeds (wear rubber gloves)
eight 10-inch wooden skewers, soaked in
    water to cover for 30 minutes
1 pound fresh sweet Italian sausage links, cut
    into ¾-inch-thick pieces
1 pound eggplant, cut into 1-inch cubes,
    blanched in boiling salted water for
    1 minute, and drained

In a bowl whisk together the garlic, the sugar, the anchovy paste, the lime juice, the *jalapeños*, and salt and pepper to taste. On each skewer thread alternately 4 pieces of the sausage and 4 pieces of the eggplant, arrange the kebabs in one layer in a shallow dish, and pour the *jalapeño* mixture over them. Let the kebabs marinate, covered and chilled, for 2 hours or overnight. Broil the kebabs on the oiled rack of a foil-lined broiler pan under a preheated broiler about 4 inches from the heat, turning them once, for 15 minutes, or until the sausage is cooked through. Serves 8 as a first course or 4 as an entrée.

Braised Sausage with Olives and Potatoes

1 tablespoon vegetable oil
2 pounds fresh Italian sausage links
1 onion, chopped fine
2 garlic cloves, crushed
a 28-ounce can plum tomatoes including
    the juice
1½ pounds boiling potatoes
½ cup Kalamata or other brine-cured
    black olives

In a heavy kettle heat the oil over moderately high heat until it is hot but not smoking, in it brown the sausage in batches, transferring it as it is browned to paper towels to drain, and pour off all but 1 tablespoon of the fat. In the fat remaining in the kettle cook the onion and the garlic over moderate heat, stirring, until the onion is golden, stir in the tomatoes with the juice, breaking up the tomatoes, and the sausage, and simmer the mixture,

covered, for 30 minutes. Stir in the potatoes, peeled and cut into ¾-inch pieces, and the olives, simmer the mixture, covered partially, for 15 to 20 minutes, or until the potatoes are tender, and season it with salt and pepper. Serves 4 to 6.

LAMB

Lamb Chops with Minted Potatoes and Zucchini

4 rib lamb chops (about 1½ pounds)
2 tablespoons olive oil
a ½-pound russet (baking) potato
1 zucchini, scrubbed and cut into ¼-inch dice
1 tablespoon fresh lemon juice
1 tablespoon water
2 tablespoons finely chopped fresh
    mint leaves

In a heavy skillet large enough to hold the lamb chops without touching heat the oil over moderately high heat until it is hot but not smoking and in it sauté the potato, peeled and cut into ¼-inch dice, turning the pieces constantly with a metal spatula, for 6 to 8 minutes, or until they are golden. Transfer the potato pieces with a slotted spoon to paper towels and let them drain. In the oil remaining in the skillet sauté the lamb chops, patted dry and seasoned with salt and pepper, over moderately high heat for 5 minutes on each side for medium-rare meat and transfer them to a heated platter. Remove the skillet from the heat, pour off the fat, and add the zucchini. Cook the zucchini over moderate heat, stirring, for 1 minute, stir in the lemon juice and the water, and cook the mixture, stirring, for 1 minute. Stir in the potato pieces, the mint, and salt and pepper to taste and spoon the mixture around the lamb chops. Serves 2.

Mustard-Crusted Lamb Chops

four ¾-inch-thick loin lamb chops
1 tablespoon Dijon-style mustard
all-purpose flour seasoned with salt and
 pepper for dredging the chops
1 tablespoon olive oil
½ cup coarsely chopped onion
2 tablespoons dry red wine
2 tablespoons water
¼ teaspoon dried tarragon, crumbled
¼ teaspoon sugar

Pat the lamb chops dry, rub them with the mustard, and dredge them in the flour, shaking off the excess. In a heavy skillet heat the oil over moderately high heat until it is hot but not smoking and in it sauté the chops for 4 minutes on each side for medium-rare meat. Transfer the chops to 2 heated plates and keep them warm, covered. Pour off the fat from the skillet and in the skillet cook the onion over low heat, stirring, for 3 minutes. Add the wine, the water, the tarragon, and the sugar and simmer the mixture, stirring, until the liquid is almost evaporated. Season the mixture with salt and pepper and spoon it over the chops. Serves 2.

Grilled Lamb Chops with Yogurt and Mint Marinade

six ¾-inch-thick shoulder-blade lamb chops
1 cup firmly packed fresh mint leaves, rinsed,
 spun dry, and minced
⅓ cup white-wine vinegar
2 teaspoons sugar
1 tablespoon water
¾ cup plain yogurt
2 garlic cloves, forced through a garlic press
 or minced

Arrange the lamb chops in one layer in a large shallow dish. In a bowl combine well the mint, the vinegar, the sugar, and salt and pepper to taste and transfer 2 tablespoons of the mixture to a small bowl. Stir the water into the small bowl and reserve the sauce, covered and chilled. Stir the yogurt and the garlic into the remaining mint mixture, pour the yogurt marinade over the chops, coating them thoroughly, and let the chops marinate, covered and chilled, overnight.

Grill the chops with the marinade clinging to them, the remaining marinade discarded, on an oiled rack set 5 to 6 inches over glowing coals for 5 minutes on each side for medium-rare meat. Transfer the chops to a platter, let them stand for 5 minutes, and serve them with the reserved mint sauce. Serves 6.

Boneless Leg of Lamb Stuffed with Swiss Chard and Feta

1 pound Swiss chard, the stems discarded and
 the leaves chopped coarse
6 large garlic cloves, sliced thin lengthwise
3 tablespoons olive oil
¼ pound Feta, crumbled (about ¾ cup)
an 8-pound leg of lamb, boned, butterflied,
 and trimmed well (4 to 5 pounds boneless)
1½ teaspoons dried rosemary, crumbled,
 or to taste
1 onion, sliced
1 cup dry red wine
1½ cups beef broth
½ cup water
1 tablespoon cornstarch dissolved in
 2 tablespoons cold water
spiced quinoa timbales (recipe follows) and
 honey-glazed baby carrots (page 173) as
 accompaniments

Wash the Swiss chard well, drain it, and in a heavy saucepan steam it in the water clinging to the leaves, covered, over moderate heat for 3 to 5 minutes, or until it is wilted. Drain the chard in a colander, refresh it under cold water, and squeeze it dry in a kitchen towel. In a skillet cook the garlic in 2 tablespoons of the oil over moderate heat, stirring, until it is pale golden and transfer it with a slotted spoon to a bowl. To the skillet add the chard, cook it, stirring, for 1 minute, or until any excess liquid is evaporated, and transfer it to the bowl. Let the chard mixture cool and stir in the Feta.

Pat the lamb dry, arrange it, boned side up, on a work surface, and season it with salt and pepper. Spread the lamb evenly with the chard mixture, leaving a 1-inch border around the edges, beginning with a short side roll it up jelly-roll fashion, and tie it tightly with kitchen string. (The rolled and tied roast may look ungainly, but it will improve in appearance when cooked.)

Transfer the lamb to a roasting pan and rub it all over with the remaining 1 tablespoon oil, 1 teaspoon of the rosemary, and salt and pepper to taste. Roast the lamb in the middle of a preheated 325° F. oven for 30 minutes, scatter the onion around it in the pan, and roast the lamb for 1 to 1¼ hours more (a total of 20 minutes cooking time for each pound of boneless meat), or until a meat thermometer registers 140° F. for medium-rare meat. Transfer the lamb to a cutting board and let it stand for 20 minutes.

While the lamb is standing, skim the fat from the pan drippings and set the roasting pan over moderately high heat. Add the wine, deglaze the pan, scraping up the brown bits, and boil the mixture until it is reduced by half. Strain the mixture through a fine sieve into a saucepan, add the broth, the remaining ½ teaspoon rosemary, the water, and any juices that have accumulated on the cutting board, and boil the mixture until it is reduced to about 2 cups. Stir the cornstarch mixture, add it to the wine mixture, whisking, and simmer the sauce for 2 minutes. Season the sauce with salt and pepper and keep it warm.

Discard the strings from the lamb, arrange the lamb on a heated platter, and surround it with the quinoa timbales and clusters of the carrots. Strain the sauce into a heated sauceboat and serve it with the lamb, sliced. Serves 6.

PHOTO ON PAGE 32

Spiced Quinoa Timbales

1 cup quinoa (small, flat, disk-shaped seeds, available at natural foods stores and many specialty foods shops)
1 small onion, minced
1 tablespoon olive oil

1 teaspoon ground cumin
½ teaspoon cinnamon
a rounded ¼ teaspoon turmeric
1 cup chicken broth
⅔ cup water
⅓ cup dried currants or raisins
¼ cup chopped drained canned tomatoes
½ teaspoon salt
3 tablespoons finely chopped fresh
    parsley leaves

In a fine sieve rinse the quinoa under cold water for 1 minute and drain it well. In a heavy saucepan cook the onion in the oil over moderately low heat, stirring, until it is softened, add the cumin, the cinnamon, and the turmeric, and cook the mixture, stirring, for 30 seconds. Add the quinoa and cook the mixture, stirring, for 1 minute. Add the broth, the water, the currants, the tomatoes, and the salt and simmer the mixture, covered, for 15 minutes, or until the liquid is absorbed. Remove the pan from the heat, let the mixture stand, covered, for 5 minutes, and stir in the parsley. Divide the quinoa mixture among 6 buttered ½-cup timbale molds, packing it, and invert the timbales onto a platter. Serves 6.

PHOTO ON PAGE 32

Rack of Lamb with Cumin and Thyme

⅓ cup fine dry bread crumbs
1 tablespoon olive oil
2 teaspoons fresh thyme leaves
1½ teaspoons ground cumin
1 small garlic clove, minced
a 1¼-pound trimmed and frenched rack of
    lamb (7 or 8 ribs)
1 teaspoon Dijon-style mustard

In a small bowl combine well the bread crumbs, the oil, the thyme, the cumin, and the garlic. Season the lamb with salt and pepper and rub the fat side with the mustard. Pat the crumb mixture evenly over the mustard and arrange the lamb, crumb side up, in a roasting pan. Roast the lamb in the middle of a preheated 475° F. oven for 15 minutes, or until a meat thermometer registers 130° to 135° for medium-rare meat, transfer it carefully to a cutting board, and let it stand, uncovered, for 10 minutes. Cut the lamb between the ribs and divide it between 2 plates. Serves 2.

PHOTO ON PAGE 21

Grilled Pineapple Curry Lamb Shanks

six 1-pound lamb shanks
1 large fresh pineapple, peeled and cored
2 teaspoons curry powder
½ onion, cut into pieces
3 tablespoons vegetable oil
1½ teaspoons freshly ground black pepper
1 teaspoon salt

In a kettle combine the lamb shanks with enough water to cover them by 1 inch, bring the water to a boil, and simmer the shanks for 1 hour. Drain the shanks and trim off some of the excess fat and membranes. Chop enough of the pineapple to measure 1½ cups, cut the remaining pineapple into 6 rings, and arrange the rings in a large shallow dish. In a blender purée the chopped pineapple with the curry powder, the onion, the oil, the pepper, and the salt, arrange the shanks on the pineapple rings, and pour the pineapple marinade over them, coating the shanks thoroughly. Let the shanks marinate at room temperature for 1 hour. (Do not let the shanks marinate longer or the meat will break down.)

Grill the shanks, covered, on an oiled rack set 5 to 6 inches over glowing coals, turning them occasionally, for 15 minutes, or until they are browned. Grill the pineapple rings, the marinade discarded, for 5 minutes on each side, or until they are golden. Serves 6.

Braised Lamb Shanks with Tomatoes and Rosemary

6 lamb shanks (about 1 pound each)
2 tablespoons olive oil
4 cups chopped onion
4 garlic cloves, minced
two 28- to 32-ounce cans tomatoes, drained and chopped
1½ cups dry white wine
1½ cups chicken broth
1½ teaspoons dried rosemary, crumbled
¾ teaspoon ground allspice
1 tablespoon minced fresh parsley leaves
1 tablespoon minced fresh rosemary leaves

Pat the shanks dry, season them with salt and pepper, and in a large heavy kettle brown them, 3 at a time, in the oil over moderately high heat, transferring them as they are browned to a roasting pan just large enough to hold them in one layer. To the kettle add the onion, cook it over moderate heat, stirring, until it is softened, and stir in the garlic. Cook the mixture for 3 minutes, stir in the tomatoes, the wine, the broth, the dried rosemary, the allspice, and salt and pepper to taste, and bring the sauce to a boil. Ladle the sauce over the shanks. Braise the shanks, covered tightly with foil, in the middle of a preheated 350° F. oven for 1½ hours, or until they are tender, transfer them to a heatproof platter, and keep them warm, covered. Pour the sauce into the kettle, cleaned, and boil it for 10 minutes, or until it is reduced to about 4 cups. *The shanks and the sauce may be made 2 days in advance, kept covered and chilled. Reheat the shanks in the sauce in a 350° F. oven and transfer them to the heatproof platter.* Into the sauce stir 2 teaspoons of the parsley and 2 teaspoons of the fresh rosemary. Divide the shanks among 6 heated plates, spoon the sauce over them, and sprinkle it with the remaining parsley and fresh rosemary. Serves 6.

PHOTO ON PAGE 71

Lamb Patties with Mint Sauce

1 tablespoon fresh lemon juice
2 tablespoons cider vinegar
2 tablespoons water
1½ teaspoons soy sauce
1 small garlic clove, minced
1 tablespoon sugar
⅛ teaspoon anchovy paste
½ teaspoon dried hot red pepper flakes
¼ cup minced fresh mint leaves
1 large egg, beaten lightly
¾ pound ground lamb
¼ teaspoon cinnamon
a pinch of freshly grated nutmeg
½ cup minced onion
¼ cup fresh fine bread crumbs

In a small bowl stir together the lemon juice, the vinegar, the water, the soy sauce, the garlic, the sugar, the anchovy paste, the red pepper flakes, and the mint until the sugar is dissolved. In a bowl combine well the egg, the lamb, the cinnamon, the nutmeg, the onion, the bread crumbs, and salt and pepper to taste, form the mixture into four ½-inch-thick patties, and broil the patties on the rack of a foil-lined broiler pan under a preheated broiler about 6 inches from the heat for 6 minutes. Turn the patties and broil them for 6 minutes more, or until they are just cooked through. Transfer the patties to 2 plates and spoon the sauce over them. Serves 2.

POULTRY

CHICKEN

*Grilled Chicken Breast
with Arugula and Olive Thyme Vinaigrette*

4 large Kalamata or other brine-cured black
    olives, pitted
1 garlic clove,
    chopped
1 teaspoon Dijon-style mustard
1 tablespoon balsamic vinegar
1½ teaspoons fresh thyme leaves
3 tablespoons olive oil plus additional
    for brushing the chicken and
    the bell pepper
1 plum tomato, seeded
1 tablespoon water
1 whole boneless chicken breast with skin
    (about 1 pound), halved
1 large red bell pepper, quartered
4 cups packed *arugula* leaves, washed well
    and spun dry
1 small Belgian endive, trimmed and sliced
    thin crosswise

In a blender or small food processor blend together
the olives, the garlic, the mustard, the vinegar, ½ teaspoon of the thyme, and salt and pepper to taste, with
the motor running add 3 tablespoons of the oil in a
stream, and blend the vinaigrette until it is emulsified.
Add the tomato and the water and blend the vinaigrette
until it is smooth. Brush the chicken and the bell pepper
with the additional oil, season them with salt and pepper, and grill them on an oiled rack set 5 to 6 inches over
glowing coals, or in a hot well-seasoned ridged grill
pan, covered, over moderately high heat for 5 minutes
on each side, or until the bell pepper is just tender and
the chicken is cooked through. Transfer the chicken and
bell pepper to a cutting board, cut the bell pepper into
thin strips, and slice the chicken on the diagonal into
¼-inch-thick pieces. In a bowl toss the chicken pieces
with the remaining 1 teaspoon thyme and salt and pepper to taste. Divide the *arugula*, the endive, the bell
pepper, and the chicken between 2 plates and pour half
the vinaigrette over each serving. Serves 2.

Chicken Breast Amandine

1 tablespoon vegetable oil
1 large whole boneless chicken breast with
    the skin (about 1 pound), halved
¼ cup sliced almonds
¼ cup dry white wine
¼ cup water
1 garlic clove, minced and mashed to a
    paste with a pinch of salt
1 tablespoon unsalted butter
2 tablespoons minced fresh parsley leaves
fresh lemon juice to taste

In a heavy skillet heat the oil over moderately high
heat until it is hot but not smoking and in it brown the
chicken, patted dry and seasoned with salt and pepper,
for 2 minutes on each side. Reduce the heat to moderately low, cook the chicken for 6 minutes more on each
side, or until it is cooked through, and transfer it to
2 heated plates.

Cook the almonds in the oil remaining in the skillet
over moderate heat, stirring, for 1 minute, or until they
are golden, and transfer them with a slotted spoon to
paper towels to drain. Add to the skillet the wine, the
water, and the garlic paste and boil the mixture until it is
reduced by half. Remove the skillet from the heat, stir in
the butter, the parsley, the almonds, the lemon juice,
and salt and pepper to taste, and spoon the almond sauce
over the chicken. Serves 2.

Brussels Sprout and Chicken Stir-Fry

1 large egg white
1 tablespoon plus 1 teaspoon cornstarch
1 whole boneless skinless chicken breast
  (about ¾ pound), cut into ¾-inch pieces
2 pints Brussels sprouts, trimmed and halved
¼ cup peanut or vegetable oil
1 shallot, minced
1 garlic clove, minced
1 tablespoon plus 1 teaspoon minced peeled
  fresh gingerroot
1 red bell pepper, cut into ¾-inch pieces
6 scallions, cut diagonally into ¾-inch pieces
3 tablespoons soy sauce
1 teaspoon sugar
1½ tablespoons rice vinegar (available at
  Oriental markets and many supermarkets)
⅓ cup chicken broth
1 teaspoon Oriental sesame oil
1 teaspoon cold water
an 8-ounce can water chestnuts, sliced thin,
  blanched in boiling water for 30 seconds,
  and refreshed under cold water

In a bowl whisk together the egg white and 1 table-spoon of the cornstarch, add the chicken, and let the mixture stand for 10 minutes. In a large saucepan of boiling salted water cook the Brussels sprouts for 2½ minutes, or until they are just crisp-tender, drain them in a colander, and refresh them under cold water.

Heat a wok over moderately high heat and in it heat the peanut oil until it is hot but not smoking. Add the chicken, drained, stir-fry it for 45 seconds to 1 minute, or until it is opaque and just firm, and transfer it with a slotted spoon to a bowl. Heat the oil remaining in the wok until it is hot but not smoking and in it stir-fry the shallot, the garlic, and the gingerroot for 30 seconds. Add the bell pepper and stir-fry the mixture for 2 minutes. Add the scallions and the Brussels sprouts and stir-fry the mixture for 1 minute. In a small bowl whisk together the soy sauce, the sugar, the vinegar, the broth, the sesame oil, the remaining 1 teaspoon cornstarch, and the cold water, make a well in the center of the vegetables, and whisk the soy sauce mixture into the well. Bring the liquid to a boil, stir together the vegetable mixture to combine it well, and simmer it for 1 minute. Stir in the chicken and the water chestnuts, season the stir-fry with salt and pepper, and cook it for 30 seconds, or until the chicken is heated through. Serves 6.

Chicken and Corn Stew with Corn Wafers

For the corn wafers
½ stick (¼ cup) unsalted butter, softened
2 teaspoons sugar
1 large egg white
½ teaspoon salt
3 tablespoons yellow cornmeal
1 tablespoon all-purpose flour
2 tablespoons freshly grated Parmesan

1 tablespoon vegetable oil
2 whole boneless chicken breasts (2 pounds)
1 tablespoon unsalted butter
3 tablespoons all-purpose flour
1 small onion, chopped fine
1 small green bell pepper, chopped fine
1 rib of celery, chopped fine
1¼ cups chicken broth
4 fresh or canned plum tomatoes, chopped
1 teaspoon chili powder
1 cup fresh corn kernels including the pulp
  scraped from the cobs (cut from about
  2 ears of corn)
½ cup thinly sliced scallion greens
¼ cup loosely packed fresh basil leaves,
  chopped fine

Make the corn wafers: In a bowl with an electric mixer cream the butter, add the sugar, and beat the mixture until it is light and fluffy. Add the egg white and the salt and beat the mixture at low speed for 5 seconds, or until it is just combined. (The mixture will be lumpy.) Add the cornmeal, the flour, and the Parmesan and stir the mixture until it is just combined. Transfer the mixture to a small bowl and chill it, covered, for at least 4 hours or overnight. Arrange rounded teaspoons of the mixture 3 inches apart on buttered baking sheets and with a fork dipped in cold water flatten them carefully to form 2-inch rounds. Bake the wafers in batches in the middle of a preheated 425° F. oven for 5 to 6 minutes, or until the edges are golden brown, with a spatula transfer the wafers immediately to racks, and let them cool.

In a 9-inch cast-iron skillet heat the oil over moderately high heat until it is hot but not smoking and in it brown the chicken, patted dry and seasoned with salt and pepper, in batches, transferring it as it is browned to a bowl. To the fat remaining in the skillet add the butter and the flour and cook the *roux* over moderately low heat, stirring constantly, until it is the color of peanut butter. Stir in the onion, the bell pepper, and the celery and cook the mixture, stirring occasionally, until the vegetables are softened. Add the broth, the tomatoes, the chili powder, and the chicken with any juices that have accumulated in the bowl, simmer the stew, covered, for 15 to 20 minutes, or until the chicken is cooked through, and stir in the corn. Transfer the chicken to a work surface and let it cool until it can be handled. Cut the chicken into bite-size pieces and stir it into the stew. *The stew may be prepared up to this point 1 day in advance and kept covered and chilled.* Stir in the scallion greens and the basil, season the stew with salt and pepper, and serve it in bowls topped with the corn wafers. Serves 4 to 6.

Chicken Breasts with Leeks and Mushrooms

¼ cup flour
¼ teaspoon paprika
1 whole boneless chicken breast with skin
   (about ¾ pound), halved
1 tablespoon olive oil
the white part of 2 medium leeks, sliced,
   washed well, and patted dry
6 mushrooms, sliced
¼ cup dry red wine
¼ cup chicken broth
½ teaspoon dried thyme, crumbled

8 Kalamata or other brine-cured black olives,
   pitted and chopped
1 teaspoon drained bottled capers, chopped
fresh lemon juice to taste

In a shallow bowl stir together the flour, the paprika, and salt and pepper to taste and dredge the chicken breasts in the flour mixture, shaking off the excess. In a heavy (preferably cast-iron) skillet heat the oil over moderately high heat until it is hot but not smoking and in it sauté the chicken, turning it once, until it is golden brown. Reduce the heat to moderately low and stir in the leeks, the mushrooms, the wine, the broth, and the thyme. Cook the mixture, covered partially, for 25 to 30 minutes, or until the chicken is cooked through, and transfer the chicken to a platter. To the skillet add the olives, the capers, and the lemon juice and cook the mixture, stirring, for 1 minute. Serve the chicken topped with the leek mixture. Serves 2.

Grilled Lemon-and-Gin-Marinated Chicken and Onions

2 tablespoons fresh lemon juice
2 tablespoons gin
¼ teaspoon dried orégano, crumbled
½ teaspoon salt
½ teaspoon sugar
3 tablespoons vegetable oil
2 whole skinless boneless chicken breasts
   (about ½ pound each)
2 cups thinly sliced onions

In a shallow dish whisk together the lemon juice, the gin, the orégano, the salt, the sugar, and pepper to taste, add the oil in a stream, whisking, and whisk the marinade until it is emulsified. Add the chicken, coating it well with the marinade, and let it marinate, covered and chilled, for 20 minutes. Grill the chicken, reserving the marinade, on an oiled rack set about 6 inches over glowing coals for 7 minutes on each side, or until it is cooked through. While the chicken is grilling, in a heavy skillet combine the reserved marinade and the onions and boil the mixture, covered, over high heat, stirring occasionally, for 3 minutes, or until the onions begin to brown. Reduce the heat to moderately low and cook the mixture, uncovered, stirring constantly, for 5 minutes. Transfer the chicken to a heated platter and with a slotted spoon scatter the onions around it. Serves 2.

Chicken Breasts with Scallions, Shiitake Mushrooms, and Tomatoes

2 tablespoons olive oil
3 whole boneless chicken breasts, halved
1 tablespoon minced garlic
½ cup minced shallot
2 thyme sprigs plus 1 tablespoon fresh thyme
    leaves, or 1 teaspoon dried thyme,
    crumbled
2 tablespoons white-wine vinegar
¼ pound fresh *shiitake* mushrooms, stems
    discarded and the mushrooms sliced
½ cup dry white wine
1½ cups chicken broth
2 bunches of scallions, dark green parts
    reserved for another use and the scallions
    split lengthwise and cut crosswise into
    1-inch pieces (about 1 cup)
2½ teaspoons arrowroot
3 plum tomatoes, seeded and
    diced fine
6 additional thyme sprigs for garnish
    if desired

In a large heavy skillet heat the oil over moderately high heat until it is hot but not smoking and in it cook the chicken, patted dry and seasoned with salt and pepper, skin sides down, for 3 to 4 minutes, or until it is golden. Turn the chicken and cook it over moderate heat, covered, for 7 to 8 minutes more, or until it is cooked through. Transfer the chicken to a platter and keep it warm. To the skillet add the garlic, the shallot, and the 2 thyme sprigs (or the dried thyme) and cook the mixture, stirring, until the shallot is softened. Add the vinegar, boil the mixture until the vinegar is almost evaporated, and add the mushrooms. Cook the mixture over moderate heat, stirring, for 1 minute, add the wine, and boil the mixture until the wine is almost evaporated. Add 1¼ cups of the broth and the scallions and simmer the mixture for 1 minute. In a small bowl whisk together the remaining ¼ cup broth and the arrowroot and add the mixture to the skillet with the tomatoes and the fresh thyme leaves. Simmer the sauce, stirring, for 1 minute, or until it is thickened, stir in any juices that have accumulated around the chicken, and add salt and pepper to taste. Transfer the chicken breasts to 6 dinner plates, spoon some of the sauce over them, and garnish each serving with 1 of the additional thyme sprigs. Serves 6.

PHOTO ON PAGE 41

Chicken Breasts with Tarragon Vinaigrette

1 whole skinless boneless chicken breast
    (about ¾ pound), halved
1 tablespoon plus 2 teaspoons vegetable oil
⅓ cup chicken broth
½ teaspoon Dijon-style mustard
1 tablespoon fresh lemon juice
1 tablespoon minced fresh tarragon
1 tablespoon minced scallion

In a microwave-safe glass pie plate coat the chicken with 2 teaspoons of the oil, arrange it with the thickest parts toward the edge of the plate, and pour the broth over it. Microwave the chicken, its surface covered with an oiled round of wax paper, at high power (100%) for 4 minutes. Turn the chicken, microwave it, covered with the wax paper, at high power for 3 minutes, and microwave it at medium power (50%) for 3 minutes more, or until it is just springy to the touch. Let the chicken stand for 5 minutes.

While the chicken is standing, in a small bowl whisk together the mustard, the lemon juice, the tarragon, the scallion, and salt to taste and whisk in 3 tablespoons of the cooking liquid and the remaining 1 tablespoon oil. Transfer the chicken to a shallow dish, spoon the vinaigrette over it, and let the chicken cool. Serve the chicken at room temperature. Serves 2.

Cold Poached Chicken Breasts with Tuna Basil Sauce

3 large whole chicken breasts with skin and
    bone (about 1¼ pounds each)
a 6½-ounce can tuna packed in olive oil,
    drained well
½ cup mayonnaise
¼ cup plain yogurt
3 anchovy fillets
1 tablespoon drained bottled capers plus
    additional for garnish
2 tablespoons fresh lemon juice,
    or to taste
⅓ cup finely chopped fresh basil leaves,
    or to taste, plus, if desired,
    6 basil sprigs for garnish
lemon slices for garnish
mixed brine-cured black olives such as
    Niçoise and Kalamata as an
    accompaniment

In a kettle combine the chicken with enough cold water to cover it by 1 inch and remove it. Bring the water to a boil, add salt to taste, and return the chicken to the kettle. Poach the chicken at a bare simmer for 18 minutes, remove the kettle from the heat, and let the chicken cool in the liquid for 30 minutes. Drain the chicken and let it stand until it is cool enough to be handled. Discard the skin and bones from the chicken, removing each breast half carefully from the bone in one piece, and chill the chicken, wrapped well in plastic wrap, for at least 6 hours or overnight.

In a blender or food processor blend together the tuna, the mayonnaise, the yogurt, the anchovies, 1 tablespoon of the capers, the lemon juice, and salt and pepper to taste until the sauce is smooth, transfer the sauce to an airtight container, and chill it for at least 6 hours or overnight.

Cut the chicken breasts diagonally into ¼-inch-thick slices and transfer a breast to each of 6 dinner plates. Just before serving, stir the chopped basil and salt and pepper to taste into the sauce. Spoon some of the sauce over each breast, garnish the chicken with the additional capers, the basil sprigs, and the lemon slices, and serve it with the olives. Serves 6.

PHOTO ON PAGE 59

Oven-Fried Chipotle Chili Chicken

2 whole canned *chipotle* chilies in *adobo*
    (available at Mexican and Hispanic markets
    and some specialty foods shops) or
    2 teaspoons chili powder
¾ cup mayonnaise
6 chicken drumsticks (about 1½ pounds)
6 chicken wings (about 1 pound)
2¼ cups fine fresh white bread crumbs
¼ teaspoon cayenne, or to taste

In a food processor blend together the *chipotles*, the mayonnaise, and salt and pepper to taste until the mixture is smooth. In a baking pan arrange the chicken pieces in one layer and coat them completely with the mayonnaise mixture. Chill the chicken, covered, for at least 1 hour or overnight.

In a large bowl combine the bread crumbs, the cayenne, and salt and pepper to taste and coat each piece of chicken with the bread crumb mixture, patting the mixture on lightly. Arrange the chicken on the lightly oiled racks of 2 roasting pans and bake it in a preheated 425° F. oven, turning it once carefully, for 30 minutes. Reduce the temperature to 375° F. and bake the chicken for 10 to 20 minutes more, or until it is cooked through. Serves 6.

PHOTO ON PAGE 64

Maple Rosemary Glazed Chicken Legs

3 tablespoons maple syrup
1 tablespoon unsalted butter
¼ teaspoon dried rosemary, crumbled
2 teaspoons cider vinegar
2 whole chicken legs

In a small saucepan combine the syrup, the butter, and the rosemary, simmer the mixture, stirring occasionally, for 7 minutes, and stir in the vinegar. Let the glaze cool slightly. Line a shallow baking pan with foil, butter the foil, and on it arrange the chicken, patted dry and seasoned with salt and pepper. Bake the chicken in the middle of a preheated 450° F. oven for 10 minutes, spread the glaze on top of it, and bake the chicken, basting it once or twice, for 15 minutes more, or until it is cooked through. Serves 2.

Chinese-Style Roast Chicken Thighs

2 garlic cloves, chopped
a 1-inch cube of peeled fresh gingerroot, quartered
2 tablespoons soy sauce
1 tablespoon cider vinegar
2 teaspoons honey
¼ teaspoon aniseed
¼ teaspoon salt
1 pound chicken thighs

In a blender purée the garlic and the gingerroot with the soy sauce, the vinegar, the honey, the aniseed, and the salt. In a resealable plastic bag combine the marinade with the chicken thighs and let the chicken marinate at room temperature for 15 minutes. Arrange the chicken on the rack of a foil-lined broiler pan, discarding the marinade, and roast it in the middle of a preheated 425° F. oven for 20 to 25 minutes, or until it is cooked through. Serves 2.

ASSORTED FOWL

Roast Cornish Hens with Sage Butter

3 tablespoons unsalted butter, softened
2 teaspoons dried sage, crumbled
1 teaspoon freshly grated lemon zest
½ teaspoon salt
two 1½-pound Cornish hens, rinsed and patted dry

In a small bowl blend together well 2 tablespoons of the butter with the sage, the zest, and the salt. Loosen the skin covering the breast meat on each hen by slipping your fingers under the skin and sliding them between the skin and the meat. Divide the butter mixture between the hens, inserting it under the skin of each hen and smoothing it evenly by rubbing the outside of the skin, season the hens with salt and pepper, and tie the legs together with kitchen string.

In a large ovenproof heavy skillet or small flameproof roasting pan heat the remaining 1 tablespoon butter over moderately high heat until the foam subsides, in it sauté the hens, breast sides up, for 1 to 2 minutes, or until the undersides are golden brown, and roast them in the middle of a preheated 450° F. oven, basting them with the pan juices every 10 minutes, for 30 to 35 minutes, or until a meat thermometer inserted in the fleshy part of the thigh registers 180° F. Let the hens stand for 5 minutes and discard the string. Serves 2.

Chutney-Glazed Cornish Hens with Hazelnut and Dried-Fruit Stuffing

For the stuffing
1 large shallot, minced
1 onion, minced
1 garlic clove, minced
¾ stick (6 tablespoons) unsalted butter
¾ teaspoon dried sage, crumbled
⅛ teaspoon ground cloves
⅓ cup golden raisins
½ cup chopped dried apricots
½ cup dry white wine
4 cups cubed stale homemade-type white
    bread (about 8 slices), toasted
¾ cup skinned, lightly toasted hazelnuts
    (procedure follows), chopped fine

6 Cornish hens, each weighing about
    1¼ pounds, rinsed and patted dry
½ stick unsalted butter, melted and cooled
⅓ cup fresh lemon juice
an 8½-ounce jar mango chutney (about ¾ cup)

Make the stuffing: In a skillet cook the shallot, the onion, and the garlic in the butter over moderate heat, stirring, until the vegetables are golden. Stir in the sage, the cloves, the raisins, the apricots, and salt and pepper to taste and cook the mixture, stirring, for 1 minute. Stir in the wine and boil the mixture until the liquid is evaporated. Remove the skillet from the heat and stir in the bread cubes, the hazelnuts, and salt and pepper to taste. Let the mixture cool before stuffing the hens.

Divide the stuffing among the cavities of the hens, packing the cavities loosely. Truss the hens, sprinkle them with salt and pepper, and arrange them so that they do not touch on the rack of a large, foil-lined broiler pan. Brush the hens with the butter and roast them in the upper third of a preheated 400° F. oven for 1 hour.

While the hens are roasting, in a pan combine the juice, the chutney, and salt and pepper to taste, bring the glaze just to a boil, stirring, and in a blender purée it. Brush the hens with the glaze, roast them for 15 to 25 minutes more, or until they are golden brown and cooked through, and discard the trussing string. Serves 6.

PHOTO ON PAGE 26

To Toast and Skin Hazelnuts

Toast the hazelnuts in one layer in a baking pan in a preheated 350° F. oven for 10 to 15 minutes, or until they are colored lightly and the skins blister. Wrap the nuts in a kitchen towel and let them steam for 1 minute. Rub the nuts in the towel to remove as much of the skins as possible and let them cool.

Five-Spice Roasted Guinea Hens

3 tablespoons five-spice powder*
4 tablespoons vegetable oil
four 2½-pound guinea hens**, rinsed and
    patted dry
For the sauce
1 cup dry white wine
the zest of 1½ navel oranges, removed in
    strips with a vegetable peeler
eight ¼-inch-thick slices of fresh gingerroot,
    crushed lightly with the flat side of a knife
3 whole star anise*
2½ cups chicken broth
½ cup water
3 tablespoons soy sauce
2 tablespoons cornstarch, dissolved in
    2 tablespoons cold water

steamed broccoli rabe (recipe follows) as an
    accompaniment

*available at Asian markets, specialty foods
    shops, and some supermarkets
**available at some butcher shops and from
    D'Artagnan, Tel. (800) D ARTAGNAN or,
    in New Jersey, Tel. (201) 792-0748

In a small bowl stir together the five-spice powder and 2 tablespoons of the oil, rub the mixture on the guinea hens, and season the hens with salt. In a large heavy skillet heat the remaining 2 tablespoons oil over moderately high heat until it is hot but not smoking and in it brown the hens lightly, 1 at a time. Arrange the browned hens, breast sides down, in 2 roasting pans and roast them in a preheated 350° F. oven, switching the pans from one rack to the other after 30 minutes, for 50 minutes to 1 hour, or until a meat thermometer inserted in the fleshy part of the thigh registers 170° F. Transfer the hens to a cutting board and let them stand, covered loosely with foil, for 15 minutes.

Make the sauce while the hens are standing: Skim the fat from the pan juices, divide the wine between the pans, and deglaze the pans over high heat, scraping up the brown bits. Transfer the mixtures to a large saucepan, add the zest, the gingerroot, and the star anise, and boil the mixture until the liquid is reduced to about ⅓ cup. Add the broth, the water, and the soy sauce and cook the mixture at a slow boil for 5 minutes. Stir the cornstarch mixture, stir it into the zest mixture, and simmer the sauce for 2 minutes. Strain the sauce through a fine sieve into a saucepan and keep it warm.

Carve the guinea hens, divide the broccoli rabe among 8 heated plates, and arrange the meat on it. Spoon some of the sauce over each serving and serve the remaining sauce separately. Serves 8.

PHOTO ON PAGE 68

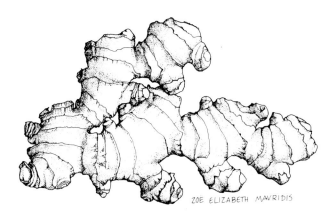

ZOE ELIZABETH MAVRIDIS

Steamed Broccoli Rabe

2½ pounds broccoli rabe (available at
    specialty produce markets and some
    supermarkets) or *choi sum* (Chinese
    flowering cabbage, available at Asian
    markets)

Trim and discard any yellow or coarse leaves and the tough stem ends from the broccoli rabe and wash the broccoli rabe well in several changes of cold water. In a steamer set over boiling water steam the broccoli rabe, covered, for 4 to 5 minutes, or until the stems are tender. Serves 8.

PHOTO ON PAGE 68

s.C.

*Roast Turkey with Herbed Oyster Stuffing
and Giblet Gravy*

For the stuffing
two ½-pound loaves of day-old Italian or
    French bread, cut into ¾-inch cubes
    (about 12 cups)
½ pound bacon, cut into ½-inch pieces
1 tablespoon minced garlic
2 cups finely chopped onion
1½ cups chopped celery
3 tablespoons minced fresh thyme leaves or
    1 tablespoon dried thyme, crumbled
1 tablespoon minced fresh sage leaves or
    2 teaspoons dried sage, crumbled
⅔ cup finely chopped fresh parsley leaves
1 stick (½ cup) unsalted butter, melted
18 oysters, shucked (procedure follows)
    and chopped, reserving the liquor for
    another use

a 12- to 14-pound turkey, the neck and giblets
    (excluding the liver) reserved for making
    turkey giblet stock (recipe opposite)
1½ sticks (¾ cup) unsalted butter,
    softened
1 cup turkey giblet stock or chicken broth
For the gravy
1 cup dry white wine
6 tablespoons all-purpose flour
4 cups turkey giblet stock, including
    the reserved cooked neck
    and giblets

parsley sprigs and thyme sprigs for garnish

Make the stuffing: In 2 shallow baking pans or jelly-roll pans arrange the bread cubes in one layer, bake them in a preheated 325° F. oven for 10 to 15 minutes, or until they are golden, and transfer them to a large bowl. In a large skillet cook the bacon over moderately low heat, stirring, until it is crisp, transfer it with a slotted spoon to paper towels to drain, and pour off all but about ¼ cup of the fat. In the fat remaining in the skillet cook the garlic, the onion, and the celery with the thyme and the sage over moderately low heat, stirring, until the vegetables are softened and transfer the mixture to the bowl. Add the parsley, the melted butter, the oysters, the bacon, and salt and pepper to taste, toss the stuffing well, and let it cool completely. *The stuffing may be made 1 day in advance and kept covered and chilled. (To prevent bacterial growth do not stuff the turkey cavities in advance.)*

Rinse the turkey, pat it dry, and season it inside and out with salt and pepper. Pack the neck cavity loosely with some of the stuffing, fold the neck skin under the body, and fasten it with a skewer. Pack the body cavity loosely with some of the remaining stuffing and truss the turkey. Transfer the remaining stuffing to a buttered 3-quart baking dish and reserve it, covered and chilled.

Spread the turkey with ½ stick of the butter and roast it on a rack in a roasting pan in a preheated 425° F. oven for 30 minutes. Reduce the temperature to 325° F., baste the turkey with the pan juices, and drape it with a piece of cheesecloth, soaked in the remaining 1 stick butter, melted and cooled. Roast the turkey, basting it every 20 minutes, for 2½ to 3 hours more, or until a meat thermometer inserted in the fleshy part of the thigh registers 180° F. and the juices run clear when the thigh is pierced with a skewer. During the last 1½ hours of roasting, drizzle the reserved stuffing with the stock, bake it, covered, in the 325° F. oven for 1 hour, and bake it, uncovered, for 30 minutes more. Discard the cheesecloth and string from the turkey, transfer the turkey to a heated platter, reserving the juices in the roasting pan, and keep it warm, covered loosely with foil.

Make the gravy: Skim all of the fat from the roasting pan juices, reserving ⅓ cup of the fat, and add the wine to the pan. Deglaze the pan over moderately high heat, scraping up the brown bits, and boil the mixture until it is reduced by half. In a saucepan combine the reserved fat and the flour and cook the *roux* over moderately low heat, whisking, for 3 minutes. Add the stock and the wine mixture in a stream, whisking, and simmer the gravy, stirring occasionally, for 10 minutes. Add the reserved cooked giblets and neck meat, chopped, and salt and pepper to taste, simmer the gravy for 2 minutes, and transfer it to a heated sauceboat.

Garnish the turkey with the parsley and thyme sprigs and serve it with the gravy and the stuffing. Serves 8.

PHOTO ON PAGES 74 AND 75

To Shuck Oysters

Scrub the oysters thoroughly with a stiff brush under running cold water. Hold each oyster flat side up on a work surface with the hinged end away from you, insert an oyster knife between the shells at the hinged end, twisting the knife to pop open the shell, and slide the blade against the flat upper shell to cut the large muscle and free the upper shell. If the shell crumbles and cannot be opened at the hinge, insert the knife between the shells at the curved end of the oyster, pry the shells open, and sever the large muscle. Break off and discard the upper shell and slide the knife under the oyster to release it from the bottom shell.

Turkey Giblet Stock

the neck and giblets (excluding the liver) from
   a 12- to 14-pound turkey
5 cups chicken broth
5 cups water
1 rib of celery, chopped
1 carrot, chopped
1 onion, quartered
1 bay leaf
½ teaspoon dried thyme, crumbled
1 teaspoon black peppercorns

In a large saucepan combine the neck and giblets, the broth, the water, the celery, the carrot, and the onion and bring the liquid to a boil, skimming the froth. Add the bay leaf, the thyme, and the peppercorns, cook the mixture at a bare simmer for 2 hours, or until it is reduced to about 5 cups, and strain the stock through a fine sieve into a bowl, reserving the neck meat and the giblets for the gravy. *The stock may be made 2 days in advance, cooled, uncovered, and kept chilled or frozen in an airtight container.* Makes about 5 cups.

Turkey Roulades with Corn Bread, Jalapeño, and Monterey Jack Filling

⅓ cup minced onion
¼ cup minced red bell pepper
½ teaspoon minced garlic
1 tablespoon minced bottled *jalapeño*
a pinch of ground cumin
4 teaspoons vegetable oil
1 large corn muffin, crumbled
   (about 1 cup)
¼ cup grated Monterey Jack
4 turkey cutlets (about ¾ pound total),
   pounded 1/16 inch thick between sheets of
   dampened plastic wrap
¾ cup chicken broth
¾ teaspoon white-wine vinegar

In a skillet cook the onion, the bell pepper, the garlic, the *jalapeño*, and the cumin in the oil over moderately low heat, stirring occasionally, until the vegetables are softened, stir in the corn muffin crumbs and the Monterey Jack, and cook the filling, stirring, until it is combined well and the cheese is melted. Season the filling with salt and pepper and let it cool for 5 minutes. Spread about 3 tablespoons of the filling on each cutlet and roll up each cutlet jelly-roll fashion, tucking in the sides and fastening them with wooden picks. Transfer the *roulades*, seam sides down, with a spatula to a lightly oiled small baking dish, pour in the broth, and bake the *roulades* in the middle of a preheated 375° F. oven, basting them occasionally, for 18 minutes, or until the turkey is cooked through. Transfer the *roulades* with a slotted spoon to 2 heated plates. Pour the cooking liquid through a fine sieve into a small saucepan, add the vinegar and salt and pepper to taste, and boil the sauce until it is thickened slightly. Pour the sauce over the *roulades*. Serves 2.

Turkey Chipotle Chili

2 canned whole *chipotle* chilies in *adobo** or
    2 dried whole *chipotle* chilies*
1 cup water, boiling hot if using the
    dried chilies
2 pounds fresh tomatillos (available at
    Hispanic markets and many supermarkets)
    or three 18-ounce cans whole tomatillos*,
    drained
2 large onions, chopped
8 garlic cloves
3 tablespoons vegetable oil
2 tablespoons ground cumin
4 pounds ground turkey
2 cups chicken broth
1 bay leaf
1½ teaspoons dried orégano, crumbled
2 teaspoons salt, or to taste
1 green bell pepper, chopped
two 4-ounce cans mild green chilies, drained
    and chopped
1 tablespoon cornmeal
a 19-ounce can (about 2 cups) white beans,
    rinsed and drained
½ cup chopped fresh coriander
sour cream as an accompaniment if desired

* available at Hispanic markets, some
    specialty foods shops, and some
    supermarkets or by mail order from
    Adriana's Bazaar, New York City,
    Tel. (212) 877-5757

If using the canned *chipotle* chilies, in a blender purée them with the water and reserve the purée. If using dried *chipotle* chilies, stem and seed them wearing rubber gloves, in a small bowl let them soak in the boiling hot water for 20 minutes, and in a blender purée the mixture, reserving the purée. If using fresh tomatillos, discard the papery husks, wash the tomatillos well, and blanch them in boiling water for 5 minutes. Drain the blanched tomatillos and in a blender purée them or the canned tomatillos, reserving the purée.

In a large heavy kettle cook the onions and 6 of the garlic cloves, minced, in the oil over moderate heat, stirring, until the onions are softened, add the cumin, and cook the mixture, stirring, for 30 seconds. Add the turkey and cook the mixture, stirring and breaking up the lumps, until the turkey is no longer pink. Add the reserved *chipotle* purée, the reserved tomatillo purée, the broth, the bay leaf, the orégano, and the salt and simmer the mixture, uncovered, adding more water if necessary to keep the turkey barely covered, for 1 hour. Stir in the bell pepper, the canned green chilies, and the cornmeal and simmer the mixture, stirring occasionally, for 30 minutes. Stir in the white beans, the coriander, the remaining 2 garlic cloves, minced, and salt to taste, simmer the chili for 3 to 5 minutes, or until the beans are heated through, and discard the bay leaf. *The chili may be frozen or made 3 days in advance, cooled, uncovered, and kept covered and chilled.* Serve the chili with the sour cream. Makes 14 cups, serving 6 to 8.

Turkey Sausage and Peppers

½ pound (4 links) Italian-style turkey sausage
½ cup water plus additional if necessary
½ cup thinly sliced red onion
½ cup thinly sliced fennel bulb
½ cup thinly sliced red bell pepper
½ cup thinly sliced yellow bell pepper
2 scallions, minced

In a skillet cook the sausage in ½ cup of the water, covered, over moderate heat for 20 minutes and add the onion, the fennel, and the bell peppers. Increase the heat to moderately high, sauté the mixture, uncovered, stirring frequently and adding more water if necessary to keep the mixture from sticking, for 20 minutes, or until the vegetables are tender, and sprinkle it with the scallions. Serves 2.

Smoked Turkey and Stilton Sandwiches

6 ounces Stilton, crumbled (about 1½ cups)
    and softened
2 tablespoons mayonnaise
2 tablespoons bottled mango chutney, or to
    taste, any large pieces chopped
1 to 2 tablespoons minced fresh parsley leaves
fresh lemon juice to taste
four 5-inch lengths of Italian or French bread,
    halved horizontally and toasted
¾ pound thinly sliced smoked turkey breast
arugula or lettuce leaves

In a small bowl mash together with a fork the Stilton, the mayonnaise, the chutney, the parsley to taste, the lemon juice, and salt and pepper to taste until the mixture is combined well, spread the halves of the bread with the Stilton mixture, and divide the turkey between the bottom halves of the bread. Top the turkey with the *arugula* and cover the sandwiches with the top halves of the bread. Makes 4 sandwiches.

ZOE
MAVRIDIS

STUFFINGS

All of the stuffing recipes below can be used to stuff a 12- to 14-pound turkey. Alternatively, they can be baked separately in a 3- to 4-quart casserole or shallow baking dish for a slightly drier and more crisp stuffing.

Corn Bread, Sausage, and Scallion Stuffing
For the corn bread
1 cup all-purpose flour
1⅓ cups yellow cornmeal
1 tablespoon double-acting baking powder
1 teaspoon salt
1 cup milk
1 large egg
3 tablespoons unsalted butter, melted and cooled

¾ pound bulk pork sausage
¾ stick (6 tablespoons) unsalted butter, plus an additional 2 tablespoons if baking the stuffing separately
2 cups finely chopped onion
1½ cups finely chopped celery
2 teaspoons dried sage, crumbled
1 teaspoon dried marjoram, crumbled
1 teaspoon dried rosemary, crumbled
½ cup thinly sliced scallion
1½ cups chicken broth if baking the stuffing separately

Make the corn bread: In a bowl stir together the flour, the cornmeal, the baking powder, and the salt. In a small bowl whisk together the milk, the egg, and the butter, add the milk mixture to the cornmeal mixture, and stir the batter until it is just combined. Pour the batter into a greased 8-inch-square baking pan and bake the corn bread in the middle of a preheated 425° F. oven for 20 to 25 minutes, or until a tester comes out clean. Let the corn bread cool in the pan for 5 minutes, invert it onto a rack, and let it cool completely. *The corn bread may be made 2 days in advance and kept wrapped tightly in foil at room temperature.*

Into a jelly-roll pan crumble the corn bread coarse, bake it in the middle of a preheated 325° F. oven, stirring occasionally, for 30 minutes, or until it is dry and golden, and let it cool. In a skillet cook the sausage over moderate heat, stirring occasionally, until it is no longer pink and transfer it with a slotted spoon to a bowl. To the fat in the skillet add 6 tablespoons of the butter and in the fat cook the onion and the celery over moderately low heat, stirring occasionally, until the vegetables are softened. Add the sage, the marjoram, the rosemary, and salt and pepper to taste and cook the mixture, stirring, for 3 minutes. Transfer the mixture to a bowl, add the sausage, the corn bread, the scallion, and salt and pepper to taste, and combine the stuffing gently but thoroughly. Let the stuffing cool completely before using it to stuff a 12- to 14-pound turkey.

The stuffing can also be baked separately: Spoon the stuffing into a buttered 3- to 4-quart casserole, drizzle it with the broth, and dot the top with the additional 2 tablespoons butter, cut into bits. Bake the stuffing, covered, in the middle of a preheated 325° F. oven for 30 minutes and bake it, uncovered, for 30 minutes more. Serves 8 to 10.

Green Chili Stuffing

2 cups finely chopped onion
2 cups finely chopped celery
1 stick (½ cup) unsalted butter plus an
    additional 2 tablespoons if baking the
    stuffing separately
two 4-ounce cans chopped mild green chilies
    including the juice
2 pickled *jalapeños*, minced
    (about 1 tablespoon), or to taste
    (wear rubber gloves)
¾ teaspoon chili powder
½ teaspoon dried thyme, crumbled
½ teaspoon dried orégano, crumbled
1½ teaspoons ground cumin
1 cup finely chopped pecans, toasted lightly
a 1-pound loaf of homemade-type white
    bread, cut into ½-inch cubes, toasted,
    and cooled
¾ cup chicken broth if baking the stuffing
    separately

In a large skillet cook the onion and the celery in 1 stick of the butter over moderate heat, stirring occasionally, until the onion is softened and light golden, add the green chilies with the juice, the *jalapeños*, the chili powder, the thyme, the orégano, the cumin, and salt and pepper to taste, and cook the mixture, stirring, for 3 minutes. Transfer the mixture to a large bowl, add the pecans, the toasted bread cubes, and salt and pepper to taste, and combine the stuffing gently but thoroughly. Let the stuffing cool completely before using it to stuff a 12- to 14-pound turkey.

The stuffing can also be baked separately: Spoon the stuffing into a buttered 3- to 4-quart casserole, drizzle it with the broth, and dot the top with the additional 2 tablespoons butter, cut into bits. Bake the stuffing, covered, in the middle of a preheated 325° F. oven for 30 minutes and bake it, uncovered, for 30 minutes more. Serves 8 to 10.

Couscous Stuffing with Golden Raisins and Pistachios

2 cups finely chopped onion
½ cup finely chopped carrot
½ cup finely chopped celery
1 large garlic clove, minced
¼ cup plus 2 tablespoons olive oil

⅔ cup finely chopped red bell pepper
⅓ cup finely chopped pistachio nuts
½ cup golden raisins
3 tablespoons finely chopped fresh
    parsley leaves
¼ teaspoon cinnamon
1 teaspoon ground cumin
1½ teaspoons ground coriander seed
¼ teaspoon dried thyme, crumbled
⅓ cup thinly sliced scallion
2¼ cups water
a 10-ounce box (1⅔ cups) couscous
¾ cup chicken broth if baking the stuffing
    separately
2 tablespoons unsalted butter if baking the
    stuffing separately

In a large skillet cook the onion, the carrot, the celery, and the garlic in ¼ cup of the oil over moderately low heat, stirring occasionally, until the vegetables are softened, add the bell pepper, and cook the mixture, stirring occasionally, for 3 minutes. Add the pistachios, the raisins, the parsley, the cinnamon, the cumin, the coriander seed, the thyme, the scallion, and salt and pepper to taste, cook the mixture, stirring, for 1 minute, and transfer it to a large bowl.

In a saucepan combine the water, the remaining 2 tablespoons oil, and salt to taste and bring the mixture to a boil. Stir in the couscous and let the mixture stand, covered, for 5 minutes, or until the liquid is absorbed. Fluff the couscous with a fork, add it to the onion mixture with salt and pepper to taste, and combine the stuffing gently. Let the stuffing cool completely before using it to stuff a 12- to 14-pound turkey.

The stuffing can also be baked separately: Spoon the stuffing into a buttered 3- to 4-quart casserole, drizzle it with the broth, and dot the top with the butter, cut into bits. Bake the stuffing, covered, in the middle of a preheated 325° F. oven for 30 minutes and bake it, uncovered, for 30 minutes more. Serves 8 to 10.

Mushroom, Walnut, and Currant Stuffing

2 cups finely chopped onion
1 cup finely chopped celery
1 stick (½ cup) unsalted butter, plus an
    additional 2 tablespoons if baking the
    stuffing separately
1½ pounds mushrooms, chopped (about 8 cups)

½ cup currants
¾ teaspoon dried sage, crumbled
¾ teaspoon dried thyme, crumbled
¾ cup finely chopped walnuts, toasted
10 slices of homemade-type white bread, cut
    into ½-inch cubes, toasted, and cooled
    (about 6 cups)
½ cup chicken broth if baking the stuffing
    separately

In a large skillet cook the onion and the celery in 1 stick of the butter over moderately low heat, stirring occasionally, until the vegetables are softened, add the mushrooms, and cook the mixture over moderate heat, stirring occasionally, until the mushrooms are tender and all but about ⅓ cup of the liquid is evaporated. Stir in the currants, the sage, the thyme, and salt and pepper to taste and cook the mixture, stirring, for 1 minute. Transfer the mixture to a large bowl, add the walnuts, the toasted bread cubes, and salt and pepper to taste, and combine the stuffing gently but thoroughly. Let the stuffing cool completely before using it to stuff a 12- to 14-pound turkey.

The stuffing can also be baked separately: Spoon the stuffing into a buttered 3- to 4-quart casserole, drizzle it with the broth, and dot the top with the additional 2 tablespoons butter, cut into bits. Bake the stuffing, covered, in the middle of a preheated 325° F. oven for 30 minutes and bake it, uncovered, for 30 minutes more. Serves 8 to 10.

Smoked Oyster, Ham, and Rye Bread Stuffing
2 cups finely chopped onion
1 cup finely chopped celery
1 green bell pepper, chopped fine
1 stick (½ cup) unsalted butter, plus an
    additional 2 tablespoons if baking the
    stuffing separately
½ pound cooked ham, chopped fine
½ teaspoon dried marjoram, crumbled
¾ teaspoon dried thyme, crumbled
cayenne to taste
a 3¾-ounce can smoked oysters, drained well
    and chopped (about ½ cup)
10 slices of rye bread, cut into ½-inch cubes,
    toasted, and cooled (about 8 cups)
¾ cup chicken broth if baking the stuffing
    separately

In a large skillet cook the onion, the celery, and the bell pepper in 1 stick of the butter over moderately low heat, stirring occasionally, until the vegetables are softened, add the ham, and cook the mixture over moderate heat, stirring occasionally, until the ham is browned lightly. Stir in the marjoram, the thyme, the cayenne, and salt and pepper to taste, cook the mixture, stirring, for 3 minutes, and stir in the oysters. Transfer the mixture to a large bowl, add the toasted bread cubes and salt and pepper to taste, and combine the stuffing gently but thoroughly. Let the stuffing cool completely before using it to stuff a 12- to 14-pound turkey.

The stuffing can also be baked separately: Spoon the stuffing into a buttered 3- to 4-quart casserole, drizzle it with the broth, and dot the top with the additional 2 tablespoons butter, cut into bits. Bake the stuffing, covered, in the middle of a preheated 325° F. oven for 30 minutes and bake it, uncovered, for 30 minutes more. Serves 8 to 10.

Mashed Potato and Sautéed Apple Stuffing

4 russet (baking) potatoes
    (about 2 pounds)
3 cups finely chopped onion
2 cups finely chopped celery
1½ sticks (¾ cup) unsalted butter,
    plus an additional 2 tablespoons if
    baking the stuffing separately
2 Granny Smith apples (about 1¼ pounds)
1 tablespoon cider vinegar
½ teaspoon dried sage, crumbled
½ teaspoon dried rosemary, crumbled
½ teaspoon dried thyme, crumbled
½ teaspoon dried marjoram, crumbled
¼ cup finely chopped fresh parsley leaves
¼ cup milk, scalded
8 slices of homemade-type white bread,
    cut into ¼-inch cubes, toasted, and
    cooled (about 5 cups)
⅓ cup chicken broth if baking the stuffing
    separately

In a steamer set over a large pan of simmering water steam the potatoes, peeled and cut into 1-inch pieces, covered, for 20 minutes, or until they are very tender.

While the potatoes are steaming, in a large skillet cook the onion and the celery in 1¼ sticks of the butter over moderately low heat, stirring occasionally, until the vegetables are softened, add the apples, peeled and chopped fine, and cook the mixture over moderate heat, stirring occasionally, until the apples are tender. Stir in the vinegar, the sage, the rosemary, the thyme, the marjoram, and the parsley and sauté the mixture over moderately high heat, stirring, for 3 minutes.

Transfer the steamed potatoes to a large bowl, mash them with a potato masher, and whisk in the milk, 2 tablespoons of the remaining butter, cut into bits, and salt and pepper to taste until the mixture is smooth.

To the mashed potatoes add the onion mixture, the toasted bread cubes, and salt and pepper to taste and combine the stuffing well. Let the stuffing cool completely before using it to stuff a 12- to 14-pound turkey.

The stuffing can also be baked separately: Spoon the stuffing into a buttered 3-quart casserole, drizzle it with the broth, and dot the top with the additional 2 tablespoons butter, cut into bits. Bake the stuffing, covered, in the middle of a preheated 325° F. oven for 30 minutes and bake it, uncovered, for 30 minutes more. Serves 8 to 10.

Raisin Bread, Cranberry, and Rosemary Stuffing

2 cups finely chopped onion
1 stick unsalted butter, plus an additional
    2 tablespoons if baking the stuffing separately
2 cups fresh cranberries, picked over and
    chopped coarse
2 tablespoons firmly packed light brown sugar
2 teaspoons dried rosemary, crumbled
½ teaspoon dried sage, crumbled
12 slices of raisin bread, cut into ½-inch
    cubes, toasted, and cooled (about 7½ cups)
½ cup fresh orange juice
½ cup chicken broth if baking the stuffing
    separately

In a skillet cook the onion in 1 stick of the butter over moderately low heat, stirring occasionally, until it is softened, add the cranberries, the brown sugar, the rosemary, the sage, and salt and pepper to taste, and cook the mixture, stirring, for 3 minutes. Transfer the mixture to a large bowl, add the toasted bread cubes, the orange juice, and salt and pepper to taste, and combine the stuffing gently but thoroughly. Let the stuffing cool completely before using it to stuff a 12- to 14-pound turkey.

The stuffing can also be baked separately: Spoon the stuffing into a buttered 3-quart casserole, drizzle it with the broth, and dot the top with the additional 2 tablespoons butter, cut into bits. Bake the stuffing, covered, in the middle of a preheated 325° F. oven for 30 minutes and bake it, uncovered, for 30 minutes more. Serves 8 to 10.

Dirty Rice Stuffing

1¼ pounds chicken giblets including the livers
2½ cups chicken broth, plus an additional
    ½ cup if baking the stuffing separately
5 cups cold water
½ teaspoon black peppercorns
2 large onions
5 slices of bacon, chopped fine
¼ cup all-purpose flour
1 green bell pepper, chopped fine
2 ribs of celery, chopped fine
2 cups long-grain rice
cayenne to taste
½ cup thinly sliced scallion
2 tablespoons unsalted butter if baking the
    stuffing separately

In a large saucepan combine the giblets, 2½ cups of the broth, 2 cups of the water, the peppercorns, 1 of the onions, halved, and salt to taste, bring the mixture to a boil, and simmer it for 10 minutes, or until the livers are just cooked through. Transfer the livers with a slotted spoon to a bowl, simmer the mixture for 30 minutes more, and strain the stock through a fine sieve set over another bowl, reserving the stock and the giblets but discarding the onion. Let the giblets cool, trim the kidneys, and remove the meat from the necks, discarding the skin and bones. Chop fine the meat, the giblets, and the livers and reserve the mixture.

In a large heavy skillet, preferably cast iron, cook the bacon until it is crisp and transfer it with a slotted spoon to paper towels to drain. Pour off all but ¼ cup of the fat from the skillet, add the flour, stirring, and cook the *roux* over moderate heat, stirring constantly with a wooden spatula, for 10 minutes, or until it is the color of milk chocolate. Add the remaining onion, chopped fine, the bell pepper, and the celery and cook the mixture, stirring occasionally, until the vegetables are softened. To the skillet add 3 cups of the reserved giblet stock and simmer the mixture, stirring occasionally, for 30 minutes.

While the mixture is simmering, in a heavy saucepan combine the rice, the remaining 3 cups cold water, and salt to taste, bring the water to a boil, and simmer the rice, covered, for 15 minutes, or until it is barely tender.

In a very large bowl combine well the rice, the reserved giblet mixture, the giblet stock mixture, the bacon, the cayenne, the scallion, and salt and pepper to taste. Let the stuffing cool completely before using it to stuff a 12- to 14-pound turkey.

The stuffing can also be baked separately: Spoon the stuffing into a buttered 3- to 4-quart casserole, drizzle it with the remaining ½ cup broth, and dot the top with the butter, cut into bits. Bake the stuffing, covered, in the middle of a preheated 325° F. oven for 30 minutes and bake it, uncovered, for 30 minutes more. Serves 8 to 10.

Sauerkraut, Apple, and Rye Bread Stuffing

2 cups finely chopped onion
1 cup finely chopped celery
1 garlic clove, minced
1 stick (½ cup) unsalted butter, plus an additional 2 tablespoons if baking the stuffing separately
2 Granny Smith apples (about 1¼ pounds)
2 tablespoons light brown sugar
2 teaspoons caraway seeds
¼ cup cider vinegar
a 1-pound bag sauerkraut, rinsed and drained well
10 slices of rye bread, cut into ½-inch cubes, toasted, and cooled (about 8 cups)
¾ cup chicken broth if baking the stuffing separately

In a skillet cook the onion, the celery, and the garlic in 1 stick of the butter over moderately low heat, stirring occasionally, until the vegetables are softened, add the apples, chopped fine, and the brown sugar, and cook the mixture over moderate heat, stirring occasionally, until the apples are tender. Stir in the caraway seeds, the vinegar, the sauerkraut, and salt and pepper to taste and cook the mixture, stirring, for 3 minutes. Transfer the mixture to a bowl, add the toasted bread cubes and salt and pepper to taste, and combine the stuffing gently but thoroughly. Let the stuffing cool completely before using it to stuff a 12- to 14-pound turkey.

The stuffing can also be baked separately: Spoon the stuffing into a buttered 3- to 4-quart casserole, drizzle it with the broth, and dot the top with the additional 2 tablespoons butter, cut into bits. Bake the stuffing, covered, in the middle of a preheated 325° F. oven for 30 minutes and bake it, uncovered, for 30 minutes more. Serves 8 to 10.

EGGS AND BREAKFAST ITEMS

EGGS

Hashed Brown Potato Cakes with Fried Eggs

2 boiling potatoes (about 1 pound)
¼ cup minced cooked ham
2 tablespoons vegetable oil
¼ cup minced onion
⅓ cup minced green bell pepper
1 tablespoon drained minced bottled pimiento
2 large eggs

In a saucepan of boiling salted water cook the potatoes, peeled, for 10 minutes, drain them, and let them cool until they can be handled. Grate the potatoes coarse into a bowl. While the potatoes are cooking, in a large skillet sauté the ham in 1 tablespoon of the oil over moderately high heat, stirring, until it is browned lightly and transfer it with a slotted spoon to paper towels to drain. To the skillet add the onion, the bell pepper, the pimiento, and salt and pepper to taste, cook the mixture over moderate heat, stirring, until the vegetables are softened, and add it to the potatoes with the ham. Season the mixture with salt and pepper and combine it well. To the skillet add the remaining 1 tablespoon oil and heat it over moderately high heat until it is hot but not smoking. Form the potato mixture into 2 cakes, fry the cakes in the oil for 4 minutes on each side, and make an indentation in each cake. Break 1 of the eggs into each indentation, season the eggs with salt and pepper, and cook them, covered, for 6 minutes, or until they are cooked through and the potato cakes are crisp and golden. Serves 2.

Bacon, Avocado, and Cheese Omelets with Tomato Salsa

⅔ cup finely chopped seeded tomato
2 tablespoons finely chopped red onion
1 pickled or fresh *jalapeño* chili, or to taste, seeded and minced (wear rubber gloves)
2 tablespoons minced fresh coriander
1 tablespoon fresh lime or lemon juice
4 large eggs
2 tablespoons water
1 tablespoon unsalted butter
3 slices of lean bacon, cooked and crumbled
1 small avocado (preferably California)
½ cup coarsely grated Monterey Jack (about 2 ounces)

In a small bowl stir together the tomato, the onion, the *jalapeño*, the coriander, the lime juice, and salt and pepper to taste until the *salsa* is combined well. In a bowl whisk together the eggs, the water, and salt and pepper to taste.

In an 8-inch skillet, preferably non-stick, heat ½ tablespoon of the butter over moderately high heat until the foam subsides, pour in half the egg mixture, tilting the skillet to spread the mixture evenly over the bottom, and cook it for 1 minute, or until it is almost set. Sprinkle half the omelet with half the bacon, half the avocado, peeled and cut into ½-inch pieces, and half the Monterey Jack and cook the omelet for 1 minute, or until it is set. Fold the omelet over the filling, transfer it to a plate, and keep it warm. Make another omelet in the same manner with the remaining butter, egg mixture, bacon, avocado, and Monterey Jack and serve the omelets with the *salsa*. Serves 2.

Ham and Egg Biscuit Pizzas

3 red, green, and yellow bell peppers, cut
  into thin strips
1 onion, sliced thin
1½ tablespoons unsalted butter
1 cup finely diced cooked ham
  (about ½ pound)
For the biscuit dough
2 cups all-purpose flour
2 teaspoons double-acting baking powder
1 teaspoon salt
1 stick (½ cup) cold unsalted butter,
  cut into bits
½ cup plus 2 tablespoons milk

2 cups grated Münster or Monterey Jack
  (about 6 ounces)
6 large eggs
watercress sprigs for garnish

In a large heavy skillet cook the bell peppers and the onion in the butter over moderate heat, stirring, until the vegetables are softened, stir in the ham, and remove the skillet from the heat. *The bell pepper mixture may be made 1 day in advance and kept covered and chilled.*

Make the biscuit dough: In a bowl whisk together the flour, the baking powder, and the salt, add the butter, and blend the mixture until it resembles coarse meal. Add the milk and stir the mixture until it just forms a dough. Gather the dough into a ball, on a lightly floured surface knead it gently 6 times, and cut it into 6 equal pieces. Roll each piece of dough into a 7-inch round, form a ½-inch-high rim on each round by turning in the edge of the dough and pinching it until the shell measures 5 inches, and transfer the shells to a buttered large baking sheet.

Divide the Münster among the shells and top it with the bell pepper mixture, making a well in the center. Crack and drop an egg carefully into the well of each shell. Bake the pizzas in the middle of a preheated 425° F. oven for 12 to 15 minutes, or until the egg yolks are just set, and garnish them with the watercress. Serves 6.

PHOTO ON PAGE 35

Sweet Potato and Gruyère Soufflé

½ cup freshly grated Parmesan
1 cup finely chopped onion
1 large garlic clove, minced
2 tablespoons unsalted butter
2 tablespoons all-purpose flour
1 cup milk
1 cup coarsely grated Gruyère
  (about 3 ounces)
2 cups mashed cooked sweet potatoes
  (about 1½ pounds)
4 large eggs, separated

Butter a 1½-quart soufflé dish and dust it with ¼ cup of the Parmesan. In a large heavy saucepan cook the onion and the garlic with salt and pepper to taste in the butter over moderately low heat, stirring, until the onion is softened, stir in the flour, and cook the *roux*, stirring, for 3 minutes. Add the milk in a stream, whisking, and simmer the mixture, whisking until it is thickened. Remove the pan from the heat, whisk in the Gruyère, whisking until the cheese is melted, and whisk in the sweet potatoes and the egg yolks, 1 at a time. In a bowl with an electric mixer beat the egg whites with a pinch of salt until they just hold stiff peaks, whisk one fourth of them into the sweet potato mixture to lighten it, and fold in the remaining whites gently but thoroughly. Pour the mixture into the prepared soufflé dish, sprinkle the remaining ¼ cup Parmesan over it, and bake the soufflé in the middle of a preheated 375° F. oven for 45 to 50 minutes, or until it is puffed and golden. Serve the soufflé immediately. Serves 4 to 6.

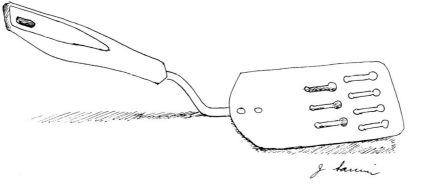

BREAKFAST ITEMS

Sausage Cheese Grits

6 cups water
1½ cups quick-cooking grits
2¾ cups grated Monterey Jack
   (about ¾ pound)
2 tablespoons unsalted butter
two 2-inch pickled *jalapeño* chilies, minced,
   including the seeds (wear rubber gloves)
4 scallions, chopped fine
¾ pound bulk fresh sausage
1 tablespoon vegetable oil
1 onion, chopped fine
1 large green bell pepper, chopped fine
4 large eggs
2 teaspoons Worcestershire sauce

In a large heavy saucepan bring the water to a boil,
stir in the grits slowly, and simmer them, covered, stirring occasionally, for 7 minutes. Stir in 1½ cups of the
Monterey Jack, the butter, the *jalapeños*, the scallions,
and salt and pepper to taste, stirring until the cheese is
melted, and spread the mixture in a buttered 13- by
9-inch baking dish.

In a heavy skillet brown the sausage over moderate
heat, stirring and breaking up the lumps, transfer it with
a slotted spoon to paper towels to drain, and pour off the
fat. Add the oil to the skillet and in it cook the onion and
the bell pepper over moderately low heat, stirring, until
the vegetables are softened. In a bowl whisk together
the eggs, the Worcestershire sauce, and salt to taste, stir
in the sausage and the vegetables, and spread the mixture over the grits. Sprinkle the sausage mixture with
the remaining 1¼ cups Monterey Jack and bake the grits
in the middle of a preheated 350° F. oven for 30 to 35
minutes, or until the eggs are firm. Serves 8 to 10.

Caviar Pancakes

2 tablespoons unsalted butter if desired
6 buttermilk pancakes (recipe follows)
about ⅓ cup sour cream
about 2 tablespoons caviar (about 2 ounces)
1 hard-boiled large egg yolk, forced through
   a sieve
½ scallion, minced

In a small saucepan cook the butter over moderate
heat, swirling the pan occasionally, until it is golden
brown, being careful not to let it burn, and keep it warm.

154

Spread each pancake with about 1 tablespoon of the sour cream, or to taste, top the sour cream with about 1 teaspoon of the caviar, or to taste, and sprinkle each pancake with some of the egg yolk and some of the scallion. Stack 3 pancakes on each of 2 plates and drizzle each stack with some of the brown butter. Serves 2.

Buttermilk Pancakes

1 cup all-purpose flour
1 teaspoon baking soda
½ teaspoon salt
1 large egg, beaten lightly
1 cup buttermilk plus additional
  if necessary
vegetable oil for brushing
  the griddle

In a bowl whisk together the flour, the baking soda, the salt, the egg, and 1 cup of the buttermilk, whisking the batter until it is smooth. *The batter may be made 3 days in advance and kept covered and chilled. It will thicken as it stands. Thin the batter to the desired consistency with the additional buttermilk or with water, 1 tablespoon at a time.*

Heat a griddle over moderate heat until it is hot enough to make drops of water scatter over its surface and brush it with some of the oil. Working in batches and using a ¼-cup measure filled halfway, pour the batter onto the griddle, cook the pancakes for 1 minute on each side, or until they are golden, and keep them warm. Use the pancakes for caviar pancakes or serve them plain with syrup. Makes 6 pancakes.

Corn and Bacon Pancakes

1 cup yellow cornmeal
½ cup all-purpose flour
1 tablespoon sugar
2 teaspoons double-acting baking powder
¼ teaspoon salt
1 cup fresh corn kernels including the pulp
  scraped from the cobs (cut from about
  2 ears of corn)
2 large eggs
¾ cup milk
2 tablespoons unsalted butter, melted and
  cooled, plus additional, melted, for
  brushing the griddle

5 slices of lean bacon, cooked until crisp
maple syrup as an accompaniment

In a bowl whisk together the cornmeal, the flour, the sugar, the baking powder, and the salt. In a food processor purée coarse the corn. In another bowl whisk together the corn purée, the eggs, the milk, and 2 tablespoons of the melted butter, add the egg mixture to the cornmeal mixture, and stir the batter until it is just combined. Let the batter stand, covered, for 10 minutes and stir in the bacon, crumbled.

Heat a griddle over moderate heat until it is hot and brush it lightly with some of the additional melted butter. Working in batches, pour the batter onto the griddle by ¼-cup measures and cook the pancakes for 1 minute on each side, or until they are golden, transferring them as they are cooked to a heated platter and brushing the griddle with some of the additional melted butter as necessary. Serve the pancakes with the syrup. Makes about 12 pancakes.

Lemon Brown Sugar Blueberry Pancakes

1 large egg
1 tablespoon freshly grated lemon zest
¾ cup milk
3 tablespoons firmly packed dark brown sugar
2 tablespoons unsalted butter, melted, plus
  additional melted butter for brushing
  the griddle
¾ cup plus 2 tablespoons all-purpose flour
1 teaspoon double-acting baking powder
½ teaspoon salt
1 cup blueberries, picked over
maple syrup as an accompaniment

In a small bowl whisk together the egg, the zest, the milk, the brown sugar, and 2 tablespoons of the butter. In a bowl whisk together the flour, the baking powder, and the salt, add the milk mixture, and whisk the batter until it is just combined. Stir in the blueberries. Heat a griddle over moderately high heat until it is hot enough to make drops of water scatter over its surface and brush it with some of the additional melted butter. Pour the batter onto the griddle by ⅓-cup measures and cook the pancakes for 2 minutes on each side, or until they are golden. Transfer the pancakes as they are cooked to a plate and keep them warm. Serve the pancakes with the syrup. Makes about six 5-inch pancakes.

PASTA AND GRAINS

PASTA

Herbed Farfalle

¾ pound *farfalle* (bow-tie–shaped pasta)
3 to 4 tablespoons extra-virgin olive oil,
or to taste
2 tablespoons minced fresh mint leaves
2 tablespoons minced fresh parsley leaves

In a kettle of boiling salted water cook the *farfalle* until it is *al dente*, drain it well, and in a bowl toss it with the oil, the mint, the parsley, and salt and pepper to taste. Serves 6.

PHOTO ON PAGE 41

Fettuccine with Morels, Asparagus, and Goat Cheese

½ cup minced shallot
2 tablespoons unsalted butter
½ cup dry white wine
½ cup chicken broth
½ pound fresh morels (available in the spring
at specialty produce markets and some
supermarkets), washed well, patted dry,
and trimmed
½ cup heavy cream
6 ounces mild goat cheese such as
Montrachet, crumbled (about 1½ cups)
¾ pound asparagus, trimmed, cut into ½-inch
pieces, and cooked in boiling salted water
for 2 to 3 minutes, or until tender
¼ cup minced fresh chives
¾ pound fettuccine

In a heavy skillet cook the shallot in the butter over moderately low heat, stirring, until it is softened, add the wine, and simmer the mixture until the wine is reduced by half. Add the broth and the morels, sliced crosswise, and simmer the mixture, covered, for 10 minutes, or until the morels are tender. Add the cream and the goat cheese and cook the mixture over low heat, stirring, until the cheese is melted. Stir in the asparagus, the chives, and salt and pepper to taste and keep the sauce warm. In a kettle of boiling salted water cook the fettuccine until it is *al dente*, drain it well, and in a bowl toss the pasta with the sauce. Serves 4 to 6 as a first course.

Whole-Wheat Fettuccine with Brussels Sprouts and Red Bell Peppers in Brown Butter

2 onions, sliced thin
1 stick (½ cup) unsalted butter
1½ tablespoons minced garlic
3 pints Brussels sprouts, trimmed and the
leaves separated
½ cup water
½ cup thinly sliced scallion
2 red bell peppers, cut into thin strips
1 pound whole-wheat fettuccine
⅓ cup freshly grated Parmesan, or to taste

In a kettle cook the onions in 3 tablespoons of the butter over moderate heat, stirring occasionally, until they are golden. Add the garlic, the Brussels sprouts, the water, the scallion, the bell peppers, and salt and pepper to taste and cook the mixture, stirring occasionally, for 15 minutes, or until the vegetables are crisp-tender.

While the vegetables are cooking, in another kettle cook the fettuccine in boiling salted water for 10 to 12 minutes, or until it is *al dente*, and drain it well. Stir the pasta into the vegetables and keep the mixture warm. In a small skillet cook the remaining 5 tablespoons butter over moderate heat, swirling the skillet, until it is browned, add it to the pasta mixture with the Parmesan and salt and pepper to taste, and toss the mixture well. Serves 6 to 8.

Asparagus Lasagne

4 pounds asparagus, trimmed
3 tablespoons extra-virgin olive oil
six 7- by 6¼-inch sheets of instant (no-boil)
  lasagne (available at specialty foods shops
  and some supermarkets)
½ stick (¼ cup) unsalted butter
¼ cup all-purpose flour
1½ cups chicken broth
½ cup water
7 ounces mild goat cheese such as Montrachet
1 teaspoon freshly grated lemon zest,
  or to taste
1⅔ cups freshly grated Parmesan
1 cup heavy cream

Cut the tips off each asparagus spear and reserve them. In each of 2 large shallow baking pans toss half the asparagus stalks with half the oil, coating them well, and roast them in a preheated 500° F. oven, shaking the pans every few minutes, for 5 to 10 minutes, or until they are crisp-tender. Sprinkle the asparagus with salt to taste and let it cool. Cut the roasted asparagus into ½-inch lengths and reserve it.

In a large bowl of cold water let the sheets of lasagne soak for 15 minutes, or until they are softened. In a saucepan melt the butter, add the flour, and cook the *roux* over moderately low heat, stirring, for 3 minutes. Add the broth and the water in a stream, whisking, simmer the mixture for 5 minutes, and whisk in the goat cheese, the zest, and salt to taste, whisking until the sauce is smooth.

Drain the pasta well, arrange 1 sheet of it in each of 2 buttered 8-inch-square baking dishes, and spread each sheet with one fourth of the sauce. Top the sauce in each dish with one fourth of the reserved roasted asparagus

and sprinkle the asparagus with ⅓ cup of the Parmesan. Continue to layer the pasta, the sauce, the asparagus, and the Parmesan in the same manner, ending with a sheet of pasta. In a bowl beat the cream with a pinch of salt until it holds soft peaks. Arrange the reserved asparagus tips decoratively on the pasta, spoon the cream over the pasta and the asparagus tips, spreading it with the back of the spoon, and sprinkle the remaining ⅓ cup Parmesan on top. Bake the lasagne in the middle of a preheated 400° F. oven for 20 to 30 minutes, or until it is golden and bubbling, and let it stand for 10 minutes before serving. Serves 8.

Linguine with Beets and Horseradish

¼ pound *linguine*
1 large garlic clove, minced
1 tablespoon unsalted butter
½ pound raw beets, peeled and grated coarse
  (about 1½ cups)
⅓ cup heavy cream
⅓ cup water
1 tablespoon drained bottled horseradish,
  or to taste
2 tablespoons minced fresh parsley leaves

In a large saucepan of salted boiling water cook the *linguine* until it is *al dente*. While the *linguine* is cooking, in a heavy skillet cook the garlic in the butter over moderately low heat, stirring, until it is golden, add the beets, the cream, and the water, and simmer the mixture for 6 minutes, or until the beets are tender. Stir in the horseradish and salt and pepper to taste, drain the *linguine* well, and in a bowl toss it with the beet mixture. Divide the pasta between 2 plates and sprinkle it with the parsley. Serves 2 as a first course.

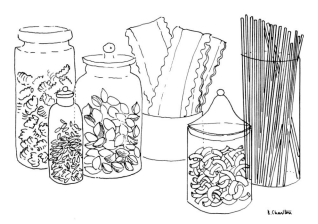

Linguine with Uncooked Tomato, Arugula, and Olive Sauce

1 garlic clove, minced and mashed to a paste
    with ¼ teaspoon salt
4 fresh plum tomatoes,
    chopped
1 bunch of *arugula*, coarse stems discarded
    and the leaves washed well, spun dry, and
    chopped coarse (about 1 cup)
6 Kalamata or other brine-cured black olives,
    pitted and chopped
2 tablespoons olive oil
1½ tablespoons balsamic vinegar,
    or to taste
½ pound *linguine*

In a large bowl stir together the garlic paste, the tomatoes, the *arugula*, the olives, the oil, the vinegar, and salt and pepper to taste and let the mixture marinate for 20 minutes. In a large saucepan of boiling salted water cook the *linguine* for 10 minutes, or until it is *al dente*, drain it, and while it is still hot, toss it with the sauce. Serve the pasta warm or at room temperature. Serves 2.

Baked Orzo and Cheddar with Pepperoni

½ cup ¼-inch dice of pepperoni
½ cup chopped onion
2 tablespoons all-purpose flour
¾ cup chicken broth
1½ cups coarsely grated Cheddar
    (about ¼ pound)
¾ cup *orzo* (rice-shaped pasta)
¼ cup fresh bread crumbs

In a saucepan cook the pepperoni over moderately high heat, stirring, for 2 minutes, add the onion, and cook the mixture, stirring, for 4 minutes. Reduce the heat to low, add the flour, and cook the *roux*, stirring, for 3 minutes. Whisk in the broth and simmer the sauce, whisking, for 2 minutes. Whisk in the Cheddar, whisking until the sauce is smooth, and keep the sauce warm. In a large saucepan of boiling salted water boil the *orzo* until it is *al dente*, drain it well, and stir it into the sauce. Turn the mixture into a buttered 10-inch oval gratin dish, sprinkle the top with the bread crumbs, and bake the mixture in the middle of a preheated 450° F. oven for 15 minutes, or until it is golden and bubbling. Serves 2 as a main course.

Penne with Pumpkin Sauce

1 onion, chopped fine
1 red bell pepper, chopped fine
2 large garlic cloves, minced
2 tablespoons unsalted butter
½ cup canned solid-pack pumpkin
1 cup chicken broth
½ cup water
2 tablespoons heavy cream
freshly grated nutmeg to taste
½ pound *penne* or other tubular pasta
3 tablespoons minced fresh parsley leaves
freshly grated Parmesan as an accompaniment

In a large skillet cook the onion, the bell pepper, and the garlic in the butter over moderate heat, stirring, until the vegetables are softened, stir in the pumpkin, the broth, the water, the cream, the nutmeg, and salt and pepper to taste, and simmer the sauce, stirring occasionally, for 10 minutes. While the sauce is simmering, in a kettle of salted boiling water boil the *penne* until it is *al dente*, ladle out and reserve about 1 cup of the cooking water, and drain the *penne* well.

Add the *penne* to the sauce, cook the mixture over moderate heat, stirring and thinning the sauce as desired with some of the reserved cooking water, for 1 to 2 minutes, or until the pasta is coated well, and stir in the parsley. Divide the pasta between 2 plates and serve it with the Parmesan. Serves 2.

Artichoke Heart and Brin d'Amour Ravioli with Three-Pepper Sauce

For the filling

¼ pound *brin d'amour* (Corsican sheep's milk
    cheese, available at specialty foods shops),
    herbed coating discarded and the cheese
    grated (about ⅓ cup)
2 tablespoons soft mild goat cheese such
    as Montrachet
¼ cup finely chopped drained marinated
    artichoke hearts

For the sauce

3 small red, yellow, and orange bell peppers,
    cut into julienne strips
1 tablespoon olive oil
1 garlic clove, chopped
½ cup chicken broth

12 won ton wrappers (available at Oriental
    markets and many supermarkets),
    thawed if frozen

Make the filling: In a bowl stir together well the cheeses, the artichoke hearts, and pepper to taste and chill the filling for 1 hour, or until it is cold.

Make the sauce: In a large heavy skillet cook the bell peppers in the oil over moderately low heat, stirring, until they are softened, stir in the garlic and the broth, and simmer the mixture for 15 minutes. Transfer about 2 tablespoons of the bell peppers with a slotted spoon to a bowl and reserve them for garnish. In a blender purée the remaining bell pepper mixture with salt and pepper to taste until it is smooth, transfer the sauce to a small saucepan, and keep it warm, covered, while preparing the ravioli.

Cut out a heart from each won ton wrapper with a heart-shaped cutter (about 3 inches at the widest point). Put 1 heart on a lightly floured surface, mound 1 teaspoon of the filling on each lobe of the heart, and brush the edges with water. Put a second heart over the first, pressing down around the filling to force out the air, and seal the edges well. Make ravioli with the remaining wrappers and filling in the same manner, transferring them as they are formed to a kitchen towel, and let them dry slightly, turning them occasionally.

Bring a large saucepan of boiling salted water to a gentle boil and in it cook the ravioli for 2 minutes, or until they rise to the surface and are tender. (Do not let the water boil vigorously once the ravioli have been added.)

Transfer the ravioli as they are cooked with a slotted spoon to a kitchen towel to drain. Divide the sauce between 2 plates, arrange 3 ravioli on each plate, and garnish each serving with some of the reserved bell peppers. Serves 2.

PHOTO ON PAGE 20

Spaghetti with Garlic Oil and Tomato

½ pound spaghetti
3 large garlic cloves, sliced
    thin lengthwise
2 tablespoons olive oil
3 tablespoons finely chopped fresh
    parsley leaves
⅓ cup canned tomato purée

In a large saucepan of salted boiling water cook the spaghetti until it is *al dente*. While the spaghetti is cooking, in a large heavy skillet cook the garlic in the oil over moderately low heat, stirring, until it is golden, being careful not to let it get too brown, stir in the parsley, the tomato purée, and salt and pepper to taste, and cook the sauce, stirring, for 1 minute. Keep the sauce warm. Ladle out and reserve about ⅓ cup of the pasta water, drain the spaghetti, and add it to the sauce with ¼ cup of the reserved water. Toss the spaghetti mixture over low heat for 1 minute, adding the remaining reserved pasta water if desired, divide it between 2 heated plates, and season it with pepper. Serves 2.

Ziti with Herbs and Red Bell Pepper

1 small red bell pepper, chopped fine
1 garlic clove, minced
2 tablespoons olive oil
2 tablespoons minced fresh parsley leaves
1 tablespoon chopped fresh chives
1 teaspoon fresh thyme leaves, minced
1 teaspoon fresh rosemary leaves, minced
½ pound *ziti*

In a heavy skillet cook the bell pepper and the garlic in the oil over moderately low heat, stirring, until the pepper is crisp-tender, transfer the mixture to a bowl, and add the herbs.

In a large saucepan of boiling salted water cook the *ziti* until it is *al dente*, drain it well, and toss it with the herb mixture and salt and pepper to taste. Serves 2.

Pasta with Kielbasa and Broccoli Rabe

1 pound *kielbasa* (Polish smoked sausage),
    quartered lengthwise and cut into
    ½-inch-thick pieces
6 garlic cloves, minced
1 bunch of broccoli rabe (about 1 pound),
    stems peeled and cut into ½-inch pieces and
    the leaves and flowerets chopped coarse
1 cup water
1 pound spiral-shaped pasta such as *rotelle*
    or *fusilli*
3 tablespoons olive oil, or to taste

In a heavy skillet brown the *kielbasa* over moderate heat, stirring, transfer it with a slotted spoon to paper towels to drain, and pour off all but 1 tablespoon of the fat. In the fat remaining in the skillet cook the garlic over moderately low heat, stirring, until it is golden, add the broccoli rabe, and cook the mixture, stirring, for 1 minute, or until the broccoli rabe is wilted. Add the water, simmer the mixture, stirring occasionally, for 5 to 7 minutes, or until the broccoli rabe is tender, and stir in the *kielbasa*. In a kettle of boiling salted water cook the pasta until it is *al dente* and drain it well. In a large bowl toss together the pasta, the oil, the *kielbasa* mixture, and salt and pepper to taste. Serves 4 to 6.

Sun-Dried Tomato, Garlic, and Jalapeño Pasta

1 tablespoon minced garlic
¼ cup minced shallot
2 tablespoons olive oil
1 tablespoon unsalted butter
⅓ cup finely chopped drained sun-dried
    tomatoes packed in oil
2 to 4 tablespoons finely chopped pickled
    whole *jalapeño* chilies, or to taste
    (wear rubber gloves)
½ pound lasagne noodles, broken into
    bite-size pieces, or wide egg noodles
2 tablespoons minced fresh parsley leaves
freshly grated Parmesan as an accompaniment

In a heavy skillet cook the garlic and the shallot in the oil and the butter over moderately low heat, stirring, for 5 minutes, add the tomatoes, the *jalapeños*, and salt to taste, and cook the mixture, stirring occasionally, for 20 minutes. To a kettle of boiling salted water add the lasagne gradually, stirring, and boil it, stirring, until it

is tender. Drain the pasta in a colander and rinse it briefly under hot water. Add the pasta and the parsley to the skillet and toss the mixture well. Serve the pasta with the Parmesan. Serves 2.

GRAINS

Lemon Barley Spring Rolls

For the filling
¾ cup pearl barley, rinsed well and drained
2¼ cups water
3 cups finely shredded red cabbage
    (about 1 pound)
1½ teaspoons vegetable oil
1 tablespoon cider vinegar
1 cup finely shredded carrot
4 scallions, chopped fine
1 teaspoon freshly grated lemon zest

8 spring-roll wrappers (available at Asian
    markets, some specialty foods shops,
    and many supermarkets)
a paste made by stirring together
    2 tablespoons all-purpose flour and
    2 tablespoons water
vegetable oil for deep frying

Make the filling: In a saucepan combine the barley, the water, and salt to taste, bring the water to a boil, and cook the barley, covered, over low heat for 40 minutes, or until the water is absorbed and the barley is tender. In a skillet sauté the cabbage in the oil with the vinegar and salt to taste over moderately high heat for 4 to 5 minutes, or until it is wilted. In a bowl toss together the barley, the cabbage mixture, the carrot, the scallions, the zest, and salt and pepper to taste and let the filling cool. *The filling may be made 1 day in advance and kept covered and chilled.*

On a work surface arrange 1 spring-roll wrapper with a corner facing you and keep the remaining wrappers covered with plastic wrap. Spread about ½ cup of the filling horizontally across the center of the wrapper, leaving a 2-inch border at each end, and fold the corner closest to you tightly over the filling. Brush the edges with some of the paste, fold the left and right corners over the filling, and, rolling away from you, roll up the filling tightly in the wrapper. Make more spring rolls with the remaining wrappers, filling, and paste in the same manner, transferring them as they are made to a wax-paper–lined baking sheet and keeping them covered with plastic wrap. In a deep skillet or deep fryer heat 1 inch of the oil to 375° F. on a deep-fat thermometer and in it fry the spring rolls in 2 batches, turning them, for 2 to 3 minutes, or until they are golden, transferring them as they are fried with tongs to paper towels to drain. *The spring rolls may be made 2 days in advance, cooled completely, wrapped in plastic wrap, and chilled. Reheat the rolls on a rack set in a jelly-roll pan in a preheated 450° F. oven, turning them once, for 10 to 15 minutes, or until they are crisp.* Cut each spring roll on the diagonal into 3 pieces. Makes 8 spring rolls.

PHOTO ON PAGE 68

Vicky

Mushroom Barley "Risotto"

2 tablespoons unsalted butter
¼ pound mushrooms, sliced
1 garlic clove, minced
¼ teaspoon salt, or to taste
½ cup pearl barley
2½ cups water
¼ cup freshly grated Parmesan
2 tablespoons minced fresh parsley leaves

In a 3-quart microwave-safe casserole with a tight-fitting lid microwave 1 tablespoon of the butter, uncov-

ered, at high power (100%) for 1 minute, or until it is melted, stir in the mushrooms, the garlic, and the salt, and microwave the mixture, uncovered, at high power for 5 minutes. Add the barley and the water, microwave the mixture, covered, at high power for 12 minutes, and microwave it, covered, at medium power (50%) for 25 minutes, or until most of the liquid is absorbed and the barley is *al dente*. Stir in the remaining 1 tablespoon butter, cut into bits, the Parmesan, the parsley, and salt and pepper to taste. Serves 2.

Carrot Couscous with Thyme

1 carrot, grated coarse
1½ tablespoons olive oil
1 teaspoon fresh lemon juice
¼ teaspoon sugar
1 cup plus 1 tablespoon water
½ teaspoon finely chopped fresh thyme leaves
  or a pinch of dried thyme, crumbled
¾ cup couscous

In a small heavy saucepan cook the carrot in the oil over moderate heat, stirring, for 1 minute. Add the lemon juice, the sugar, 1 tablespoon of the water, the thyme, and salt to taste and simmer the mixture, covered, for 1 minute. Add the remaining 1 cup water, bring the liquid to a boil, and stir in the couscous. Cover the pan, remove it from the heat, and let the couscous stand for 5 minutes. Fluff the couscous with a fork. Serves 2.

Chili-Flavored Couscous

1 small onion, chopped fine
1 tablespoon olive oil
1 teaspoon chili powder
¾ cup chicken broth
½ cup couscous
2 tablespoons thinly sliced scallion greens

In a heavy saucepan cook the onion in the oil over moderate heat, stirring occasionally, until it is golden, add the chili powder, and cook the mixture, stirring, for 1 minute. Add the broth, bring the liquid to a boil, and stir in the couscous. Cover the pan, remove it from the heat, and let the couscous stand for 5 minutes. Fluff the couscous with a fork and stir in the scallion greens. Serves 2.

Lemon Couscous

¾ cup water
¼ teaspoon freshly grated lemon zest
1 teaspoon vegetable oil
½ cup couscous
2 tablespoons chopped fresh chives

In a small saucepan bring the water to a boil, stir in the zest, the oil, the couscous, and salt and pepper to taste, and let the mixture stand, covered, off the heat for 5 minutes. Fluff the couscous with a fork and stir in the chives. Serves 2.

Polenta with Vegetables

1 cup water
¾ cup chicken broth
½ cup yellow cornmeal
¼ cup heavy cream
¼ teaspoon salt
1 small carrot, halved lengthwise and sliced
    thin crosswise
⅓ cup thinly sliced red onion
2 mushrooms, stems discarded and the
    mushrooms sliced thin
1 garlic clove, minced
1 tablespoon olive oil
⅓ cup freshly grated Parmesan
a pinch of dried hot red pepper flakes,
    or to taste

In a 2-quart microwave-safe round glass casserole with a lid stir together the water, the broth, the cornmeal, the cream, and the salt and microwave the mixture, covered, at high power (100%), stirring every 2 minutes, for 6 minutes, or until the cornmeal is cooked but the mixture is still soft. In a small heavy skillet sauté the carrot, the onion, the mushrooms, and the garlic in the oil over moderately high heat, stirring frequently, for 3 minutes, or until the vegetables are crisp-tender and golden, and stir into the polenta the vegetable mixture, the Parmesan, and the red pepper flakes. Serves 2 generously.

Spiced Basmati Rice

2 tablespoons vegetable oil
two 3-inch cinnamon sticks
8 cloves
1 bay leaf
2 cups chopped onion
1 tablespoon minced peeled fresh gingerroot
1 large garlic clove, minced
⅛ teaspoon turmeric
1 cup *basmati* rice (available at specialty
    foods shops and East Indian markets),
    picked over and rinsed
1½ cups chicken broth
1 cup water

In a 2½-quart microwave-safe casserole combine the oil, the cinnamon sticks, the cloves, and the bay leaf and microwave the mixture, uncovered, at high power (100%) for 2 minutes, or until it is fragrant. Stir in the onion, the gingerroot, the garlic, and the turmeric and microwave the mixture at high power, stirring after 2 minutes, for 4 minutes, or until the onion is softened. Stir in the rice, the broth, the water, and salt to taste and microwave the mixture, uncovered, stirring every 4 minutes, for 8 to 10 minutes, or until the liquid has been absorbed. Cover the casserole and microwave the mixture at high power for 4 minutes more, or until the rice is tender. Let the rice stand, covered, for 5 minutes and fluff it with a fork.

The spices, which are left whole in Indian rice dishes, are not meant to be eaten. Serves 4 to 6.

Mexican Rice and Pea Timbales with Coriander

1 large onion, chopped
1 large garlic clove, chopped
¾ teaspoon cuminseed
¼ cup vegetable oil
1 large tomato, quartered
1 cup chicken broth
1 cup plus 2 tablespoons water
2 tablespoons fresh lime juice
1½ cups medium- or long-grain white rice
¼ cup chopped fresh coriander plus sprigs
    for garnish
1 cup thawed frozen peas
lime slices, halved, for garnish if desired

In a large deep skillet cook the onion, the garlic, and the cuminseed in 2 tablespoons of the oil over moderate heat, stirring, until the onion is golden, add the tomato, and sauté the mixture over moderately high heat, stirring, for 1 minute. In a blender purée the mixture with the broth, pour the purée into a saucepan, and stir in the water and the lime juice. Bring the mixture to a simmer and keep it warm. In the skillet heat the remaining 2 tablespoons oil over moderate heat until it is hot but not smoking and in it cook the rice, stirring, for 5 to 7 minutes, or until it is golden. Remove the skillet from the heat, stir in the broth mixture slowly, and cook the rice, covered, over moderately low heat for 15 minutes. Remove the skillet from the heat, sprinkle the chopped coriander and the peas over the rice, and let the mixture stand, covered, for 5 minutes. Fluff the rice with a fork, distributing the peas evenly. Using a ⅔-cup timbale mold and forming 1 timbale at a time, pack the rice mixture into the mold and invert it onto plates. Garnish the timbales with the coriander sprigs and the lime slices. Serves 10.

Tomato Paella with Spicy Squid and Peas

1 pound squid, cleaned (procedure follows)
    and cut into ¼-inch slices
¼ cup plus 2 tablespoons vegetable oil
2 cups chicken broth
1 cup tomato juice
1 cup water
1 teaspoon paprika
1 teaspoon ground cumin
2 garlic cloves, minced
1½ cups paella rice or Arborio rice (both
    available at specialty foods shops and some
    supermarkets) or other medium-grain rice
1½ cups thawed frozen peas
lemon wedges for garnish

Pat the squid dry with paper towels. In a heavy skillet, measuring 9½ inches across the bottom and 13 inches across the top, heat ¼ cup of the oil over moderately high heat until it is hot but not smoking and in it sauté the squid for 1 minute, or until it is golden. Transfer the squid to paper towels and let it drain. In a saucepan combine the broth, the tomato juice, the water, the paprika, and the cumin and bring the liquid to a boil. Wipe out the skillet and in it cook the garlic in the remaining 2 tablespoons oil over moderately low heat, stirring, until it is softened. Add the rice to the skillet and cook the mixture, stirring, for 3 minutes. Add the hot broth mixture and simmer the mixture, uncovered, stirring occasionally, for 5 minutes. Stir in salt and pepper to taste and simmer the mixture, undisturbed, for 10 minutes

more. Scatter the squid over the rice and cook the mixture, covered, over moderately low heat for 5 minutes. Scatter the peas over the squid and rice and cook the mixture, covered, for 5 minutes. Remove the skillet from the heat and let the paella steam, covered with a double thickness of kitchen towels, for 5 minutes. Serve the paella with the lemon wedges. Serves 4 to 6.

To Clean Squid

Pull the head and body of the squid apart, cut off the tentacles just below the eyes, and reserve the tentacles and body sac. Discard the transparent quill from inside the body sac, rinse the body sac well, and peel off the purple membrane covering it. Pull off the flaps gently from the body sac to avoid tearing the sac and reserve them.

Make the sauce while the risotto mixture is being chilled: In a small saucepan cook the onion and the garlic in the oil over moderate heat, stirring, until the onion is softened. Add the peppers, the cumin, the tomatoes, and the broth and bring the mixture to a boil. In a blender purée the mixture until it is smooth and add salt and pepper to taste. *The sauce may be made 2 days in advance and kept covered and chilled.*

Form heaping tablespoons of the risotto mixture into logs. Have the egg whites and the bread crumbs ready in separate bowls. Working with 1 croquette at a time, dip the croquettes into the egg whites, letting the excess drip off, coat them in the bread crumbs, shaking off the excess, and arrange them in a shallow baking pan lined with wax paper. *The croquettes may be prepared up to this point 1 day in advance and kept uncovered and chilled.* In a large saucepan fry the croquettes, 3 at a time, in 2 inches of 375° F. oil for 1 minute, or until they are golden, transferring them as they are fried to paper towels to drain. Serve the croquettes with the sauce, heated, and garnished with the parsley sprigs. Serves 4 as a first course or light luncheon entrée.

Mozzarella Risotto Croquettes with Tomato Red Pepper Sauce

½ cup grated mozzarella
1 recipe parsleyed mushroom risotto
   (recipe follows), omitting the mushrooms
For the sauce
1 small onion, chopped
1 garlic clove, minced
1 tablespoon vegetable oil
a 7-ounce jar roasted red peppers,
   drained well
¾ teaspoon ground cumin
a 14- to 16-ounce can tomatoes, drained well
¼ cup chicken broth

2 large egg whites, beaten lightly
1 cup fine dry bread crumbs
vegetable oil for deep-frying
parsley sprigs for garnish

Stir the mozzarella into the risotto and spread the mixture in a greased shallow baking dish. Chill the mixture for at least 2 hours or overnight.

Parsleyed Mushroom Risotto

4 cups chicken broth
1 cup water
1 onion, chopped
2 tablespoons olive oil
¼ pound mushrooms, chopped fine
3 tablespoons minced fresh parsley leaves
   (preferably flat-leafed)
¾ cup Arborio rice (available at specialty
   foods shops and some supermarkets) or
   other medium-grain rice
½ cup freshly grated Parmesan, or to taste

In a saucepan combine the broth and the water, bring the liquid to a boil, and keep it at a bare simmer. In a large heavy saucepan cook the onion in the oil over moderate heat, stirring, until it is softened, add the mushrooms, the parsley, and salt to taste, and sauté the mixture over moderately high heat, stirring, until the liquid the mushrooms give off is evaporated. (If omitting the mushrooms, add the parsley and salt to taste and sauté the mixture over moderately high heat, stirring, for 1 minute.) Stir in the rice and cook the mixture, stirring with a wooden spatula, for 1 minute. Add about ½ cup of the broth and cook the mixture, stirring, for 3 minutes, or until the liquid is absorbed. Add more of the broth, ½ cup at a time, stirring and cooking the mixture for 3 minutes, or until the liquid is absorbed, after each addition, until the rice begins to soften. (About 3 cups of the broth will have been absorbed.) Add more of the broth, about ⅓ cup at a time, stirring and simmering the mixture over moderately low heat for 3 minutes, or until the liquid is absorbed, after each addition, until the rice is *al dente*. (The mixture should be creamy.) Remove the pan from the heat and stir in the Parmesan and pepper to taste. Serves 2 as a main course or 4 as a first course or side dish.

Sun-Dried Tomato Risotto

1 ounce sun-dried tomatoes (not packed in oil)
1 cup water
2½ cups chicken broth
1 cup finely chopped onion
1 garlic clove, minced
4 tablespoons olive oil
1 cup Arborio rice
¼ cup freshly grated Parmesan
finely chopped fresh parsley leaves
    for sprinkling the risotto
    if desired

In a small saucepan simmer the tomatoes in the water for 1 minute, drain them, reserving the liquid, and chop them. In a saucepan combine the reserved cooking liquid and the broth, bring the liquid to a simmer, and keep it at a bare simmer. In a large saucepan cook the onion and the garlic in the oil over moderately low heat, stirring, until they are softened, add the rice, stirring until each grain is coated with oil, and stir in the tomatoes. Add ½ cup of the simmering liquid and cook the mixture over moderate heat, stirring constantly, until the liquid is absorbed. Continue adding the liquid, ½ cup at a time, stirring constantly and letting each portion be absorbed before adding the next, until the rice is tender but still *al dente*. (The rice should take about 17 minutes to become *al dente*.) Stir in the Parmesan and salt and pepper to taste and sprinkle the risotto with the parsley. Serves 4 to 6.

VEGETABLES

Artichokes with Scallion Tomato Vinaigrette

two ½-pound artichokes
½ lemon
½ cup water
4 teaspoons white-wine vinegar
¼ cup olive oil
2 tablespoons minced scallion greens
1 small tomato, peeled, seeded, and chopped

Cut off and discard the stems of the artichokes with a stainless-steel knife, break off the tough outer leaves, and cut off the top fourth of the artichokes. Snip off the tips of the artichoke leaves with scissors and rub the cut edges with the lemon half. In a 3-quart microwave-safe casserole with a lid combine the water and the artichokes, microwave the artichokes, covered, at high power (100%) for 15 minutes, or until the bases are tender, and let them stand, covered, for 5 minutes.

In a bowl whisk together the vinegar, the oil, and salt and pepper to taste, whisking the dressing until it is emulsified, and whisk in the scallion greens and the tomato. Arrange the artichokes on 2 plates, spoon the dressing over them, and serve the artichokes at room temperature. Serves 2.

Asparagus Napoleons
with Oriental Black Bean Sauce

For the pastry rectangles
½ pound frozen puff pastry,
   thawed
an egg wash made by beating 1 large egg yolk
   with 2 teaspoons water
For the sauce
1 tablespoon cornstarch
⅓ cup water
⅔ cup chicken broth
1½ tablespoons soy sauce
1½ tablespoons Scotch or medium-dry Sherry
2 teaspoons sugar
1 tablespoon vegetable oil

1 tablespoon fermented black beans (available
   at Oriental markets and specialty foods
   shops), rinsed well and drained
2 tablespoons fine julienne strips of orange zest
1½ tablespoons minced peeled fresh gingerroot
1 tablespoon minced garlic
1½ pounds asparagus, trimmed and peeled

Make the pastry rectangles: Roll out the pastry ⅛ inch thick on a lightly floured surface, cut out six 5- by 2-inch rectangles, and transfer them to a dampened baking sheet. Brush the tops of the rectangles with some of the egg wash, being careful not to let the egg wash drip down the sides, score them in a crosshatch pattern with the back of a paring knife, and brush them again with some of the egg wash. Bake the rectangles in the upper third of a preheated 400° F. oven for 12 to 15 minutes, or until they are puffed and golden, transfer them with a spatula to racks, and let them cool. *The pastry rectangles may be made 1 day in advance, kept in an airtight container at room temperature, and reheated.* Halve the rectangles horizontally with a serrated knife and with a fork pull out carefully any uncooked dough.

Make the sauce: In a small bowl dissolve the cornstarch in the water and stir in the broth, the soy sauce, the Scotch, and the sugar. In a heavy saucepan heat the oil over moderately high heat until it is hot but not smoking and in it stir-fry the beans, the zest, the gingerroot, and the garlic for 1 minute, or until the mixture is very fragrant. Stir the broth mixture and add it to the bean mixture. Bring the sauce to a boil, stirring, simmer it for 2 minutes, and keep it warm. *The sauce may be made 1 day in advance, kept covered and chilled, and reheated.*

In a large deep skillet of boiling salted water cook the asparagus for 3 to 5 minutes, or until the stalks are just tender but not limp, and drain it well. Arrange the bottom half of each pastry rectangle on a plate and divide the asparagus among the pastries. Spoon the sauce over the asparagus and around the pastries on each plate and top the asparagus with the top halves of the pastries. Serves 6 as a first course.

Black Bean Ancho Chili

1 pound (about 2½ cups) dried black beans,
  picked over and rinsed
2 medium onions, chopped
6 garlic cloves
3 tablespoons vegetable oil
1 tablespoon ground cumin
7½ cups water
3 ounces (about 6) dried *ancho* chilies*,
  stemmed, seeded, and torn into pieces
  (wear rubber gloves)
a 28-ounce can tomatoes including the juice,
  puréed coarse
1 cup chicken broth
1 red bell pepper, chopped
1 teaspoon dried orégano, crumbled
⅓ cup chopped fresh coriander,
  or to taste
2 tablespoons fresh lime juice,
  or to taste
avocado *salsa* (recipe follows) as an
  accompaniment if desired
sour cream as an accompaniment
  if desired

*available at Hispanic markets, some
  specialty foods shops, and some
  supermarkets or by mail order from Los
  Chileros de Nueva Mexico, Santa Fe, NM,
  Tel. (505) 471-6967 or Adriana's Bazaar,
  New York City, Tel. (212) 877-5757

In a large bowl let the beans soak in enough water to cover them by 2 inches for 1 hour and drain them. In a large heavy kettle cook the onions and 4 of the garlic cloves, minced, in the oil over moderate heat, stirring, until the onions are softened, add the cumin, and cook the mixture, stirring, for 30 seconds. Add the beans and 6 cups of the water and simmer the mixture, uncovered, adding more water if necessary to keep the beans barely covered, for 1 hour, or until the beans are tender.

While the beans are simmering, in a small saucepan bring the remaining 1½ cups water to a boil, add the chilies, and remove the pan from the heat. Let the mixture stand for 20 minutes and in a blender purée the chilies with the liquid. Add the chili purée to the bean mixture with the tomato purée, the broth, the bell pepper, the orégano, and salt to taste and simmer the mixture, uncovered, stirring occasionally, for 30 minutes.

Stir in the coriander, the lime juice, and the remaining 2 garlic cloves, minced, and simmer the chili for 5 minutes. *The chili may be frozen or made 4 days in advance, cooled, uncovered, and kept covered and chilled.* Serve the chili with the avocado *salsa* and the sour cream. Makes about 10 cups, serving 4 to 6.

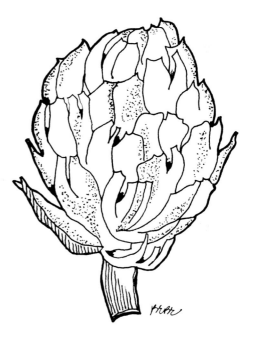

Avocado Salsa

1 avocado (preferably California)
1½ tablespoons fresh lime juice, or to taste
½ cup finely chopped red onion
1 fresh or pickled *jalapeño*, seeded and
  minced (wear rubber gloves)

Halve and peel the avocado and cut it into ¼-inch dice. In a bowl toss the avocado with the lime juice, the onion, the *jalapeño*, and salt and pepper to taste. Makes 1½ cups.

Brazilian-Style Black Bean Stew

2½ quarts water
2 pounds (about 4 cups) dried black beans,
    picked over, soaked overnight in water to
    cover them by 2 inches, and drained well
6 slices of lean bacon, chopped fine
1 pound lean boneless beef chuck, cut into
    2-inch pieces
1 pound cured *chorizo* (spicy pork sausage,
    available at Hispanic markets and some
    specialty foods shops), cut into
    1-inch-thick pieces
½ pound Canadian bacon, cut
    into 1-inch pieces
1½ cups finely chopped onion
1 tablespoon finely chopped garlic
¼ cup olive oil
a 28-ounce can tomatoes, drained well and
    chopped
2 tablespoons minced seeded fresh or
    pickled *jalapeño* peppers, or to taste
    (wear rubber gloves)
Tabasco to taste
½ pound fresh kale, coarse stems discarded
    and the leaves washed well and
    chopped fine
½ cup long-grain rice
½ cup finely chopped fresh coriander
⅓ cup fresh orange juice
warm flour tortillas as an accompaniment
    if desired

In a large heavy kettle bring the water to a boil and stir in the beans and the lean bacon. Bring the mixture to a boil, skimming the froth, and simmer it, covered, for 45 minutes. Stir in the beef and simmer the mixture, covered, stirring occasionally and skimming the fat, for 45 minutes. Stir in the *chorizo* and the Canadian bacon, simmer the mixture, covered, for 30 minutes, or until the beans are tender, and skim the fat from the surface.

In a large skillet cook the onion and the garlic in the oil over moderately low heat, stirring occasionally, until the onion is softened, stir in the tomatoes, the *jalapeño* peppers, the Tabasco, and salt and pepper to taste, and simmer the mixture, stirring occasionally, for 5 minutes. Transfer 2 cups of the beans with a slotted spoon from the kettle to the skillet and mash them with the back of a wooden spoon thoroughly into the onion mixture, adding 2 cups of the bean liquid gradually.

Simmer the mixture, stirring occasionally, for 15 minutes, or until it is thickened and transfer it to the kettle. Stir in the kale and the rice, simmer the mixture, stirring occasionally, for 20 minutes, or until the rice is tender, and stir in the coriander, the orange juice, and salt and pepper to taste. Serve the stew with the tortillas. Serves 8.

Curried Green Beans

½ pound green beans, trimmed and cut into
    1½-inch pieces
2 teaspoons unsalted butter, cut into bits
½ teaspoon curry powder
¼ cup water

In an 8-inch-square microwave-safe baking dish stir together the green beans, the butter, the curry powder, the water, and salt and pepper to taste. Microwave the mixture, covered partially, at high power (100%) for 6 minutes, or until the beans are just tender, and let it stand for 5 minutes. Serves 2.

Lemon Rosemary Green Beans

2 pounds green beans, trimmed and cut
    into 1-inch pieces
3 tablespoons unsalted butter
1 teaspoon freshly grated lemon zest
1 tablespoon minced fresh rosemary leaves, or
    1 teaspoon dried rosemary, crumbled

In a kettle of boiling salted water cook the beans for 5 minutes, or until they are crisp-tender, and drain them. While the beans are cooking, in a small saucepan melt the butter over low heat with the zest, the rosemary, and salt and pepper to taste and keep the mixture warm. Transfer the beans to a serving dish, add the butter mixture, and toss the mixture well. Serves 8.

PHOTO ON PAGES 74 AND 75

Minted Green Beans with Red Onion

2 pounds green beans, trimmed
1 teaspoon Dijon-style mustard
1 tablespoon white-wine vinegar
¼ cup olive oil
3 tablespoons minced fresh mint leaves
½ cup finely chopped red onion

In a kettle of boiling water cook the beans for 2 to 4 minutes, or until they are crisp-tender, transfer them with a slotted spoon to a bowl of ice and cold water to stop the cooking, and drain them well. Pat the beans dry with paper towels and chill them, covered, for at least 3 hours or overnight.

In a large bowl whisk together the mustard, the vinegar, and salt and pepper to taste, add the oil in a stream, whisking, and whisk the dressing until it is emulsified. Add the beans, the mint, and the onion and toss the mixture until it is combined well. Serves 6.

PHOTO ON PAGE 59

Sautéed Green Beans

2 pounds green beans, trimmed and cut
  on the diagonal into
  1½-inch pieces
2 tablespoons unsalted butter

In a kettle of boiling salted water cook the beans for 4 minutes, or until they are barely tender, drain them, and plunge them into a bowl of ice and cold water to stop the cooking. Drain the beans well and transfer them to a bowl. *The beans may be prepared up to this point 1 day in advance and kept covered and chilled.* In a large heavy skillet heat the butter over moderately high heat until the foam subsides, in it sauté the green beans, stirring, for 3 minutes, or until they are crisp-tender, and season them with salt and pepper. Serves 10.

PHOTO ON PAGE 14

Pinto Bean and Vegetable Chili

1 pound (about 2½ cups) dried pinto beans,
  picked over and rinsed
2 large onions, chopped
6 garlic cloves
3 tablespoons vegetable oil
⅓ cup chili powder
1 tablespoon ground cumin
½ teaspoon cayenne, or to taste
6 cups water
3 cups chicken broth
a 28-ounce can tomatoes, drained and chopped
1 red bell pepper, chopped fine
a 10-ounce package frozen corn
¾ cup bulgur
2 zucchini, scrubbed and cut into ¾-inch pieces
2 tablespoons Worcestershire sauce, or to taste
¾ cup Kalamata olives, pitted and chopped
⅓ cup chopped fresh coriander if desired

In a large bowl let the pinto beans soak in enough water to cover them by 2 inches overnight and drain them or quick-soak them (procedure follows) and drain them. In a large heavy kettle cook the onions and 4 of the garlic cloves, minced, in the oil over moderate heat, stirring, until the onions are softened, add the chili powder, the cumin, and the cayenne, and cook the mixture, stirring, for 30 seconds. Add the beans and the water and simmer the mixture, uncovered, adding more water if necessary to keep the beans barely covered, for 45 minutes to 1 hour, or until the beans are tender. Add the broth, the tomatoes, the bell pepper, and the corn and simmer the mixture, stirring occasionally, for 20 minutes. Add the bulgur and the zucchini and simmer the mixture, stirring occasionally, for 20 minutes, or until the zucchini is just tender. Stir in the remaining 2 garlic cloves, minced, the Worcestershire sauce, the olives, and salt and pepper to taste, simmer the chili for 5 minutes, and stir in the coriander. *The chili may be frozen or made 4 days in advance, cooled, uncovered, and kept covered and chilled.* Makes about 12 cups, serving 6 to 8.

To Quick-Soak Dried Beans

In a large saucepan combine dried beans, picked over and rinsed, with triple their volume of cold water. Bring the water to a boil and cook the beans, uncovered, over moderate heat for 2 minutes. Remove the pan from the heat and let the beans soak for 1 hour.

Cassoulet
(White Bean Casserole with Pork, Lamb, and Duck)

For the bean mixture
2 quarts chicken broth
2 quarts water
2 pounds (about 4 cups) dried white beans,
    picked over, soaked in water to cover by
    2 inches overnight, and drained
a ½-pound piece salt pork, simmered in water
    to cover for 15 minutes and drained
1 pound smoked pork sausage such as
    kielbasa, cut into 1-inch pieces
3 onions, halved lengthwise
3 garlic cloves, crushed lightly and left whole
1 teaspoon dried thyme, crumbled
a *bouquet garni* of 4 parsley sprigs, 3 celery
    tops, the white and pale green part of 1 leek,
    and 2 bay leaves, tied in a cheesecloth bag

5 slices of lean bacon, chopped fine
1 pound boneless pork loin, cut into
    1-inch pieces
1 pound boneless lamb shoulder, cut into
    1-inch pieces
1 cup finely chopped onion
½ cup finely chopped celery
1 tablespoon finely chopped garlic
1 cup dry white wine
a 28-ounce can plum tomatoes, drained,
    reserving ½ cup of the juice, and chopped
a 4-pound duck, cut into 8 pieces
about 3 cups fine dry bread crumbs

Make the bean mixture: In a large heavy kettle combine the broth and the water and bring the liquid to a boil. Stir in the beans, the salt pork, and the sausage and bring the liquid to a boil, skimming the froth. Stir in the onions, the garlic, the thyme, the *bouquet garni*, and pepper to taste and simmer the mixture, uncovered, for 1½ to 1¾ hours, or until the beans are tender. Discard the salt pork, the onions, and the *bouquet garni*, strain the mixture through a colander set over a large bowl, and in separate bowls reserve the bean mixture and the broth. *The bean mixture and the broth may be made 1 day in advance and kept covered and chilled.*

In a large skillet cook the bacon over moderate heat, stirring, until it is crisp and transfer it with tongs to paper towels to drain. In the fat remaining in the skillet brown the pork and the lamb over moderately high heat,

turning the pieces once, for 8 minutes and transfer the meat with a slotted spoon to a large casserole. In the fat remaining in the skillet cook the onion, the celery, and the garlic with salt and pepper to taste over moderately low heat, stirring occasionally, until the vegetables are softened. Stir in the wine and boil the mixture until the liquid is reduced by half. Stir in the tomatoes with the reserved juice and the bacon and simmer the mixture, stirring occasionally, for 5 minutes. Transfer the mixture to the casserole and braise it, covered, in a preheated 325° F. oven for 1 hour.

Arrange the duck pieces, skin sides down, on a rack in a roasting pan and broil them under a preheated broiler about 4 inches from the heat for 10 minutes. Turn the duck pieces and broil them for 10 minutes more, or until the juices run clear and the meat is cooked through. Transfer the duck with tongs to a cutting board and reserve ¼ cup of the duck fat.

In a 6-quart casserole layer one third of the reserved bean mixture, half the braised meat mixture, 4 pieces of duck, half the remaining bean mixture, the remaining braised meat mixture, the remaining duck pieces, and the remaining bean mixture. Pour 6 cups of the reserved broth, skimmed of any fat, slowly over the mixture, sprinkle the top with 2 cups of the bread crumbs, and drizzle it with 2 tablespoons of the reserved duck fat. Bake the cassoulet, uncovered, in the middle of a preheated 325° F. oven for 30 minutes. Press the bread crumb layer lightly into the cassoulet, top it with the remaining 1 cup bread crumbs, and drizzle the top with the remaining 2 tablespoons duck fat. Bake the cassoulet for 1¾ hours more, or until the crust is golden brown. Serves 8.

PHOTO ON PAGE 16

White Bean and Watercress Gratin

1 pound dried white beans such as Great
    Northern or navy, picked over
4 cups chopped onion
2½ quarts water
3 tablespoons olive oil
2 teaspoons white-wine vinegar
1 teaspoon salt
1½ cups packed tender watercress sprigs plus
    additional sprigs for garnish if desired
1 cup fine day-old bread crumbs
1 cup grated Gruyère
1 garlic clove, minced

In a kettle combine the beans with enough cold water to cover them by 2 inches, bring the water to a boil, and simmer the beans, uncovered, for 2 minutes. Remove the kettle from the heat and let the beans soak, covered, for 1 hour. Drain the beans in a colander, return them to the kettle, and stir in the onion and the 2½ quarts water. Simmer the beans for 35 to 45 minutes, or until they are tender, drain them in the colander set over a large bowl, and transfer them to a 3-quart gratin dish. Return the cooking liquid to the kettle and boil it for 5 to 10 minutes, or until it is reduced to about 1½ cups. In a blender purée 1 cup of the beans with the reduced cooking liquid, the oil, the vinegar, and the salt and stir the purée with 1½ cups of the watercress into the whole beans. *The gratin may be prepared up to this point 2 days in advance and kept covered and chilled.*

In a bowl toss together the bread crumbs, the Gruyère, and the garlic, sprinkle the topping over the gratin, and bake the gratin in the middle of a preheated 425° F. oven for 20 minutes, or until it is bubbly and golden. Divide the gratin among 6 to 8 plates and garnish each serving with some of the additional watercress. Serves 6 to 8.

PHOTO ON PAGE 71

Beet Flowers and Beet Greens Vinaigrette
12 small beets with the greens
    (about 4 pounds)
½ teaspoon Dijon-style mustard
1½ tablespoons red-wine vinegar
¼ cup olive oil
1 scallion, sliced thin diagonally

Cut the beet greens from the beets, leaving about 1 inch of the stems attached to the beets, and reserve 16 of the beet leaves. Scrub the beets, wrap them in small groupings tightly in foil, and in a baking pan roast them in a preheated 350° F. oven for 1 to 1½ hours, or until they are tender. Unwrap the beets carefully, discarding any liquid that may have accumulated in the foil, and let them cool until they can be handled. *The beets may be roasted 1 day in advance and kept covered and chilled.*

Rinse the reserved beet leaves, in a steamer set over simmering water steam them, covered, for 1 minute, and transfer them with tongs to paper towels to drain. In a small bowl whisk together the mustard, the vinegar, and salt to taste, add the oil in a stream, whisking, and whisk the dressing until it is emulsified.

Peel the beets and trim the stem ends flat. Standing each beet on its stem end, cut parallel slices into but not through the beet at ¼-inch intervals, stopping about ½ inch above the root end. Rotate each beet 90 degrees and cut parallel slices in the same manner to form a crosshatch pattern, keeping the stem end intact. Arrange 4 of the beet leaves on each of 4 plates and arrange the beets on the leaves. Drizzle the beets with the dressing and sprinkle them with the scallions. Serves 4.

PHOTO ON PAGE 29

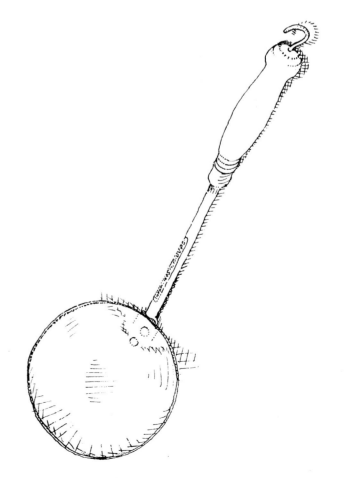

Roasted Beets with Horseradish Cream

about 3½ pounds beets including
    the greens
⅔ cup *crème fraîche* or sour cream
2 to 3 tablespoons finely grated peeled fresh
    horseradish or drained bottled horseradish
½ teaspoon freshly grated lemon zest
2 tablespoons unsalted butter
1 tablespoon minced fresh chives

Cut the greens from the beets, leaving about 1 inch of the stems attached, and reserve the greens. Scrub the beets, wrap them tightly in 2 foil packages, and roast them on a baking sheet in the middle of a preheated 350° F. oven for 1 to 1½ hours, or until they are tender. Unwrap the beets carefully, discarding any liquid that may have accumulated in the foil, and let them cool until they can be handled. Peel and halve the beets and cut them into ¼-inch slices.

In a small bowl stir together the *crème fraîche*, the horseradish to taste, the zest, and salt and pepper to taste. Wash well and drain the reserved greens, in a large skillet cook them with salt and pepper to taste in 1 tablespoon of the butter over moderately high heat, stirring, for 3 to 4 minutes, or until they are wilted, and transfer them to a platter. In the skillet cook the beets with salt and pepper to taste in the remaining 1 tablespoon butter over moderately high heat, stirring, for 2 to 3 minutes, or until they are hot, and spoon them over the greens. Top the beets with the horseradish cream and sprinkle the cream with the chives and salt and pepper to taste. Serves 6.

Lemon-Buttered Broccoli Spears

2 pounds broccoli, trimmed and cut into
    spears, the stems reserved for another use
3 tablespoons unsalted butter
fresh lemon juice to taste
freshly grated lemon zest for sprinkling
    the broccoli

In a steamer set over boiling water steam the broccoli, covered, for 4 minutes, or until it is crisp-tender. In a skillet heat the butter over moderate heat until the foam subsides, in it toss the broccoli until it is coated well, and sprinkle the broccoli with the lemon juice, salt and pepper to taste, and the zest. Serves 6.

PHOTO ON PAGE 26

Broccoli with Lemon and Red Pepper Flakes

2 bunches of broccoli (about 1½ pounds each)
the zest of 1 lemon removed with a vegetable
    peeler and minced
dried hot red pepper flakes to taste
¼ cup extra-virgin olive oil

Trim the broccoli, peel the stems, and slice them thin. Cut the flowerets into 2-inch pieces and reserve them. In a large steamer set over boiling water steam the broccoli stems, covered, for 5 minutes, or until they are crisp-tender, and transfer them to a bowl. In the steamer steam the reserved flowerets, covered, for 3 to 5 minutes, or until they are crisp-tender, and transfer them to another bowl. Sprinkle the stems and the flowerets with the zest, the red pepper flakes, and salt to taste, drizzle the oil over them, and toss the mixtures well. Arrange the stems and the flowerets on a platter. Serves 8.

PHOTO ON PAGE 80

Brussels Sprouts with Shallots

2 shallots, sliced thin
1 tablespoon olive oil
¾ pound (about 14) Brussels sprouts,
    trimmed, cored, and shredded
½ cup water
2 teaspoons balsamic vinegar, or to taste

In a skillet sauté the shallots in the oil over moderately high heat for 1 to 2 minutes, or until they are softened, and stir in the Brussels sprouts and the water. Cook the mixture, stirring occasionally, for 6 to 8 minutes, or until the sprouts are tender, and stir in the vinegar and salt and pepper to taste. Serves 2.

Cabbage with Caraway Seeds

3 cups thinly sliced cabbage
½ teaspoon caraway seeds, toasted lightly
1 tablespoon extra-virgin olive oil
1 scallion, chopped fine
coarse salt to taste
fresh lemon juice to taste

In a saucepan of boiling salted water cook the cabbage for 3 minutes, or until it is just tender, drain it, and in a bowl toss it with the caraway seeds, the oil, the scallion, the salt, the juice, and pepper to taste. Serves 2.

Honey-Glazed Baby Carrots

1¼ pounds baby carrots, trimmed and peeled
1 tablespoon unsalted butter
1½ tablespoons honey
1 tablespoon fresh lemon juice

In a steamer set over boiling water steam the carrots for 4 to 8 minutes, or until they are just tender, and transfer them to a bowl. In a skillet melt the butter with the honey and the lemon juice, stirring until the mixture is smooth, and add the carrots. Cook the mixture over moderately low heat, stirring, for 1 to 2 minutes, or until the carrots are glazed evenly and heated through, and season it with salt and pepper. Serves 6.

PHOTO ON PAGE 32

Carrots with Peanuts and Coriander

¾ pound carrots (about 7), cut crosswise on
    the diagonal into ½-inch slices
1 tablespoon unsalted butter
2 teaspoons fresh lemon juice
1 teaspoon honey, or to taste
2 tablespoons finely chopped dry-roasted
    peanuts
1 tablespoon chopped fresh coriander,
    or to taste

In a steamer set over boiling water steam the carrots, covered, for 8 minutes, or until they are just tender. In a skillet melt the butter over moderate heat and stir in the lemon juice, the honey, the peanuts, and salt and pepper to taste. Add the carrots and cook the mixture, stirring, for 1 minute, or until the carrots are coated well. Sprinkle the carrot mixture with the coriander. Serves 2.

Diced Carrots and Turnips

2 pounds carrots, cut into
    ½-inch dice
1½ pounds turnips, peeled and
    cut into ½-inch dice
3 tablespoons unsalted butter
freshly grated nutmeg
    to taste

In a kettle of boiling salted water cook the carrots for 3 minutes, add the turnips, and boil the vegetables for 3 to 5 minutes, or until they are tender. Drain the vegetables and transfer them to a serving dish. Add the butter, cut into bits, the nutmeg, and salt and pepper to taste and toss the mixture until the butter is melted. Serves 8.

PHOTO ON PAGE 74

Cauliflower Parmesan Gratin

1 tablespoon unsalted butter
¼ teaspoon ground cumin
1 tablespoon all-purpose flour
¾ cup milk
5 tablespoons freshly grated Parmesan
½ cauliflower, cut into 1½-inch flowerets
    (about 2½ cups)

In a small heavy saucepan melt the butter over moderately low heat, add the cumin and the flour, and cook the *roux*, stirring, for 3 minutes. Add the milk in a slow stream, whisking, bring the mixture to a boil, whisking, and simmer the sauce for 1 minute. Stir in 4 tablespoons of the Parmesan and salt and pepper to taste and cook the sauce over low heat, stirring, until the cheese is just melted. Remove the pan from the heat and keep the sauce warm.

In a steamer set over boiling water steam the cauliflower, covered, for 5 minutes, or until it is just tender, and transfer it to a buttered 3-cup baking dish. Drizzle the cauliflower with the sauce, sprinkle it with the remaining 1 tablespoon Parmesan, and bake the gratin in the upper third of a preheated 400° F. oven for 15 minutes, or until it is golden and bubbly. Serves 2.

Fried Chick-Pea Sandwiches with Coriander Yogurt

a 19-ounce can chick-peas, rinsed well and
    patted dry
1 large garlic clove, chopped
½ teaspoon ground cumin
1 teaspoon salt
¼ cup thinly sliced scallion
4 tablespoons chopped fresh coriander
2 teaspoons sesame seeds
all-purpose flour for dredging the patties
2 tablespoons vegetable oil
2 *pita* loaves, warmed, halved crosswise, and
    opened into pockets
4 slices of tomato
¼ cup plain yogurt

In a food processor purée the chick-peas with the garlic, the cumin, the salt, and pepper to taste until the mixture is smooth. Transfer the mixture to a bowl, stir in the
scallion, 3 tablespoons of the coriander, and the sesame
seeds, and form the mixture into four ½-inch-thick patties. Dredge the patties in the flour and freeze them on a
wax paper–lined plate for 10 minutes. In a heavy skillet
heat the oil over moderately high heat until it is hot but
not smoking and in it sauté the patties, turning them
carefully with a spatula, for 3 minutes on each side, or
until they are golden brown. (The patties will be very
soft.) Transfer each patty to a *pita* pocket and insert a
tomato slice in each pocket. In a small bowl stir together
the yogurt, the remaining 1 tablespoon coriander, and
salt and pepper to taste and divide the sauce among the
sandwiches. Makes 4 sandwiches, serving 2 as a main
course.

Corn and Potato Cakes

two ½-pound russet (baking) potatoes
½ cup finely chopped green bell pepper
1½ cups fresh corn kernels including the
    pulp scraped from the cobs (cut from
    about 2 ears of corn)
4 scallions, chopped fine
1 teaspoon ground cumin
3 tablespoons all-purpose flour
2 tablespoons unsalted butter
4 tablespoons sour cream

Peel the potatoes, grate them coarse, and squeeze
them with the bell pepper between several thicknesses
of paper towels to remove any excess moisture. In a
bowl toss together the potato and pepper mixture, the
corn, the scallions, the cumin, the flour, and salt and
pepper to taste.

In a non-stick skillet measuring 6 inches across the
bottom heat ½ tablespoon of the butter over moderate
heat until the foam subsides, add ¾ cup of the corn mixture, tamping it down with a spatula, and cook the corn
and potato cake for 6 minutes, or until the underside is
golden and crisp. Invert the cake onto a plate and slide it
back into the skillet, cooked side up. Cook the cake for
6 minutes more, or until the underside is golden and
crisp, slide it onto a plate, and keep it warm, covered.
Make 3 more corn and potato cakes in the same manner
with the remaining butter and corn mixture. Spread 2 of
the cakes with the sour cream, arrange the remaining
cakes on the sour cream, and cut the corn and potato
cakes into wedges. Serves 4 to 6 as a side dish.

Cajun-Style Corn and Tomato with Fried Okra

1 onion, sliced thin
2 tablespoons unsalted butter
1 tablespoon vegetable oil plus
   additional for frying
   the okra
3 cups fresh corn kernels including
   the pulp scraped from the
   cobs (cut from about
   4 ears of corn)
1 tomato, seeded and
   chopped
½ cup heavy cream
¼ cup water
¼ pound okra, rinsed well and
   patted dry
cornmeal seasoned with salt and pepper for
   coating the okra

In a heavy saucepan cook the onion in the butter and 1 tablespoon of the oil over moderate heat, stirring occasionally, until it is golden, add the corn, the tomato, the cream, and the water, and cook the mixture, covered, over moderately low heat, stirring occasionally, for 20 minutes. Season the corn mixture with salt and pepper and keep the mixture warm, covered.

Cut the okra into ¼-inch-thick slices, in a bowl toss it with the seasoned cornmeal, and shake it in a coarse sieve to knock off the excess cornmeal. In a deep skillet heat ½ inch of the additional oil over moderately high heat until it is hot but not smoking and in it fry the okra in batches for 1 to 2 minutes, or until it is golden, transferring it with a slotted spoon as it is fried to paper towels to drain. Serve the corn mixture topped with the fried okra. Serves 6.

Vegetable- and Ricotta-Stuffed Collard Rolls with Tomato Sauce

For the sauce
1 cup chopped onion
2 tablespoons unsalted butter
3 tablespoons dry red wine
a 28-ounce can plum tomatoes, drained and
   chopped
⅛ teaspoon sugar
¼ teaspoon dried rosemary,
   crumbled

½ teaspoon dried orégano,
   crumbled
⅛ teaspoon dried hot red pepper flakes,
   or to taste
For the rolls
20 to 24 large collard leaves,
   washed well
a 15-ounce container of whole-milk ricotta
½ pound whole-milk mozzarella, cut into
   ¼-inch dice
1 large egg, beaten lightly
2 small red bell peppers,
   chopped
a 10-ounce package frozen corn kernels,
   thawed and patted dry
½ cup thinly sliced scallion

¼ cup minced fresh parsley leaves

Make the sauce: In a saucepan cook the onion in the butter over moderately low heat, stirring occasionally, until it is softened, add the wine, and simmer the mixture for 2 minutes. Add the tomatoes, the sugar, the rosemary, the orégano, the red pepper flakes, and salt to taste, simmer the sauce, stirring occasionally, until it is very thick and the liquid is almost evaporated, and spread it in the bottom of a large shallow casserole or baking dish.

Make the rolls: In a kettle of boiling water boil the collards for 10 minutes, or until they are crisp-tender, drain them, and refresh them in a large bowl of cold water. In another large bowl combine well the ricotta, the mozzarella, the egg, the bell peppers, the corn, the scallion, and salt and pepper to taste. Cut out the tough center rib and stem one third of the way up one of the collard leaves and pat the leaf dry. Mound 2 heaping tablespoons of the cheese mixture at the top end of the leaf and roll up the leaf, tucking in the ends to form a roll. Make rolls with the remaining collard leaves and cheese mixture in the same manner.

Arrange the collard rolls in one layer on the sauce in the casserole and bake the rolls, covered, in the middle of a preheated 375° F. oven for 45 to 50 minutes, or until the sauce is bubbling and the rolls are cooked through. Transfer the collard rolls carefully with tongs to a platter and keep them warm, covered. Transfer the tomato sauce to a saucepan and boil it until it is thickened. Stir in the parsley and pour the sauce over the rolls. Serves 4 to 6.

Greek-Style Stuffed Eggplant

three ½-pound eggplants
1 teaspoon salt
4 tablespoons olive oil
2 cups chopped onion
2 garlic cloves,
  minced
⅓ cup minced fresh parsley leaves
3 tablespoons minced fresh mint leaves
3 plum tomatoes, halved lengthwise,
  seeded, and cut into
  julienne strips
1 cup crumbled Feta cheese

Halve 2 of the eggplants lengthwise, score their pulp deeply with a sharp knife, being careful not to pierce the skins, and with a grapefruit knife scoop out the pulp, reserving it and leaving ½-inch-thick shells. Sprinkle the shells with salt and invert them on paper towels to drain for 30 minutes. Cut the reserved pulp and the remaining whole eggplant into ½-inch pieces, in a colander toss the pieces with the salt, and let them drain for 30 minutes.

Pat the shells dry with paper towels, brush them with 1 tablespoon of the oil, and broil them on the rack of a broiler pan under a preheated broiler about 4 inches from the heat for 5 minutes, or until they are tender. In a skillet heat the remaining 3 tablespoons oil over moderately high heat until it is hot but not smoking and in it sauté the eggplant pieces, patted dry, stirring, until they are golden. Stir in the onion and the garlic and cook the mixture over moderate heat, stirring, until the onion is softened. Remove the skillet from the heat, stir in the parsley, the mint, the tomatoes, the Feta, and salt and pepper to taste, and divide the filling among the shells, mounding it. Broil the stuffed eggplants in a large flameproof baking dish for 5 minutes, or until the filling is bubbling and golden. Serves 4.

Sautéed Eggplant with Tomato and Onion Topping

1 eggplant (about 1 pound),
  trimmed
1 onion, chopped fine
3 tablespoons olive oil
2 garlic cloves,
  minced
2 tomatoes (about ½ pound),
  chopped fine
½ teaspoon dried orégano, crumbled
½ cup dry red wine
2 tablespoons freshly grated Parmesan
2 tablespoons minced fresh parsley leaves

Cut the eggplant lengthwise into ½-inch-thick slices, sprinkle both sides of 4 center slices with salt to taste, reserving the remaining eggplant for another use, and let the slices drain in a colander for 30 minutes. While the eggplant is draining, in a heavy skillet cook the onion in 1 tablespoon of the oil over moderate heat, stirring, until it is golden, stir in the garlic, the tomatoes, the orégano, and the wine, and simmer the mixture, stirring occasionally, for 10 minutes, or until the liquid is almost evaporated. Stir in the Parmesan, the parsley, and salt and pepper to taste, transfer the topping to a bowl, and keep it warm, covered.

In the skillet, cleaned, heat 1 tablespoon of the remaining oil over moderately high heat until it is hot but not smoking and in it brown 2 slices of the eggplant, patted dry. Reduce the heat to moderately low, cook the eggplant, turning it, for 5 minutes more, or until it is tender, and transfer it to a plate. Cook the remaining eggplant in the remaining 1 tablespoon oil in the same manner and transfer it to another plate. Spoon the tomato and onion topping onto the eggplant. Serves 2.

Hearts of Fennel with Lemon and Coriander

2 small fennel bulbs (sometimes called anise,
  available in most supermarkets), trimmed,
  reserving 6 of the leaves for garnish
  if desired
1 tablespoon olive oil
1 tablespoon unsalted butter
1 tablespoon fresh lemon juice
2 tablespoons minced fresh coriander

In a kettle of boiling salted water cook the fennel for 15 minutes, or until it is barely tender. Transfer the fennel to a cutting board, let it cool, and cut it lengthwise into ⅓-inch-thick slices. In a large skillet heat the oil and the butter over moderately high heat until the butter is foaming and in the fat sauté the fennel slices for 3 minutes on each side, or until they are golden. Sprinkle the fennel with the lemon juice, the coriander, and salt and pepper to taste, divide it between 2 plates, and garnish it with the reserved fennel leaves. Serves 2.

PHOTO ON PAGE 21

Steamed Fiddleheads
with Horseradish Scallion Sauce

1 pound fiddleheads (available in the spring at
  specialty produce markets and some
  supermarkets), cleaned (procedure follows)
½ cup plain yogurt
½ cup mayonnaise
1 tablespoon fresh lemon juice, or to taste
2 teaspoons Dijon-style mustard
1 tablespoon drained bottled horseradish,
  or to taste
3 tablespoons finely chopped scallion green

In a steamer set over boiling water steam the fiddleheads for 5 minutes, or until they are crisp-tender, transfer them with a slotted spoon to a bowl of ice and cold
water to stop the cooking, and transfer them to paper
towels to drain. In a small bowl whisk together the
yogurt, the mayonnaise, the lemon juice, the mustard,
the horseradish, the scallion, and salt and pepper to
taste, whisking until the sauce is smooth, and serve the
fiddleheads topped with the sauce. Serves 4 to 6.

To Clean Fresh-Picked Fiddleheads

Snap off the crisp, bright green fiddlehead tops from
ostrich ferns, leaving about 2 inches of stem attached.
Rub off the dry brown casings by hand or put the fiddleheads in a wire salad basket and whirl the basket outdoors to remove the casings. Let the fiddleheads soak in
a sink half full of cold water, changing the water several
times to remove any grit or casing particles, and drain
them. The fiddleheads keep, covered and chilled, for up
to 1 week.

Beer-Batter-Fried Kale

1 cup plus 2 tablespoons beer
  (not dark)
1 cup all-purpose flour
½ teaspoon table salt
½ teaspoon freshly ground pepper
vegetable oil for deep-frying the kale leaves
12 small kale leaves, washed well
  and spun dry
coarse salt for sprinkling the leaves
lemon wedges as an accompaniment

In a blender blend the beer, the flour, the table salt,
and the pepper for 20 seconds, or until the batter is
smooth, transfer the batter to a bowl, and let it stand,
covered, for 1 hour.

In a large deep skillet heat 1 inch of the oil until it registers 360° F. on a deep-fat thermometer. Dip each leaf
into the batter, coating it thoroughly and knocking off
the excess batter on the side of the bowl, and fry it in the
oil for 30 seconds on each side, or until it is golden.
Transfer the kale as it is fried to paper towels to drain
and sprinkle it lightly with the coarse salt. Serve the kale
with the lemon wedges. Serves 6.

Discard the bay leaf, season the stew with salt, and serve the stew on the couscous or rice. Makes about 14 cups, serving 8 to 10.

German-Style Stuffed Kohlrabi

8 kohlrabies, bulbs peeled, stems discarded,
  and the leaves trimmed of tough center ribs
½ cup finely chopped onion
1 garlic clove, chopped fine
½ stick (¼ cup) unsalted butter
1 pound ground pork
¼ cup cooked long-grain rice
2 tablespoons finely chopped fresh parsley
  leaves plus additional for garnish if desired
2 tablespoons sweet paprika
¼ teaspoon dried marjoram, crumbled
¼ teaspoon caraway seeds
1½ tablespoons tomato paste
2 large eggs, beaten lightly
3½ cups chicken broth
2 tablespoons all-purpose flour
½ cup heavy cream

Trim ¼ inch from the root end of each kohlrabi bulb so the bulb will stand upright, scoop out the pulp from the opposite end with a small melon-ball cutter or spoon, leaving ¼-inch-thick shells, and chop it fine (there will be about 2¾ cups). In a large kettle of boiling salted water cook the kohlrabi leaves for 3 minutes, or until they are just tender, drain them well, and chop them fine (there will be about 2 cups).

In a large skillet cook the onion and the garlic in 2 tablespoons of the butter over moderate heat, stirring, until the onion is golden and transfer the mixture to a large bowl. To the bowl add the pork, the rice, 2 tablespoons of the parsley, the paprika, the marjoram, the caraway seeds, the tomato paste, the eggs, ½ cup of the kohlrabi pulp, ¼ cup of the chopped kohlrabi leaves, and salt and pepper to taste and combine the mixture well. Divide the mixture among the kohlrabi shells, mounding it, and arrange the shells in a shallow flameproof baking dish just large enough to hold them in one layer. Scatter the remaining pulp and leaves in the dish and pour in the broth. Bring the broth to a boil and simmer the shells, covered partially, for 30 to 50 minutes, or until they can be pierced easily with a sharp knife. Transfer the shells with a slotted spoon to a plate, reserving the cooking mixture in the baking dish, and keep them warm.

Spicy Kale and Chick-Pea Stew

1½ cups dried chick-peas, soaked overnight in
  enough water to cover them by 4 inches,
  drained, and rinsed
10 cups water
2 large onions, chopped coarse
3 large garlic cloves, minced
¼ cup olive oil
2 green bell peppers, chopped coarse
1½ pounds kale, coarse stems discarded and
  the leaves washed well and chopped
two 28-ounce cans plum tomatoes including
  the juice, chopped
a 6-ounce can tomato paste
2½ tablespoons chili powder
1 teaspoon dried thyme, crumbled
1 teaspoon dried orégano, crumbled
1 teaspoon dried hot red pepper flakes
1 teaspoon ground cumin
1 teaspoon sugar
1 bay leaf
steamed couscous or rice as an
  accompaniment

In a large saucepan simmer the chick-peas in the water, covered partially, for 1½ hours, or until they are tender. In a heavy kettle cook the onions and the garlic in the oil over moderate heat, stirring occasionally, until the vegetables are golden, add the bell peppers, and cook the mixture, stirring, for 10 minutes. Add the chick-peas with the cooking liquid, the kale, the tomatoes with the juice, the tomato paste, the chili powder, the thyme, the orégano, the red pepper flakes, the cumin, the sugar, and the bay leaf, bring the liquid to a boil, and simmer the stew, stirring occasionally, for 1 hour.

In a small saucepan cook the flour in the remaining 2 tablespoons butter over moderate heat, whisking, for 3 minutes and whisk in the cream. Bring the mixture to a boil, whisking, simmer it for 1 minute, and stir it into the reserved cooking mixture, a little at a time. Add salt and pepper to taste and cook the sauce over moderate heat, stirring occasionally, for 5 to 10 minutes, or until it is thickened. Return the stuffed shells to the baking dish and garnish them with the additional parsley. Serves 4 to 8.

Creamed Leeks with Tarragon, Tomato, and Bacon

2 slices of lean bacon, chopped fine
1 leek (about 1 pound), halved lengthwise,
    sliced thin crosswise, and washed well
½ cup finely chopped seeded tomato
¾ teaspoon finely chopped fresh tarragon
    leaves or ¼ teaspoon dried, crumbled
⅓ cup half-and-half
⅓ cup chicken broth

In a skillet cook the bacon until it is crisp and transfer it to paper towels to drain. In the fat remaining in the skillet cook the leek, covered, over moderately low heat, stirring occasionally, for 10 minutes, or until it is softened, and stir in the tomato, the tarragon, the half-and-half, the broth, and salt and pepper to taste. Bring the liquid to a boil, cook the mixture over moderate heat, stirring occasionally, for 5 minutes, or until it is thickened, and stir in the bacon. Serves 2.

Creamed Onions and Carrots with Cumin

1 cup ½-inch pieces of carrot
1 onion, cut into 1-inch pieces
½ cup water
½ teaspoon sugar
½ tablespoon unsalted butter
1 tablespoon heavy cream
⅛ teaspoon ground cumin,
    or to taste

In a small saucepan combine the carrot, the onion, the water, the sugar, and the butter and boil the mixture, stirring occasionally, for 25 minutes, or until the water is evaporated and the vegetables begin to brown. Remove the pan from the heat and stir in the cream, the cumin, and salt and pepper to taste. Serves 2.

Parsnips in Maple Mustard Sauce

2 tablespoons pure maple syrup
1 teaspoon Dijon-style mustard
2 tablespoons unsalted butter,
    cut into bits
2 large parsnips (about ½ pound), peeled and
    cut into 3- by ¼-inch sticks

In a microwave-safe shallow baking dish combine the syrup, the mustard, the butter, and salt and pepper to taste, add the parsnips, and toss them to coat them well. Microwave the parsnips, covered partially, at high power (100%) for 10 minutes, or until they are tender. Serves 2.

Peas with Sautéed Bread Crumbs

¼ cup finely chopped onion
¼ cup water
1 cup frozen peas
1 tablespoon unsalted butter
⅓ cup fresh fine bread crumbs

In a small saucepan simmer the onion in the water, covered, for 4 minutes, stir in the peas, and simmer the mixture, covered, for 4 minutes, or until the peas are just tender. In a small heavy skillet heat the butter over moderately high heat until the foam subsides, add the bread crumbs, and sauté them, stirring, for 3 minutes, or until they are golden. Drain the pea mixture, add it to the bread crumbs with salt and pepper to taste, and sauté the mixture, stirring, for 1 minute. Serves 2.

Pea and Watercress Purée

two 10-ounce packages frozen peas
2 bunches of watercress, coarse stems
    discarded and the watercress rinsed and
    spun dry (about 4 cups)
¼ cup water
2 tablespoons unsalted butter

In a large saucepan combine the peas, the watercress, and the water and boil the mixture, covered, for 5 minutes, or until the peas and watercress are tender. Transfer the mixture to a food processor, add the butter and salt and pepper to taste, and purée the mixture. Makes about 3 cups, serving 6.

PHOTO ON PAGE 41

Onion- and Olive-Stuffed Bell Peppers

8 assorted bell peppers
4 tablespoons olive oil
3 tablespoons balsamic vinegar
3 large onions, halved lengthwise and sliced
  thin lengthwise
3 garlic cloves, sliced thin
12 Kalamata or other brine-cured black
  olives, pitted and sliced thin

Halve 3 of the bell peppers lengthwise, leaving the stem ends intact, and core and seed them. Arrange the halves on a steamer rack set over simmering water, steam them, covered, for 3 to 5 minutes, or until they are tender, and invert them on paper towels to drain. In a small bowl whisk together 1 tablespoon of the oil and 1 teaspoon of the vinegar and brush the insides of the halves with the mixture. In a large heavy skillet cook the onions in the remaining 3 tablespoons oil over moderate heat, stirring, until they are softened, stir in the garlic and the remaining 5 bell peppers, cut into julienne strips, and cook the mixture until the peppers are just tender. Remove the skillet from the heat, stir in the olives, the remaining vinegar, and salt and pepper to taste, and divide the filling among the bell pepper halves. Serve the stuffed bell peppers at room temperature. Serves 6.

Spanish-Style Stuffed Bell Peppers

four ½-pound whole green or red bell peppers
  plus ¼ cup minced red bell pepper
3 tablespoons olive oil
1 onion, chopped
1 tomato, peeled, seeded, and chopped
1 garlic clove, minced
¾ cup long-grain rice
2¼ cups chicken broth
2 tablespoons slivered almonds, toasted
  lightly
½ cup fresh or thawed frozen peas
½ pound zucchini, scrubbed and cut into
  ¼-inch cubes
½ teaspoon ground cumin
lemon wedges for garnish

Halve 3 of the whole bell peppers lengthwise, leaving the stem ends intact, core and seed them, and in a large saucepan of boiling salted water blanch them for 3 min-utes, or until they are just tender. Remove the peppers and invert them on paper towels to drain (they will soft-en while they stand).

In a heavy 11- to 12-inch skillet heat the oil over mod-erately high heat until it is hot but not smoking and in it sauté the onion, the remaining whole bell pepper, chopped, the tomato, and the garlic over moderate heat, stirring, for 15 minutes. Stir in the rice and cook the mixture, stirring, for 1 minute. Stir in the broth, heated, and salt and pepper to taste, bring the liquid to a boil, and simmer the mixture, uncovered, for 20 minutes, or until the rice is barely tender. Stir in the almonds, the peas, the minced bell pepper, the zucchini, and the cumin and divide the mixture among the bell pepper shells, mounding it. Bake the stuffed bell peppers in an oiled baking dish, covered, in a preheated 325° F. oven for 15 minutes, or until the rice is tender, and serve them with the lemon wedges. Serves 6.

Potatoes Parisienne

2 russet (baking) potatoes, peeled
3 tablespoons clarified butter (procedure follows)

Scoop out balls from the potatoes with a small melon-ball cutter and dry them well. In a heavy skillet heat the butter over moderately high heat until it is hot but not smoking and in it sauté the potatoes, shaking the skillet, until they are golden brown. Sprinkle the potatoes with salt and pepper to taste, reduce the heat to moderately low, and cook the potatoes, covered, shaking the skillet occasionally, for 12 to 15 minutes, or until they are tender. Serves 2.

PHOTO ON PAGE 21

To Clarify Butter

unsalted butter, cut into 1-inch pieces

In a heavy saucepan melt the butter over low heat. Remove the pan from the heat, let the butter stand for 3 minutes, and skim the froth. Strain the butter through a sieve lined with a double thickness of rinsed and squeezed cheesecloth into a bowl, leaving the milky solids in the bottom of the pan. Pour the clarified butter into a jar or crock and store it, covered, in the refrigera-tor. The butter keeps, covered and chilled, indefinitely. When clarified, butter loses about one fourth of its orig-inal volume.

Potatoes with Bacon and Scallions

4 slices of lean bacon, chopped fine
1 pound boiling potatoes
1 onion, chopped fine (about ½ cup)
1 garlic clove, minced
2 scallions, sliced thin
1 tablespoon finely chopped fresh
   parsley leaves

In a skillet cook the bacon over moderate heat, stirring, for 5 minutes, or until it is crisp, transfer it to paper towels to drain, and in the fat remaining in the skillet cook the potatoes, peeled, sliced thin, and patted dry, and the onion, covered, stirring occasionally, for 5 minutes, or until the potatoes are browned. Reduce the heat to moderately low, stir in the garlic, and cook the mixture, uncovered, stirring occasionally, for 15 minutes. Stir in the bacon, the scallions, the parsley, and salt and pepper to taste and cook the mixture, covered, stirring occasionally, for 5 minutes, or until the potatoes are tender. Serves 2.

Paprika Potato Rosettes

4 russet (baking) potatoes
   (about 2¼ pounds)
1 tablespoon unsalted butter
⅔ cup buttermilk
1 teaspoon paprika plus additional for
   sprinkling the rosettes

In a large saucepan combine the potatoes with enough salted cold water to cover them by 2 inches, bring the water to a boil, and simmer the potatoes for 1 hour, or until they are very tender. Drain the potatoes and let them cool until they can be handled. Peel the potatoes and force them through a ricer into a bowl. In a small saucepan heat the butter and the buttermilk over moderately low heat, stirring, until the butter is melted, pour the mixture over the potatoes, and add 1 teaspoon of the paprika and salt and pepper to taste. Stir the mixture until it is combined well, transfer it to a large pastry bag fitted with a large decorative tip, and pipe six 3-inch rosettes onto a well-buttered baking sheet. *The potato rosettes may be prepared up to this point 1 hour in advance and kept at room temperature.* Sprinkle the rosettes with the additional paprika, bake them in the upper third of a preheated 425° F. oven for 6 minutes, or until they are hot, and transfer them carefully with a metal spatula to a platter. Serves 6.

PHOTO ON PAGE 47

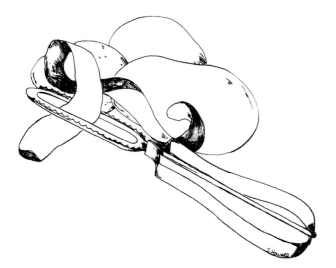

Roasted Potatoes and Cauliflower with Chives

3 large russet (baking) potatoes
3 tablespoons olive oil
1 small head of cauliflower, cut into small
   flowerets
⅓ cup thinly sliced fresh chives plus 8 whole
   chives for garnish if desired

Peel the potatoes, with a melon-ball cutter scoop out as many balls as possible from them, and in a jelly-roll pan toss the balls with the oil and salt and pepper to taste. Roast the potatoes in the middle of a preheated 450° F. oven, turning them occasionally, for 15 minutes. Add the cauliflower, toss the mixture well, and roast it for 10 minutes, or until the cauliflower is tender and golden in spots. Toss the vegetables with the sliced chives and salt and pepper to taste and serve them garnished with the whole chives. Serves 4.

PHOTO ON PAGE 62

Scalloped Potato, Cheddar, and Chive Pie

2 recipes *pâte brisée* (page 233)
raw rice for weighting the shell
1¼ pounds small red potatoes
3 quarts water
1½ cups grated sharp Cheddar (6 ounces)
¼ cup chopped fresh chives
3 large eggs
¾ cup milk
1 cup sour cream

Divide the dough into 2 pieces, one twice the size of the other, and chill the smaller piece, wrapped in wax paper. Roll out the larger piece of dough ⅛ inch thick on a floured surface, fit it into a 10-inch pie plate (preferably ovenproof glass), and trim the edge. Chill the shell. Roll out the smaller piece of dough ⅛ inch thick on the floured surface and with a 1-inch decorative cutter cut out about 90 shapes. Moisten the edge of the shell and press the shapes onto it, 1 at a time, overlapping them slightly, until the edge is covered. Line the shell with foil, fill the foil with the rice, being careful not to disturb the decorative edge, and bake the shell in the lower third of a preheated 425° F. oven for 10 minutes. Remove the rice and foil carefully and bake the shell for 8 minutes more, or until it is pale golden. Let the shell cool in the plate on a rack.

In a food processor fitted with a ⅛-inch slicing disk or with a hand-held slicing device slice the potatoes thin. In a kettle bring the water to a boil, in it boil the potatoes for 5 minutes, or until they are just tender, and drain them in a colander. Plunge the potatoes into a bowl of cold water to stop the cooking and drain them very well. Arrange one fifth of the potato slices, overlapping them, in the shell with one fifth of the Cheddar and chives and salt and pepper to taste. Make 4 more layers in the same manner with the remaining potatoes, Cheddar, and chives and salt and pepper to taste.

In a bowl whisk together the eggs, the milk, the sour cream, and salt and pepper to taste, pour the mixture slowly over the potatoes, letting it seep between the layers, and bake the pie on a baking sheet in the middle of a preheated 375° F. oven for 40 minutes, or until the custard is pale golden and the potatoes are tender. Transfer the pie to a rack and let it cool for 10 minutes. *The pie may be made 1 day in advance, kept covered and chilled, and reheated in a 375° F. oven for 15 minutes.* Serve the pie warm or at room temperature. Serves 8.

PHOTO ON PAGES 82 AND 83

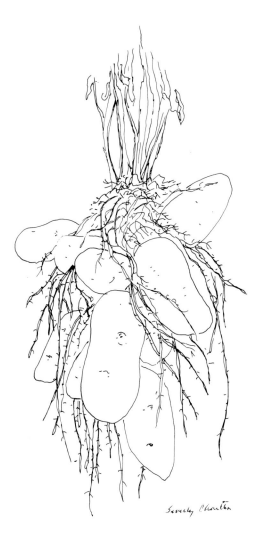

Potato, Chestnut, and Celery Root Purée

¾ cup finely chopped onion
3 tablespoons unsalted butter
2 cups trimmed, peeled, and coarsely chopped celery root (about 1 pound) or 2 cups thinly sliced celery
3 pounds (about 6) russet (baking) potatoes
¾ pound (about 2 cups) canned or vacuum-packed whole chestnuts (rinsed, drained well, and patted dry if using canned)
2 cups chicken broth
2 to 3 cups water
celery leaves for garnish

In a large saucepan cook the onion in 1½ tablespoons of the butter over moderately low heat, stirring, until it is softened, add the celery root, the potatoes, peeled and cut into 1-inch pieces, the chestnuts, the broth, and enough of the water to just cover the mixture, and simmer the mixture, covered, for 15 to 20 minutes, or until the vegetables are very tender. Drain the mixture, reserving the cooking liquid, force it through a food mill fitted with the medium disk or a ricer into a bowl, and stir in the remaining 1½ tablespoons butter, salt and pepper to taste, and enough of the reserved cooking liquid to achieve the desired consistency. *The purée may be made 1 day in advance, kept covered and chilled, and reheated.* Transfer the purée to a serving dish and garnish it with the celery leaves. Serves 8.

PHOTO ON PAGE 75

Grilled Potato Wedges with Chili Salt

two ½-pound russet (baking) potatoes
vegetable oil for brushing the potatoes
2 teaspoons chili powder
½ teaspoon paprika

Scrub the potatoes, cut each potato into 4 wedges, and brush the wedges with some of the oil. Grill the potatoes on a rack set about 6 inches over glowing coals, turning them, for 10 to 15 minutes, or until they are tender. In a small bowl combine well the chili powder, the paprika, and salt to taste. Transfer the potatoes to a platter, brush them lightly with some of the oil, and sprinkle them with the chili salt. Serves 2.

Garlic Potato Purée with Shiitake Ragout and Potato Crisps

For the crisps
2 tablespoons vegetable oil
1 large russet (baking) potato, scrubbed
For the purée
2 pounds russet (baking) potatoes
1 large head of garlic (about 22 cloves),
    separated into cloves and peeled
¾ stick (6 tablespoons) unsalted butter, cut
    into bits and softened
¾ cup milk, scalded
For the ragout
2 tablespoons olive oil

1 pound fresh *shiitake* mushrooms, stems
    discarded and the caps quartered
1 cup medium-dry Sherry
1 cup chicken broth
3 tablespoons soy sauce
2 teaspoons cornstarch, dissolved in
    1 tablespoon cold water
3 tablespoons minced fresh parsley leaves

Make the crisps: Brush a baking sheet well with some of the oil. In a food processor fitted with the 2-millimeter slicing disk or with a hand-held slicing device slice thin the potato on the diagonal (cut one end of the potato on the diagonal to facilitate this) and arrange the slices immediately in one layer on the sheet. Brush the slices with the remaining oil, sprinkle them with salt to taste, and bake them in the middle of a preheated 400° F. oven for 12 to 15 minutes, or until they are golden brown. While they are still warm transfer the crisps with a metal spatula to a rack and let them cool. *The crisps may be made several days in advance and kept in a plastic bag at room temperature.*

Make the purée: Peel the potatoes, quarter them lengthwise, and cut them into 1-inch pieces. Reserving 3 of the garlic cloves for the ragout, in a steamer set over boiling water steam the remaining garlic cloves with the potatoes, covered, for 12 to 15 minutes, or until the potatoes are very tender. Force the steamed garlic and the potatoes through a ricer or a food mill fitted with the medium disk into a large bowl, stir in the butter, the milk, and salt and pepper to taste, and keep the purée warm, covered. *The purée may be made 1 day in advance, kept covered and chilled, and reheated.*

Make the ragout: In a large heavy skillet heat the oil over moderately high heat until it is hot but not smoking and in it sauté the mushrooms with the reserved garlic cloves, minced, and salt and pepper to taste for 5 minutes, or until the mushrooms are softened and any liquid they give off is evaporated. Add the Sherry and boil the mixture until almost all the liquid is evaporated. Add the broth and the soy sauce and bring the mixture to a boil. Stir the cornstarch mixture, stir it into the sauce, and simmer the ragout, stirring occasionally, for 2 minutes. Stir in the parsley. *The ragout may be made 1 day in advance, kept covered and chilled, and reheated.*

Divide the purée among 8 heated small plates, mounding it, arrange 3 crisps decoratively in each mound, and spoon the ragout over and around the purée. Serves 8.

Potato, Kale, and Kielbasa Casserole

3 pounds russet (baking) potatoes (about 6)
½ stick (¼ cup) unsalted butter
¾ cup chicken broth
2 tablespoons cider vinegar
2½ pounds kale, coarse stems discarded and
  the leaves washed well
½ pound Münster, grated coarse
  (about 2 cups)
1 pound smoked *kielbasa*, cut crosswise into
  ¼-inch-thick pieces
2 large onions, halved lengthwise and sliced
  thin crosswise

In a kettle combine the potatoes, peeled and quartered, with enough water to cover them by 2 inches, bring the water to a boil, and boil the potatoes for 15 minutes, or until they are tender. Transfer the potatoes with a slotted spoon to a colander, reserving the cooking liquid, and force them through a ricer into a bowl. Add the butter, ½ cup of the broth, the vinegar, and salt and pepper to taste and combine the mixture well. Bring the reserved cooking liquid to a boil, add the kale, and boil it for 20 minutes, or until it is crisp-tender. Drain the kale in the colander, refresh it under cold water, and press out the excess water. Stir the kale and 1 cup of the Münster into the potato mixture and spread the mixture in a buttered 13- by 9-inch baking dish.

In a large skillet brown the *kielbasa* over moderate heat and transfer it to a bowl with the slotted spoon. In the fat remaining in the skillet cook the onions over moderate heat, stirring, until they are golden and stir them into the *kielbasa*. Scatter the *kielbasa* mixture on top of the potato mixture, sprinkle it with the remaining Münster, and pour the remaining ¼ cup broth on top. *The casserole may be prepared up to this point 1 day in advance and kept covered and chilled.* Bake the casserole in the middle of a preheated 400° F. oven for 20 minutes, or until it is heated through. Serves 6.

Potato Nests with Sautéed Shiitake Mushrooms

For the potato nests
3 large russet (baking) potatoes
vegetable oil for deep-frying the nests
a 3¾-inch potato nest fryer (available at
  Bridge Kitchenware, New York City,
  Tel. 212-688-4220)
kosher salt for sprinkling the nests

For the mushroom mixture
½ stick (¼ cup) unsalted butter
1 pound fresh *shiitake* mushrooms, stems
  discarded and the caps sliced thin
¼ cup medium-dry Sherry
2 tablespoons heavy cream
2 tablespoons finely chopped fresh
  parsley leaves

Make the potato nests: Peel the potatoes, transferring them as they are peeled to a bowl of cold water, and grate them coarse, returning them as they are grated to the bowl of water. Drain the potatoes well and pat them dry thoroughly with paper towels. In a deep-fat fryer or deep kettle heat 4 inches of the oil until it registers 375° F. on a deep-fat thermometer. Dip the larger basket of the potato nest fryer into the oil, remove it, and line the bottom and side with some of the potatoes, being careful not to burn your fingers. Dip the smaller basket into the oil, press it into the potato-lined larger basket, and clamp the basket handles together firmly. Plunge the fryer into the oil and fry the potato nest for 1 to 3 minutes, or until it is crisp, golden, and cooked through at the bottom. Remove the fryer from the oil, detach the larger basket, and let the potato nest cool on the smaller basket for 3 minutes. Using a small sharp knife, pry off the potato nest carefully from the smaller basket, inserting the knife tip between the wires to loosen the nest. Make 5 more nests in the same manner with the remaining potatoes, sprinkle all the nests with the salt, and keep them warm. *The nests may be made 3 hours in advance and reheated in a 350° F. oven.*

Make the mushroom mixture: In a large skillet heat the butter over moderately high heat until the foam subsides and in it sauté the mushrooms, stirring, until they are tender. Stir in the Sherry, boil the mixture for 1 minute, or until the liquid is evaporated, and stir in the cream, the parsley, and salt and pepper to taste.

Divide the mushroom mixture among the potato nests. Serves 6.

PHOTO ON PAGE 26

Waffled Sweet-Potato Chips

1 large sweet potato
vegetable oil for deep-frying

Peel the sweet potato. Adjust the fluted blade of a *mandoline* to ¼ inch and with the *mandoline* slice the sweet potato, turning it a quarter turn after each slice to produce a waffle pattern. In a deep skillet heat 1 inch of the oil over moderately high heat to 375° F. on a deep-fat thermometer, in it fry the slices in batches, turning them, for 1 minute, or until they are golden, and transfer the chips as they are fried with a slotted spoon to paper towels to drain. *The chips may be made 1 day in advance and kept in an airtight container. Just before serving arrange the chips in one layer in shallow baking pans and heat them in a preheated 400° F. oven for 5 minutes.* Sprinkle the chips with salt to taste and serve them warm.

PHOTO ON PAGE 20

Roasted Sweet Potato Slices

1 tablespoon olive oil
1 tablespoon unsalted butter, melted
¾ pound sweet potatoes, scrubbed, left
    unpeeled, and cut into ⅛-inch-thick slices
coarse salt for sprinkling the potatoes

In a small bowl whisk together the oil, the butter, and salt and pepper to taste. Arrange the potato slices, not touching, in rows on an oiled baking sheet, brush them with the oil mixture, and roast them in the upper third of a preheated 450° F. oven, turning them once with a spatula, for 18 to 22 minutes, or until they are golden and crisp. Transfer the potatoes to paper towels to drain, sprinkle them with the coarse salt and pepper to taste, and serve them warm. Serves 2.

Sweet Potato and Apple Purée

2 pounds sweet potatoes
1 cup finely chopped onion
2 large Granny Smith apples
2 tablespoons unsalted butter
3 tablespoons *crème fraîche* or sour cream,
    or to taste
freshly grated nutmeg to taste
hot water for thinning the purée if necessary

In a large saucepan boil the sweet potatoes, peeled and cut into 1-inch pieces, in water to cover for 10 to 12 minutes, or until they are very tender. While the sweet potatoes are boiling, in a large skillet cook the onion and the apples, peeled, cored, and sliced thin, with salt and pepper to taste in the butter over moderate heat, stirring,

for 5 to 10 minutes, or until the apples are very tender. Drain the sweet potatoes well, in a food processor purée them with the apple mixture until the mixture is smooth, and with the motor running add the *crème fraîche*, the nutmeg, salt and pepper to taste, and enough hot water to thin the purée to the desired consistency. Serves 6 to 8.

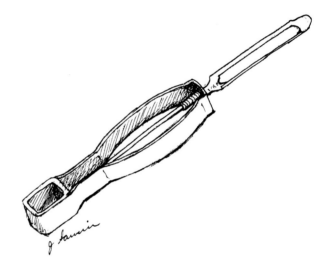

Radishes and Scallions

20 radishes, trimmed and sliced very thin
    (about 2 cups)
2 scallions, minced
1 tablespoon unsalted butter
2 teaspoons minced fresh parsley leaves
a pinch of freshly grated lemon zest

In a non-stick skillet cook the radishes and the scallions in the butter over moderate heat for 3 to 5 minutes, or until the radishes are tender. Remove the skillet from the heat and stir in the parsley, the zest, and salt and pepper to taste. Serves 2.

¼ cup snipped fresh chives, or to taste, plus,
  if desired, additional for garnish

In a large saucepan cook the leek and the onion with salt and pepper to taste in the butter over moderately low heat, stirring, until the vegetables are softened, add the potatoes, peeled and cut into 1-inch pieces, the broth, and the water, and simmer the mixture, covered, for 10 to 15 minutes, or until the potatoes are very tender. Stir in the sorrel and simmer the mixture for 1 minute. Purée the mixture in a blender in batches, transferring it as it is puréed to a bowl, and let it cool. Stir in the cream, the chives, and salt and pepper to taste, chill the soup, covered, for at least 4 hours or overnight, and serve it sprinkled with the additional chives. Makes about 8 cups, serving 6 to 8.

Spinach with Sour Cream and Toasted Pine Nuts

2 teaspoons pine nuts
1 tablespoon olive oil
1 small onion, chopped fine
1 pound fresh spinach, coarse stems discarded
  and the leaves washed well, spun dry, and
  chopped coarse
1 tablespoon sour cream
1 teaspoon fresh lemon juice

In a large skillet cook the pine nuts in the oil over moderate heat, stirring, for 2 minutes, or until they are golden, and transfer them with a slotted spoon to a small dish. In the skillet cook the onion, stirring occasionally, until it is golden, add the spinach, and cook the mixture, covered, stirring once every minute, for 3 minutes, or until the spinach is wilted and tender. Stir in the sour cream, the lemon juice, and salt and pepper to taste, remove the skillet from the heat, and sprinkle the mixture with the pine nuts. Serves 2.

Sorrel Vichyssoise

1 cup finely chopped white and pale green
  part of leek, washed well
½ cup finely chopped onion
2 tablespoons unsalted butter
1 pound boiling potatoes
4 cups chicken broth
2 cups water
½ pound fresh sorrel (available in the
  spring at specialty produce markets
  and some supermarkets), stems discarded
  and the leaves rinsed, spun dry,
  and shredded coarse (about 8 cups)
½ cup heavy cream

Maple-Glazed Acorn Squash with Currants

3 acorn squash (each about 1½ pounds),
  halved crosswise and the seeds and strings
  discarded
½ stick (¼ cup) unsalted butter, softened
⅓ cup pure maple syrup
¼ teaspoon ground allspice, or to taste
3 tablespoons dried currants

Spread the cavity of each squash half with about ½ teaspoon of the butter, sprinkle the halves with salt and pepper to taste, and arrange them, cut sides down, in a large baking pan. Add enough water to reach about ¼ inch up the sides of the squash halves and bake the squash in the middle of a preheated 400° F. oven for 30 minutes. While the squash is baking, in a small saucepan combine the remaining butter, the maple syrup, the allspice, the currants, and a pinch of salt and heat the mixture over moderately low heat, stirring, until the butter is melted and the currants are plumped. Remove the squash from the oven, turn it cut sides up, and brush it generously with some of the maple mixture. Return the squash to the oven and bake it, brushing it with the maple mixture occasionally and adding more water to the pan as necessary to keep the bottom covered, for 20 to 30 minutes more, or until it is very tender. Season the squash with salt and pepper. Serves 6.

Roasted Butternut Squash with Curry and Coriander

2 tablespoons unsalted butter
2 tablespoons olive oil
1 tablespoon plus 1 teaspoon curry powder
4 pounds butternut squash, peeled and
    cut into 1-inch pieces
    (about 8 cups)
2 tablespoons minced fresh coriander

In a small saucepan heat the butter with the oil, the curry powder, and salt and pepper to taste over moderately low heat, stirring, until it is melted and in a roasting pan just large enough to hold the squash in one layer toss the squash with the curry mixture until it is coated well. Roast the squash in the middle of a preheated 375° F. oven, shaking the pan occasionally, for 25 minutes, or until it is tender. Season the squash with salt and pepper, add the coriander, and toss the mixture gently. Serves 6.

Succotash on Fried Cheddar Grits

2½ cups water
½ cup quick-cooking grits
1 cup grated sharp Cheddar
1 tablespoon unsalted butter
2 slices of lean bacon
1 green bell pepper, chopped fine
½ cup fresh or frozen baby lima beans

1½ cups fresh corn kernels including the pulp
    scraped from the cobs (from 2 ears of corn)
1 large egg beaten with 1 tablespoon water
fine dry bread crumbs for coating the grits
vegetable oil for frying the grits

In a heavy saucepan bring 2 cups of the water to a boil, add the grits in a stream, stirring, and cook them, covered, over moderate heat, stirring occasionally, for 7 minutes, or until they are very thick. Add the Cheddar, the butter, and salt to taste, stir the mixture until the cheese is melted, and spread it in an 8-inch-square baking dish. Chill the grits mixture, covered, overnight.

In a heavy skillet cook the bacon over moderate heat until it is crisp, transfer it to paper towels to drain, and crumble it fine. In the fat remaining in the skillet cook the bell pepper over moderate heat, stirring, until it is softened, stir in the lima beans, the corn, and the remaining ½ cup water, and simmer the succotash, covered partially, for 8 to 10 minutes, or until the lima beans are tender.

Have ready in separate bowls the egg mixture and the bread crumbs. In a kettle heat ¾ inch of the oil over moderately high heat until it registers 360° F. on a deep-fat thermometer. While the oil is heating cut the grits mixture into 9 squares. Working in batches, dip the squares into the egg mixture, letting the excess drip off, coat them with the bread crumbs, and fry them in the oil, turning them carefully, for 2 minutes on each side, or until they are golden, transferring them as they are fried to paper towels to drain. Serve the succotash spooned over the grits squares. Serves 6 to 8 as a side dish.

Sugar Snap Peas with Lemon Butter

1 pound sugar snap peas, trimmed
1½ tablespoons unsalted butter
¾ teaspoon freshly grated lemon zest

In a large saucepan of boiling salted water blanch the snap peas for 1 minute, drain them, and plunge them into a bowl of ice and cold water to stop the cooking. Drain the peas well. *The peas may be prepared up to this point 1 day in advance and kept covered and chilled.* In a large heavy skillet melt the butter with the zest, add the peas and salt and pepper to taste, and heat the peas over moderately low heat, stirring, until they are hot. Serves 6.

PHOTO ON PAGES 46 AND 47

Panfried Tofu with Oriental Garlic Sauce

a 1-pound block of extra-firm tofu, rinsed
4 teaspoons cornstarch
1 cup water
2 to 3 tablespoons soy sauce
1 tablespoon cider vinegar
1 tablespoon Scotch
2 teaspoons sugar
⅛ teaspoon salt
2½ tablespoons vegetable oil
3 large garlic cloves, minced
a 1-inch cube of peeled fresh gingerroot,
   minced
1 teaspoon Oriental sesame oil
1 scallion, minced
cooked rice as an accompaniment if desired

Cut the tofu crosswise into 4 slices and let the slices drain between a double thickness of paper towels for 20 minutes.

While the tofu is draining, in a small bowl dissolve the cornstarch in ¼ cup of the water and stir in the remaining ¾ cup water, the soy sauce to taste, the vinegar, the Scotch, the sugar, and the salt. In a heavy saucepan heat 1½ tablespoons of the vegetable oil over moderately high heat until it is hot but not smoking and in it stir-fry the garlic until it is pale golden, being careful not to let it burn. Add the gingerroot and stir-fry the mixture for 30 seconds. Stir the soy sauce mixture, add it to the garlic mixture, stirring, and bring the sauce to a boil, stirring. Simmer the sauce for 2 minutes, stir in the sesame oil, and keep the sauce warm.

In a non-stick skillet heat the remaining 1 tablespoon vegetable oil over high heat until it is hot but not smoking and in it brown the tofu on all sides, turning it with tongs and transferring it as it is browned to paper towels to drain. Divide the tofu between 2 plates and spoon the sauce over it. Sprinkle the scallion over each serving and serve the tofu with the rice. Serves 2.

Baked Herbed Tomatoes

2 tomatoes, halved horizontally and seeded
½ cup fine fresh bread crumbs
¼ cup finely chopped onion
½ teaspoon minced garlic
½ cup finely chopped fresh basil leaves
¼ teaspoon dried thyme, crumbled
2 teaspoons extra-virgin olive oil

Sprinkle the insides of the tomatoes with salt, arrange the tomato halves, cut sides down, on layers of paper towels, and let them drain for 1 hour. In a bowl stir together the bread crumbs, the onion, the garlic, the basil, the thyme, and salt and pepper to taste and stir in the oil. Arrange the tomato halves, cut sides up, in a shallow baking pan and divide the bread crumb mixture among them. *The tomatoes may be prepared up to this point 4 hours in advance and kept at room temperature.*

Bake the tomatoes in the upper third of a preheated 450° F. oven for 10 minutes, or until the topping is golden. (Do not overcook the tomatoes or they will lose their shape.) Serves 4.

PHOTO ON PAGE 62

Couscous-Stuffed Tomatoes with Currants and Herbs

four ½-pound tomatoes
¼ cup dried currants
about 1⅔ cups chicken broth
3 tablespoons olive oil
1 cup couscous
⅓ cup finely chopped scallion
3 tablespoons minced fresh dill
3 tablespoons minced fresh mint leaves
1 to 2 tablespoons fresh lemon juice

Halve each tomato horizontally, scoop out and discard the seeds, and with a grapefruit knife scoop out the pulp, reserving it and leaving ⅓-inch-thick shells. Sprinkle the insides of the tomatoes with salt and invert the tomato shells onto a rack to drain for 30 minutes.

In a small saucepan combine the currants with 1 cup of the broth and simmer them for 5 minutes. Drain the currants in a sieve set over a 2-cup measure, add enough of the remaining broth to measure 1½ cups, and transfer the broth to the pan. Add 1 tablespoon of the oil to the broth and bring the mixture to a boil. Stir in the couscous and let it stand, covered, off the heat for 5 minutes. Stir the couscous with a fork, breaking up any lumps, and toss it in a bowl with the currants, the reserved tomato pulp, chopped, the remaining 2 tablespoons oil, the scallion, the dill, the mint, the lemon juice, and salt and pepper to taste. Divide the couscous mixture among the tomato shells, mounding it, arrange the stuffed tomatoes in an oiled baking dish just large enough to hold them, and bake them, covered, in a preheated 325° F. oven for 10 minutes. Serve the stuffed tomatoes warm or at room temperature. Serves 8.

Tomatoes with Moroccan-Style Fish Stuffing

four ½-pound tomatoes
4 tablespoons olive oil,
  or to taste
1 pound scrod fillet or other firm-fleshed
  white fish fillet
2 tablespoons dry white wine
2 tablespoons finely chopped peel from
  quick preserved lemons
  (recipe follows)
1 tablespoon brine from quick preserved
  lemons (recipe follows)
2 tablespoons minced fresh coriander
2 teaspoons fresh lemon juice,
  or to taste

Cut off the top third of each tomato, scoop out the seeds and pulp with a grapefruit knife, leaving ⅓-inch-thick shells, and reserve the tops and pulp for another use. Sprinkle the insides of the tomatoes with salt and invert the tomatoes on a rack to drain for 30 minutes.

In a non-stick skillet heat 1 tablespoon of the oil over moderately high heat until it is hot but not smoking and in it sauté the scrod for 1 minute on each side. Add the wine to the skillet and cook the fish, covered, over moderately low heat for 3 to 6 minutes, or until it just flakes. Remove the skillet from the heat and let the fish cool. Flake the fish into a bowl and stir in the preserved lemon peel and brine, the coriander, the lemon juice, and 2 tablespoons of the remaining oil. Divide the mixture among the tomato shells and drizzle it with the remaining 1 tablespoon oil. Serves 4.

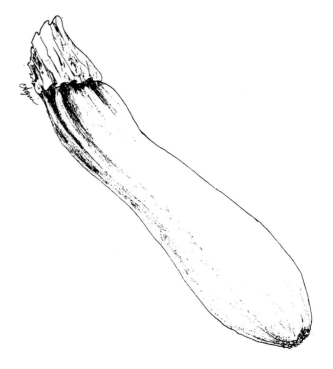

Quick Preserved Lemons

6 thin-skinned lemons, scrubbed, trimmed
  at both ends, and cut lengthwise
  into sixths
6 tablespoons kosher salt
about 1 cup fresh lemon juice

In a baking dish just large enough to hold the lemons in one layer toss the lemons with the salt, pour enough of the lemon juice over them to just cover them, and bake the lemons, covered, in a preheated 200° F. oven, stirring occasionally, for 3 hours. Let the lemons cool and transfer them with their brine to an airtight container. The preserved lemons keep, covered and chilled, indefinitely. Makes about 1 pint.

Roasted Zucchini with Yogurt

3 zucchini, scrubbed, halved lengthwise, and
  cut into ¼-inch-thick slices
1 tablespoon olive oil
1 scallion, chopped fine
2 tablespoons plain yogurt
cayenne to taste

In a shallow baking pan toss the zucchini with the oil and salt to taste and roast it in the upper third of a preheated 500° F. oven for 20 minutes, or until it is golden brown. In a bowl toss the zucchini with the scallion, the yogurt, and the cayenne. Serves 2.

Mixed Vegetables Vinaigrette

1½ pounds small red potatoes
¾ pound *haricots verts* (thin French green
    beans)*, trimmed
1 pound "baby" Pattypan squash*,
    trimmed
4 bunches of baby carrots*
    (about 24), trimmed and peeled
3 bunches of small radishes
    (about 24), trimmed
For the vinaigrette
1 large shallot, chopped
1 large garlic clove, chopped
2 teaspoons coarse-grained mustard
2 tablespoons fresh lemon juice
2 teaspoons balsamic vinegar
⅓ cup olive oil

*available at specialty foods shops and
    specialty produce markets

In a large saucepan combine the potatoes with enough cold water to cover them by 1 inch and simmer them, covered, for 10 to 15 minutes, or until they are tender. Drain the potatoes, let them cool completely, and cut them into ¼-inch-thick slices. In a kettle of boiling water cook separately the *haricots verts*, the squash, and the carrots for 3 to 5 minutes each, or until each vegetable is crisp-tender, transferring them as they are cooked with a slotted spoon to a bowl of ice and cold water to stop the cooking. Transfer the vegetables with the slotted spoon to paper towels and pat them dry. In the kettle of boiling water cook the radishes for 2 to 3 minutes, or until they are crisp-tender, and transfer them with the slotted spoon to the bowl of ice and cold water. Drain the radishes and pat them dry. Transfer the vegetables to 5 separate bowls and chill them, covered. *The vegetables may be cooked 1 day in advance and kept covered and chilled.*

Make the vinaigrette: In a blender or food processor blend together the shallot, the garlic, the mustard, the lemon juice, the vinegar, and salt and pepper to taste until the mixture is smooth, with the motor running add the oil in a stream, and blend the dressing until it is emulsified.

Divide the vinaigrette evenly among the 5 bowls, toss each vegetable to coat it with the dressing, and arrange the vegetables decoratively on a large platter. Serves 12.

PHOTO ON PAGE 45

Mixed Grilled Vegetables

3 red or yellow bell peppers, quartered
    lengthwise
6 small eggplants (about 1 pound total), each
    cut into 3 lengthwise slices
twelve ¼-inch-thick lengthwise slices of red
    onion with root ends intact (about 4 onions)
olive oil for brushing the vegetables

Brush the vegetables lightly with the oil, and grill them in batches on a rack set 4 inches over glowing coals, turning them, for 15 to 20 minutes, or until they are tender, transferring them to a platter as they are done. Season the vegetables with salt and pepper and keep them warm, covered with foil. (Alternatively, the vegetables may be roasted in batches on the rack of a broiler pan under a preheated broiler about 4 inches from the heat, turning them, for 10 to 15 minutes, transferring them to a jelly-roll pan set on the bottom rack of the oven as they are done.) Serves 6.

PHOTO ON PAGES 38 AND 39

Spring Vegetable Ragout

½ pound fiddleheads*, cleaned
    (procedure on page 177)
½ pound miniature pattypan squash*,
    trimmed

½ pound baby carrots*, trimmed
¾ cup shelled fresh peas
½ stick (¼ cup) unsalted butter
½ pound pearl onions, blanched in boiling
    water for 1 minute, peeled, and trimmed
2 thyme sprigs
1 bay leaf
1 cup chicken broth
¼ pound fresh morels*, washed well, patted
    dry, and trimmed
3 tablespoons minced fresh parsley leaves
1½ tablespoons minced fresh mint leaves
1 large garlic clove, minced

*available seasonally at specialty produce
    markets and some supermarkets

In a kettle of boiling salted water boil the fiddleheads for 4 minutes, or until they are crisp-tender, transfer them with a slotted spoon to a bowl of ice and cold water to stop the cooking, and transfer them to paper towels to drain. In the kettle boil the squash and the carrots for 3 minutes, or until they are crisp-tender, transfer the vegetables with the slotted spoon to the bowl of ice and cold water to stop the cooking, and transfer them to paper towels to drain. In the kettle boil the peas for 2 to 3 minutes, or until they are just tender, and drain them.

In a large heavy skillet combine 2 tablespoons of the butter, the onions, the thyme, the bay leaf, ¼ cup of the broth, and salt and pepper to taste and simmer the mixture, covered, for 5 minutes. Add the morels, halved lengthwise or sliced crosswise, and ½ cup of the remaining broth and simmer the mixture, covered, for 10 minutes, or until the morels are tender. Add the fiddleheads, the squash, the carrots, and the remaining ¼ cup broth and simmer the mixture, covered, for 1 minute. Add the peas, the parsley, the mint, and the garlic, simmer the ragout, covered, for 1 minute, and stir in the remaining 2 tablespoons butter, cut into bits, stirring until the butter is just melted. Discard the bay leaf and season the ragout with salt and pepper. Serves 6.

Steamed Root Vegetables and Cabbage with Dill
1 small head of cabbage
1 pound carrots, peeled and cut into fine
    julienne
1 pound turnips, peeled and cut into fine
    julienne

1 pound parsnips, peeled and cut into
    fine julienne
2 tablespoons unsalted butter, softened
2 tablespoons cider vinegar
2 tablespoons minced fresh dill plus dill sprigs
    for garnish

In a kettle of boiling water blanch the cabbage for 1 minute, transfer it with tongs to a work surface, and let it cool until it can just be handled. Cut the outermost cabbage leaf free at the core, remove the leaf gently in one piece, being careful not to tear it, and remove 3 more leaves in the same manner. Arrange a leaf on each of 4 plates. Cut enough of the remaining cabbage into ⅛-inch-thick shreds to measure 2 cups packed loosely, reserving the rest for another use. In a steamer set over boiling water arrange in order the carrots, the turnips, the parsnips, and the shredded cabbage, steam the vegetables, covered, for 8 to 10 minutes, or until they are just tender, and in a heated bowl toss them with the butter, the vinegar, the minced dill, and salt and pepper to taste. Mound the vegetable mixture in the cabbage leaves and garnish it with the dill sprigs. Serves 4.

PHOTO ON PAGE 28

Mashed Root Vegetables with Horseradish
2 turnips, peeled and cut into ½-inch pieces
3 parsnips, peeled and cut into ½-inch pieces
2 russet (baking) potatoes (about 1 pound)
¼ cup heavy cream
½ stick (¼ cup) unsalted butter
2 to 3 tablespoons finely grated peeled fresh
    horseradish or drained bottled horseradish

In a large saucepan of boiling salted water cook the turnips and the parsnips for 10 minutes, add the potatoes, peeled and cut into ½-inch pieces, and boil the vegetables for 10 to 12 minutes, or until they are tender. While the vegetables are cooking, in a small saucepan heat the cream, the butter, and the horseradish to taste over low heat until the mixture is hot and keep it warm. Drain the vegetables, in the pan cook them over high heat, shaking the pan, for 30 seconds, or until any excess liquid is evaporated, and remove the pan from the heat. Add the cream mixture to the potato mixture, straining it through a fine sieve and pressing hard on the solids if desired. Mash the vegetables with a potato masher and stir in salt and pepper to taste. Serves 4.

SALADS

ENTRÉE SALADS

*White Bean, Pasta, and Grilled Duck Salad
with Orange Cumin Vinaigrette*

1 pound dried white beans such as *cannellini*
    or Great Northern, picked over and soaked
    in enough cold water to cover them by
    2 inches overnight, or 1¾ pounds canned
    white beans (about 2½ cups),
    rinsed well and drained
1 whole boneless duck breast with skin
    (about 1⅓ pounds, available at many
    butcher shops and some supermarkets)
For the vinaigrette
¾ cup fresh orange juice
2 tablespoons white-wine vinegar
1 teaspoon ground cumin
⅓ cup olive oil
dried hot red pepper flakes to taste

½ pound *ziti*, *penne*, or other tubular pasta
1 red onion, minced, soaked in
    ice water for 10 minutes,
    and drained well
2 garlic cloves, minced
1¼ cups finely chopped celery
1 red bell pepper, sliced thin
1 yellow bell pepper, sliced thin
3 tablespoons finely chopped fresh coriander
    plus coriander sprigs for garnish
1 tablespoon finely chopped fresh mint leaves

2 navel oranges, the zest, pith, and
    membranes cut away with a serrated knife
    and the flesh cut into sections
⅓ cup finely chopped pitted black olives

If using dried beans, in a kettle combine them with enough water to cover them by 2 inches, bring the water to a boil, and cook the beans, covered, at a bare simmer, stirring occasionally, for 1 hour, or until they are just tender. Drain the beans well.

On an oiled rack set 5 to 6 inches over glowing coals or in a well-seasoned ridged grill pan over moderately high heat grill the duck for 7 minutes on each side. Transfer the duck to a roasting pan and roast it in a pre-heated 450° F. oven for 7 minutes for medium-rare meat. Transfer the duck to a cutting board and let it stand for 15 minutes.

Make the vinaigrette: In a bowl whisk together the orange juice, the vinegar, and the cumin, add the oil in a stream, whisking, and whisk the dressing until it is emulsified. Whisk in the red pepper flakes and salt and pepper to taste.

In a kettle of boiling salted water cook the pasta until it is tender, rinse it under cold water, and drain it well. In a very large bowl toss together the beans, the pasta, the onion, the garlic, the celery, the bell peppers, the chopped coriander, the mint, the orange sections, the olives, and the duck, cut into thin slices. Add the vinai-grette and salt and pepper to taste and toss the salad gently but thoroughly. Divide the salad among 8 plates and garnish the plates with the coriander sprigs. Serve the salad at room temperature. Serves 8.

PHOTO ON PAGE 56

Beef and Orange Salad
with Red Onion Mustard Vinaigrette

1½ tablespoons red-wine vinegar
1 tablespoon Dijon-style mustard
¼ cup olive oil
2 tablespoons finely chopped red onion
1 tablespoon finely chopped fresh
   parsley leaves
¾ pound sirloin steak, about 1 inch thick
1 garlic clove, halved
Boston lettuce, shredded, for lining
   the plates
1 navel orange, peeled, the zest and pith cut
   away with a serrated knife and the sections
   cut away from the membranes

In a bowl whisk together the vinegar, the mustard, and salt and pepper to taste, add the oil in a stream, whisking, and whisk the dressing until it is emulsified. Stir in the onion and the parsley. Rub the steak with the garlic, discard the garlic, and sprinkle the steak with salt and pepper to taste. Broil the steak on the rack of a broiler pan under a preheated broiler about 4 inches from the heat for 4 to 5 minutes on each side for medium-rare meat and let it stand for 5 minutes. Divide the lettuce between 2 plates, arrange decoratively on the top the steak, sliced thin diagonally, and the orange sections, and drizzle some of the dressing over each salad. Serve the remaining dressing separately. Serves 2.

Warm Caesar Salad with Grilled Shrimp and Scallops

2 garlic cloves, minced and mashed to a paste
   with a pinch of salt
5 tablespoons olive oil
1½ cups ½-inch bread cubes
1½ teaspoons anchovy paste
2 teaspoons fresh lemon juice
8 shrimp (about ½ pound), shelled
8 sea scallops (about ½ pound), halved
   horizontally if desired
½ head of romaine, washed well, spun dry,
   and torn into small pieces (about 4 cups)
2 tablespoons freshly grated Parmesan

In a small bowl whisk together half the garlic paste, 2 tablespoons of the oil, and salt and pepper to taste, add the bread cubes, and toss the mixture well. Bake the bread cubes on a baking sheet in the middle of a preheat-ed 350° F. oven for 12 to 15 minutes, or until the croutons are golden.

In a large bowl whisk together the remaining garlic paste, 2 tablespoons of the remaining oil, the anchovy paste, the lemon juice, and salt and pepper to taste until the dressing is combined well. In a bowl toss the shrimp and the scallops with the remaining 1 tablespoon oil and salt and pepper to taste and grill them in a ridged grill pan or on an oiled rack set about 6 inches over glowing coals for 2 to 3 minutes on each side, or until the shrimp are cooked through and the scallops are opaque. Transfer the shellfish to the large bowl, add the romaine and 1 tablespoon of the Parmesan, and toss the salad well. Divide the salad between 2 plates and sprinkle the croutons and ½ tablespoon of the remaining Parmesan over each serving. Serves 2.

Curried Smoked Chicken and Wild Rice Salad

For the dressing
2 garlic cloves, chopped
3 tablespoons white-wine vinegar
4 tablespoons fresh lemon juice
1½ tablespoons curry powder
3 tablespoons bottled mango chutney
⅔ cup olive oil
¾ cup sour cream
3 tablespoons water
½ cup finely chopped fresh coriander
For the wild rice mixture
2½ cups wild rice, rinsed
6½ cups water
2 teaspoons salt
1 tablespoon white-wine vinegar
2 tablespoons olive oil
1 bunch of scallions including the green part,
    chopped (about ¾ cup)
1 cup golden raisins

6 whole smoked chicken breasts*
    (about 3½ to 4 pounds), skinned if desired
3 cups *mâche* (lamb's-lettuce, available at
    specialty foods shops and specialty produce
    markets), washed well and spun dry

*available at some butcher shops and
    specialty foods shops

Make the dressing: In a blender or food processor blend the garlic, the vinegar, the lemon juice, the curry powder, the chutney, and salt and pepper to taste until the mixture is smooth. With the motor running add the oil in a stream, add the sour cream and the water, adding additional water if necessary to reach the desired consistency, and blend the dressing until it is combined well. Transfer the dressing to a small bowl and stir in the coriander. *The dressing may be made 1 day in advance and kept covered and chilled.*

Make the wild rice mixture: In a large heavy saucepan combine the wild rice with the water and the salt and simmer it, covered, for 45 to 50 minutes, or until it is tender and all the water is absorbed. Transfer the wild rice to a large bowl and add the vinegar, the oil, and salt and pepper to taste. Toss the mixture well and let it cool completely. *The wild rice mixture may be prepared up to this point 1 day in advance and kept covered and chilled.* Stir in the scallions and the raisins.

Cut the chicken into ¾-inch pieces. Spoon the wild rice mixture onto one side of a large shallow serving dish, arrange the chicken on the other half, and arrange the *mâche* decoratively down the middle. Serve the dressing separately. (Alternatively, the wild rice mixture, the chicken, and the dressing may be tossed together in a large serving bowl and garnished with the *mâche*.) Serves 12.

PHOTO ON PAGES 44 AND 45

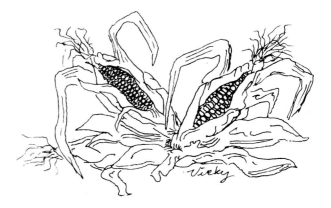

Grilled Corn and Shrimp Salad

6 ears of corn
⅓ cup olive oil plus additional for brushing
    the corn and the shrimp
1 pound medium shrimp (about 25), shelled
    and deveined
1 red onion, chopped fine
1 large fresh *jalapeño* chili including the
    seeds, minced (wear rubber gloves)
⅓ cup loosely packed fresh coriander,
    chopped fine
3 tablespoons fresh lemon juice
1 tablespoon white-wine vinegar
2 bunches of watercress, rinsed well, spun
    dry, and coarse stems discarded

Brush the corn with some of the additional oil and grill it on a rack set about 6 inches over glowing coals, turning it, for 15 minutes, or until it is golden brown. Let the corn cool until it can be handled. Working over a bowl, with a serrated knife cut the kernels from the cobs and with the back of the knife scrape the pulp from the cobs. Brush the shrimp with some of the additional oil, grill them on the rack, turning them, for 6 to 8 minutes, or until they are cooked through, and transfer them to the bowl. Stir in the onion, the *jalapeño*, and the coriander.

In a small bowl whisk together the lemon juice, the vinegar, and salt and pepper to taste, add the remaining ⅓ cup oil in a stream, whisking, and whisk the dressing until it is emulsified. Pour the dressing over the corn mixture and combine the salad well. Divide the watercress among 6 plates and spoon the salad over it. Serves 6.

Crab Salad

2 tablespoons mayonnaise
2 tablespoons *crème fraîche*
1 tablespoon fresh lemon juice
1 tablespoon chopped fresh chives
⅔ cup chopped seeded tomato plus 2 large
    whole tomatoes
⅔ cup seedless cucumber, cut into ¼-inch dice
2 cups picked-over lump crab meat, thawed
    and drained if frozen
soft-leafed lettuce, rinsed and dried, for lining
    the plates

In a bowl whisk together the mayonnaise, the *crème fraîche*, the lemon juice, and the chives. In another bowl combine gently the chopped tomato, the cucumber, the crab meat, half the mayonnaise sauce, and salt and pepper to taste. Without cutting all the way through the bottoms, core the whole tomatoes and cut them into sixths, forming tulip shapes. Line 2 plates with the lettuce, center the tomatoes on the lettuce, and mound the crab salad on top. Serve the salad with the remaining sauce. Serves 2.

Marinated Lobster Salad with Corn and Tomatoes

two 1¼-pound live lobsters
1 tablespoon fresh lemon juice
1 tablespoon white wine vinegar
1 teaspoon Pernod
¼ cup olive oil (preferably extra-virgin)
1 bunch (about ¼ pound) *arugula*, trimmed,
    washed well, and spun dry
1 cup cooked corn kernels
16 cherry tomatoes, halved
chive blades for garnish if desired

Plunge the lobsters into a kettle of salted boiling water and simmer them, covered, for 8 minutes from the time the water returns to a simmer. Transfer the lobsters with tongs to a colander and let them cool until they can be handled. Crack the shells, remove the meat, keeping the claws and tail meat in one piece, and cut the tail meat crosswise into ¾-inch slices. In a bowl whisk together the lemon juice, the vinegar, the Pernod, and salt and pepper to taste, add the oil in a stream, whisking, and whisk the dressing until it is emulsified. Add the lobster to the dressing, tossing it to coat it well, and let it marinate at room temperature, stirring occasionally, for 30 minutes.

Arrange the *arugula* decoratively on two plates. With a slotted spoon transfer the lobster to the plates, arranging it decoratively, and sprinkle the corn over each salad. Arrange the tomatoes decoratively on each salad, drizzle each serving with some of the dressing, and garnish each salad with the chive blades. Serves 2.

FRONTISPIECE

Warm Scallop, Black Bean, and Bell Pepper Salad
For the dressing
1 garlic clove, minced and mashed to a paste
    with ¼ teaspoon salt
2½ tablespoons white-wine vinegar
3 tablespoons finely chopped fresh coriander
⅛ teaspoon cayenne
3 tablespoons olive oil

¾ pound sea scallops, rinsed and patted dry
1 cup canned black beans, rinsed and
    drained well
½ cup chopped red bell pepper
2 tablespoons thinly sliced scallion

Make the dressing: In a bowl whisk together the garlic paste, the vinegar, the coriander, the cayenne, and the oil and whisk the dressing until it is emulsified.

Add the scallops to the dressing, tossing them to coat them well, and in another bowl toss together the beans, the bell pepper, and the scallion. Heat a heavy skillet over moderately high heat until it is hot, remove the scallops from the dressing, letting the excess drip off and reserving it, and in the skillet sauté them for 3 to 4 minutes, or until they are just cooked through. Remove the skillet from the heat, transfer the scallops to a platter, and stir the reserved dressing into the skillet. Add the simmering dressing to the bean mixture, toss the bean mixture well, and spoon it around the scallops. Serves 2.

Baked Scrod "Seviche" Salad

four 6- to 8-ounce scrod fillets, seasoned with
    salt and pepper
2 tablespoons olive oil plus additional for
    brushing the fish
½ cup fresh orange juice
½ cup fresh lemon juice
¼ cup fresh lime juice
1 teaspoon Dijon-style mustard
1 teaspoon Tabasco,
    or to taste
1 tablespoon white-wine vinegar
1 teaspoon salt
1½ cups minced red onion
the white and pale green parts of 6 scallions,
    minced
1 tablespoon minced garlic
⅓ cup finely chopped fresh coriander
lettuce for lining the plates
slices of French or Italian bread, toasted, as
    an accompaniment

In a large greased jelly-roll pan arrange the scrod fillets in one layer and brush them with the additional oil. Bake the fish in the middle of a preheated 400° F. oven for 15 to 20 minutes, or until it just flakes, transfer it to a bowl, and flake it into small pieces.

In another bowl whisk together the citrus juices, the remaining 2 tablespoons oil, the mustard, the Tabasco, the vinegar, the salt, the onion, the scallions, the garlic, the coriander, and pepper to taste, add the fish, and toss the salad well. Line 6 plates with the lettuce, divide the salad among the plates, and serve it with the toast. Serves 6.

Grilled Seafood Salad Niçoise

For the dressing
3 tablespoons red-wine vinegar
1 tablespoon Dijon-style mustard
1 teaspoon anchovy paste
½ teaspoon dried thyme, crumbled
¼ teaspoon sugar
⅓ cup olive oil

1 pound 1-inch-thick tuna steak, cut into
    6 pieces
1 large yellow squash, cut into
    ¼-inch-thick slices

9 jumbo shrimp, shelled and halved
    lengthwise
12 large sea scallops
1 pound green or wax beans or a combination,
    trimmed and cut into 2-inch lengths
red-leaf lettuce for lining the plates
1 red bell pepper, roasted (procedure follows)
    and cut into 2-inch pieces
1 pint red or yellow cherry tomatoes or a
    combination, quartered
1 cup drained Niçoise olives
    (available at specialty foods shops
    and some supermarkets)

Make the dressing: In a small bowl whisk together the vinegar, the mustard, the anchovy paste, the thyme, the sugar, and salt and pepper to taste, add the oil in a stream, whisking, and whisk the dressing until it is emulsified.

Reserve 2 tablespoons of the dressing in another small bowl, arrange the tuna pieces and the squash slices on a baking sheet, and brush them lightly with the reserved dressing. In a bowl toss the shrimp and the scallops with 2 tablespoons of the remaining dressing. Let the mixtures stand for 15 minutes. In a kettle of boiling water cook the beans for 5 minutes, or until they are crisp-tender, drain them in a colander, and refresh them under cold water. In another bowl toss the beans with 3 tablespoons of the remaining dressing.

On a rack set 4 to 6 inches over glowing coals grill the tuna for 2½ minutes on each side, the shrimp for 4 minutes on each side, and the scallops and the squash for 6 minutes on each side, transferring the seafood and the squash as it is cooked to a platter. Line 6 plates with the lettuce, on each plate arrange 2 scallops, halved horizontally, 3 shrimp halves, and 1 piece of tuna, sliced diagonally, and divide the squash, beans, roasted pepper, tomatoes, and olives among the plates. Drizzle the remaining dressing over the salads or serve it separately. Serves 6.

PHOTO ON PAGE 50

To Roast Peppers

Using a long-handled fork char the peppers over an open flame, turning them, for 2 to 3 minutes, or until the skins are blackened. (Or broil the peppers on the rack of a broiler pan under a preheated broiler about 2 inches from the heat, turning them every 5 minutes, for 15 to

25 minutes, or until the skins are blistered and charred.) Transfer the peppers to a bowl and let them steam, covered, until they are cool enough to handle. Keeping the peppers whole, peel them starting at the blossom end, cut off the tops, and discard the seeds and ribs. (Wear rubber gloves when handling chilies.)

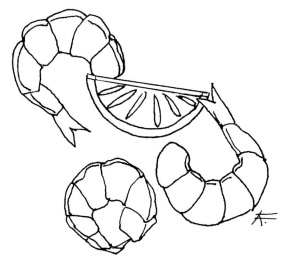

Stir-Fried Shrimp, Snow Pea, and Walnut Salad

1 tablespoon water
1 tablespoon plus 1 teaspoon white-wine
  vinegar
1 teaspoon soy sauce
½ teaspoon Oriental sesame oil
a pinch of sugar
12 medium shrimp (about ½ pound), shelled
1 garlic clove, minced and mashed to a paste
  with ½ teaspoon salt
2 tablespoons olive oil
3 tablespoons coarsely chopped walnuts
¼ pound snow peas, trimmed
1 large Belgian endive
3 cups watercress sprigs, coarse stems discarded

In a small bowl stir together the water, 1 tablespoon of the vinegar, the soy sauce, the sesame oil, the sugar, and a pinch of salt. In a bowl toss the shrimp with the garlic paste and 1 teaspoon of the olive oil and let the shrimp marinate for 10 minutes. In a non-stick skillet heat 2 teaspoons of the remaining olive oil over moder-

ately high heat until it is hot but not smoking and in it sauté the walnuts, stirring, for 30 seconds. Add the snow peas, sauté the mixture, stirring, for 45 seconds, or until the snow peas are crisp-tender, and transfer it to a bowl. In the skillet sauté the shrimp for 1 minute on each side, add the soy sauce mixture, and simmer the shrimp, covered, for 1 minute, or until they are cooked through. Add the shrimp mixture to the snow pea mixture. In a large bowl toss the endive, sliced thin crosswise, and the watercress with the remaining 1 tablespoon olive oil, the remaining 1 teaspoon vinegar, and salt and pepper to taste, divide the greens between 2 dinner plates, and top them with the shrimp mixture. Serves 2.

SALADS WITH GREENS

Tomato, Arugula, and Ricotta Salata Salad
For the dressing
1 garlic clove, minced and mashed to a paste
  with ¼ teaspoon salt
1 tablespoon balsamic vinegar
1 tablespoon red-wine vinegar
¼ cup plus 2 tablespoons olive oil

3 bunches of *arugula*, coarse stems discarded
  and the leaves washed well and spun dry
6 small tomatoes (about 1½ pounds), cut
  crosswise into ¼-inch slices
¼ pound *ricotta salata* (available at specialty
  foods shops) or Feta, crumbled
  (about 1 cup)
1 tablespoon finely shredded fresh orégano
  leaves

Make the dressing: In a blender blend together the garlic paste, the vinegars, and salt and pepper to taste, with the motor running add the oil in a stream, and blend the dressing until it is emulsified.
Divide the *arugula* among 6 salad plates and arrange one sixth of the tomato slices on each plate. Divide the *ricotta salata* and the orégano among the plates. Drizzle each salad with about 1½ tablespoons of the dressing. Serves 6.

PHOTO ON PAGE 58

Boston Lettuce, Orange, and Onion Salad with Citrus Chili Vinaigrette

3 tablespoons fresh orange juice
1 teaspoon fresh lemon juice
⅓ cup olive oil
2 heads of Boston lettuce, separated into leaves, rinsed, and spun dry
1 red onion, cut into thin rounds, soaked in ice and cold water for 1 hour, and patted dry
4 navel oranges, rind and pith cut away with a serrated knife and the flesh cut crosswise into 4 rounds
chili powder to taste

In a small bowl whisk together the juices and salt and pepper to taste, add the oil in a stream, whisking, and whisk the vinaigrette until it is emulsified. On each of 8 chilled salad plates arrange some of the lettuce leaves, some of the onion slices, and 2 orange slices, drizzle the vinaigrette over the salads, and sprinkle the salads with the chili powder. Serves 8.

Chicory and Carrot Salad

2 teaspoons Sherry vinegar (available at specialty foods shops and some supermarkets)
1 teaspoon Dijon-style mustard
¼ teaspoon sugar
1 teaspoon water
3 tablespoons olive oil
1 bunch of chicory, rinsed, spun dry, and torn into pieces (about 4 cups packed)
½ cup coarsely grated carrot

·In a bowl whisk together the vinegar, the mustard, the sugar, the water, and salt and pepper to taste, add the oil in a stream, whisking, and whisk the dressing until it is emulsified. Add the chicory and the carrot and toss the salad well. Serves 4.

Red and Green Endive and Walnut Salad

1½ teaspoons Dijon-style mustard
½ teaspoon sugar
2 tablespoons minced shallot
2 tablespoons red-wine vinegar
¼ cup walnut oil
¼ cup vegetable oil

8 green Belgian endives, trimmed
8 red endives (also known as Belles Rouges, available at some supermarkets and specialty produce markets or by mail from California Vegetable Specialties, P.O. Box 916, Dixon, CA 95620, Tel. or fax 707-447-3310), trimmed
1 cup walnut pieces

In a small bowl whisk together the mustard, the sugar, the shallot, the vinegar, and salt to taste, add the oils in a stream, whisking, and whisk the dressing until it is emulsified. Line a large salad bowl with some of the endive leaves, cut the remaining endives crosswise into ½-inch slices, and add them to the bowl with the walnuts. Just before serving, drizzle the salad with the dressing and toss it to combine it well. Serves 8.

PHOTO ON PAGES 82 AND 83

Frisée Salad with Goat Cheese Croques-Monsieurs

2 tablespoons minced shallot
1 teaspoon Dijon-style mustard
3 tablespoons red-wine vinegar
⅓ cup olive oil
For the goat cheese croques-monsieurs
3½ ounces (½ cup) soft mild goat cheese such as Montrachet, at room temperature
4 tablespoons olive oil
eight ⅓-inch-thick slices of French bread, cut on the diagonal so that each slice is about 3 inches long

1 pound *frisée* (French curly chicory, available at specialty produce markets), rinsed, spun dry, and torn into bite-size pieces (about 8 cups)

In a salad bowl whisk together the shallot, the mustard, the vinegar, and salt to taste and let the mixture stand for 10 minutes. Add the oil in a stream, whisking, and whisk the dressing until it is emulsified.

Make the goat cheese *croques-monsieurs*: In a small bowl cream together the goat cheese and 1 tablespoon of the oil. Spread 4 slices of the bread with the mixture and top them with the remaining slices, pressing the sandwiches lightly. In a small non-stick skillet heat 1½ tablespoons of the remaining oil over moderately high heat until it is hot but not smoking, in it sauté 2 of the sandwiches for 1½ minutes on each side, or until they are golden, and transfer them to a plate. Sauté the remaining 2 sandwiches in the remaining 1½ tablespoons oil in the same manner.

Cut the *croques-monsieurs* into 1-inch squares. Add the *frisée* to the salad bowl, toss it to coat it with the dressing, and add the *croque-monsieur* squares, tossing the salad gently. Serves 6.

Mesclun Salad

8 cups (about ½ pound) *mesclun* (mixed baby greens), rinsed and spun dry
2½ tablespoons extra-virgin olive oil, or to taste
2 teaspoons Sherry vinegar (available at specialty foods shops and some supermarkets) or other wine vinegar

In a salad bowl toss the *mesclun* well with the oil and drizzle it with the vinegar. Season the salad with salt and pepper and toss it well. Serves 6.

Mixed Green Salad

2 tablespoons white-wine vinegar
¼ cup extra-virgin olive oil
1 head of *frisée* (French curly chicory, available at specialty produce markets), rinsed, spun dry, and torn into pieces
1 bunch of *arugula*, coarse stems discarded and the leaves rinsed, spun dry, and torn into pieces
2 shallots, halved lengthwise and sliced thin

In a small bowl whisk together the vinegar and salt and pepper to taste, add the oil in a stream, whisking, and whisk the dressing until it is emulsified. In a large bowl toss together the *frisée*, the *arugula*, and the shallots, drizzle the dressing over the salad, and toss the salad well. Serves 8.

PHOTO ON PAGES 16 AND 17

Wilted Mustard Greens Salad with Bacon

½ pound mustard greens, stems and center ribs cut out and discarded and the leaves cut crosswise into ½-inch-wide strips

3 tablespoons olive oil
1½ teaspoons mustard seeds
1 small onion, chopped fine
1½ tablespoons balsamic vinegar
2 slices of bacon, cooked until crisp and crumbled

Wash the mustard greens, spin them dry, and put them in a large heatproof bowl. In a skillet heat the oil with the mustard seeds, covered partially to keep the seeds from popping out, over moderate heat for 2 to 4 minutes, or until the popping subsides, add the onion, and cook the mixture, stirring, until the onion is softened. Remove the skillet from the heat, stir in the vinegar, and bring the mixture to a boil. Drizzle the dressing immediately over the mustard greens and toss the salad. Add the bacon and salt and pepper to taste and toss the salad well. Serves 2.

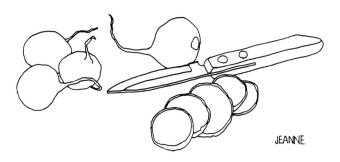
JEANNE

Red-Leaf Lettuce, Radish, and Pine Nut Salad

5 teaspoons red-wine vinegar
6 tablespoons olive oil
8 cups shredded red-leaf lettuce plus 18 whole leaves for lining the plates (about 2 heads total, rinsed and spun dry)
1 cup julienne strips of radish
⅓ cup pine nuts, toasted lightly

In a large bowl whisk together the vinegar and salt and pepper to taste, add the oil, whisking, and whisk the dressing until it is emulsified. Add the shredded lettuce, the radish, and the pine nuts and toss the salad well. Line each of 6 plates with 3 whole lettuce leaves and divide the salad among the plates. Serves 6.

Stilton and Pear Salad

2 tablespoons white-wine vinegar
½ teaspoon Dijon-style mustard
¼ cup olive oil
6 cups red- or green-leaf lettuce (preferably
    young lettuce, available at specialty
    produce markets and some supermarkets),
    or a combination of both, rinsed and
    spun dry
1 large red Bartlett pear
¼ pound Stilton, crumbled (about 1 cup)
½ cup pecans, toasted lightly, cooled,
    and chopped

In a small bowl whisk together the vinegar, the mustard, and salt and pepper to taste, add the oil in a stream, whisking, and whisk the dressing until it is emulsified. In a bowl toss the lettuce with half the dressing and divide the salad among 4 plates. Halve and core the pear and cut it lengthwise into ¼-inch-thick slices. Arrange one-fourth of the pear slices decoratively on each plate, divide the Stilton and the pecans among the salads, and drizzle the remaining dressing on top. Serves 4.

Green Salad with Oranges and Black Olives

1 navel orange, rind and pith cut away with
    a serrated knife and the flesh sectioned
¼ red onion, sliced thin
6 oil-cured black olives, pitted and cut
    into slivers
1½ tablespoons olive oil (preferably
    extra-virgin)
1 teaspoon Sherry vinegar or
    cider vinegar
a pinch of ground cumin
2 cups shredded romaine, washed well
    and spun dry

In a bowl stir together the orange sections, the onion, the olives, the oil, the vinegar, the cumin, and salt and pepper to taste, add the romaine, and toss the salad well. Serves 2.

Spinach and Endive Salad with Blue Cheese Dressing

2 tablespoons blue cheese
1 tablespoon red-wine vinegar, or to taste
3 tablespoons olive oil

a dash of Worcestershire sauce
4 cups spinach leaves, washed well and
    spun dry
1 Belgian endive, sliced thin crosswise

In a bowl with a fork mash the blue cheese and whisk in the vinegar, the oil, the Worcestershire sauce, and salt and pepper to taste, whisking until the dressing is emulsified. In a large bowl toss the spinach and the endive with the dressing until the salad is combined well. Serves 2.

Watercress, Bell Pepper, and Daikon Radish Salad

1½ tablespoons white-wine vinegar
¼ cup olive oil
3 bunches of watercress, coarse stems
    discarded, rinsed well and spun dry
    (about 12 cups)
2 red bell peppers, cut into julienne strips
½ pound *daikon* radish (available at specialty
    produce markets and some supermarkets),
    peeled and cut into julienne strips

In a large bowl whisk together the vinegar and salt and pepper to taste, add the oil in a stream, whisking, and whisk the dressing until it is emulsified. Add the watercress, the bell peppers, and the *daikon* and toss the salad well. Serves 8.

VEGETABLE SALADS

Green Bean, Red Onion, and Roast Potato Salad
with Rosemary Vinaigrette

3 pounds red boiling potatoes
⅔ cup olive oil
1 garlic clove
¼ cup red-wine vinegar
1 tablespoon fresh rosemary leaves or
    1 teaspoon dried, crumbled, plus rosemary
    sprigs for garnish
1 red onion, halved lengthwise and sliced thin
    lengthwise
2 pounds green beans, trimmed and cut into
    1-inch pieces

24 Kalamata or Niçoise olives, pitted and
   halved

Halve the potatoes, unpeeled, and cut them into
1-inch wedges. In a large roasting pan heat ⅓ cup of the
oil in the middle of a preheated 425° F. oven for 5 minutes, add the potatoes, tossing them to coat them with
the oil, and roast them, stirring them every 10 minutes,
for 30 minutes, or until they are tender. Let the potatoes
cool in the pan. In a blender purée the garlic, the vinegar, the rosemary leaves, and salt to taste, with the motor running add the remaining ⅓ cup oil in a stream, and
blend the dressing until it is emulsified. In a small bowl
of ice and cold water let the onion soak for 5 minutes,
drain it well, and pat it dry. In a kettle of boiling salted
water boil the green beans for 5 minutes, or until they
are crisp-tender, and drain them in a colander. Refresh
the beans under cold water and pat them dry. In a very
large bowl combine the potatoes, the onion, the green
beans, and the olives, add the dressing, and toss the salad gently. Serve the salad, garnished with the rosemary
sprigs, at room temperature. Serves 8 to 10.

Warm Green Bean and Walnut Salad

2 tablespoons walnuts, toasted lightly and
   chopped fine
2 teaspoons white-wine vinegar
2 tablespoons olive oil
¾ pound green beans, trimmed and cut into
   ¾-inch pieces

In a blender or mini-processor purée 1 tablespoon of
the walnuts with the vinegar, the oil, and salt and pepper
to taste. In a steamer set over boiling water steam the
beans, covered, for 5 to 8 minutes, or until they are
crisp-tender, transfer them to a bowl, and toss them
with the dressing and the remaining chopped walnuts.
Serves 2.

Three-Bean Salad with Coriander Chili Dressing

1 pound dried black beans, picked over
1 pound dried white beans, picked over
2 garlic cloves
2 bottled pickled *jalapeño* chilies, seeded if
   desired (wear rubber gloves)
2 cups loosely packed fresh coriander, rinsed
   and spun dry
⅓ cup plus 2 tablespoons fresh lemon juice
1 cup vegetable oil
1 pound green beans, trimmed and cut into
   1-inch pieces

*Note: It is important to soak and cook the black beans
and the white beans separately because one bean variety can become mushy in the few minutes it takes another to become tender.*

In a large saucepan combine the black beans with triple their volume of cold water and in another large
saucepan combine the white beans with the same pro-
portion of cold water. Bring the water to a boil and simmer the beans, uncovered, for 2 minutes. Remove the
pans from the heat and let the beans soak for 1 hour.
Drain each pan of beans separately in a colander. In
each pan put 2½ quarts water and stir the black beans
into the water in one pan, the white beans into the water
in the other. Cook the beans at a bare simmer, testing for
doneness every 5 minutes, for 15 to 40 minutes, or until
they are just tender but still hold their shape. Drain the
beans and let them cool to warm.
   In a blender purée 1 of the garlic cloves, the *jalapeños*, and 1 cup of the coriander with ⅓ cup of the lemon juice, ⅔ cup of the oil, and salt to taste, scraping
down the side of the blender, until the dressing is
smooth. In a large bowl toss the beans with the dressing
and let them marinate, covered and chilled, stirring occasionally, overnight. *The salad may be prepared up to
this point 1 day in advance and kept chilled.*
   In a saucepan of boiling salted water boil the green
beans for 5 minutes, or until they are crisp-tender, and
drain them. Refresh the beans under cold water and pat
them dry. In the blender purée the remaining garlic clove
and the remaining 1 cup coriander with the remaining
2 tablespoons lemon juice, the remaining ⅓ cup oil, and
salt to taste, scraping down the side of the blender, until
the dressing is smooth. Add the green beans and the
dressing to the bowl of dressed beans, toss the salad
well, and serve it at room temperature. Serves 10 to 12.

Minted Beet Salad

2 pounds beets, trimmed, leaving 1 inch of
   the stems intact, and scrubbed
1 tablespoon balsamic vinegar
1 tablespoon rice vinegar
¼ teaspoon sugar
2½ tablespoons olive oil
¼ cup loosely packed fresh mint leaves,
   rinsed, spun dry, and shredded fine
soft-leafed lettuce, rinsed and spun dry, for
   lining the plates

Wrap the beets together tightly in foil in 2 batches and roast them in the middle of a preheated 350° F. oven for 1½ hours, or until they are tender. *The beets may be roasted 2 days in advance and kept covered and chilled.* Unwrap the beets carefully and let them cool until they can be handled. Slip the skins off the beets, cut off the stems, and cut the beets into ¼-inch pieces. In a large bowl whisk together the vinegars, the sugar, and salt to taste, add the oil in a stream, whisking, and whisk the dressing until it is emulsified. Add the beets to the bowl with two thirds of the mint and toss the salad until it is combined well. Line 4 plates with the lettuce leaves, divide the beet mixture among them, and sprinkle each salad with some of the remaining mint. Serves 4.

Warm Brussels Sprout and Spinach Salad with Bacon

4 slices of bacon
1 pint Brussels sprouts, trimmed, steamed
   for 3 minutes, and chopped fine
   (about 1¾ cups)
1½ teaspoons caraway seeds
3 tablespoons vegetable oil
3 tablespoons white-wine vinegar
¼ teaspoon sugar, or to taste
½ pound spinach, tough stems discarded and
   the leaves washed well and spun dry
   (about 8 cups)

In a heavy skillet cook the bacon over moderate heat until it is crisp and transfer it to paper towels to drain. Heat the fat remaining in the skillet over moderately high heat until it is hot but not smoking and in it sauté the Brussels sprouts with the caraway seeds, stirring, for 1 to 2 minutes, or until the sprouts are tender and pale golden. Remove the skillet from the heat, stir in the oil, the vinegar, and the sugar, and add the spinach. Sauté

the mixture over moderately high heat, tossing it, for 1 minute, or until the spinach is wilted. Season the salad with pepper and sprinkle it with the bacon, crumbled. Serves 6.

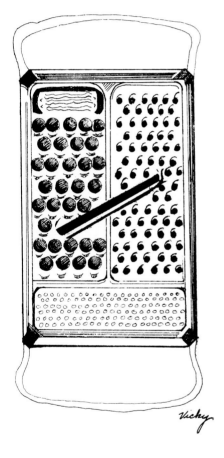

Vicky

Carrot, Apple, and Horseradish Salad

2½ cups coarsely grated carrot
2 large Granny Smith apples
½ cup sour cream
2 to 3 tablespoons finely grated peeled fresh
   horseradish or drained bottled horseradish
2 tablespoons finely chopped fresh parsley
   leaves
1 teaspoon fresh lemon juice
1 teaspoon sugar

In a bowl stir together the carrots, the apples, peeled and grated coarse, the sour cream, the horseradish to taste, the parsley, the lemon juice, the sugar, and salt and pepper to taste and chill the salad, covered, for 1 hour, or until it is cold. Serves 4 to 6.

Spicy Chick-Pea Salad

a 19-ounce can chick-peas, rinsed and
    drained well
2 tablespoons olive oil
1 garlic clove,
    minced
fresh lemon juice to taste
⅛ teaspoon crushed dried hot red pepper
    flakes, or to taste
2 tablespoons minced fresh parsley leaves

In a bowl stir together the chick-peas, the oil, the garlic, the lemon juice, the red pepper flakes, the parsley, and salt and pepper to taste and chill the salad, covered, for 30 minutes. Serves 2.

Cucumber, Radish, and Tomato Salad with Citrus Dressing

2 tablespoons fresh lemon juice
2 tablespoons fresh lime juice
1 garlic clove, minced and mashed to a paste
    with ¼ teaspoon salt
¼ cup olive oil
⅓ cup finely chopped fresh coriander,
    or to taste, plus coriander sprigs
    for garnish
2 tomatoes (about 1¼ pounds), seeded
    and chopped fine
2 cucumbers, peeled, seeded, and chopped
    fine (about 2½ cups)
¾ pound radishes, trimmed and chopped fine
6 scallions, sliced thin

In a large bowl whisk together the juices and the garlic paste, add the oil in a stream, whisking, and whisk the dressing until it is emulsified. Whisk in the chopped coriander and salt and pepper to taste. Add the tomatoes, the cucumbers, the radishes, and the scallions, toss the salad to combine it well, and garnish it with the coriander sprigs. Serves 6.

PHOTO ON PAGE 64

Kohlrabi and Apple Salad with Creamy Mustard Dressing

½ cup heavy cream
2 tablespoons fresh lemon juice
1 tablespoon coarse-grained mustard
3 tablespoons finely chopped fresh parsley
    leaves
½ teaspoon sugar
2 bunches kohlrabi (about 2 pounds), bulbs
    peeled and cut into julienne strips, stems
    discarded, and the leaves reserved for
    another use
1 Granny Smith apple

In a bowl whisk the cream until it holds soft peaks and whisk in the lemon juice, the mustard, the parsley, the sugar, and salt and pepper to taste. Stir in the kohlrabi strips and the apple, peeled, cored, and diced, and combine the salad well. Serves 8.

Roasted Vidalia Onion, Cherry Tomato, and Bacon Salad

4 Vidalia onions (about 2 pounds, available
    seasonally at specialty produce markets and
    some supermarkets), peeled
2 cups cherry tomatoes, quartered
6 slices of lean bacon, cooked until crisp and
    crumbled
⅓ cup minced fresh basil or parsley leaves
1 large garlic clove, minced and mashed
    to a paste with ¼ teaspoon salt
1 tablespoon balsamic vinegar
1 tablespoon red-wine vinegar
¼ cup olive oil

Season the onions with salt and pepper, wrap them individually in foil, and bake them in the middle of a preheated 350° F. oven for 45 minutes to 1 hour, or until they are tender. Let the onions cool in the foil and discard the foil. Chop the onions coarse, discarding the root ends, and in a bowl toss them with the tomatoes, the bacon, and the basil. In a small bowl whisk together the garlic paste, the vinegars, and salt and pepper to taste, add the oil in a stream, whisking, and whisk the dressing until it is emulsified. Pour the dressing over the salad, toss the salad well, and serve it, chilled or at room temperature, with grilled chicken or beef. Serves 6.

Collard Potato Salad with Mustard Dressing

2 pounds small red potatoes, scrubbed
1 pound collards, coarse stems discarded
    and the leaves washed well and cut into
    1-inch pieces
2 tablespoons Dijon-style mustard
2 tablespoons red-wine vinegar
⅓ cup olive oil
6 slices of lean bacon, cooked until crisp,
    drained, and crumbled
3 tablespoons thinly sliced scallion

In a kettle combine the potatoes with enough water to cover them by 2 inches, bring the water to a boil, and simmer the potatoes for 15 to 20 minutes, or until they are tender. Transfer the potatoes with a slotted spoon to a colander, reserving the cooking liquid, and in the reserved cooking liquid boil the collards, stirring occasionally, for 10 minutes. Drain the collards in a sieve, refresh them under cold water, and squeeze them dry in a kitchen towel. In a bowl whisk together the mustard, the vinegar, and salt and pepper to taste, add the oil in a stream, whisking, and whisk the dressing until it is emulsified. Quarter the potatoes and add them to the dressing. Add the collards, pulling them apart to separate the leaves, the bacon, and the scallion and toss the salad well. Serves 6.

Horseradish Dill Potato Salad

1 pound small red potatoes
¼ cup water
2 tablespoons mayonnaise
2 tablespoons plain yogurt
1 teaspoon Dijon-style mustard
1 teaspoon balsamic vinegar
1 teaspoon drained bottled horseradish,
    or to taste
2 tablespoons minced fresh dill
1 large carrot, shredded coarse
    (about 1 cup)
¼ cup finely chopped red onion

In a microwave-safe bowl combine the potatoes, cut into 1-inch pieces, and the water and microwave the potatoes, covered with microwave-safe plastic wrap, at high power (100%) for 6 to 8 minutes, or until they are tender. Let the potatoes stand, covered, for 3 minutes, drain them, and let them cool completely. In a bowl whisk together the mayonnaise, the yogurt, the mustard, the vinegar, the horseradish, the dill, and salt and pepper to taste, add the carrot, the onion, and the potatoes, and toss the salad until it is combined well. Serves 2.

Layered Vegetable Salad with Caper and Thyme Dressing

8 cups thinly sliced Napa cabbage
    (about 1½ pounds)
4 cups thinly sliced red onions, soaked in
    cold water to cover for 10 minutes,
    drained, and patted dry
3 cups chopped yellow bell peppers
    (about 3 large)
two 10-ounce packages frozen peas, cooked
    in boiling salted water for 1 minute,
    drained, and patted dry
¾ cup plain yogurt
¾ cup mayonnaise
2 tablespoons drained bottled capers, minced
1½ teaspoons fresh thyme leaves, minced

In a large glass bowl make separate layers with the cabbage, the onions, the bell peppers, and the peas. In a bowl whisk together the yogurt, the mayonnaise, the capers, the thyme, and salt and pepper to taste, pour the dressing over the peas, spreading it evenly, and chill the salad, covered, for 6 hours. *The salad may be made 1 day in advance and kept covered and chilled.* Combine the salad well and serve it with additional salt and pepper to taste. Serves 8.

PHOTO ON PAGES 76 AND 77

SLAWS

Carrot and Bell Pepper Slaw

2 tablespoons plain yogurt
2 tablespoons mayonnaise
1 teaspoon Dijon-style mustard
1 teaspoon fresh lemon juice
1 cup coarsely grated carrot
1 red bell pepper, cut into 1-inch julienne strips
1 scallion, chopped fine

In a bowl whisk together the yogurt, the mayonnaise, the mustard, and the lemon juice, add the carrot, the bell pepper, and the scallion, and toss the slaw until it is combined well. Season the slaw with salt and pepper. Serves 2.

Waldorf Coleslaw

a 2½-pound white cabbage, cored and
    chopped (about 12 cups)
4 Granny Smith apples, cut into julienne
    strips, plus apple slices for garnish
4 ribs of celery, sliced thin diagonally
1½ cups walnuts
½ cup mayonnaise
½ cup plain yogurt
1 tablespoon Dijon-style mustard
3 tablespoons sugar
¼ cup vegetable oil
¾ teaspoon salt, or to taste
¼ cup red-wine vinegar

In a very large bowl stir together the cabbage, the apple strips, the celery, and the walnuts. In a small bowl whisk together the mayonnaise, the yogurt, the mustard, the sugar, the oil, the salt, and the vinegar until the dressing is smooth, pour the dressing over the cabbage mixture, and toss the slaw well. Chill the slaw, covered, for 2 hours. *The slaw may be made 1 day in advance and kept covered and chilled.* Serve the slaw topped with the apple slices. Serves 10 to 12.

GRAIN SALADS

*Barley, Corn, and Cherry Tomato Salad
with Basil Dressing*

2 cups medium barley
1 teaspoon salt
⅓ cup white-wine vinegar
1½ cups packed fresh basil leaves, rinsed and
    spun dry
⅔ cup vegetable oil
3 cups cooked fresh corn kernels
    (cut from about 6 ears)
2 pints cherry tomatoes, halved or, if large,
    quartered

In a kettle bring 10 cups water to a boil, stir in the barley and the salt, and simmer the barley, covered, for 40 minutes, or until it is tender. Drain the barley in a colander, rinse it under cold water, and drain it well. In a blender blend the vinegar, the basil, the oil, and salt to taste until the dressing is emulsified. In a very large bowl toss the barley with the dressing and the corn and stir in the tomatoes gently. Chill the salad, covered, for 1 hour. *The salad may be made 1 day in advance and kept covered and chilled.* Serves 10 to 12.

Couscous Tabbouleh

1 cup chicken broth
1 cup water
½ cup fresh lemon juice
⅓ cup plus 2 tablespoons olive oil
1½ cups couscous
1 seedless cucumber, cut into ¼-inch pieces,
　　plus cucumber slices for garnish
8 plum tomatoes, seeded and cut into ¼-inch
　　dice, plus tomato slices for garnish
¾ cup finely chopped scallion
2 cups loosely packed fresh parsley leaves,
　　minced
1 cup loosely packed fresh mint leaves,
　　minced, plus mint sprigs for garnish

In a saucepan combine the broth, the water, ¼ cup of the lemon juice, and 2 tablespoons of the oil, bring the mixture to a boil, and stir in the couscous. Cover the pan, remove it from the heat, and let the couscous stand for 5 minutes. Fluff the couscous with a fork and let it cool in the pan. In a very large bowl stir together the cucumber pieces, the tomato dice, the scallion, the remaining ⅓ cup oil, the remaining ¼ cup lemon juice, and salt to taste and let the mixture stand for 15 minutes. Add the couscous, the parsley, and the mint leaves, stir the salad well, and chill it, covered, for 1 hour. *The salad may be made 2 days in advance and kept covered and chilled.* Serve the salad garnished with the mint sprigs and the cucumber and tomato slices. Serves 8 to 10.

Arborio Rice Salad with Cucumber and Mint

1 pound Arborio rice (available at specialty
　　foods shops and some supermarkets)
3 tablespoons white-wine vinegar
1 tablespoon fresh lemon juice
½ cup olive oil
1 pound cucumber, peeled, seeded, and
　　chopped
¾ cup fresh mint leaves,
　　minced
radishes as an accompaniment if desired

To a kettle of boiling salted water add the rice, stirring, return the water to a boil, stirring, and boil the rice, stirring occasionally, for 10 to 12 minutes, or until it is tender. Drain the rice in a large colander or sieve, rinse it under cold water until it is cooled, and drain it well.

Transfer the rice to a large bowl. *The rice may be cooked 3 days in advance and kept covered and chilled.*

In a bowl whisk together the vinegar, the lemon juice, and salt and pepper to taste, add the oil in a stream, whisking, and whisk the dressing until it is emulsified. To the rice add the dressing, the cucumber, and the mint, toss the salad well, and serve it with the radishes. *The salad may be made several hours in advance and kept covered and chilled.* Serves 6.

PHOTO ON PAGES 38 AND 39

Warm Hoppin' John and Brown Rice Salad

1 pound dried black-eyed peas,
　　picked over
1 large onion, stuck with 3 cloves
½ bay leaf
8 cups cold water
½ pound ham steak, trimmed and cut into
　　¼-inch dice
3 tablespoons white-wine vinegar
¾ teaspoon salt
2 tablespoons minced bottled pickled *jalapeño*
　　peppers (wear rubber gloves)
⅓ cup vegetable oil
2 tablespoons fresh lemon juice
2 cups chopped scallion
1 cup minced celery
1½ cups brown rice

In a kettle combine the black-eyed peas with enough cold water to cover them by 2 inches, bring the water to a boil, and boil the black-eyed peas for 2 minutes. Remove the kettle from the heat and let the black-eyed peas soak for 1 hour. Drain the black-eyed peas in a colander, rinse them, and in the kettle combine them with the onion, the bay leaf, and the water. Bring the water to a boil and simmer the mixture, stirring occasionally, for 15 minutes. Add the ham and simmer the mixture for 10 minutes, or until the black-eyed peas are just tender. Drain the black-eyed pea mixture in a colander set over a large saucepan, reserving the cooking liquid, remove the onion, and discard the bay leaf and the cloves. Keep the black-eyed pea mixture warm, covered, and chop the onion. In a bowl whisk together the vinegar, the salt, and the *jalapeño* peppers, add the oil in a stream, whisking, and whisk the dressing until it is emulsified. Add the warm black-eyed pea mixture to the dressing and stir it to coat it with the dressing. Stir in the lemon juice, the scallion, the celery, and salt and pepper to taste and let the black-eyed pea mixture marinate, stirring occasionally. Bring the reserved black-eyed pea cooking liquid to a boil with a pinch of salt, stir in the rice, and bring the liquid to a boil, stirring. Simmer the rice, covered, for 35 to 40 minutes, or until it is tender, and drain it. Divide the rice among 8 plates and spoon the black-eyed pea mixture over it. Serves 8.

Curried Rice Salad with Melon, Raisins, and Peanuts

2 cups long-grain rice
1½ teaspoons salt
2½ teaspoons curry powder
3 tablespoons white-wine vinegar
⅓ cup vegetable oil
¾ cup golden raisins
1 cantaloupe, seeded and cut into
  ½-inch cubes
1 cup plain yogurt
¼ cup Major Grey's chutney
⅓ cup unsalted roasted peanuts

In a large saucepan bring 4 quarts water to a boil, stir in the rice and the salt, stirring until the water returns to a boil, and boil the rice for 10 minutes. Drain the rice in a large sieve and rinse it. Set the sieve over a large saucepan of simmering water and steam the rice, covered with a folded kitchen towel and the lid, for 15 minutes, or until it is fluffy and dry. Transfer the rice to a very large bowl and let it cool to lukewarm.

In a small bowl whisk together 1½ teaspoons of the curry powder, the vinegar, the oil, and salt to taste, add the vinaigrette to the rice, and toss the mixture well. Stir in the raisins and the cantaloupe. In a blender blend the yogurt, the chutney, and the remaining 1 teaspoon curry powder until the dressing is smooth, pour the dressing over the rice mixture, and toss the salad well. Chill the salad, covered, for 1 hour. *The salad may be made 2 days in advance and kept covered and chilled.* Serve the salad sprinkled with the peanuts. Serves 10 to 12.

Rice Salad with Lemon and Pine Nuts

1 cup water
½ cup long-grain rice
1 tablespoon fresh lemon juice
1 teaspoon white-wine vinegar
½ teaspoon freshly grated lemon zest
1 tablespoon olive oil
2 tablespoons pine nuts, toasted lightly
2 tablespoons finely chopped scallion greens

In a small heavy saucepan bring the water to a boil, add the rice with salt to taste, and cook it, covered, over low heat for 15 minutes, or until the water is absorbed and the rice is tender. In a bowl whisk together the lemon juice, the vinegar, the zest, the oil, and salt and pepper to taste, whisking until the vinaigrette is emulsified. Fluff the rice with a fork, add it with the pine nuts and the scallion greens to the vinaigrette, and combine the salad well. Serves 2.

Wild Rice and Spiced Shrimp Salad

2 cups wild rice, rinsed and drained
5⅓ cups water
5 tablespoons white-wine vinegar
½ cup vegetable oil
1 bay leaf
1 teaspoon black peppercorns
3 cloves
1 teaspoon coriander seeds
2 teaspoons salt
1½ pounds medium shrimp
   (about 32), shelled
   and deveined
1 small red bell pepper, chopped fine
1 small yellow bell pepper,
   chopped fine
½ cup minced fresh parsley leaves plus
   parsley sprigs for garnish

In a large heavy saucepan combine the wild rice, the water, and salt to taste and simmer the wild rice, covered, for 45 to 50 minutes, or until it is tender and all the water is absorbed. In a bowl whisk together 1 tablespoon of the vinegar and 2 tablespoons of the oil, fluff the wild rice with a fork, and toss it with the vinegar mixture. Let the wild rice mixture cool. *The wild rice mixture may be made 2 days in advance and kept covered and chilled.*

In a large saucepan combine the bay leaf, the peppercorns, the cloves, the coriander seeds, and the salt with enough water to cover the shrimp by 1 inch, bring the mixture to a boil, and boil it for 5 minutes. Stir in the shrimp, cook them over high heat, stirring occasionally, for 3 minutes, or until they are just cooked through, and drain the shrimp mixture well. In a bowl whisk together the remaining 4 tablespoons vinegar and salt and pepper to taste, add the remaining 6 tablespoons oil in a stream, whisking, and whisk the dressing until it is emulsified. Stir in the shrimp mixture and let it marinate, covered and chilled, for at least 6 hours or overnight.

Reserve 10 shrimp for garnish, cut the remaining shrimp into ½-inch pieces, and strain the dressing through a sieve into a small bowl, discarding the spices. In a bowl stir together the cut shrimp, the wild rice mixture, the bell peppers, the minced parsley, and ⅓ cup of the dressing, divide the salad among 10 plates, and garnish each serving with 1 of the reserved shrimp and a parsley sprig. Serves 10.

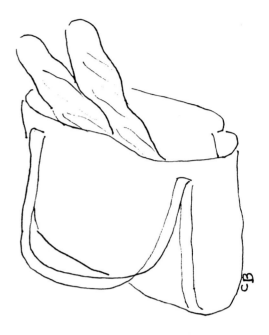

PASTA SALADS

Antipasto Pasta Salad

1 pound *rotini* or *fusilli*
   (corkscrew-shaped pastas)
2 garlic cloves
1 tablespoon Dijon-style mustard
⅓ cup red-wine vinegar
2 tablespoons balsamic vinegar
1 tablespoon water
½ cup vegetable oil
1 ounce (½ cup) sun-dried tomatoes (not
   packed in oil), soaked in hot water for
   5 minutes and drained well
½ pound smoked mozzarella, cut into
   ½-inch cubes
a 1-pound can garbanzo beans, drained
   and rinsed
3½ ounces sliced hard salami, cut into
   julienne strips
10 to 20 bottled small *peperoncini*
   (pickled Tuscan peppers)
½ teaspoon dried hot red pepper flakes
1 cup loosely packed fresh flat-leafed parsley
   leaves, minced

In a kettle of boiling salted water cook the *rotini* until it is tender and drain it. Refresh the pasta under cold water and drain it well. In a blender blend the garlic, the mustard, the vinegars, the water, the oil, and salt to taste until the dressing is emulsified. In a very large bowl toss the pasta well with the dressing and stir in the sun-dried tomatoes, the mozzarella, the garbanzos, the salami, the Tuscan peppers, the red pepper flakes, and the parsley. Chill the salad, covered, for 1 hour. *The salad may be made 2 days in advance and kept covered and chilled.* Serves 8 to 10.

Herbed Penne and Cucumber Salad

½ cup loosely packed fresh mint leaves, rinsed and spun dry
1 cup loosely packed fresh fine dill sprigs, rinsed and spun dry
1 cup loosely packed fresh parsley leaves (preferably flat-leafed), rinsed and spun dry
1 cup coarsely chopped scallion
1 cup mayonnaise
1 cup buttermilk
1 pound small *penne rigata* or other macaroni
1 seedless cucumber, halved lengthwise and cut into ¼-inch-thick slices

In a blender purée the mint, the dill, the parsley, and the scallion with the mayonnaise, the buttermilk, and salt to taste until the dressing is smooth. In a kettle of boiling salted water cook the *penne* until it is tender and drain it in a colander. Refresh the pasta under cold water and drain it well. In a very large bowl toss the pasta well with the dressing and the cucumber and chill the salad, covered, for 1 hour. *The salad may be made 1 day in advance and kept covered and chilled.* Serves 8 to 10.

SAUCES

SAVORY SAUCES

Jellied Apple Cranberry Sauce

a 12-ounce bag of cranberries, picked over
2 large Granny Smith apples (about 1 pound)
1 cup dry white wine
1½ cups sugar
mint sprigs for garnish

In a large saucepan combine the cranberries, the apples, chopped coarse (not peeled or cored), the wine, and the sugar, bring the mixture to a boil, stirring, and simmer it, covered, stirring occasionally, for 15 minutes. Simmer the mixture, uncovered, stirring occasionally, for 20 to 25 minutes more, or until it is very thick and reduced to about 3 cups. Force the mixture through a food mill fitted with the fine disk into a bowl, spoon it into an oiled 3- to 4-cup decorative mold, and chill it, covered, overnight. Run a thin knife around the edge of the mold and dip the mold into warm water for 10 seconds. Invert the mold onto a serving plate and garnish the cranberry sauce with the mint sprigs. Serves 8.

PHOTO ON PAGE 74

Lemon-Pepper Dill Sauce

1 cup mayonnaise
1 teaspoon freshly grated lemon zest
2 tablespoons fresh lemon juice
1 tablespoon minced fresh dill
½ teaspoon coarsely ground black pepper

In a bowl stir together the mayonnaise, the zest, the lemon juice, the dill, and the pepper. Serve the sauce with cooked asparagus or other vegetables or as a dip with *crudités*. Makes about 1 cup.

Jalapeño Garlic Sauce

1 cup mayonnaise
3 whole pickled *jalapeño* chilies, stems
    discarded, plus ½ *jalapeño*
    for garnish
2 tablespoons tomato paste
1 garlic clove, chopped
1 teaspoon red-wine vinegar
½ teaspoon Worcestershire sauce

In a blender blend together the mayonnaise, the whole *jalapeños*, the tomato paste, the garlic, the vinegar, and the Worcestershire sauce until the mixture is smooth, transfer the sauce to a bowl, and garnish it with the *jalapeño* half. Serve the sauce with meat or chicken. Makes about 1¼ cups.

Creamy Apple Horseradish Sauce

1 cup mayonnaise
¾ cup applesauce
3 tablespoons horseradish
1 teaspoon balsamic vinegar

In a bowl stir together the mayonnaise, the applesauce, the horseradish, the vinegar, and pepper to taste. Serve the sauce with roast pork. Makes about 2 cups.

Caesar Mayonnaise Dressing

2 small garlic cloves, minced and mashed to
 a paste with ¼ teaspoon salt
1 teaspoon anchovy paste
2 tablespoons fresh lemon juice
1 teaspoon Dijon-style mustard
1 teaspoon Worcestershire sauce
1 cup mayonnaise
½ cup freshly grated Parmesan

In a bowl whisk together the garlic paste, the anchovy paste, the lemon juice, the mustard, and the Worcestershire sauce, add the mayonnaise, the Parmesan, and pepper to taste, and whisk the dressing until it is combined well. Toss the dressing with salad greens or serve it as a dip with *crudités*. Makes about 1⅓ cups.

Curry Mayonnaise

1 cup mayonnaise
2 teaspoons curry powder
1 tablespoon fresh lime juice
⅛ teaspoon cayenne
paprika for garnish

In a bowl stir together the mayonnaise, the curry powder, the lime juice, and the cayenne. Chill the mayonnaise, covered, for 1 hour and garnish it with the paprika. Serve the mayonnaise with chicken or vegetables. Makes about 1 cup.

Gribiche Sauce
(Egg, Pickle, and Caper Mayonnaise)

½ cup mayonnaise
½ cup plain yogurt
3 tablespoons finely chopped dill pickle
3 tablespoons minced shallot
3 tablespoons minced fresh parsley leaves
2 tablespoons chopped drained bottled capers
1 teaspoon minced fresh thyme leaves plus
 a thyme sprig for garnish
1 hard-boiled large egg, chopped fine

In a bowl stir together the mayonnaise, the yogurt, the pickle, the shallot, the parsley, the capers, the minced thyme, the egg, and pepper to taste and garnish the sauce with the thyme sprig. Serve the sauce with fish or shellfish. Makes about 1½ cups.

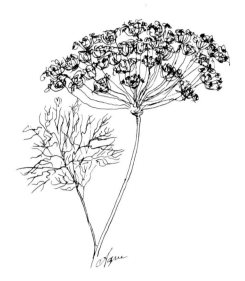

Three-Mustard Mayonnaise

1 cup mayonnaise
1½ tablespoons coarse-grained mustard
1 tablespoon English-style prepared mustard
 (not dry)
2 teaspoons Dijon-style mustard
2 teaspoons fresh lemon juice
1 teaspoon honey

In a bowl stir together the mayonnaise, the mustards, the lemon juice, the honey, and pepper to taste. Serve the mayonnaise with meat, chicken, or vegetables. Makes about 1¼ cups.

English Mint Sauce with Raspberry Vinegar

1 cup packed fresh mint leaves, rinsed and
 spun dry
2 tablespoons sugar
1½ tablespoons boiling water
4 tablespoons raspberry vinegar
 (available at specialty foods shops
 and some supermarkets)

In a food processor chop fine the mint with the sugar and transfer the mixture to a small bowl. Stir the water into the mixture, stirring until the sugar is dissolved, and stir in the vinegar. Let the sauce stand, covered, for 15 minutes or chill it, covered, overnight. Serve the sauce at room temperature with lamb. Makes about ⅓ cup.

Spinach Herb Sauce

a 10-ounce package frozen spinach, cooked,
  rinsed, and squeezed dry
1 cup mayonnaise
½ cup plain yogurt
2 teaspoons minced fresh tarragon
1 teaspoon fresh lemon juice
2 teaspoons minced fresh chives

In a blender purée the spinach with the mayonnaise, the yogurt, the tarragon, and the lemon juice until the mixture is smooth and stir in the chives. Serve the sauce with chicken. Makes about 2 cups.

CONDIMENTS

Spicy Coconut Mint Chutney

1 *serrano* or 2 *jalapeño* chilies, seeded and
  chopped coarse (wear rubber gloves)
⅔ cup sweetened flaked coconut
1 teaspoon salt, or to taste
2 teaspoons freshly grated lemon zest
3 tablespoons fresh lemon juice, or to taste
2 cups packed fresh mint leaves
2 tablespoons water
½ cup plain yogurt

In a food processor blend the chilies, the coconut, the salt, the zest, the lemon juice, the mint, the water, and the yogurt until the mixture is ground fine. The chutney keeps, covered and chilled, for 2 days. Serve the chutney with grilled or broiled chicken or fish. Makes about 1¼ cups.

Cranberry Horseradish Relish

a 12-ounce bag of cranberries,
  picked over
2 firm-ripe pears, peeled and cut into pieces
½ cup plus 2 tablespoons firmly packed
  brown sugar
4 to 6 tablespoons finely grated peeled
  fresh horseradish or drained
  bottled horseradish
2 tablespoons raspberry vinegar
  (available at specialty foods shops and
  some supermarkets)

In a food processor chop coarse the cranberries and the pears with the brown sugar, pulsing the motor. Transfer the mixture to a small bowl and stir in the horseradish to taste, the vinegar, and salt and pepper to taste. The relish keeps, covered and chilled, for 2 weeks. Serve the relish with roasted poultry or pork. Makes about 3 cups.

Pineapple and Mint Chutney

1½ cups loosely packed fresh mint leaves,
  rinsed, spun dry, and chopped fine
a 4½-pound pineapple, peeled, cored, and cut
  into ⅓-inch dice
⅓ cup minced red onion
¼ cup sugar, or to taste

In a bowl combine the mint with the pineapple, the onion, the sugar, and a pinch of salt and stir the mixture until it is combined well. Let the chutney stand, covered, for 1 hour. *The chutney may be made 1 week in advance and kept covered and chilled.* Serve the chutney with grilled meat and fish. Makes about 3 cups.

DESSERTS

CAKES

*Chocolate Buttermilk Layer Cake with
Chocolate Pudding Frosting*

For the cake
2 cups cake flour (not self-rising)
½ cup unsweetened cocoa powder
   (not Dutch process)
½ teaspoon baking soda
2 teaspoons double-acting baking powder
1 teaspoon salt
1¾ cups sugar
½ stick (¼ cup) unsalted butter, softened
3 large eggs
1 teaspoon vanilla
1 cup buttermilk
For the frosting
1 cup sugar
3½ tablespoons cornstarch
2 ounces unsweetened chocolate,
   chopped fine
1 cup boiling water
1 tablespoon orange-flavored liqueur
2 tablespoons unsalted butter, cut into pieces
   and softened

Make the cake: Line the bottoms of 3 buttered 8-inch round (2-inch-deep) cake pans with wax paper, butter the paper, and dust the pans with flour, knocking out the excess. Into a bowl sift together the flour, the cocoa powder, the baking soda, the baking powder, and the salt. In a large bowl with an electric mixer beat together the sugar and the butter until the mixture is combined well, add the eggs, 1 at a time, beating well after each addition, and beat in the vanilla. Beat in the flour mixture alternately with the buttermilk in batches, beginning and ending with the flour mixture and beating well after each addition, divide the batter among the pans, smoothing the tops, and bake the layers in the middle of a preheated 350° F. oven for 25 to 30 minutes, or until a tester comes out clean. Let the layers cool in the pans on racks for 10 minutes. Run a thin knife around the edge of each pan, invert the layers onto the racks, and let them cool completely. *The cake layers may be made 2 days in advance and kept chilled, wrapped tightly in plastic wrap.*

Make the frosting: In a heavy saucepan whisk together the sugar, the cornstarch, a pinch of salt, and the chocolate and whisk in the boiling water. Bring the mixture to a boil over moderate heat, whisking constantly, and simmer it, whisking, for 2 minutes. Whisk in the liqueur, transfer the mixture to a metal bowl, and with an electric mixer beat in the butter, beating until the butter is incorporated. Set the bowl in a larger bowl of ice and cold water and beat the frosting until it is light and holds soft peaks.

Assemble the cake: On a cake stand arrange 1 cake layer, spread the top with some of the frosting, and top the frosting with a second cake layer. Spread the second layer with some of the remaining frosting and top the frosting with the remaining layer. Spread the side and top of the cake with the remaining frosting. *The cake may be assembled 4 hours in advance and kept at room temperature.*

Bittersweet Chocolate Pecan Bourbon Cake

For the cake

6 ounces fine-quality bittersweet chocolate,
   chopped

2 ounces unsweetened chocolate,
   chopped

1 stick (½ cup) unsalted butter, softened

¾ cup sugar

6 large eggs, separated

¼ cup bourbon

1 tablespoon all-purpose flour

½ cup pecans, toasted lightly, cooled, and
   chopped fine

For the glaze

6 ounces fine-quality bittersweet chocolate,
   chopped

½ cup heavy cream

4 pecan halves

lightly sweetened whipped cream as an
   accompaniment

Make the cake: Line the bottom of a buttered 8½-inch springform pan with wax paper, butter the paper, and dust the pan with flour, shaking out the excess. In a metal bowl set over a saucepan of barely simmering water melt the chocolates, stirring until the mixture is smooth, remove the bowl from the pan, and let the chocolate cool until it is room temperature. In the bowl of an electric mixer cream together the butter and the sugar until the mixture is pale and fluffy, add the chocolate, and beat the mixture until it is combined well. Beat in the egg yolks, 1 at a time, beating well after each addition, and beat in the bourbon and the flour. In a large bowl beat the egg whites with a pinch of salt until they just hold stiff peaks, stir one third of them into the chocolate mixture to lighten it, and fold in the remaining whites and the chopped pecans gently but thoroughly. Turn the batter into the prepared pan and bake the cake in the middle of a preheated 350° F. oven for 35 to 40 minutes, or until a tester inserted 2 inches from the rim comes out clean. (The center of the cake will remain moist.) Transfer the cake to a rack and let it cool completely. Remove the cake from the pan, invert it onto the rack, and remove the wax paper carefully. *The cake may be made 1 day in advance and kept wrapped in plastic wrap at room temperature.*

Make the glaze: Put the chocolate in a small bowl, in a saucepan bring the cream to a boil, and pour it over the chocolate. Stir the mixture until the chocolate is melted and the glaze is smooth.

Invert the cake onto a rack set on wax paper, pour the glaze over it, smoothing the glaze over the top and side with a spatula, and arrange the pecan halves in the center of the cake. Let the cake stand for 2 hours, or until the glaze is set, and serve it with the whipped cream.

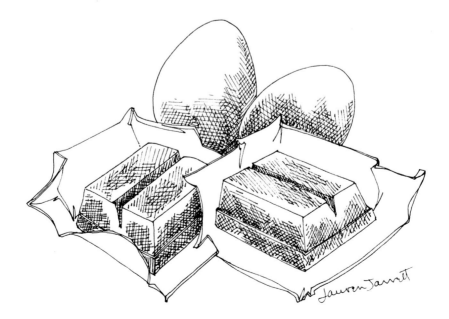

Chocolate-Frosted Devil's Food Cake with Pecan and Coconut Filling

For the cake layers
4 ounces unsweetened chocolate, chopped
½ cup water
3 cups cake flour (not self-rising)
1 teaspoon baking soda
1 teaspoon salt
2 sticks (1 cup) unsalted butter, softened
1 cup firmly packed light brown sugar
1 cup granulated sugar
3 large eggs
1½ teaspoons vanilla
1 cup buttermilk
For the filling
1 cup heavy cream
1 cup granulated sugar
1 stick (½ cup) unsalted butter
3 large egg yolks, beaten lightly
1 teaspoon vanilla
1 cup pecans, chopped fine and toasted lightly
1⅓ cups sweetened flaked coconut, toasted lightly
For the frosting
5 tablespoons unsalted butter, softened
3 tablespoons heavy cream
1 teaspoon vanilla
2 ounces unsweetened chocolate, melted and cooled
2 cups confectioners' sugar

Make the cake layers: Line the bottoms of 3 buttered 9- by 1½-inch round cake pans with rounds of wax paper, butter the paper, and dust the pans with flour, knocking out the excess. In a small metal bowl set over a saucepan of barely simmering water melt the chocolate with the water, stirring occasionally, remove the bowl from the heat, and let the mixture cool. Into a bowl sift together the flour, the baking soda, and the salt. In the large bowl of an electric mixer cream together the butter and the sugars until the mixture is light and fluffy, add the eggs, 1 at a time, beating well after each addition, and beat in the vanilla and the chocolate mixture. Beat in the flour mixture and the buttermilk alternately in batches, beginning and ending with the flour mixture, and beat the batter until it is smooth. Divide the batter among the prepared pans, smoothing the tops, rap each pan twice on a hard surface to expel any air bubbles, and bake the layers in the middle of a preheated 350° F. oven for 25 to 30 minutes, or until a tester comes out clean. Let the layers cool in the pans on racks for 10 minutes,

run a knife around the edge of each pan, and invert the layers onto the racks. Remove the wax paper and let the layers cool completely. *The cake layers may be made 2 days in advance and kept, wrapped in plastic wrap, at room temperature.*

Make the filling: In a saucepan combine the cream, the granulated sugar, and the butter and cook the mixture over moderately low heat, stirring, until the sugar is dissolved. Whisk ½ cup of the cream mixture into the yolks, whisk the yolk mixture into the remaining cream mixture, and cook the mixture over moderately low heat, whisking, for 10 minutes, or until it is thickened (do not boil). Stir in the vanilla, the pecans, and the coconut and let it cool, stirring occasionally.

Make the frosting: In a bowl beat together the butter, the cream, the vanilla, the chocolate, and the confectioners' sugar until the frosting is fluffy.

Assemble the cake: On a cake stand arrange 1 cake layer, spread the layer with ¾ cup of the filling, and top the filling with a second layer. Spread the second layer with ¾ cup of the remaining filling and top the filling with the remaining layer. Spread the top and side of the cake with the frosting and spread the remaining filling on top of the cake, letting it drip down the side of the cake. *The cake may be assembled 1 day in advance and kept covered loosely and chilled. Let the cake return to room temperature before serving.*

PHOTO ON PAGE 15

Chocolate Mint Icebox Cake

⅓ cup loosely packed fresh mint leaves, rinsed, spun dry, and chopped fine, plus, if desired, mint sprigs for garnish
3 tablespoons sugar
1 tablespoon unsweetened cocoa powder
1 cup heavy cream, chilled
a 9-ounce package chocolate wafers

In the bowl of an electric mixer combine the mint leaves, the sugar, the cocoa powder, and the cream, beat the mixture until it holds soft peaks, and spread about 1 mounded teaspoon of it on one side of the wafer. On a platter sandwich the wafers together on their sides to form a log and ice the log with the remaining cream mixture, covering it completely. Chill the cake, covered loosely with plastic wrap, for at least 6 hours or overnight. Cut the cake diagonally into ¾-inch-thick slices and serve it garnished with the mint sprigs.

Enchanted Forest Cake

butter cake layers (recipe follows)
cream-cheese frosting (recipe opposite)
ganache frosting (recipe opposite)
chocolate meringue sticks (recipe opposite)
chocolate twig candies (available at
    specialty foods shops)
about 2½ cups sweetened flaked coconut,
    toasted lightly and some of it tinted with
    green food coloring
small Chiclets
rock candy (available at specialty foods
    shops or from The Chocolate Gallery,
    New York City, Tel. 212-675-2253)
1 silver dragée candy
1 cotton swab

Arrange 1 cake layer, rounded side down, on a wooden board at least 10 by 12 inches, spread the top with some of the cream-cheese frosting, and top the frosting with another cake layer, rounded side down. Spread the top with some of the *ganache* frosting and chill the cake for 15 minutes. Arrange another cake layer, rounded side down, on top of the *ganache* frosting and spread the top with some of the remaining cream-cheese frosting. Arrange the remaining cake layer, rounded side up, on top of the cream-cheese frosting and chill the cake for 1 hour, or until the frosting is firm.

Using the photograph (page 27) as a guide, with a small sharp knife trim one side of the bottom 2 layers about ½ inch deep so that the top 2 layers form an overhang (this side becomes the front of the cake). Cut out a 1-inch-deep corner from each side of the bottom 2 layers of the front, reserving the trimmings. Score an outline of a triangle on the top 2 layers of the front and trim away the cake from the sides to define a gable. If the gable is not steep enough, attach a piece of the cake trimmings with some of the remaining *ganache* frosting to the top of the triangle to make it steeper.

Trim the top 2 layers in a sloping manner to form a rounded roof. Cut a piece of the trimmings into a 2- by ¾-inch chimney, cut out a square in a rear corner of the roof, and insert the chimney into it, attaching the chimney with some of the remaining cream-cheese frosting. Cut a piece of the trimmings into a 3- by 2-inch rectangular roof extension and attach it to the roof with some of the remaining *ganache* frosting.

Spread the bottom 2 layers with the remaining cream-cheese frosting and arrange some of the thicker meringue sticks, trimming them with a small sharp knife as necessary, to resemble wooden logs along the sides and back of the house. Arrange the thinner meringue sticks decoratively on the door, the gable, and the front of the house to resemble posts.

Spread the top 2 layers with the remaining *ganache* frosting and arrange some of the thicker meringue sticks, trimming them as necessary, on the 4 sides of the chimney. Arrange some of the chocolate twigs on either side of the gable and sprinkle the roof with the plain toasted coconut to resemble thatch.

Arrange some more of the chocolate twigs, trimmed to fit, on the front of the house to form a window, fill in the window with the Chiclets, and sprinkle the green toasted coconut over the wooden board to resemble grass. Cut small pieces of the cake trimmings to form tree trunks and insert several more chocolate twigs in the trunks to form trees. Arrange the rock candy to form a path and attach the silver dragée to the door as a doorknob. Feather the cotton at one end of the swab so that it resembles a puff of smoke and insert the swab, feathered side up, into the chimney. Arrange the remaining meringue sticks decoratively around the board.

PHOTO ON PAGE 27

Butter Cake Layers

4½ cups cake flour (not self-rising)
4 teaspoons double-acting baking powder
½ teaspoon salt
3 sticks (1½ cups) unsalted butter,
    softened
3 cups sugar
6 large eggs
2 cups milk
1 tablespoon vanilla
a 12-ounce bag mini–chocolate chips
    (about 2 cups)

Into a bowl sift together the flour, the baking powder, and the salt. In the large bowl of an electric mixer cream the butter with the sugar, beating the mixture until it is light and fluffy, add the eggs, 1 at a time, beating well after each addition, and beat the mixture until it is smooth. Add the flour mixture in batches alternately with the milk, beginning and ending with the flour mixture, and stir in the vanilla and the chocolate chips.

Spoon the batter into 4 buttered and floured 9-inch-square baking pans and bake the cakes in a preheated

350° F. oven for 30 to 35 minutes, or until a tester comes out clean. Let the cake layers cool on racks for 5 minutes, turn them out onto the racks, and let them cool completely. *The cake layers may be made 1 week in advance, wrapped tightly, and kept frozen. Defrost the cake layers before proceeding with the Enchanted Forest cake (recipe opposite).*

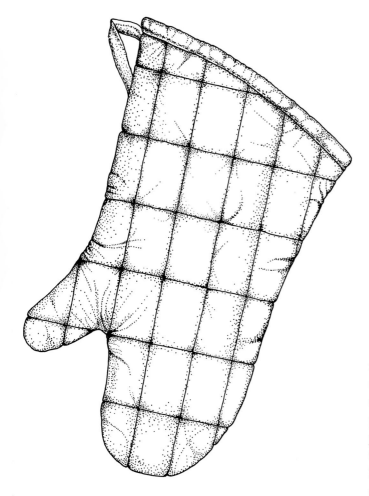

ZOE MAVRIDIS

Cream-Cheese Frosting

8 ounces cream cheese, cut into bits and
  softened
½ stick (¼ cup) unsalted butter, softened
1½ cups confectioners' sugar, sifted
2 teaspoons vanilla

In the large bowl of an electric mixer cream together the cream cheese and the butter, add the confectioners' sugar, a little at a time, beating well after each addition, and beat in the vanilla and a pinch of salt.

Ganache Frosting

1½ cups heavy cream
8 ounces semisweet chocolate chips
  (about 1½ cups)

In a small heavy saucepan combine the cream with the chocolate chips and cook the mixture over moderate heat, stirring, until the chocolate is melted and the mixture is thickened slightly. Transfer the *ganache* to a bowl and chill it until it is thickened and holds its shape on a spoon, but do not let it solidify. With an electric mixer beat the *ganache* until it holds soft peaks. (Do not overbeat the frosting or it will become granular.)

Chocolate Meringue Sticks

¼ cup unsweetened cocoa powder
1 cup confectioners' sugar
5 large egg whites
⅔ cup granulated sugar

Into a bowl sift together the cocoa powder and the confectioners' sugar. In another bowl with an electric mixer beat the egg whites until they hold soft peaks, add the granulated sugar, a little at a time, and beat the whites until they hold stiff peaks. Fold in the cocoa mixture gently but thoroughly. Onto parchment-lined baking sheets with a pastry bag fitted with a ½-inch tip pipe three fourths of the mixture into sticks the length of the sheets. With the pastry bag fitted with a ¼-inch tip, pipe the remaining mixture into sticks onto another parchment-lined baking sheet in the same manner. Bake the meringue sticks in a preheated 300° F. oven for 1¼ hours, transfer them to a rack, and let them cool completely. *The sticks may be made 3 days in advance and kept in an airtight container.*

Chocolate Raspberry Cake

For the cake layers

1¾ cups cake flour (not self-rising)
1 teaspoon baking soda
¼ teaspoon salt
½ cup Dutch-process cocoa powder
1 cup warm water
1¼ sticks (10 tablespoons) unsalted butter,
    softened
1 cup granulated sugar
1 cup firmly packed light brown sugar
2 large eggs, beaten lightly
2½ teaspoons vanilla
½ cup sour cream

For the ganache

1½ cups heavy cream
6 ounces fine-quality bittersweet chocolate,
    chopped

2 cups raspberries,
    picked over

For the glaze

12 ounces fine-quality bittersweet chocolate,
    chopped
1½ sticks (12 tablespoons) unsalted butter

fresh raspberries, mint leaves,
    and confectioners' sugar
    for decorating the cake

Make the cake layers: Line the bottoms of 2 buttered 8-inch round (2-inch deep) cake pans with wax paper, butter the paper, and dust the pans with flour, knocking out the excess. Into a bowl sift together the flour, the baking soda, and the salt. In a small bowl whisk together the cocoa powder and ½ cup of the water until the mixture is smooth. In a bowl with an electric mixer cream the butter with the sugars and beat the mixture until it is light and fluffy. Add the eggs, a little at a time, beating, and beat in the cocoa mixture and the vanilla. In a bowl whisk together the remaining ½ cup water and the sour cream. With the mixer on low speed, add alternately the flour mixture and the sour cream mixture to the cocoa mixture in batches, beginning and ending with the flour mixture and beat the batter until it is just combined. Divide the batter between the pans, smoothing the tops, and bake the cake layers in the middle of a preheated 350° F. oven for 35 to 40 minutes, or until a

tester comes out clean. Let the layers cool in the pans on racks for 5 minutes, invert them onto racks to cool completely, and peel off the wax paper.

Make the *ganache*: In a saucepan bring the cream just to a simmer, remove it from the heat, and add the chocolate. Stir the mixture until it is smooth, transfer it to a bowl, and chill it, covered, until it is cold but not set. In a bowl with an electric mixer beat the chocolate cream until it holds soft peaks (being careful not to overbeat the *ganache* as it will become grainy).

With a serrated knife halve each layer horizontally. Put 1 tablespoon of the *ganache* in the center of a 7-inch cardboard round and set one of the cake layers, bottom side down, on the cardboard. Spread the cake layer thinly with some of the *ganache* and top the *ganache* with about ⅔ cup of the raspberries. Cover the raspberries with another thin layer of the *ganache* and top the *ganache* with another cake layer, bottom side up. Continue to layer the cake in the same manner with some of the remaining *ganache* and the remaining raspberries, ending with the remaining cake layer, bottom side up. Spread the remaining *ganache* around the side of the cake, filling in between the layers, and chill the cake, covered loosely, until it is cold.

Make the glaze: In a metal bowl set over a pan of barely simmering water melt the chocolate and the butter, stirring, until the mixture is smooth. Transfer the glaze to a bowl and let it stand for 30 minutes.

Set the cake on a rack over a jelly-roll pan and pour the glaze over it, smoothing the glaze with a spatula to completely cover the cake. Chill the cake, uncovered, for 30 minutes and chill it, covered loosely with plastic wrap, until the glaze is set. Before serving, decorate the top of the cake with the raspberries and the mint leaves and sprinkle the raspberries and the mint leaves with the confectioners' sugar.

PHOTO ON FRONT JACKET

Gingerbread Roll with Lemon Cream Filling

4 large eggs, separated
1 cup sugar
a pinch of cream of tartar
¼ cup cornstarch
¼ cup all-purpose flour
1½ teaspoons ground ginger
¼ teaspoon freshly grated nutmeg
⅛ teaspoon ground cloves
½ teaspoon cinnamon

½ cup unsulfured molasses

For the filling

3 large egg yolks

½ cup sugar

¼ cup strained fresh lemon juice

1 teaspoon unflavored gelatin, softened in
1 tablespoon cold water

1½ teaspoons freshly grated lemon zest

2 tablespoons unsalted butter,
softened

½ cup heavy cream

confectioners' sugar for sifting over the cake

Line a buttered jelly-roll pan, 15½ by 10½ by 1 inches, with parchment paper, leaving a 2-inch overhang on the short sides, and butter the paper. In a large bowl with an electric mixer beat the egg yolks, add ½ cup of the sugar, and beat the mixture until it forms a ribbon when the beaters are lifted. In a bowl with cleaned beaters beat the egg whites with the cream of tartar and a pinch of salt until they hold soft peaks, add the remaining ½ cup sugar, a little at a time, and beat the meringue until it holds stiff glossy peaks. Onto a sheet of wax paper sift together the cornstarch, the flour, the ginger, the nutmeg, the cloves, and the cinnamon. Stir the cornstarch mixture and the molasses into the yolk mixture and stir the batter until it is combined well. Stir one fourth of the meringue into the batter to lighten it and fold in the remaining meringue gently but thoroughly. Turn the batter into the

prepared pan, spreading it evenly, and bake the cake in the middle of a preheated 350° F. oven for 15 to 17 minutes, or until the paper pulls away easily from the sides of the cake. Let the cake cool in the pan, covered with a slightly dampened kitchen towel. (The cake will puff up when baking but will sink as it cools.)

Make the filling: In a heavy saucepan whisk together the egg yolks, the sugar, the lemon juice, the gelatin mixture, and the zest and cook the mixture over moderate heat, whisking, for 8 minutes, or until it is thickened. Remove the pan from the heat and whisk in the butter. Transfer the mixture to a bowl set over a large bowl of ice and cold water and chill it, stirring, for 8 to 10 minutes, or until it is very thick but not set. In a bowl with an electric mixer beat the cream until it holds stiff peaks, fold it into the egg yolk mixture gently but thoroughly and chill the filling, covered, for 30 minutes.

Cover the cake with a sheet of parchment paper, invert a baking sheet over the paper, and invert the cake onto it. Peel off the top sheet of the parchment paper carefully and spread the filling over the cake, leaving a 1-inch border all around. With a long side facing you and using the parchment paper as a guide, roll up the cake jelly-roll fashion, wrap it in the paper, and chill it on the baking sheet for 30 minutes. *The cake may be made 4 hours in advance and kept covered and chilled.* Transfer the cake to a platter, remove the paper, and trim the ends on the diagonal. Sift the confectioners' sugar decoratively over the cake and serve the cake at room temperature.

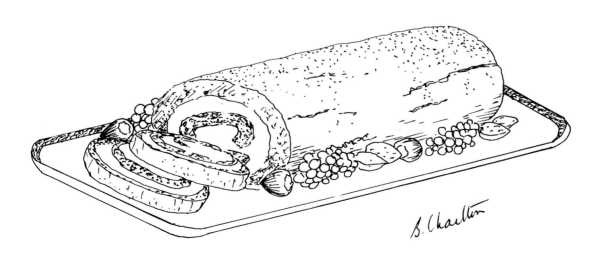

Key Lime Cheesecake

For the crust

1½ cups fine graham cracker crumbs
2 tablespoons sugar
½ stick (¼ cup) unsalted butter, melted and
  cooled

1¼ pounds (2½ eight-ounce packages) cream
  cheese, softened
¾ cup sugar
1 cup sour cream
3 tablespoons all-purpose flour
3 large eggs
¾ cup Key lime juice (available at specialty
  foods shops or by mail order from
  Adriana's Bazaar, New York City,
  Tel. 212-877-5757) or fresh lime juice
1 teaspoon vanilla
a drop of green food coloring
  if desired
whipped cream for garnish
lime slices, quartered,
  for garnish
mint sprigs for garnish

Make the crust: In a bowl stir together the crumbs and the sugar and stir the butter in well. Pat the mixture evenly onto the bottom and ½ inch up the side of a buttered 10-inch springform pan and bake the crust in the middle of a preheated 375° F. oven for 8 minutes. Transfer the pan to a rack and let the crust cool.

In a bowl with an electric mixer beat together the cream cheese and the sugar until the mixture is smooth, beat in the sour cream, the flour, the eggs, 1 at a time, beating well after each addition, the lime juice, the vanilla, and the food coloring, and beat the mixture until it is smooth. Pour the filling over the crust. Bake the cheesecake in the middle of a preheated 375° F. oven for 15 minutes, reduce the temperature to 250° F., and bake the cheesecake for 50 to 55 minutes more, or until the center is barely set. (The cheesecake will continue to set as it cools.) Let the cheesecake cool on a rack and chill it, covered, overnight.

Remove the cheesecake from the pan and transfer it to a cake stand. With a pastry bag fitted with a decorative tip pipe the whipped cream into rosettes on the cheesecake. Garnish the cheesecake with the lime slices and the mint sprigs.

PHOTO ON PAGE 57

Orange Chiffon Cake

For the cake

2¼ cups cake flour (not self-rising)
1½ cups sugar
1 tablespoon double-acting baking powder
½ teaspoon salt
½ cup vegetable oil
7 large egg yolks
¾ cup fresh orange juice
2 tablespoons freshly grated orange zest
2 teaspoons vanilla
9 large egg whites
1 teaspoon cream of tartar

For the whipped cream frosting

2 cups well-chilled heavy cream
3 tablespoons Grand Marnier or other
  orange-flavored liqueur
2 teaspoons freshly grated orange zest
¼ cup sugar
¼ teaspoon orange-flower water
  (available at specialty foods shops),
  or to taste, if desired

candied mimosa balls and candied violets
  (both available at specialty foods shops or
  by mail order from The Chocolate Gallery,
  New York City, Tel. 212-675-2253) for
  garnish if desired
fresh orange sections, membranes discarded,
  for garnish if desired

Make the cake: Into a large bowl sift together the flour, ¾ cup of the sugar, the baking powder, and the salt. In a bowl whisk together the oil, the egg yolks, the orange juice, the zest, and the vanilla and whisk the mixture into the flour mixture, whisking until the batter is smooth. In the large bowl of an electric mixer beat the egg whites with a pinch of salt until they are foamy, add the cream of tartar, and beat the whites until they hold soft peaks. Add the remaining ¾ cup sugar, a little at a time, and beat the whites until they hold stiff glossy peaks. Stir one third of the whites into the batter to lighten it and fold in the remaining whites gently but thoroughly. Spoon the batter into an ungreased 10-inch tube pan, 4 inches deep, with feet and a removable bottom, and bake the cake in the middle of a preheated 325° F. oven for 1 hour, or until a tester comes out clean. Invert the pan immediately onto a rack and let the cake cool completely in the pan upside down on the rack. Run a long thin knife around the outer and tube edges of the pan and turn the cake out of the pan onto the rack. Using a serrated knife cut the cake in half horizontally.

Make the whipped cream frosting: In a large bowl, chilled, with an electric mixer beat together the cream, the Grand Marnier, the zest, the sugar, the orange-flower water, and a pinch of salt until the mixture holds stiff peaks.

Transfer the bottom layer of the cake to a platter, spread some of the frosting on it, and top it with the remaining layer. Spread the remaining frosting on the top layer and side of the cake and garnish the cake with the candied mimosa balls, the candied violets, and the orange sections.

Orange Poppy-Seed Cake
with Berries and Crème Fraîche

For the cake
1½ cups cake flour (not self-rising)
¾ teaspoon salt
1 teaspoon baking soda
½ teaspoon double-acting baking powder
¼ cup poppy seeds
1½ sticks (¾ cup) unsalted butter, softened
1¼ cups sugar
2 teaspoons freshly grated orange zest
4 large eggs, separated
⅔ cup sour cream
2 teaspoons vanilla
¼ teaspoon cream of tartar
For the syrup
1 cup fresh orange juice
¼ cup plus 2 tablespoons Grand Marnier,
    or other orange-flavored liqueur
3 tablespoons sugar
¼ cup julienne strips of orange zest
    (preferably removed with a zester)

3 cups mixed berries
confectioners' sugar for sifting over the cake
crème fraîche as an accompaniment

Make the cake: Into a bowl sift together the flour, the salt, the baking soda, and the baking powder and stir in the poppy seeds. In a large bowl with an electric mixer cream the butter with 1 cup of the sugar and the zest until the mixture is light and fluffy. In a small bowl whisk together the yolks, the sour cream, and the vanilla until the mixture is combined well and beat the flour mixture and the yolk mixture into the butter mixture alternately, beginning and ending with the flour mixture and beating well after each addition. In another bowl with cleaned beaters beat the whites with a pinch of salt until they are foamy, add the cream of tartar, and beat the whites until they hold soft peaks. Add the remaining ¼ cup sugar, a little at a time, beating, and beat the meringue until it holds stiff peaks. Stir about one third of the meringue into the batter to lighten it, fold in the remaining meringue gently, and pour the batter into a buttered and floured 10-inch springform pan, smoothing the top. Bake the cake in the middle of a preheated 350° F. oven for 40 to 45 minutes, or until a tester comes out clean.

Make the syrup while the cake is baking: In a small saucepan combine the juice, the liqueur, the sugar, and the zest, heat the mixture over moderately high heat, stirring, until the sugar is dissolved, and remove the pan from the heat.

Transfer the zest with a fork to a bowl, pour ⅓ cup of the syrup into the bowl, reserving the remaining syrup, and add the berries to the bowl. Toss the mixture until it is combined well and chill it, covered, for at least 2 hours and up to 24 hours.

Remove the cake from the oven, transfer it in the pan to a rack, and poke the top immediately all over with a skewer. Brush the top of the cake generously with half the reserved syrup, letting some of it run down between the cake and the side of the pan, and let the cake stand for 10 minutes. Run a thin knife around the edge of the pan, remove the side of the pan, and invert the cake onto the rack. Poke the cake all over with the skewer and brush it generously with the remaining syrup. Re-invert the cake onto another rack and let it cool completely. *The cake may be made 1 day in advance and kept wrapped well in plastic wrap or in an airtight container at room temperature.* Just before serving, sift the confectioners' sugar over the top of the cake and serve the cake with the macerated berries and the *crème fraîche*.

Pistachio Praline Dacquoise

For the meringue layers

⅔ cup shelled natural pistachio nuts
¾ cup plus 2 tablespoons sugar
2 teaspoons cornstarch
4 large egg whites
¼ teaspoon cream of tartar
¼ teaspoon salt if using unsalted
    pistachio nuts
2 drops of green food coloring if desired

For the filling

½ cup plus 2 tablespoons sugar
⅓ cup shelled natural pistachio nuts
2 tablespoons cornstarch
1 cup milk
1 large whole egg
1 large egg yolk
2 tablespoons unsalted butter,
    cut into bits
2 tablespoons kirsch, or to taste
1 envelope (1 tablespoon) unflavored gelatin
¼ cup cold water
1 cup well-chilled heavy cream

confectioners' sugar for dusting the *dacquoise*
10 shelled natural pistachio nuts, blanched
    and peeled, for garnish

Line 2 buttered baking sheets with foil or parchment paper and trace a total of three 13- by 4-inch rectangles on the sheets of foil (2 on one sheet and 1 on the other).

Make the meringue layers: In a food processor grind fine the pistachio nuts with ¼ cup plus 2 tablespoons of the sugar and the cornstarch. In a large bowl with an electric mixer beat the egg whites with the cream of tartar and the salt until they hold soft peaks, beat in the remaining ½ cup sugar, a little at a time, and the food coloring, and beat the whites until they hold stiff glossy peaks. Fold in the pistachio mixture gently but thoroughly and transfer the meringue to a pastry bag fitted with a ½-inch plain tip. Starting along an edge of a rectangle, pipe the meringue onto the prepared foil, filling in 2 of the rectangles. Outline the edges of the remaining rectangle with 2 rows of the meringue, leaving the center free, and bake the meringues in a preheated 250° F. oven, switching the sheets from one rack to the other after 30 minutes, for 1 to 1¼ hours, or until the meringues are firm and dry when touched. Let the meringues cool on the sheets, slide the foil off the sheets, and peel the meringues off the foil carefully. *The meringues may be made 1 day in advance and kept wrapped in plastic wrap at room temperature.*

Make the filling: In a small skillet, preferably non-stick, cook ¼ cup of the sugar, undisturbed, over moderate heat until it begins to melt, cook it, stirring with a fork, until it is melted completely and turns a golden caramel, and add the pistachio nuts, stirring until they are coated well. Pour the mixture immediately onto a piece of foil and let it cool completely. Break the praline into pieces and grind it fine in a food processor. In a heavy saucepan dissolve the cornstarch in ¼ cup of the milk, stir in the remaining ¾ cup milk and the remaining ¼ cup plus 2 tablespoons sugar, and bring the mixture just to a boil, stirring. In a heatproof bowl whisk together the whole egg and the egg yolk, add the milk mixture in a stream, whisking, and transfer the pastry cream to the pan. Bring the pastry cream to a boil, whisking, and simmer it, whisking, for 2 minutes. Remove the pan from the heat, whisk in the butter and the kirsch, whisking until the butter is incorporated, and force the pastry cream through a fine sieve into a metal bowl. Stir in the praline and let the pastry cream cool completely, its surface covered with plastic wrap. *The filling may be prepared up to this point 1 day in advance and kept covered and chilled.* In a small saucepan sprinkle the gelatin over the water, let it soften for 1 minute, and heat the mixture over moderately low heat, stirring, until the gelatin is dissolved and the liquid is hot. Whisk the gelatin mixture into the pastry cream, set the bowl in a larger bowl of ice and cold water, and stir the pastry cream until it is thickened but not set. Remove the bowl from the ice water. In a chilled bowl with an electric mixer beat the heavy cream until it just holds stiff peaks, whisk one third of it into the pastry cream to lighten it, and fold in the remaining cream gently but thoroughly. Transfer the filling to a pastry bag fitted with a medium star tip.

Arrange a solid meringue rectangle, rough side up, on a platter and pipe some of the filling decoratively in rows down the length of it to cover it. Top the filling with the remaining solid meringue rectangle, rough side up, and pipe some of the remaining filling on the meringue in the same manner. Dust the remaining meringue, rough side up, with the confectioners' sugar and set it on top of the filling. Pipe rosettes of the remaining filling on the meringue, garnish them with the pistachios, and chill the *dacquoise* for at least 2 hours and up to 4 hours. Serves 8.

PHOTO ON PAGE 69

DESSERTS

Strawberry Rhubarb Shortcakes

For the filling

1½ pounds rhubarb, trimmed and
   cut into ¾-inch pieces
   (about 4 cups)
⅓ cup sugar
2 tablespoons fresh orange juice
1 pint strawberries,
   hulled and sliced

For the shortcakes

2 cups all-purpose flour
3 tablespoons sugar
½ teaspoon salt
1 tablespoon double-acting baking powder
1½ teaspoons ground cardamom
1½ tablespoons freshly grated orange zest
½ stick (¼ cup) cold unsalted butter,
   cut into bits
2 tablespoons cold vegetable shortening
¼ cup milk
1 large egg
1 teaspoon vanilla

1 cup well-chilled heavy cream
1 to 2 tablespoons sugar, or to taste
½ teaspoon orange-flower water (available
   at specialty foods shops) or
   vanilla, or to taste

Make the filling: In a heavy saucepan combine the rhubarb, the sugar, and the juice and simmer the mixture, stirring occasionally, for 5 to 10 minutes, or until the rhubarb is tender. Transfer the mixture to a bowl, stir in the strawberries, and let the mixture cool. Chill the filling, covered, for at least 2 hours or overnight.

Make the shortcakes: Into a bowl sift together the flour, the sugar, the salt, the baking powder, and the cardamom and blend in the orange zest, the butter, and the shortening until the mixture resembles meal. In a small bowl whisk together the milk, the egg, and the vanilla, add the milk mixture to the flour mixture, and stir the mixture with a fork until it just forms a dough. Turn the dough out onto a floured surface and knead it gently for 20 seconds. Pat the dough into a 6-inch round, cut it into 6 wedges, and transfer the wedges to a buttered baking sheet. Bake the shortcakes in the middle of a preheated 425° F. oven for 12 to 15 minutes, or until they are golden, transfer them to a rack, and let them cool.

In a bowl with an electric mixer beat the cream until it just forms soft peaks and add the sugar, beating. Beat in the orange-flower water and beat the cream until it forms stiff peaks. Split the shortcakes horizontally with a fork, arrange the bottom halves on 6 plates, and spoon the filling over them. Spoon the whipped cream over the filling and cover it with the top halves of the shortcakes. Serves 6.

223

Walnut Spice Cake with Lemon Glaze

2 cups all-purpose flour

1½ teaspoons cinnamon

1½ teaspoons allspice

1½ teaspoons freshly grated nutmeg

1 teaspoon baking soda

1 teaspoon double-acting baking powder

½ teaspoon salt

2 sticks (1 cup) unsalted butter, softened

1 cup sugar

3 large eggs, separated

1 teaspoon vanilla

1¼ cups sour cream

1 cup walnuts, toasted lightly, cooled, and
  chopped fine

For the glaze

1 cup confectioners' sugar

2 tablespoons fresh lemon juice

For the cranberry cluster garnish

½ cup light corn syrup

¼ cup sugar

½ cup cranberries, picked over

mint sprig for garnish

Butter well a 3-quart (5-inch-deep) decorative cake pan. Into a bowl sift together the flour, the cinnamon, the allspice, the nutmeg, the baking soda, the baking powder, and the salt. In the bowl of an electric mixer cream together the butter and the sugar until the mixture is light and fluffy, beat in the egg yolks, 1 at a time, beating well after each addition, and beat in the vanilla. Beat in the flour mixture alternately with the sour cream in batches, beginning and ending with the flour mixture and beating well after each addition. In another bowl with cleaned beaters beat the egg whites until they just hold stiff peaks, fold them and the walnuts into the batter gently but thoroughly, and spoon the batter into the buttered pan, smoothing the top. Bake the cake in the middle of a preheated 350° F. oven for 45 to 50 minutes, or until a tester comes out clean, transfer it to a rack for 10 minutes, and invert it onto the rack to cool completely. *The cake may be made 1 day in advance and kept wrapped tightly in plastic wrap.*

Make the glaze: In a small bowl whisk together the sugar and the lemon juice until the glaze is smooth.

Transfer the glaze to a heavy-duty resealable plastic bag and cut a small opening with scissors in one corner of the bag. Drizzle the glaze over the cake in a circular motion and let the cake stand until the glaze is set. *The cake may be glazed 6 hours in advance and kept covered loosely.* Transfer the cake to a cake plate.

Make the cranberry cluster garnish: In a small heavy saucepan combine the corn syrup and the sugar, bring the mixture to a boil over moderate heat, stirring until the sugar is dissolved, and boil the syrup until it is a golden caramel and registers 320° F. on a candy thermometer. While the syrup is boiling, oil lightly a 12-inch-square sheet of foil. Working quickly over the foil, with a fork stir the cranberries into the syrup, lift them out, and transfer them immediately to the foil, forming them into a cluster with the fork. Let the cluster cool completely. *The cluster may be made 2 hours in advance (preferably not on a damp day) and kept in a cool, dry place.*

Pry the cluster gently from the foil, arrange it on the cake plate, and garnish it with the mint sprig.

PHOTO ON PAGE 81

Almond Cupcakes with Orange Icing

1 cup all-purpose flour

½ cup natural almonds (with skin),
  toasted lightly, cooled, and ground fine
  in a blender

1¼ teaspoons double-acting baking powder

⅓ cup vegetable shortening

½ cup granulated sugar

1 large egg

¼ teaspoon almond extract

⅓ cup water

1 cup plus 2 tablespoons confectioners' sugar

1½ tablespoons unsalted butter,
  softened

½ teaspoon freshly grated orange zest

1 tablespoon orange juice

In a bowl whisk together the flour, the almonds, the baking powder, and a pinch of salt. In another bowl with an electric mixer cream together the shortening and the granulated sugar, beat in the egg and the almond extract, and beat in the flour mixture alternately with the water, beating well after each addition. Divide the batter among 12 paper-lined ½-cup muffin tins and bake the cupcakes in the middle of a preheated 350° F. oven for 15 to 20 minutes, or until a tester comes out clean. Turn the cupcakes out onto a rack and let them cool completely.

In another bowl beat together the confectioners' sugar, the butter, the zest, and the juice, beating until the icing is fluffy, and spread the icing on the cupcakes. Makes 12 cupcakes.

Chocolate Cupcakes with Butterscotch Icing

⅓ cup Dutch-process cocoa powder
½ cup boiling water
1 cup all-purpose flour
½ teaspoon baking soda
¾ stick (6 tablespoons) unsalted butter, softened
½ cup sugar
1 whole large egg
1 large egg yolk
¾ cup butterscotch chips
¼ cup heavy cream

In a small bowl whisk together the cocoa powder and the water until the cocoa powder is dissolved and let the mixture cool to room temperature. In a bowl whisk together the flour, the baking soda, and a pinch of salt. In another bowl with an electric mixer cream together the butter and the sugar and beat in the whole egg and the egg yolk, beating until the mixture is combined well. Beat in the cocoa mixture alternately with the flour mixture, beating well after each addition, divide the batter among 12 paper-lined ½-cup muffin tins, and bake the cupcakes in the middle of a preheated 350° F. oven for 25 to 30 minutes, or until a tester comes out clean. Turn the cupcakes out onto a rack and let them cool completely.

In another bowl combine the butterscotch chips and the cream, scalded, let the chips soften, and whisk the mixture until it is smooth. Let the icing cool completely, whisk it until it is fluffy, and spread it on the cupcakes. Makes 12 cupcakes.

Peanut Butter Chocolate-Chip Cupcakes with Chocolate Icing

1 cup all-purpose flour
1½ teaspoons double-acting baking powder
½ cup firmly packed dark brown sugar
¼ cup chunky peanut butter
3 tablespoons unsalted butter, softened
1 large egg
½ teaspoon vanilla
½ cup milk
1¼ cups semisweet chocolate chips
¼ cup heavy cream

In a bowl whisk together the flour, the baking powder, and a pinch of salt. In another bowl with an electric mixer cream together the brown sugar, the peanut butter, and the butter and beat in the egg and the vanilla. Beat in the flour mixture alternately with the milk, beating well after each addition, and stir in ½ cup of the chocolate chips. Divide the batter among 12 paper-lined ½-cup muffin tins and bake the cupcakes in the middle of a preheated 350° F. oven for 20 to 25 minutes, or until a tester comes out clean. Turn the cupcakes out onto a rack and let them cool completely.

In another bowl combine the remaining ¾ cup chocolate chips and the cream, scalded, let the chips soften, and whisk the mixture until it is smooth. Let the icing cool completely, whisk it until it is fluffy, and spread it on the cupcakes. Makes 12 cupcakes.

Spice Cupcakes with Cream-Cheese Icing

1¼ cups all-purpose flour
1 teaspoon baking soda
1 teaspoon cinnamon
½ teaspoon freshly grated nutmeg
¼ teaspoon ground cloves
¼ cup vegetable shortening
¼ cup granulated sugar
1 large egg
½ cup unsulfured molasses stirred together
    with ½ cup boiling water
4 ounces cream cheese, softened
2 tablespoons unsalted butter, softened
½ cup confectioners' sugar

In a bowl whisk together the flour, the baking soda, the spices, and a pinch of salt. In another bowl with an electric mixer cream together the shortening and the granulated sugar, beat in the egg, and beat in the flour mixture alternately with the molasses mixture, beating well after each addition. Divide the batter among 12 paper-lined ½-cup muffin tins and bake the cupcakes in the middle of a preheated 350° F. oven for 15 to 20 minutes, or until a tester comes out clean. Turn the cupcakes out onto a rack and let them cool completely.

In another bowl beat together the cream cheese, the butter, and the confectioners' sugar until the icing is fluffy and spread the icing on the cupcakes. Makes 12 cupcakes.

COOKIES

Apple Date-Nut Bars

2 large Granny Smith apples, peeled, cored,
    and chopped fine
2 tablespoons granulated sugar
2 tablespoons fresh lemon juice
2 tablespoons water
1½ cups pitted dates, chopped
2 sticks (1 cup) unsalted butter, cut into bits
    and softened
1 cup packed light brown sugar
1 teaspoon salt
2½ cups all-purpose flour
1½ cups finely chopped pecans
1½ teaspoons cinnamon

In a heavy saucepan combine the apples, the granulated sugar, the lemon juice, and the water and simmer the mixture, covered, stirring occasionally, for 5 to 10 minutes, or until the apples are tender. Add the dates, simmer the mixture, uncovered, stirring it and mashing the dates, for 3 to 5 minutes, or until the dates are soft and the mixture is almost smooth, and let the purée cool. In a bowl combine the butter, the brown sugar, the salt, the flour, the pecans, and the cinnamon and blend the mixture well. Press half the flour mixture evenly into a buttered 13- by 9-inch baking pan, spread the purée over it, and crumble the remaining flour mixture over the purée, pressing it lightly to form an even layer. Bake the mixture in the middle of a preheated 375° F. oven for 35 to 40 minutes, or until it is golden, let it cool completely in the pan on a rack, and cut it into 36 bars. Makes 36 cookies.

Chocolate Nut Cookies

2 cups all-purpose flour
1 teaspoon double-acting baking powder
¼ teaspoon salt
½ cup unsweetened cocoa powder
½ cup walnuts
⅔ cup plus 2 tablespoons sugar
⅔ cup almond paste (about 7 ounces)
1 stick (½ cup) unsalted butter, softened
1 teaspoon vanilla
2 large egg whites

In a bowl whisk together the flour, the baking powder, the salt, and the cocoa powder. In a food processor grind fine the walnuts with 2 tablespoons of the sugar, add the almond paste, and grind the mixture until it forms a paste. In the bowl of an electric mixer cream together the butter and the remaining ⅔ cup sugar, add the nut paste and the vanilla, and beat the mixture until it is combined well. Beat in the flour mixture at low speed until a dough is formed and beat in the egg whites until they are incorporated.

Working with half the dough at a time, roll out the dough ¼ inch thick between sheets of plastic wrap, cut out diamond shapes with a 2-inch-wide cutter, and arrange them 1½ inches apart on buttered baking sheets. Press ridges into the diamonds with the tines of a fork and bake the cookies in batches in the middle of preheated 350° F. oven for 10 minutes. Let the cookies cool on the sheets on a rack for 2 minutes, transfer them carefully with a spatula to racks, and let them cool completely. *The cookies may be made 3 days in advance and kept in airtight containers*. Makes about 40 cookies.

Beverly Charlton

Chocolate-Dipped Coconut Macaroons

4 large egg whites
1⅓ cups sugar
½ teaspoon salt
1½ teaspoons vanilla
2½ cups sweetened flaked coconut
¼ cup plus 2 tablespoons all-purpose flour
8 ounces fine-quality bittersweet chocolate, chopped

In a heavy saucepan stir together the egg whites, the sugar, the salt, the vanilla, and the coconut, sift in the flour, and stir the mixture until it is combined well. Cook the mixture over moderate heat, stirring constantly, for 5 minutes, increase the heat to moderately high, and cook the mixture, stirring constantly, for 3 to 5 minutes more, or until it is thickened and begins to pull away from the bottom and side of the pan. Transfer the mixture to a bowl, let it cool slightly, and chill it, its surface covered with plastic wrap, until it is just cold. Drop heaping teaspoons of the dough 2 inches apart onto buttered baking sheets and bake the macaroons in batches in the middle of a preheated 300° F. oven for 20 to 25 minutes, or until they are pale golden. Transfer the macaroons to a rack and let them cool.

In a small metal bowl set over a pan of barely simmering water melt the chocolate, stirring until it is smooth, remove the bowl from the heat, and dip the macaroons, 1 at a time, into the chocolate, coating them halfway and letting any excess drip off. Transfer the macaroons as they are dipped to a foil-lined tray and chill them for 30 minutes to 1 hour, or until the chocolate is set. The macaroons keep, chilled and separated by layers of wax paper, in an airtight container for 3 days. (If the macaroons are made in advance, let them stand at room temperature for 20 minutes before serving.) Makes about 30 macaroons.

Triple-Chocolate Fudge Brownies

6 ounces fine-quality bittersweet chocolate, chopped
2 ounces unsweetened chocolate, chopped
1½ sticks (¾ cup) unsalted butter
1½ cups sugar
2 teaspoons vanilla
4 large eggs
1 teaspoon salt
1 cup all-purpose flour
1 cup semisweet chocolate chips

In a metal bowl set over a pan of barely simmering water melt the bittersweet chocolate and the unsweetened chocolate with the butter, stirring until the mixture is smooth, remove the bowl from the heat, and let the mixture cool until it is lukewarm. Stir in the sugar and the vanilla and add the eggs, 1 at a time, stirring well after each addition. Stir in the salt and the flour, stirring until the mixture is just combined, and stir in the chocolate chips. Pour the batter into a well-buttered and floured 13- by 9-inch baking pan, smooth the top, and bake the mixture in the middle of a preheated 350° F. oven for 25 to 30 minutes, or until a tester comes out with crumbs adhering to it. Let the mixture cool completely in the pan on a rack and cut it into 24 bars. Makes 24 brownies.

Coconut Blondies

1½ sticks (¾ cup) unsalted butter, softened
1½ cups firmly packed light brown sugar
2 large eggs
2 teaspoons vanilla
½ teaspoon salt
1½ teaspoons double-acting baking powder
1½ cups all-purpose flour
1½ cups semisweet chocolate chips
2 cups sweetened flaked coconut, toasted
  and cooled

In a bowl with an electric mixer cream together the butter and the brown sugar, beating the mixture until it is light and fluffy, add the eggs, 1 at a time, beating well after each addition, and beat in the vanilla. In a small bowl whisk together the salt, the baking powder, and the flour, add the flour mixture to the butter mixture, and beat the batter until it is just combined. Stir in the chocolate chips and the coconut, spread the batter evenly in a buttered and floured 13- by 9-inch baking pan, and bake it in the middle of a preheated 350° F. oven for 25 to 30 minutes, or until it begins to pull away from the sides of the pan and crumbs adhere to a tester. Let the mixture cool completely in the pan on a rack and cut it into squares. Makes about 32 blondies.

Candied Ginger Shortbread Hearts

2 sticks (1 cup) unsalted butter, softened
½ cup firmly packed light brown sugar
½ teaspoon ground ginger
2 cups all-purpose flour
¼ teaspoon salt
¾ cup finely chopped candied ginger
confectioners' sugar for sprinkling the cookies

In a bowl with an electric mixer cream together the butter, the brown sugar, and the ground ginger until the mixture is light and fluffy and add the flour and the salt. Beat the dough until it is just combined and beat in the candied ginger. Halve the dough, roll out each half ¼ inch thick between sheets of wax paper, and freeze the dough on baking sheets for 10 to 15 minutes, or until it is very firm. Working with half the dough at a time, remove the top sheets of wax paper and cut out cookies with a 2¼-inch heart-shaped cutter. (The dough should be cold so that the cookies retain their shape.) Arrange the cookies 2 inches apart on the baking sheets, bake

them in batches in the middle of a preheated 300° F. oven for 25 to 30 minutes, or until they are pale golden, and transfer them to a rack. Gather the scraps, reroll the dough, and make more cookies in the same manner. Let the cookies cool completely and sprinkle them with the confectioners' sugar, sifted. The cookies keep in an airtight container for 5 days. Makes about 40 cookies.

Hermit Bars

1¾ cups all-purpose flour
½ teaspoon baking soda
½ teaspoon salt
1 teaspoon cinnamon
½ teaspoon freshly grated nutmeg
¼ teaspoon ground cloves
1 stick (½ cup) unsalted butter, softened
⅔ cup packed dark brown sugar
1 large egg
¼ cup molasses
½ cup raisins or currants
½ cup chopped walnuts

In a bowl whisk together the flour, the baking soda, the salt, the cinnamon, the nutmeg, and the cloves. In another bowl with an electric mixer cream the butter with the brown sugar, beat in the egg, and beat in the molasses. Add the flour mixture, beating the mixture until it is just combined, and stir in the raisins and the walnuts. Spread the mixture in a buttered and floured 13- by

9-inch baking pan and bake it in the middle of a preheated 350° F. oven for 15 to 20 minutes, or until a tester comes out clean. Let the mixture cool completely in the pan on a rack and cut it into 24 bars. Makes 24 cookies.

Lemon Poppy-Seed Shortbread Bars

1 stick (½ cup) unsalted butter, softened
½ cup confectioners' sugar plus additional
    for sprinkling the bars
1½ tablespoons freshly grated lemon zest
¾ teaspoon vanilla
1½ tablespoons poppy seeds
1 cup all-purpose flour
½ teaspoon salt

In a bowl with an electric mixer cream the butter with ½ cup of the confectioners' sugar and beat the mixture until it is light and fluffy. Beat in the zest and the vanilla, add the poppy seeds, the flour, and the salt, and beat the mixture until it is just combined. Press the mixture evenly into a buttered 8-inch-square baking pan and bake it in the middle of a preheated 300° F. oven for 30 to 35 minutes, or until it is pale golden. Let the shortbread cool in the pan on a rack for 10 minutes, cut it into 24 bars, and let the bars cool completely in the pan. Sprinkle the bars with the additional confectioners' sugar. Makes 24 cookies.

Peanut Butter Coconut Bars

1½ sticks (¾ cup) unsalted butter, softened
1 cup sugar
1 cup smooth peanut butter
1 large egg
1 teaspoon vanilla
½ teaspoon salt
2 cups all-purpose flour
2 cups sweetened flaked coconut
½ cup finely chopped salted roasted peanuts

In a bowl with an electric mixer cream the butter with the sugar and beat the mixture until it is light and fluffy. Add the peanut butter, beat the mixture until it is combined well, and beat in the egg, the vanilla, and the salt. Add the flour, beat the mixture until it is just combined, and stir in the coconut. Spread the mixture evenly in a buttered jelly-roll pan, 15½ by 10½ by 1 inches, sprinkle the peanuts over it, pressing them into the mixture

lightly, and bake the mixture in the middle of a preheated 350° F. oven for 20 to 25 minutes, or until a tester comes out clean. Let the mixture cool completely in the pan on a rack, cut it into 24 bars, and cut each bar in half diagonally to form 2 triangles. Makes 48 cookies.

PIES AND TARTS
_____

Sour Cream Apple Pie

1 recipe *pâte brisée* (page 233)
For the topping
3 tablespoons unsalted butter, softened
¼ cup plus 2 tablespoons sugar
1 teaspoon cinnamon
2 tablespoons all-purpose flour
For the filling
1⅓ cups sour cream
⅔ cup sugar
¼ teaspoon salt
2 teaspoons vanilla
2 large eggs
3 tablespoons all-purpose flour
5 large Granny Smith apples (about 2¼ pounds)

ginger whipped cream (page 230) as
    an accompaniment

Roll out the dough ⅛ inch thick on a lightly floured surface, fit it into a 10-inch (6-cup capacity) pie plate, and flute the edge decoratively. Chill the shell while making the topping and the filling.

Make the topping: In a small bowl blend together the butter, the sugar, the cinnamon, and the flour until the mixture is combined well and chill the topping, covered, while making the filling.

Make the filling: In a large bowl whisk together the sour cream, the sugar, the salt, the vanilla, the eggs, and the flour until the mixture is smooth, add the apples, peeled, cored, and sliced thin, and stir the filling until it is combined well.

Spoon the filling into the chilled shell, smoothing the top, and crumble the topping evenly over it. Bake the pie in the middle of a preheated 350° F. oven for 1 to 1¼ hours, or until it is golden and the apples are tender, transfer it to a rack, and let it cool completely. Serve the pie with the ginger whipped cream.

Ginger Whipped Cream

1½ cups well-chilled heavy cream
3 tablespoons confectioners' sugar, or to taste
½ teaspoon ground ginger
¼ cup finely chopped candied ginger plus
    additional for garnish

In a bowl with an electric mixer beat the cream until it just holds stiff peaks, add the confectioners' sugar and the ground ginger, and beat the mixture until it holds stiff peaks. Fold in ¼ cup of the candied ginger, transfer the whipped cream to a bowl, and garnish it with the additional candied ginger. Makes about 3 cups.

Black Bottom Butterscotch Cream Pie

For the shell
1 cup pecans
2 tablespoons sugar
1¼ cups all-purpose flour
¾ stick cold unsalted butter, cut into bits
½ teaspoon salt
3 tablespoons ice water
raw rice for weighting the shell

6 ounces fine-quality bittersweet chocolate
    (not unsweetened)
¼ cup heavy cream
For the filling
1 tablespoon bourbon
2 tablespoons water
1 envelope unflavored gelatin
1 cup firmly packed dark brown sugar
1 cup milk
¾ teaspoon salt
2 tablespoons unsalted butter
3 large egg yolks
½ teaspoon vanilla
freshly grated nutmeg to taste
¾ cup heavy cream
For the decoration
¼ cup sugar
8 to 10 pecan halves
1 cup heavy cream

Make the shell: In a food processor grind coarse the pecans with the sugar and transfer the mixture to a bowl. In the food processor blend together the flour, the butter, and the salt until the mixture resembles meal and add the flour mixture to the pecan mixture. Add the ice water, toss the mixture until the water is incorporated, and press it onto the bottom and up the side of a 9-inch (1-quart) pie plate, crimping the edge decoratively. Chill the shell for 1 hour, prick it all over with a fork, and line it with foil. Fill the foil with the rice, bake the shell in the lower third of a preheated 425° F. oven for 10 minutes, and remove the foil and rice carefully. Reduce the heat to 375° F., bake the shell for 12 to 15 minutes more, or until it is golden brown, and let it cool on a rack.

In a small metal bowl set over a pan of barely simmering water melt the chocolate with the cream, stirring until the mixture is smooth, spread the mixture in the bottom and halfway up the side of the shell, and let it cool. Chill the shell.

Make the filling while the shell is chilling: In a large metal bowl combine the bourbon and the water, sprinkle the gelatin over the liquid, and let it soften. In a saucepan heat the brown sugar, the milk, and the salt over moderate heat, stirring, until the mixture is hot and the sugar is dissolved and whisk in the butter. (The mixture will appear slightly curdled.) In a bowl whisk together the egg yolks, add the hot milk mixture in a stream, whisking, and pour the mixture into the pan. Cook the custard over moderately low heat, whisking constantly, until it is thickened and registers 160° F. on a candy thermometer and add it to the gelatin mixture. Stir in the vanilla and the nutmeg and stir the mixture until the gelatin is dissolved. Set the bowl in another bowl of ice and cold water, stir the mixture until it is cold and the consistency of raw egg whites, and remove the bowl from the ice water. In another bowl with an electric mixer beat the cream until it holds stiff peaks, fold it into the custard mixture gently but thoroughly, and pour the filling into the chilled shell. Chill the pie for 6 hours or overnight.

Decorate the pie: In a very small skillet or saucepan cook the sugar over moderate heat, undisturbed, until it begins to melt, cook it, stirring with a fork, until it is melted completely and turns a golden caramel, and reduce the heat to low. Working quickly, add the pecans, turning them to coat them thoroughly with the caramel, and with the fork transfer them, 1 at a time, to a piece of foil to cool. In a chilled bowl with chilled beaters beat the cream until it holds stiff peaks, drop it by heaping tablespoons around the edge of the pie, and arrange a caramelized pecan in the center of each dollop.

PHOTO ON PAGE 63

Grapefruit and Coconut Angel Pie

For the shell

4 large egg whites at room temperature

¼ teaspoon salt

¼ teaspoon cream of tartar

1 cup sugar

1 cup sweetened flaked coconut

For the filling

1 envelope (about 1 tablespoon) unflavored
   gelatin

¾ cup strained fresh grapefruit juice

4 large egg yolks

½ cup sugar

8 ounces cream cheese, softened

1 cup well-chilled heavy cream

2 cups fresh grapefruit sections (cut from
   about 3 large grapefruit), cut into ½-inch
   pieces and drained well

fresh grapefruit sections for garnish if desired

Make the shell: In a bowl with an electric mixer beat the egg whites with the salt until they are foamy, beat in the cream of tartar, and beat the whites until they hold soft peaks. Beat in the sugar, a little at a time, beat the meringue for 5 to 7 minutes, or until it is stiff and glossy and the sugar is dissolved, and fold in the coconut. Drop heaping tablespoons of the meringue evenly around the edge of a well-buttered 9-inch (1-quart) pie plate, spreading the meringue with the back of the spoon to form the side of the shell, and spread the remaining meringue evenly over the bottom of the pie plate. Bake the shell in the middle of a preheated 250° F. oven for 1¼ to 1⅓ hours, or until it is firm and very pale golden,

turn off the oven, and let the shell cool completely in the oven with the door ajar. (Once the shell is cooled completely, it may be left overnight in the oven with the door closed.)

Make the filling: In a small bowl sprinkle the gelatin over ¼ cup of the grapefruit juice and let it soften for 1 minute. In a small saucepan whisk together the egg yolks and the sugar, add the remaining ½ cup grapefruit juice, the gelatin mixture, and a pinch of salt, and cook the mixture over moderate heat, whisking, until it registers 160° F. on a candy thermometer. Transfer the yolk mixture to a metal bowl set in a larger bowl of ice and cold water and whisk it constantly until it is thickened to the consistency of raw egg white but is not set. Remove the smaller bowl from the bowl of ice and cold water and reserve the bowl of ice and cold water for later use. In another metal bowl with an electric mixer beat the cream cheese until it is light, fluffy, and smooth, scraping down the side, add the yolk mixture, a little at a time, beating, and beat the mixture until it is smooth and combined well. Set the bowl containing the cream cheese mixture in the reserved bowl of ice and cold water and whisk the cream cheese mixture until it is thickened and forms a ribbon when the whisk is lifted. In a bowl beat the heavy cream until it holds stiff peaks and whisk about one fourth of it into the cream cheese mixture. Fold in the remaining whipped cream gently but thoroughly and fold in the grapefruit pieces gently.

Pour the filling into the shell, smoothing the top, and chill the pie, uncovered, for 4 hours, or until the filling is set completely. (If the pie is to be chilled for more than 4 hours, cover it with plastic wrap or wax paper.) Just before serving garnish the pie with the grapefruit sections.

Maple Walnut Pie

For the shell

1½ cups all-purpose flour

½ teaspoon salt

7 tablespoons cold unsalted butter,
  cut into bits

2½ tablespoons cold vegetable shortening

2 to 4 tablespoons ice water

For the filling

1½ cups pure maple syrup

2 tablespoons unsalted butter, melted

1 teaspoon cinnamon

½ teaspoon maple extract or flavor
  (available at specialty foods shops
  and some supermarkets)

1 tablespoon all-purpose flour

3 large eggs, beaten lightly

1 teaspoon freshly grated orange zest

3 tablespoons fresh orange juice

¼ teaspoon salt

½ pound chopped walnuts (about 2⅓ cups)

a thin strip of orange zest, removed with a
  vegetable peeler, for garnish if desired

whipped cream dusted with cinnamon as an
  accompaniment if desired

Make the shell: In a food processor blend together the flour, the salt, the butter, and the shortening until the mixture resembles meal and transfer the mixture to a bowl. Add 2 tablespoons of the water, toss the mixture until the water is incorporated, adding as much of the remaining 2 tablespoons water as necessary to form a dough, and form the dough into a ball. Dust the dough with flour and chill it, wrapped in wax paper, for 1 hour. Roll out the dough ⅛ inch thick on a lightly floured surface and fit it into a 9½-inch (1½-quart) deep-dish pie plate. Crimp the edge of the dough decoratively and chill the shell for 30 minutes.

Make the filling: In a bowl whisk together the syrup, the butter, the cinnamon, the maple extract, the flour, the eggs, the grated zest, the juice, and the salt until the filling is smooth and stir in the walnuts.

Pour the filling into the shell and bake the pie in the lower third of a preheated 450° F. oven for 10 minutes. Reduce the heat to 350° F., bake the pie for 30 minutes more, or until it is golden and just set, and transfer it to a rack. Let the pie cool, garnish it with the orange zest strip, and serve it with the whipped cream.

Brandied Pumpkin Pie

1½ recipes *pâte brisée* (recipe follows)

an egg wash made by beating
  1 large egg yolk with
  1 teaspoon water

2 cups canned solid-pack pumpkin

⅔ cup firmly packed light brown sugar

2 teaspoons cinnamon

1 teaspoon ground ginger

½ teaspoon salt

1 cup heavy cream

⅔ cup milk

2 large eggs

¼ cup Cognac or
  other brandy

ginger whipped cream (page 230) as
  an accompaniment

Roll out three fourths of the dough ⅛ inch thick on a lightly floured surface, fit it into a 10-inch (6-cup capacity) pie plate, and trim the edge, leaving a ½-inch overhang. Fold the overhang under the dough flush with the edge of the pie plate and with a sharp knife make ½-inch-long cuts at ¾-inch intervals all the way around the edge of the shell. Turn every other section of the dough in toward the center of the shell to form a decorative edge and chill the shell for 30 minutes.

Roll out the remaining dough ⅛ inch thick on the lightly floured surface and with a 3-inch leaf-shaped cutter cut out 3 leaves. Transfer the pastry leaves to a baking sheet, score them lightly with the back of a knife to form veins, and chill them for 15 minutes, or until they are firm. Brush the leaves lightly with some of the egg wash and bake them in the middle of a preheated 375° F. oven for 12 to 15 minutes, or until they are golden. Transfer the leaves to a rack and let them cool completely.

In a bowl whisk together the pumpkin, the brown sugar, the cinnamon, the ginger, the salt, the heavy cream, the milk, the eggs, and the Cognac until the filling is smooth and pour the filling into the shell. Brush the edge of the shell lightly with some of the remaining egg wash if desired and bake the pie in the middle of a preheated 375° F. oven for 1 hour, or until the filling is set but the center still shakes slightly. (The filling will continue to set as the pie cools.) Transfer the pie to a rack and let it cool completely. Garnish the pie with the pastry leaves just before serving and serve it with the ginger whipped cream.

Pâte Brisée

1¼ cups all-purpose flour
¾ stick (6 tablespoons) cold unsalted butter,
　　cut into bits
2 tablespoons cold vegetable shortening
¼ teaspoon salt
2 tablespoons ice water plus additional
　　if necessary

In a large bowl blend the flour, the butter, the vegetable shortening, and the salt until the mixture resembles meal. Add 2 tablespoons ice water, toss the mixture until the water is incorporated, adding more ice water if necessary to form a dough, and form the dough into a ball. Dust the dough with flour and chill it, wrapped in wax paper, for 1 hour.

Lauren Jarrett

Apricot Rice Pudding Tart

For the shell

1⅓ cups all-purpose flour
¼ cup sugar
1 stick (½ cup) cold unsalted butter,
　　cut into bits
¼ teaspoon salt
1 large egg yolk, beaten lightly with
　　1½ tablespoons ice water
raw rice for weighting the shell

For the filling

½ cup long- or medium-grain white rice
1 quart boiling salted water
2 cups milk
⅓ cup sugar
4 large eggs,
　　beaten lightly
½ cup finely chopped dried apricots

¼ cup apricot preserves, heated
　　and strained
dried apricot halves for garnish
　　if desired
fresh mint sprigs for garnish
　　if desired

Make the shell: In a large bowl blend the flour, the sugar, the butter, and the salt until the mixture resembles meal. Add the egg-yolk mixture, toss the mixture until the egg-yolk mixture is incorporated, adding more ice water if necessary to form a dough, and form the dough into a flattened round. Dust the dough with flour and chill it, wrapped in wax paper, for 1 hour. Roll out the dough ⅛ inch thick on a lightly floured surface and fit it into a 10-inch tart pan with a removable fluted rim. Prick the shell in several places with a fork and chill it for 30 minutes. Line the shell with foil, fill the foil with the rice, and bake the shell in the lower third of a preheated 425° F. oven for 15 minutes. Remove the foil and the rice carefully, bake the shell for 10 minutes more, or until it is golden, and let it cool in the pan on rack.

Make the filling: In a saucepan stir the rice into the boiling water, simmer it, stirring occasionally, for 20 minutes, or until it is tender, and drain it well. In the pan combine the rice, the milk, the sugar, and a pinch of salt, bring the liquid to a boil, and cook the mixture over moderately low heat, stirring, for 20 minutes. Whisk about 1 cup of the rice mixture into the eggs, whisk the egg mixture into the pan, and cook the mixture, stirring constantly, over moderately low heat for 3 to 5 minutes, or until it registers 160° F. on a candy thermometer. (Do not let the custard boil.) Remove the pan from the heat and stir in the chopped apricots. *The filling may be made 1 day in advance and kept covered and chilled.*

Spread the filling in the shell and bake the tart in the middle of a preheated 325° F. oven for 25 minutes. Spread the preserves on the filling and serve the tart warm or at room temperature garnished with the apricot halves and the mint sprigs.

Summer Berry Mint Cream Tart

For the shell

1 stick (½ cup) unsalted butter at room
    temperature
⅓ cup sugar
¼ teaspoon salt
½ teaspoon vanilla
1¼ cups all-purpose flour
raw rice for weighting the shell

For the mint cream

1 cup milk
⅓ cup coarsely chopped fresh mint leaves
3 large egg yolks
½ cup sugar
3 tablespoons cornstarch
1 teaspoon vanilla
½ cup well-chilled heavy cream

1 quart strawberries, hulled
2 cups blueberries
1 cup raspberries

Make the shell: In a bowl with an electric mixer cream the butter with the sugar, the salt, and the vanilla, add the flour, and blend the mixture until it forms crumbs that become a dough when pressed together. Turn the crumbs into a buttered 10-inch tart pan with a removable fluted rim, press them firmly onto the bottom and up the side of the pan, and chill the shell for 30 minutes. Prick the shell all over with a fork, line it with foil, and fill the foil with the rice. Bake the shell in the lower third of a preheated 375° F. oven for 15 minutes, remove the rice and the foil carefully, and bake the shell for 10 minutes more, or until it is golden. Let the shell cool in the pan on a rack for 5 minutes, remove the side of the pan, and let the shell cool completely. (The shell will be very crisp and cookie-like.)

Make the mint cream: In a small saucepan bring the milk to a boil with the mint, remove the pan from the heat, and let the mixture stand, covered, for 5 minutes. Strain the milk through a fine sieve into a bowl, pressing hard on the mint. In the pan, cleaned, whisk together the egg yolks, the sugar, the cornstarch, and the vanilla, whisk in the milk, and bring the mixture to a boil over moderate heat, whisking constantly. Simmer the pastry cream, whisking, for 3 minutes (it will be very thick), transfer it to a bowl, and chill it, its surface covered with plastic wrap, for 4 hours, or until it is firm. *The pastry cream may be made 1 day in advance and kept covered and chilled.* In a chilled bowl with an electric mixer beat the heavy cream until it holds stiff peaks. Whisk the pastry cream until it is smooth, whisk in half the whipped cream, and fold in the remaining whipped cream gently but thoroughly.

Arrange the shell on a large plate and fill it with the mint cream. Stand the strawberries, hulled ends down, in the mint cream, scatter the blueberries and the raspberries over and between the strawberries, and chill the tart for 1 hour. *The tart may be made 1 day in advance and kept covered loosely and chilled.*

PHOTO ON PAGE 51

Pecan Coconut Tart

For the shell
½ cup firmly packed light brown sugar
1 cup old-fashioned rolled oats
1 cup all-purpose flour
½ teaspoon double-acting baking powder
½ teaspoon salt
1 stick (½ cup) unsalted butter,
    melted and cooled
For the filling
⅓ cup honey
¾ cup firmly packed light brown sugar
1 stick (½ cup) unsalted butter
¼ cup heavy cream
1 cup old-fashioned rolled oats
½ cup sweetened flaked coconut
1¼ cups finely chopped pecans, toasted lightly
½ cup hulled sunflower seeds, toasted lightly

1 ounce fine-quality bittersweet chocolate
   (not unsweetened)
1 teaspoon unsalted butter

Make the shell: In a bowl stir together the brown sugar, the oats, the flour, the baking powder, and the salt, add the butter, and combine the mixture well. Pat the mixture evenly onto the bottom and ½ inch up the side of a well-buttered 9-inch springform pan and bake the shell in the lower third of a preheated 325° F. oven for 15 to 20 minutes, or until it is pale golden. Let the shell cool in the pan on a rack.

Make the filling: In a saucepan combine the honey, the brown sugar, and the butter, cook the mixture over moderate heat, stirring, until it is smooth and the butter is melted completely, and stir in the cream. In a bowl stir together the oats, the coconut, the pecans, the sunflower seeds, and a pinch of salt, add the butter mixture, and combine the filling well.

Pour the filling into the shell and bake the tart in the middle of a preheated 350° F. oven for 25 to 30 minutes, or until the edges are golden and the center is just set. (The center will set completely as the tart cools.) Let the tart cool on a rack for 10 minutes, remove the side of the pan, and let the tart cool completely on the rack.

In a small metal bowl set over a pan of simmering water melt the chocolate with the butter, stirring until the mixture is smooth, and let it cool slightly. Drizzle the chocolate mixture on top of the tart decoratively and let it set.

Caramelized Pineapple and Frangipane Tart

pâte brisée (page 233)
raw rice for weighting
   the shell
¾ cup blanched almonds
½ cup granulated sugar
1 stick (½ cup) unsalted butter,
   softened
1 large egg
¾ teaspoon almond extract
1 tablespoon all-purpose flour
¼ teaspoon salt
¼ cup firmly packed light
   brown sugar
1 pineapple (about 4 pounds),
   peeled, cored, cut into
   ½-inch-thick rings, and
   the rings halved
2 tablespoons dark rum

Roll out the dough ⅛ inch thick on a lightly floured surface and fit it into a 9-inch round tart pan with a removable fluted rim. Prick the bottom of the shell with a fork and chill the shell for 30 minutes. Line the shell with foil, fill the foil with the rice, and bake the shell in the bottom third of a preheated 375° F. oven for 15 minutes. Remove the rice and foil carefully and let the shell cool in the pan on a rack.

In a food processor grind the almonds fine with ¼ cup of the granulated sugar. In a large bowl cream 6 tablespoons of the butter with the remaining ¼ cup granulated sugar and beat in the egg, the almond mixture, the almond extract, the flour, and the salt. Spread the frangipane mixture evenly on the bottom of the shell and bake the tart in the bottom third of the preheated 375° F. oven for 15 minutes.

In a large skillet melt the remaining 2 tablespoons butter with the brown sugar, stirring until the mixture is smooth, and in it cook the pineapple slices, in batches if necessary, covered, over moderate heat, turning them once carefully, for 8 minutes. Transfer the pineapple slices with a slotted spatula to the tart, arranging them decoratively. Add the rum to the skillet and boil the mixture until it thickens slightly. Brush the pineapple slices with the glaze and bake the tart in the bottom third of the preheated 375° F. oven for 15 to 20 minutes, or until the crust is golden and the pineapple is tender. Let the tart cool in the pan on a rack and remove the rim carefully.

PUDDINGS

Banana Clafouti
(Baked Banana Pudding)

⅓ cup plus 1 tablespoon sugar
2 tablespoons all-purpose flour
2 large eggs
⅔ cup milk
2 teaspoons vanilla
¼ teaspoon salt
1 large banana, cut into ½-inch slices
1 tablespoon unsalted butter,
   cut into bits

In a blender blend together ⅓ cup of the sugar, the flour, the eggs, the milk, the vanilla, and the salt until the mixture is smooth. Arrange the banana slices in one layer in a buttered 3-cup gratin dish or flameproof shallow baking dish, pour the pudding over them, and bake the *clafouti* in the middle of a preheated 400° F. oven for 20 minutes, or until the top is puffed and springy to the touch. Sprinkle the top with the remaining 1 tablespoon sugar, dot it with the butter, and broil the *clafouti* under a preheated broiler about 3 inches from the heat for 1 to 2 minutes, or until it is browned lightly. Serves 2.

Pumpkin Bread Puddings

⅓ cup firmly packed light brown sugar
¼ teaspoon cinnamon
a pinch of freshly grated nutmeg
½ cup heavy cream
½ cup milk
¾ cup canned pumpkin purée
2 tablespoons raisins
1 large egg, beaten lightly
¼ teaspoon vanilla
4 slices of cinnamon-raisin bread,
   cut into ½-inch cubes (about
   2½ cups) and toasted

In a bowl whisk together the brown sugar, the cinnamon, the nutmeg, the cream, the milk, the pumpkin purée, the raisins, the egg, the vanilla, and a pinch of salt until the mixture is smooth, stir in the bread cubes, and let the mixture stand for 5 minutes. Divide the mixture between 2 buttered 1-cup microwave-safe ramekins fitted with wax-paper collars extending 2 inches above the rim, microwave the puddings at high power (100%), switching positions once, for 15 to 17 minutes, or until a tester comes out clean, and let them stand for 3 minutes. Discard the paper collars and serve the puddings warm. Serves 2.

DESSERT SOUFFLÉS

Individual Chocolate Soufflés

¼ cup granulated sugar plus additional for
   dusting the dishes
2 tablespoons all-purpose flour
2 tablespoons Dutch-process cocoa powder
1 tablespoon cold unsalted butter
½ cup milk
½ ounce unsweetened chocolate,
   chopped fine
1 large egg yolk
2 large egg whites
confectioners' sugar for dusting
   the soufflés

Butter 2 shallow ¾-cup gratin dishes and dust them with the additional granulated sugar, shaking out the excess. In a bowl blend together 2 tablespoons of the remaining granulated sugar, the flour, the cocoa powder, the butter, and a pinch of salt until the mixture resembles meal. In a saucepan bring the milk to a boil. Whisk the cocoa mixture into the milk with the chocolate, cook the mixture over moderate heat, whisking, for 1 minute, or until it is thickened, and let it cool. In a bowl beat the egg yolk slightly and beat in the chocolate mixture. In another bowl beat the egg whites with a pinch of salt until they hold soft peaks, add the remaining 2 tablespoons granulated sugar, a little at a time, beating, and beat the meringue until it holds stiff glossy peaks. Stir one fourth of the meringue into the chocolate pastry cream to lighten it and fold in the remaining meringue gently but thoroughly. Divide the mixture between the prepared dishes and bake the soufflés in a shallow baking pan in the middle of a preheated 400° F. oven for 15 minutes, or until they are puffed. Dust the soufflés decoratively with the confectioners' sugar and serve them immediately. Serves 2.

Frozen Cranberry Soufflé
with Spun Sugar Cranberry Wreath

For the cranberry mixture
2½ cups cranberries, picked over
⅔ cup sugar
⅔ cup water
For the Italian meringue
¾ cup sugar
⅓ cup water
4 large egg whites

2½ cups well-chilled heavy cream

For the spun sugar wreath
⅓ cup light corn syrup
¼ cup sugar
½ cup cranberries, picked over

mint sprigs for garnish

Make the cranberry mixture: In a heavy saucepan combine the cranberries, the sugar, and the water and bring the mixture to a boil, stirring until the sugar is dissolved. Simmer the mixture, stirring occasionally, for 5 minutes, or until it is thickened, and let it cool completely.

Make the Italian meringue: In a small heavy saucepan combine the sugar and the water and bring the mixture to a boil, stirring until the sugar is dissolved. Boil the syrup, washing down any sugar crystals clinging to the side of the pan with a brush dipped in cold water, until it registers 248° F. on a candy thermometer and remove the pan from the heat. While the syrup is boiling, in the large bowl of an electric mixer beat the egg whites with a pinch of salt until they hold soft peaks, with the motor running add the hot syrup in a stream, beating, and beat the meringue at medium speed for 8 minutes, or until it cools to room temperature.

Fold the cranberry mixture into the meringue gently but thoroughly. In another bowl with cleaned beaters beat the cream until it just holds stiff peaks and fold it into the cranberry mixture gently but thoroughly. Spoon the soufflé into a 2½-quart (8-inch diameter) freezer-proof glass serving bowl, smoothing the top, and freeze the soufflé, its surface covered with plastic wrap, overnight. *The soufflé may be made 3 days in advance and kept covered and frozen.*

Make the spun sugar wreath: In a small heavy saucepan combine the corn syrup and the sugar, bring the

mixture to a boil over moderate heat, stirring until the sugar is dissolved, and boil the syrup until it is a golden caramel and registers 320° F. on a candy thermometer. While the syrup is boiling, oil lightly a 12-inch-square sheet of foil and on it arrange the cranberries in a 6-inch-wide wreath shape. Remove the pan from the heat and let the syrup cool for 30 seconds. Dip a fork into the syrup and drizzle the syrup over the cranberries, repeating this procedure until the cranberries are covered with the syrup and a solid wreath is formed. (If the syrup becomes too thick to drizzle from a fork, reheat it over moderate heat until it is the right consistency.) Let the wreath cool completely. *The wreath may be made 2 hours in advance (preferably not on a damp day) and kept in a cool, dry place.*

Pry the wreath gently from the foil, arrange it on the soufflé, and garnish it with the mint sprigs.

PHOTO ON PAGE 81

B Choulton

237

FROZEN DESSERTS

Toasted Almond Mocha Ice-Cream Tart

For the crust
1¼ cups chocolate-wafer crumbs
    (about 25 wafers)
1 cup sliced blanched almonds, toasted
    lightly, cooled, and ground fine
½ stick (¼ cup) unsalted butter, melted
For the filling
1½ cups sliced blanched almonds, toasted
    lightly and cooled
3½ tablespoons Amaretto
2 pints coffee ice cream, softened
4 ounces fine-quality bittersweet chocolate,
    chopped fine (about 1 cup)

¼ cup sliced blanched almonds, toasted
    lightly and cooled
1 ounce fine-quality bittersweet chocolate,
    chopped fine or grated

Make the crust: In a bowl stir together with a fork the wafer crumbs, the almonds, and the butter until the mixture is combined well, pat the mixture onto the bottom and side of an oiled 10-inch fluted tart pan with a removable rim, and freeze the crust for 30 minutes, or until it is firm.

Make the filling: In a food processor blend the almonds, scraping down the side occasionally, for 5 minutes, or until they form a nut butter, and with the motor running add the Amaretto. Add the ice cream and the chocolate and pulse the motor 6 to 8 times, or until the filling is smooth and combined well.

Transfer the filling to the crust, spreading it evenly. Garnish the top of the tart with the almonds and the chocolate and freeze the tart, uncovered, for 1 hour. Cover the tart with plastic wrap and freeze it overnight.

Cappuccino Gelato

5 cups milk
⅓ cup instant espresso powder
4 tablespoons cornstarch
1½ cups sugar

In a small bowl whisk ½ cup of the milk, scalded, into the espresso powder, whisking until the powder is dis-

solved. In another small bowl stir ½ cup of the remaining milk into the cornstarch, stirring until the cornstarch is dissolved. In a large heavy saucepan combine the remaining 4 cups milk and the sugar and bring the mixture just to a boil, stirring until the sugar is dissolved. Stir the cornstarch mixture, whisk it into the milk mixture, and simmer the mixture, whisking, for 2 minutes. Whisk in the espresso mixture. Let the mixture cool to room temperature, chill it, covered, until it is cold, and freeze it in an ice-cream freezer according to the manufacturer's instructions. Makes about 1 quart.

Coconut Snowballs with Mocha Sauce

vanilla ice cream, scooped into 4 balls and
    frozen for 15 minutes
1 cup sweetened coconut (about a 3½-ounce
    can), toasted lightly if desired and
    chopped fine
⅓ cup firmly packed light brown sugar
1 tablespoon light corn syrup
2 tablespoons instant espresso powder
1½ ounces unsweetened chocolate, chopped fine
¼ cup heavy cream
1 tablespoon Kahlúa

In a shallow dish roll the ice-cream balls in the coconut, coating them heavily, and freeze the snowballs while making the mocha sauce. In a small heavy saucepan combine the brown sugar, the corn syrup, and the espresso powder, bring the mixture to a boil over moderate heat, stirring, and cook it, stirring constantly, for 3 minutes, or until the sugar is dissolved. Remove the pan from the heat, stir in the chocolate, the cream, the Kahlúa, and a pinch of salt, and stir the sauce until it is smooth. Pour some of the mocha sauce onto each of 2 plates, divide the snowballs between the plates, and serve the remaining sauce separately. Serves 2.

Vanilla Ice Cream with Amaretti and Plum Sauce

1 cup vanilla ice cream, softened slightly
½ cup crumbled *amaretti*
    (Italian almond macaroons) or other
    crisp almond macaroons
2 plums, cut into 1-inch pieces
2 to 3 tablespoons sugar
2 teaspoons fresh lemon juice
1 tablespoon dark rum, or to taste

In a small metal bowl stir together the ice cream and the *amaretti* until the mixture is combined well and freeze the mixture, its surface covered with plastic wrap, for 30 minutes. In a small saucepan combine the plums, the sugar to taste, and the lemon juice and simmer the mixture, covered, for 10 minutes, or until the plums are very tender. Force the mixture through a sieve or the medium disk of a food mill set over a bowl, discarding the skins, let the sauce cool, and stir in the rum. Divide the ice-cream mixture between 2 bowls and pour the sauce over it. Serves 2.

Gingered Grapefruit Sorbet

3 cups strained fresh grapefruit juice
¾ cup sugar
1 tablespoon grated fresh gingerroot
2 or 3 drops of Angostura bitters,
    or to taste

In a small saucepan combine 1 cup of the grapefruit juice, the sugar, and the gingerroot and boil the mixture, stirring, until the sugar is dissolved. Remove the pan from the heat and let the mixture cool completely.

Pour the mixture through a fine sieve into a bowl or large glass measure, stir in the remaining 2 cups grapefruit juice and the bitters, and chill the mixture, covered, until it is cold. Freeze the mixture in an ice-cream freezer according to the manufacturer's instructions. Makes about 1 quart.

Minted Lemon Granita

⅓ cup sugar
1 cup fresh lemon juice
1 cup packed fresh mint leaves, rinsed and
    spun dry

In a saucepan combine the sugar and the lemon juice, bring the mixture to a boil, stirring until the sugar is dissolved, and let the syrup cool. In a blender or food processor purée the mint with the syrup, transfer the mixture to 2 metal ice-cube trays without dividers or a shallow metal pan, and freeze it, stirring and crushing the lumps with a fork every 30 minutes, for 2 to 3 hours, or until it is firm but not frozen solid. Scrape the granita with a fork to lighten the texture and serve it in chilled goblets. Makes about 3 cups.

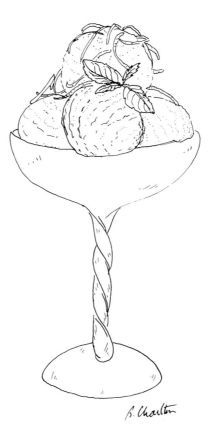

B. Charlton

Frozen Strawberry Lemon Meringue Torte

For the meringue layers

4 large egg whites
1 cup granulated sugar

For the lemon filling

1 teaspoon unflavored gelatin
2 tablespoons cold water
½ cup fresh lemon juice
⅔ cup granulated sugar
3 large egg yolks
2½ teaspoons freshly grated
    lemon zest
½ cup well-chilled heavy cream

For the strawberry filling

1½ teaspoons unflavored gelatin
2 tablespoons cold water
1½ cups sliced strawberries
⅓ cup strawberry preserves
2 tablespoons granulated sugar
3 large egg yolks
½ cup well-chilled heavy cream

For the frosting

1½ teaspoons unflavored gelatin
3 tablespoons cold water
1¼ cups well-chilled heavy cream
⅓ cup sour cream
2 tablespoons confectioners' sugar

strawberries for garnish
    if desired

Make the meringue layers: Line 2 buttered baking sheets with parchment paper or foil and on them trace 3 circles using the bottom of an 8½-inch springform pan as a guide. In a large bowl with an electric mixer beat the egg whites with a pinch of salt until they hold soft peaks, add the sugar gradually, beating, and beat the whites until they hold stiff glossy peaks. Transfer the meringue to a pastry bag fitted with a ½-inch plain tip, beginning in the middle of each parchment circle pipe the meringue in a tight spiral to fill in each circle, and smooth the tops. Bake the meringues on 2 racks in a preheated 250° F. oven, switching the baking sheets from one rack to the other every 30 minutes, for 1 to 1½ hours, or until they are firm when touched and very pale golden. Remove the parchment with the meringue from the baking sheets, let the meringue cool on it, and peel off the parchment carefully. *The meringue layers may be made 1 day in advance and kept, wrapped well in plastic wrap, at room temperature.* With a serrated knife trim the meringue layers so that they will just fit inside the 8½-inch springform pan.

Oil the pan, line it with plastic wrap, leaving an overhang, and arrange 1 of the meringue layers, smooth side down, in the bottom.

Make the lemon filling: In a heavy saucepan sprinkle the gelatin over the water, let it soften for 1 minute, and heat the mixture over low heat, stirring, until the gelatin is dissolved. Whisk in the lemon juice, the sugar, the egg yolks, and the zest and cook the mixture over moderately low heat, whisking constantly, until it registers 170° F. on a candy thermometer. Transfer the mixture to a metal bowl set in a larger bowl of ice and cold water and stir it occasionally until it is very thick but not set. In a bowl beat the cream until it holds soft peaks and fold it into the lemon mixture.

Pour the lemon filling over the meringue layer in the springform pan, top it with 1 of the remaining meringue layers, and freeze the torte for 1 hour, or until the lemon filling is firm.

Make the strawberry filling: In a heavy saucepan sprinkle the gelatin over the water, let it soften for 1 minute, and heat the mixture over low heat, stirring, until the gelatin is dissolved. In a food processor or blender purée the strawberries with the preserves and the sugar, whisk the purée and the egg yolks into the gelatin mixture, and cook the mixture over moderately low heat, whisking constantly, until it registers 170° F. on a candy thermometer. Transfer the mixture to a metal bowl set in a larger bowl of ice and cold water and stir it occasionally until it is very thick but not set. In a bowl beat the cream until it holds soft peaks and fold it into the strawberry mixture.

Pour the strawberry filling over the meringue layer in the springform pan, top it with the remaining meringue layer, smooth side up, and fold the plastic wrap overhang over the top. Freeze the torte for 2 hours, or until it is frozen. *The torte may be prepared up to this point 2 days in advance and kept wrapped well and frozen.*

Make the frosting: In a small saucepan sprinkle the gelatin over the water, let it soften for 1 minute, and heat the mixture over low heat, stirring, until the gelatin is dissolved. In a bowl beat the heavy cream and the sour cream with the confectioners' sugar until the mixture just holds stiff peaks, add the gelatin mixture in a stream, beating, and beat the frosting until it holds stiff peaks.

Remove the side of the pan and transfer the torte to a

serving plate, discarding the plastic wrap. Spread a thin layer of the frosting on the top and side of the torte and freeze the torte for 10 minutes, or until the frosting is firm. Transfer the remaining frosting to a pastry bag fitted with a decorative tip (such as a basket-weave tip), pipe it over the torte, and freeze the torte for at least 30 minutes and up to 4 hours. Let the torte stand in the refrigerator for 30 minutes before serving and garnish it with the strawberries.

PHOTO ON PAGE 33

Pastry Crisps with Vanilla Ice Cream and Orange Caramel Sauce

1 sheet (½ pound) frozen puff pastry, thawed
1 navel orange
¼ cup sugar
⅓ cup water
2 tablespoons Grand Marnier or other
 orange-flavored liqueur
vanilla ice cream

On a lightly floured surface roll out the puff pastry ⅛ inch thick and cut out as many 6-inch squares as desired, reserving any remaining dough, covered and chilled, for another use. (Extra squares, baked, keep in an airtight container at room temperature for several days.) Transfer the squares to an ungreased baking sheet, bake them in the upper third of a preheated 425° F. oven for 12 to 15 minutes, or until they are crisp and golden, and let them cool on a rack.

While the pastry is baking, remove the zest from half the orange with a vegetable peeler and chop it. With a serrated knife cut away the remaining zest and the pith from the orange, discarding them, and cut the sections free from the membranes, discarding the membranes. In a heavy skillet cook the sugar over moderate heat, undisturbed, until it begins to melt and continue cooking the sugar, swirling the skillet, until it is a golden caramel. Remove the skillet from the heat and add the water carefully with the chopped zest. Simmer the sugar mixture, stirring, until the caramel is dissolved, add the Grand Marnier, and boil the mixture until it is reduced to about ¼ cup. Strain the sauce into a bowl and let it cool until it is warm.

Put a pastry square on each of 2 dessert plates, top each pastry with a scoop of the ice cream and some of the orange sections, and drizzle each serving with some of the sauce. Serves 2.

FRUIT FINALES

Ginger-Baked Apples

1½ tablespoons unsalted butter, softened
2½ tablespoons firmly packed brown sugar
½ teaspoon ground ginger
2 tablespoons finely chopped pecans
 or walnuts
2 tablespoons raisins, chopped
two ½-pound Golden Delicious apples
½ lemon
vanilla ice cream as an accompaniment
 if desired

In a bowl stir together the butter, the brown sugar, the ginger, the pecans, and the raisins. Core the apples, peel the top third of them, and rub the peeled flesh with the lemon. Spoon the ginger mixture into the apple cavities, mounding it, arrange the apples in a deep microwave-safe dish, and microwave them, covered, at high power (100%), rotating the dish halfway through the cooking, for 8 minutes. Transfer the apples to 2 plates, spoon the cooking liquid over them, and serve the apples with the ice cream. Serves 2.

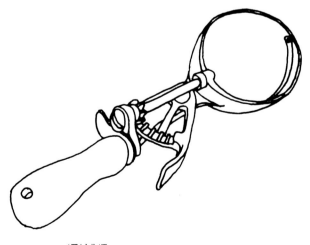

JEANNE

Babas au Calvados with Glazed Apple Rings

For the babas

1½ teaspoons active dry yeast

1 tablespoon sugar

¼ cup lukewarm milk

¾ cup all-purpose flour

1 large egg

¼ teaspoon salt

3 tablespoons unsalted butter, cut into
pieces and softened

½ teaspoon cinnamon

For the syrup

½ cup sugar

1 cup water

⅓ cup Calvados

For the glaze

¼ cup apple jelly

2 tablespoons Calvados

1 tablespoon sugar

glazed apple rings (recipe follows) and
crème fraîche for garnish

Make the babas: Butter eight ⅓-cup ring molds. In the bowl of an electric mixer proof the yeast with the sugar in the milk for 5 minutes, or until the mixture is foamy. Stir in ¼ cup of the flour, stir the mixture until it is smooth, and let the sponge rise, covered, in a warm place for 20 minutes, or until it is doubled in bulk. In a small bowl whisk together lightly the egg and the salt. To the yeast mixture add the remaining ½ cup flour in 2 batches alternately with the egg mixture, beating well after each addition. Beat in the butter, 1 piece at a time, beating well after each addition, and the cinnamon and beat the dough, scraping down the side of the bowl, for 3 minutes. (The dough will be very soft.) Divide the dough among the prepared ring molds set in a jelly-roll pan, let the babas rise, uncovered, for 15 minutes, or until they are just even with the tops of the molds, and bake them in the middle of a preheated 375° F. oven for 15 minutes, or until they are golden. Transfer the babas in the molds to a rack set over another jelly-roll pan and let them cool for 10 minutes, or until they are warm.

Make the syrup while the babas are cooling: In a small saucepan combine the sugar and the water, bring the mixture to a boil, stirring until the sugar is dissolved, and simmer the syrup for 3 minutes. Remove the pan from the heat and stir in the Calvados.

Make the glaze: In a small saucepan combine the jel-

ly, the Calvados, and the sugar, bring the mixture to a boil, and simmer it, stirring, for 2 minutes.

Run a thin, sharp knife around the center and side of each mold and invert the babas onto the rack. Reserve ½ cup of the syrup in a measuring cup, spoon the remaining syrup, heated to warm, over the babas, reusing the syrup that drips into the pan, until it is all absorbed, and let the babas stand for 15 minutes. *The babas may be prepared up to this point 1 day in advance, kept on the rack set over the jelly-roll pan, and covered with foil.*

Brush the glaze, heated to warm, carefully over the babas. *The babas may be glazed 1 hour in advance.*

Reserve 6 to 8 small apple rings. Arrange the remaining apple rings decoratively in overlapping rings on each of 6 to 8 plates, top them with the babas, and garnish each baba with a spoonful of the *crème fraîche*. Fold the reserved apple rings in half and roll the halves into cones to resemble flower buds. Garnish each baba with an apple-ring "bud" and drizzle some of the reserved syrup around it. Serves 6 to 8.

PHOTO ON PAGE 70

Glazed Apple Rings

4 Red Delicious apples

2 tablespoons unsalted butter, softened

½ cup fresh lemon juice

3 tablespoons sugar for sprinkling the apple rings

Core 2 of the apples and cut them crosswise with a hand-held slicing device into ⅛-inch-thick rings, discarding the ends. Butter a jelly-roll pan with 1 tablespoon of the butter and in it arrange the apple rings in one layer. Pour ¼ cup of the lemon juice over the apple rings, turn the rings to coat them with the juice, and broil them under a preheated broiler about 4 inches from the heat for 6 minutes, or until the edges just begin to turn golden. Sprinkle about ¼ teaspoon of the sugar over each ring, broil the rings for 2 minutes more, or until they are glazed and golden, and transfer them to another jelly-roll pan to cool. Make more glazed apple rings in the same manner with the remaining apples, butter, lemon juice, and sugar. *The glazed apple rings may be made 3 hours in advance, kept covered loosely at room temperature, and, if desired, reheated, arranged decoratively into 6 clusters of overlapping rings, in a buttered jelly-roll pan in a preheated 350° F. oven for 10 minutes before serving.*

PHOTO ON PAGE 70

⅓ cup granulated sugar
½ cup raisins
½ teaspoon cinnamon
twelve 17- by 12-inch sheets of
    phyllo, stacked between 2 sheets
    of wax paper and covered with a
    dampened kitchen towel
confectioners' sugar for dusting the strudels
For the whipped cream
1 cup well-chilled heavy cream
¼ cup sour cream
¼ cup confectioners' sugar
1 teaspoon vanilla

Make the strudels: In a small skillet cook the bread crumbs in 1½ tablespoons of the butter over moderate heat, stirring, until they are golden and transfer them to a large bowl. To the bread crumbs add the apples, the granulated sugar, the raisins, and the cinnamon and toss the mixture well. On a work surface arrange an 18-inch-long piece of wax paper with a long side facing you, cover it with 1 sheet of the *phyllo*, and brush the *phyllo* lightly with some of the remaining butter, melted. Layer 5 more sheets of the *phyllo* over the first sheet in the same manner, brushing each sheet lightly with some of the melted butter, and mound half the apple mixture evenly along the long side facing you, leaving a 2-inch border at each end. Using the wax paper as a guide and rolling away from you, roll up the strudel tightly and, with the seam side down, fold the ends under to enclose the filling. Transfer the strudel carefully to a lightly buttered jelly-roll pan and brush it with some of the remaining melted butter. Make another strudel with the remaining *phyllo*, melted butter, and apple filling in the same manner and transfer it to the jelly-roll pan. Bake the strudels in the middle of a preheated 375° F. oven for 35 to 45 minutes, or until they are golden, and let them cool to warm in the pan on a rack. *The strudels may be made 1 day in advance and kept covered loosely at room temperature. Reheat the strudels in a preheated 400° F. oven for 15 minutes.* Transfer the strudels with slotted spatulas carefully to serving platters and dust them with the confectioners' sugar.

Make the whipped cream: In a chilled bowl with an electric mixer beat the heavy cream with the sour cream, the confectioners' sugar, and the vanilla until the mixture holds soft peaks and transfer it to a bowl.

Serve the strudels warm, sliced diagonally, with the whipped cream. Makes 2 strudels.

Apple Raisin Strudels

For the strudels
½ cup fine dry bread crumbs
7½ tablespoons unsalted butter
1½ pounds tart apples, such as
    Granny Smith, peeled, quartered,
    and sliced thin crosswise

Apricot Berry Trifle

For the apricot custard
2½ cups milk
1 vanilla bean, split lengthwise
6 large egg yolks
⅔ cup sugar
3 tablespoons cornstarch
3 tablespoons apricot brandy, or to taste
½ cup *crème fraîche* (available at specialty
   foods shops and many supermarkets)
½ cup well-chilled heavy cream
6 large fresh apricots, cut into ½-inch pieces
   (about 2 cups)

For the red berry mixture
4 cups strawberries, hulled
2 cups raspberries, picked over
2 tablespoons sugar, or to taste
1 to 2 tablespoons fresh lemon juice,
   or to taste
1 to 2 tablespoons framboise or Chambord,
   or to taste

For the blackberry mixture
2½ cups blackberries, picked over
1 tablespoon sugar
1 tablespoon fresh lemon juice
1 tablespoon framboise or Chambord

lemon almond spongecake for trifle
   (recipe follows)
¼ cup apricot brandy
raspberries and blackberries for garnish
   plus additional raspberries as
   an accompaniment if desired

Make the apricot custard: In a heavy saucepan scald the milk with the vanilla bean. In a metal bowl whisk together the egg yolks, the sugar, the cornstarch, sifted, and a pinch of salt. Add the milk mixture to the yolk mixture in a stream, whisking, and transfer the mixture to the pan. Boil the custard, whisking, for 1 minute, or until it is thick and smooth, strain it through a fine sieve into a bowl, and stir in the brandy. Chill the custard, its surface covered with plastic wrap, for at least 6 hours or overnight. Whisk in the *crème fraîche*, fold in the heavy cream, beaten to stiff peaks, and the apricots, and chill the apricot custard, covered.

Make the red berry mixture: In a blender or food processor purée 2 cups of the strawberries, sliced, and 1 cup of the raspberries with the sugar, the lemon juice,

and the framboise until the mixture is smooth, force the purée through a fine sieve into a bowl, pressing hard on the solids, and stir in the remaining 2 cups strawberries and 1 cup raspberries, both crushed lightly.

Make the blackberry mixture: In a blender or food processor purée 1½ cups of the blackberries with the sugar, the lemon juice, and the framboise until the mixture is smooth, transfer the purée to a bowl, and stir in the remaining 1 cup blackberries, crushed lightly.

Assemble the trifle: Arrange one third of the cake on the bottom of a 3½- to 4-quart trifle bowl, sprinkle it with one third of the brandy, and pour half the red berry mixture evenly over the cake. Spoon one third of the apricot custard evenly over the red berry layer, top it with half the remaining cake, and sprinkle the cake with half the remaining brandy. Pour the blackberry mixture evenly over the cake, spoon half the remaining custard over it, and top the custard with the remaining cake. Sprinkle the cake with the remaining brandy, pour the remaining red berry mixture evenly over it, and spoon the remaining custard evenly over the red berry layer, covering the red berry layer completely.

Chill the trifle, covered, for at least 12 hours or overnight, garnish it with the berries, and serve it with the additional raspberries. Serves 12.

Lemon Almond Spongecake for Trifle

1 cup all-purpose flour
½ teaspoon salt
2 teaspoons double-acting baking powder
½ cup finely ground blanched almonds
5 large eggs, separated
1 cup sugar
1½ tablespoons freshly grated lemon zest
4 tablespoons fresh lemon juice
1 teaspoon vanilla
1 teaspoon almond extract

Line a greased jelly-roll pan, 15½ by 10½ by 1 inches, with wax paper, grease the paper, and dust the pan with flour, knocking out the excess. Into a bowl sift together the flour, the salt, and the baking powder and whisk in the almonds. In the bowl of an electric mixer beat together the egg yolks, ¾ cup of the sugar, and the zest until the mixture is very thick and pale, beat in the lemon juice, the vanilla, and the almond extract, and beat the mixture for 3 to 5 minutes, or until it forms a ribbon when the beater is lifted. Add the flour mixture and beat the batter until it is just combined. In another bowl with cleaned beaters beat the egg whites with a pinch of salt until they form soft peaks, beat in the remaining ¼ cup sugar, a little at a time, and beat the whites until they form stiff peaks. Whisk one third of the whites into the batter to lighten it and fold in the remaining whites gently but thoroughly.

Spread the batter evenly in the prepared pan and bake it in the middle of a preheated 350° F. oven for 15 to 20 minutes, or until the cake is golden and a tester comes out clean. Let the cake cool in the pan for 5 minutes, invert it onto a rack, and discard the wax paper. Invert the cake onto another rack and let it stand, uncovered, overnight to dry out. Cut the cake with a serrated knife into ¾-inch cubes.

Grapefruit and Banana Rum Gratins

2 large grapefruit, the zest, pith, and
    membranes cut away with a serrated knife
    and the flesh cut into sections
1 large banana, cut crosswise into
    ¼-inch-thick slices
1 cup milk
½ vanilla bean, split lengthwise
1 large whole egg
1 large egg yolk
½ cup granulated sugar
3 tablespoons all-purpose flour
2 tablespoons dark rum, or to taste
⅓ cup well-chilled heavy cream
sifted confectioners' sugar for sprinkling
    the gratins

Divide the grapefruit sections and the banana slices among four 6-inch (1- to 1¼-cup-capacity) gratin dishes. In a small saucepan combine the milk and the vanilla bean and bring the milk just to a boil. While the milk is heating, in a metal bowl whisk together the whole egg, the egg yolk, the granulated sugar, the flour, sifted, and a pinch of salt. Add the milk mixture in a stream, whisking. Transfer the pastry cream to the pan, bring it to a boil, and simmer it, whisking, for 2 minutes.

Force the pastry cream through a fine sieve into a bowl, discarding the vanilla bean, whisk in the rum, and let the pastry cream cool slightly. In another bowl with an electric mixer beat the heavy cream until it holds stiff peaks, whisk a small amount of the whipped cream into the pastry cream, and fold in the remaining whipped

cream gently but thoroughly. Pour one fourth of the cream mixture into each gratin dish, spreading it to cover the fruit completely, and sprinkle each gratin with some of the confectioners' sugar. Arrange the gratins in a large baking pan and broil them under a preheated broiler about 4 inches from the heat for 2 to 4 minutes, or until they are browned and heated through. Serves 4.

Nectarine Almond Cobbler

⅓ cup sugar
1 teaspoon cornstarch
2 nectarines (about ¾ pound), sliced thin
1 tablespoon fresh lemon juice
½ cup all-purpose flour
½ teaspoon double-acting baking powder
¼ teaspoon salt
2 tablespoons almond paste
2 tablespoons unsalted butter
¼ cup boiling water

In a bowl stir together the sugar and the cornstarch, add the nectarines and the lemon juice, and combine the mixture well. In another bowl whisk together the flour, the baking powder, and the salt, blend in the almond paste and the butter until the mixture resembles coarse meal, and stir in the boiling water, stirring the mixture until it is just combined.

Turn the nectarine mixture into a buttered 8-inch-square baking pan, drop the almond dough in 6 mounds onto it, and bake the cobbler in the middle of a preheated 400° F. oven for 20 to 25 minutes, or until the top is golden. Serves 2.

Papaya in Cinnamon Syrup

2 cups sugar
a 4-inch cinnamon stick
3½ pounds firm papayas, peeled, seeded, and cut
   lengthwise into ½-inch-thick strips

In a heavy 3-quart saucepan spread ⅔ cup of the sugar, add the cinnamon stick, and top the sugar with half the papaya strips. Sprinkle ⅔ cup of the remaining sugar on top, add the remaining papaya strips, and top the strips with the remaining ⅔ cup sugar. Cook the mixture, covered, over moderately low heat, shaking the pan occasionally (do not stir), for 35 to 45 minutes, or until the sugar is dissolved completely. Simmer the papaya strips, uncovered, for 10 minutes, or until they begin to appear translucent. Let the mixture cool and chill it, covered, overnight. The papaya in cinnamon syrup keeps, covered and chilled, for 1 month. Makes about 5 cups.

PHOTO ON PAGES 34 AND 35

Pears with Pear Sauce

3 firm-ripe small pears
3 tablespoons sugar
2 tablespoons heavy cream
⅛ teaspoon vanilla
1 tablespoon unsalted butter
a 2½- by 1-inch strip of lemon zest

Peel, core, and chop coarse 1 of the pears. In a small dry non-stick skillet sauté the pear over moderately high heat, stirring occasionally, for 5 to 6 minutes, or until it is tender and golden, and transfer it to a small food processor. In the skillet, cleaned and dried, melt the sugar over moderately low heat, stirring with a fork, and cook the syrup, swirling the skillet gently, until it is a light caramel. Remove the skillet from the heat, pour the heavy cream carefully down the side of the skillet, and whisk the mixture until the caramel is dissolved and the mixture is smooth. Add the caramel to the food processor, blending it with the cooked pear until it is smooth. Stir in the vanilla and keep the sauce warm.

Peel, halve, and core the remaining 2 pears. In the skillet, cleaned, melt the butter over moderately low heat, add the zest and the pears, and cook the pears for 4 to 5 minutes on each side, or until they are tender. Divide the pears between 2 plates and spoon the pear sauce over them. Serves 2.

Strawberries with Zabaglione

1 cup strawberries, hulled and quartered
   lengthwise
2 tablespoons Marsala
2 large eggs
2 tablespoons sugar

Divide the strawberries and 1 tablespoon of the Marsala between 2 goblets and let the strawberries macerate for 15 minutes. In a metal bowl whisk together the eggs and the sugar, set the bowl over a saucepan of simmering water, and whisk the mixture until it begins to thicken. Whisk in the remaining 1 tablespoon Marsala, continue to whisk the mixture until it is thick and foamy and registers 160° F. on a candy thermometer, and spoon the zabaglione over the strawberries. Serves 2.

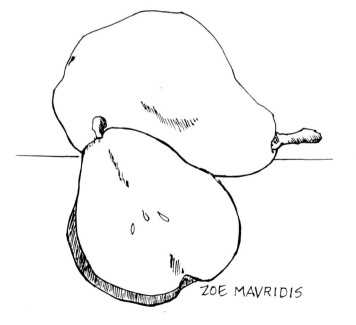

ZOE MAVRIDIS

Winter Fruit Compote with Ginger

2 to 2½ cups dried cranberries (available
    at specialty foods shops and some
    supermarkets)
2 cups fresh orange juice
a 10½-ounce jar preserved ginger
    in syrup
3 cups seedless green grapes, halved
3 large pink grapefruit, the rind and pith
    cut away with a serrated knife and the
    flesh sectioned
½ pineapple, peeled, cored, and cut into
    ½-inch pieces
1 large navel orange, the rind and pith
    cut away with a serrated knife and
    the flesh sectioned

In a bowl let the cranberries soak in the orange juice
for 30 minutes, drain them in a sieve set over a bowl,
and reserve the juice. Reserve 1 large piece of the preserved ginger and in a blender or food processor purée
the remaining ginger with the syrup and the reserved orange juice. In a deep 2-quart glass serving dish arrange
half the cranberries, drizzle them with about ½ cup of
the ginger mixture, and top them with the grapes. Drizzle the grapes with about ½ cup of the remaining ginger
mixture, top them with the grapefruit, and drizzle the
grapefruit with about ½ cup of the remaining ginger
mixture. Top the grapefruit with the pineapple, drizzle
it with the remaining ginger mixture, and arrange the remaining cranberries on top. Arrange the orange sections
over the cranberries, chill the compote, covered, for at
least 2 hours or overnight, and serve it garnished with
the reserved ginger, cut into julienne strips. Serves 8.

CONFECTIONS

Coconut Date Nut Balls

½ cup graham cracker crumbs
½ pound (about 1½ cups) pitted dried dates
1¼ cups sweetened flaked coconut, toasted
    and cooled
¼ cup honey
½ cup walnuts, chopped fine

In a food processor blend the graham cracker crumbs,
the dates, ½ cup of the coconut, and the honey until the
mixture is just combined. Add the walnuts and blend the
mixture until it forms a ball. Have ready in a shallow
dish the remaining ¾ cup coconut, form the date mixture into walnut-size balls, and roll the balls in the coconut, pressing the coconut slightly to make it adhere.
Makes about 32 confections.

Trail Mix

1¼ cups M&M's
1¼ cups salted peanuts
1¼ cups raisins
½ cup finely chopped dried apricots
chocolate twig candies (available at specialty
    foods shops) for garnish

In a large bowl toss together well the M&M's, the
peanuts, the raisins, and the apricots. Divide the trail
mix among 6 cups and garnish the cups with the chocolate twig candies. Serves 6.

PHOTO ON PAGE 27

BEVERAGES

ALCOHOLIC

Aquavit Bloody Marys

1 cup aquavit
4 cups tomato vegetable juice
2 tablespoons bottled horseradish
2 tablespoons Worcestershire sauce
3 tablespoons fresh lemon juice
½ teaspoon Tabasco
¼ teaspoon pepper
6 small celery ribs and lemon slices
   for garnish

In a pitcher combine the aquavit, the tomato vegetable juice, the horseradish, the Worcestershire sauce, the lemon juice, the Tabasco, and the pepper and stir the mixture well. Divide the Bloody Mary mixture among 6 glasses filled with ice and garnish each drink with a celery rib and a lemon slice. Serves 6.

PHOTO ON PAGE 34

Champagne Punch

1 cup triple sec
1 cup brandy
½ cup Chambord
2 cups unsweetened pineapple juice
1 quart chilled ginger ale
2 chilled 750-ml. bottles dry Champagne

In a bowl combine the triple sec, the brandy, the Chambord, and the pineapple juice and chill the mixture, covered, for at least 4 hours or overnight. In a large punch bowl combine the triple sec mixture, the ginger ale, and the Champagne and add ice cubes. Makes about 16 cups, serving 12.

"Damn the Weather" Cocktails
(Port, Pineapple Juice, and Orange Juice)

2 cups Ruby Port
1 cup unsweetened pineapple juice
1 cup fresh orange juice
1 teaspoon fresh lemon juice
chilled club soda or seltzer
6 lemon slices
   for garnish

In a large pitcher stir together well the Port, the pineapple juice, the orange juice, and the lemon juice. Divide the drink among 6 glasses filled with ice cubes. Top off the drinks with the soda and garnish them with the lemon slices. Makes 6 drinks.

PHOTO ON PAGE 64

Lillet au Citron
(Lillet and Lemon Syrup Cocktails)

¼ cup sugar
¼ cup fresh lemon juice
ice cubes if desired
1 cup white Lillet
chilled soda water
2 lemon slices for garnish
   if desired

In a small saucepan combine the sugar and the lemon juice, bring the mixture to a boil, stirring until the sugar is dissolved, and simmer it for 5 minutes. Let the lemon syrup cool completely. In each of 2 glasses filled with the ice stir together ½ cup of the Lillet and 1 to 2 tablespoons of the lemon syrup, or to taste, top off the drinks with the soda water, and garnish them with the lemon slices. Makes 2 drinks.

PHOTO ON PAGES 52 AND 53

Pernod and Water

ice cubes if desired
3 ounces (2 jiggers) Pernod,
    or to taste
water to taste

In a glass half-filled with the ice stir together the Pernod and the water (the mixture will become cloudy). Makes 1 drink.

PHOTO ON PAGE 53

Tequila Sunrises
(Tequila, Orange Juice, and Grenadine)

⅔ cup Tequila
3 cups fresh orange juice
1 tablespoon grenadine,
    or to taste
6 orange slices for garnish

In a large pitcher stir together well the Tequila, the orange juice, and the grenadine. Divide the drink among 6 glasses filled with ice cubes. Garnish the drinks with the orange slices. Makes 6 drinks.

PHOTO ON PAGE 64

"Two-Dollar Cocktail"
(Brandy and Curaçao Cocktail)

ice cubes
1½ ounces (1 jigger) French brandy
1½ ounces (1 jigger) Curaçao
a lemon twist for garnish
    if desired

In a cocktail shaker half-filled with the ice combine the brandy and the Curaçao and shake the mixture for 30 seconds. Pour or strain the drink into a tall glass, add more ice, and garnish the drink with the lemon twist. Makes 1 drink.

PHOTO ON PAGE 53

Frozen Yogurt Melon Shake

2 cups scooped-out melon, such as honeydew
    or cantaloupe
1 tablespoon Midori liqueur if desired
1 teaspoon fresh lemon juice
1½ cups frozen vanilla yogurt

In a blender purée the melon with the Midori, the lemon juice, and a pinch of salt, add the frozen yogurt, and blend the shake until it is smooth. Makes about 3 cups, serving 2.

Brandy Alexander White Hot Chocolate

3½ cups milk
½ of a vanilla bean, split lengthwise
6 ounces fine-quality white chocolate,
    chopped fine, plus shaved white chocolate
    for garnish
⅓ cup Cognac or Armagnac, or to taste
3 tablespoons dark or white *crème de cacao*,
    or to taste
whipped cream for garnish

In a large heavy saucepan combine the milk, the vanilla bean halves, and a pinch of salt and bring the mixture just to a boil over moderate heat. Remove the pan from the heat and let the mixture stand, covered, for 15 minutes. Scrape the seeds from the vanilla bean back into the mixture, discarding the pods, and reheat the mixture until it just comes to a boil. In a small heatproof bowl combine the chopped chocolate with about ⅔ cup of the hot milk mixture and whisk the mixture until the chocolate is melted and the mixture is smooth. Whisk the chocolate mixture into the remaining milk mixture and simmer the hot chocolate, whisking, for 2 minutes. Stir in the Cognac and the *crème de cacao*. (For a frothy result, in a blender blend the hot chocolate in batches.) Divide the hot chocolate among mugs and top it with the whipped cream and the shaved chocolate. Makes about 4 cups, serving 4 to 6.

Grasshopper Hot Chocolate

½ cup unsweetened cocoa powder
⅓ cup sugar
½ cup cold water
1 teaspoon vanilla
1 cup half-and-half
2½ cups milk
⅓ cup *crème de menthe*, or to taste
2 tablespoons *crème de cacao*,
  or to taste
whipped cream and shaved bittersweet
  chocolate for garnish

In a heavy saucepan combine the cocoa powder, the sugar, the water, the vanilla, and a pinch of salt and heat the mixture over low heat, whisking, until the cocoa powder is dissolved and the mixture is a smooth paste. Gradually add the half-and-half and the milk, both scalded, and simmer the hot chocolate, whisking, for 2 minutes. Stir in the *crème de menthe* and the *crème de cacao*. (For a frothy result, in a blender blend the hot chocolate in batches.) Divide the hot chocolate among mugs and top it with the whipped cream and the chocolate. Makes about 4½ cups, serving 4 to 6.

Irish Hot Chocolate

½ cup unsweetened cocoa powder
⅓ cup sugar
1 teaspoon vanilla
½ cup cold water
2¼ cups milk
¾ cup half-and-half
½ cup Baileys Original Irish Cream liqueur,
  or to taste
whipped cream and shaved bittersweet
  chocolate for garnish

In a large heavy saucepan combine the cocoa powder, the sugar, the vanilla, the water, and a pinch of salt and heat the mixture over low heat, whisking, until the cocoa powder is dissolved and the mixture is a smooth paste. Gradually add the milk and the half-and-half, both scalded, and simmer the hot chocolate, whisking, for 2 minutes. Stir in the Baileys. (For a frothy result, in a blender blend the hot chocolate in batches.) Divide the hot chocolate among mugs and top it with the whipped cream and the chocolate. Makes about 4½ cups, serving 4 to 6.

Mexican Hot Chocolate

3½ cups milk
⅓ cup firmly packed light brown sugar
¾ teaspoon ground cinnamon
1½ teaspoons vanilla
3 ounces unsweetened chocolate,
  chopped fine
½ cup Kahlúa, or to taste
cinnamon sticks for garnish

In a large heavy saucepan combine the milk, the brown sugar, the ground cinnamon, the vanilla, and a pinch of salt and bring the mixture just to a boil over moderate heat. In a small heatproof bowl combine the chocolate with about ½ cup of the hot milk mixture and whisk the mixture until the chocolate is melted and the mixture is smooth. Add the chocolate mixture to the remaining milk mixture and simmer the hot chocolate, whisking, for 2 minutes. Whisk in the Kahlúa. (For a frothy result, in a blender blend the hot chocolate in batches.) Divide the hot chocolate among mugs and serve it with the cinnamon sticks as stirrers. Makes about 4 cups, serving 4 to 6.

NONALCOHOLIC

Cranberry Apple Cocktails

4 cups cranberry juice
2 cups apple juice or cider
½ cup fresh orange juice

In a pitcher combine the juices, chill the cocktail for 1 hour, or until it is cold, and divide it among 8 glasses. Serves 8.

PHOTO ON PAGE 83

Blueberry Banana Shakes

1 banana, cut into pieces
2 cups fresh or frozen blueberries, picked over
¼ cup honey
2 cups plain yogurt

In a blender blend the banana, the blueberries, the honey, and the yogurt until the mixture is smooth and chill the mixture for 1 hour if desired. Pour the mixture into chilled glasses. (Frozen blueberries result in slightly thicker shakes.) Makes about 3¼ cups.

Cantaloupe Raspberry Shakes

a 2½-pound cantaloupe, seeded and cut into
   ¾-inch pieces (about 4 cups)
1 pint raspberry *sorbet*
1 cup ice cubes

In a blender blend 2 cups of the cantaloupe, the *sorbet*, and the ice until the mixture is almost smooth. Add the remaining 2 cups cantaloupe, blend the mixture until it is smooth, and pour it into chilled glasses. Makes about 4½ cups.

Chocolate Raspberry Shakes

1⅓ cups raspberries (about 6 ounces)
1 pint chocolate frozen yogurt
1½ cups milk

In a blender blend the raspberries, the frozen yogurt, and the milk until the mixture is smooth and pour the mixture into chilled glasses. Makes about 3½ cups.

Coffee Date Shakes

1 cup pitted dates
1 pint coffee frozen yogurt or ice cream
1 cup milk

In a blender blend the dates, the frozen yogurt, and the milk until the mixture is smooth and pour the mixture into chilled glasses. Makes about 3½ cups.

Gingered Cantaloupe Shakes

a 1¾-pound cantaloupe, seeded and cut into
   ½-inch pieces (about 2 cups), plus
   cantaloupe slices for garnish
1 tablespoon chopped crystallized ginger
1 pint vanilla frozen yogurt
   or ice cream

In a blender blend the cantaloupe pieces, the ginger, and the frozen yogurt until the mixture is smooth, pour the mixture into chilled glasses, and garnish it with the cantaloupe slices. Makes about 3 cups.

Iced Mocha Shakes

1 cup strong brewed coffee, chilled
1 cup coffee frozen yogurt
3 tablespoons unsweetened cocoa powder
½ cup milk
sugar to taste

In a blender blend the coffee, the frozen yogurt, the cocoa powder, the milk, and the sugar until the mixture is smooth and pour the mixture into chilled glasses. Makes about 3½ cups.

Papaya Citrus Shakes

a 1-pound papaya, peeled, seeded, and cut
   into ½-inch pieces
½ cup fresh lime juice
1 pint lemon *sorbet*
1 cup ice cubes
lime slices for garnish

In a blender blend the papaya, the lime juice, the *sorbet*, and the ice until the mixture is smooth. Pour the mixture into chilled glasses and garnish it with the lime slices. Makes about 3¾ cups.

Raspberry Orange Shakes

1⅓ cups raspberries
  (about 6 ounces)
¾ cup fresh orange juice
1 pint raspberry *sorbet*
1 cup ice cubes

In a blender blend the raspberries, the orange juice, the *sorbet*, and the ice until the mixture is smooth and pour the mixture into chilled glasses. Makes about 3½ cups.

Strawberry Coconut Pineapple Shakes

8 ounces strawberries, hulled and sliced
  (about 1 cup)
½ cup well-stirred canned cream of coconut
1 pint vanilla frozen yogurt
1 cup chilled unsweetened pineapple juice

In a blender blend the strawberries, the cream of coconut, the frozen yogurt, and the pineapple juice until the mixture is smooth and pour the mixture into chilled glasses. Makes about 3¼ cups.

Strawberry Mango Shakes

8 ounces strawberries, hulled and sliced
  (about 1 cup), plus whole strawberries
  for garnish
a ¾-pound mango, peeled, pitted, and cut
  into ½-inch pieces
½ pint strawberry *sorbet*
1½ cups chilled unsweetened pineapple juice

In a blender blend the sliced strawberries, the mango pieces, the strawberry *sorbet*, and the pineapple juice until the mixture is smooth. Pour the mixture into chilled glasses and garnish it with the whole strawberries. Makes about 4 cups.

Vanilla Orange Shakes

1½ cups fresh orange juice
1 pint vanilla frozen yogurt
⅛ teaspoon orange flower water if desired

In a blender blend the orange juice, the frozen yogurt, and the orange flower water until the mixture is smooth and pour the mixture into chilled glasses. Makes about 3¼ cups.

Café au Lait

4 cups hot strong coffee
4 cups scalded milk
6 cinnamon sticks for garnish

Into 6 large mugs pour equal amounts of the coffee and the milk and garnish each serving with a cinnamon stick. Serves 6.

Rich Hot Chocolate

¾ cup heavy cream
3¼ cups milk
1½ teaspoons vanilla
6 ounces fine-quality bittersweet chocolate,
  chopped fine
miniature marshmallows for garnish

In a heavy saucepan combine the cream, the milk, the vanilla, and a pinch of salt and bring the mixture just to a boil over moderate heat. In a small heatproof bowl combine the chocolate with about ⅔ cup of the hot milk mixture and whisk the mixture until the chocolate is melted and the mixture is smooth. Whisk the chocolate mixture into the remaining milk mixture and simmer the hot chocolate, whisking, for 2 minutes. (For a frothy result, in a blender blend the hot chocolate in batches.) Divide the hot chocolate among mugs and top it with the marshmallows. Makes about 4½ cups, serving 4 to 6.

PART THREE

CUISINES OF THE WORLD

THE FLAVORS OF
Italy

You may travel to Italy in search of its ancient ruins, to stroll through its galleries filled with masterpieces of past centuries, or perhaps simply to bask in the beauty of its picturesque hilltop villages, its towering cliffs, and its glimmering Mediterranean shores. But among these national treasures you will also find a warmhearted, inviting people, anxious to share their glorious cuisine. One trip to this blessed country will show you that, here, life itself is a celebration.

For the Italians good living and good food go hand in hand. Since the banquets of ancient Rome, these spirited people have been expressing their passion for life with their delight in dining. Throughout Italy, eating with family and friends is still the high point of the day. From about one o'clock until three or four (except in some urban areas), businesses and schools close for afternoon *pranzo*, and the family leisurely savors the main meal of the day. Hours are spent around the kitchen table, the center of the typical Italian household, talking, relaxing, and enjoying one another's company. In this unhurried world simple pleasures are relished, such as inviting neighbors in at twilight for some home-grown figs, a hunk of aged Parmesan, and *nonna's* (grandma's) crusty fresh bread, or whiling away the evening sipping espresso with friends at the local *caffè*.

This frank enjoyment of life is reflected in the country's cuisine. The food of Italy, like its people, is bold, bright, and direct. Unlike their French neighbors, who emphasize subtle harmonies and intricate sauces, the Italians prefer to let the genuine flavor of food stand on its own. Simple marinades of golden-green olive oil, aged balsamic vinegar, and fresh herbs enhance but do not overwhelm meat and poultry; and fresh produce is as colorful on the plate as it was in the marketplace.

To achieve the best natural flavor, the proud Italians insist on using only their own home-grown ingredients. They shy away from imports—even from neighboring areas within their own country! The twenty-three regions of Italy were not united until the mid-nineteenth century, so local pride is still strong. Different geography, climate, and history give the provinces their own distinctions, and opinions vary on what constitutes the "supreme" ingredients. A simple request for the "best" pasta recipe, for example, may elicit a variety of responses: A native of Emilia-Romagna will swear by a basic combination of flour and numerous eggs; a Ligurian cook will suggest adding water to flour and a few eggs; and a Neapolitan will praise the use of semolina flour, water, and no eggs at all! But whatever the region, the universal philosophy is to use only the best local foods—the finest produce, the most flavorful meat, and the freshest fish.

However separatist the individual provinces may be, Italy's central location on the European continent has left it open to a host of foreign influences. Many dishes that are now considered "Italian classics" are made with ingredients that were brought to the country from other lands, and, in fact, are not indigenous to the Mediterranean peninsula. Since the fifth century B.C., when the Greeks first planted wheat fields and olive trees in the south, foreign tastes have shaped the country's cuisine. The southern Italian sweet tooth was encouraged by the Arabs, who planted citrus trees and cultivated sugarcane in Sicily. And even the indispensable *pomo d'oro* ("golden apple," or tomato) did not arrive in Italy until the sixteenth century, when it was brought in from Mexico. Explorers from the New World also introduced cornmeal, the main ingredient in today's polenta.

On the following pages we offer a sampling of this diverse cuisine. We begin with information and helpful tips on some of the essentials of Italian cooking. You'll learn how to make *pasta fresca* (fresh pasta, page 257), produce a creamy polenta (page 260), discriminate between olive oils (page 262), and choose among an abundance of Italian cheeses (page 264). Our three menus put these basics to use and capture some of the authentic tastes of northern, central, and southern Italy.

With A Northern Buffet *alla Rustica* you'll sample the flavors of the region's tender livestock, abundant dairy products, and plentiful grain fields. An assortment of *antipasti* includes a Lombard cheese, Taleggio, paired with succulent Parma prosciutto and honeydew melon; flavorful Gorgonzola and fresh sage on soft focaccia; and traditional white bean and tuna salad—to name a few. Two other northern favorites are combined in the entrée of savory veal stew on grilled polenta. And the deliciously light dessert of *tiramisù* (literally, ''lift me up'') raises the feast to new heights.

Our Dinner *alla Romana* takes you to the country's capital, in central Italy. Here you will find *pasta fresca* in the classic Roman dish of fettuccine with creamy white sauce (''fettuccine Alfredo''). The entrée that follows caters to the robust appetites of the central regions with a lively dish of pepper-and-lemon-marinated chicken, accompanied by a colorful array of vegetables. We have also included a wonderful recipe for a hearty fresh bread that's the ideal accompaniment to any meal. And in typical Roman fashion, simple yet delicious almond *biscotti* and lemon ice cream are offered for a sophisticated finale to this cosmopolitan dinner.

Finally, our Southern Sunday Lunch *in Famiglia* honors the traditional family midday meal. A peppery baked ziti starter pays tribute to the spice-loving palates of the south, using *pasta secca* (dried pasta) at its best and boasting eggplants, tomatoes, and bell peppers, all vegetables that flourish in the intense southern sun. And from the seas bordering the tip of the peninsula, swordfish is paired with the much-loved fennel and an assortment of fresh herbs. Then let your guests relax over espresso and a spectacular Sicilian specialty, Cassata—a layer cake filled with ricotta, bittersweet chocolate, and candied orange.

While our menus keep Italian traditions in mind, we have adapted them to American entertaining habits. In Italy the meal is divided into several courses to allow the flavors of each dish to be separately appreciated. Soup, risotto, or pasta is often served as a first course, followed by a fish or meat entrée. Vegetable side dishes or a salad are served in the *contorno* course, usually after the entrée. And a simple dessert of fresh fruit and local cheese follows. On Sundays or holidays assorted *antipasti* begin the meal, and a more elaborate dessert of cake or pastries is accompanied by espresso. Cappuccino, usually a dessert beverage in the United States, is taken at breakfast with assorted biscuits.

Let our menus bring a bit of the Italian zest for life into your home. As you prepare these authentic dishes, allow the warm polenta to take you to hills of Piedmont, the fresh fettuccine to the kitchens of Umbria, and the incredible Cassata to a *pasticceria* (cake shop) in Sicily. Most important, remember to sit back, relax, and enjoy them for hours!

Essentials of Italian Cooking

PASTA

ucatini, fettuccine, tortellini, fusilli, penne, cannelloni, ziti . . . the list goes on and on. Italians adore their pasta. So much so that they've created over 230 varieties of this glorious food. In households from Milan to Sicily there is no dish more lovingly prepared and eagerly awaited. Pasta has been praised for centuries, and with good reason—it is economical, healthful, and versatile and appeals to the renowned restaurant chef as well as the novice cook. Whether it appears with many other ingredients in a warming baked casserole, or simply with a fresh tomato sauce, there is a pasta dish for everyone.

Although Italians have made pasta famous, its origin is unknown. Some people claim that Marco Polo returned to Italy from the Far East with intriguing noodles; others say, simply, that a clever woman in Bologna mixed together some flour and eggs to make the first tagliatelle, Italy's most popular pasta. As far back as the third century A.D., the Roman author Cicero mentions "lagani," which were thin sheets of dough made from flour and water and probably the prototype of to-day's lasagne. Whatever the case may be, pasta has been a staple in Italian cuisine for hundreds of years.

There are two types of pasta—*pasta fresca* (fresh pasta), which is homemade, and *pasta secca* (dried pasta), which is commercially produced. *Pasta fresca* is associated with the northern regions of Italy, especially Emilia-Romagna, where Bologna's Pasta Museum houses the ultimate, perfect tagliatelle—in gold—as a reminder of the area's attachment to this precious food. A supple dough made with flour, water, and usually eggs is cut into *pasta liscia* (strips of smooth, flat noodles), such as fettuccine and lasagne, or is filled and formed into *pasta ripiena* (stuffed pasta), such as ravioli. These varieties are typically paired with lighter tomato sauces and cream sauces, which adhere best to the fresh dough. *Pasta secca* originated in southern Italy, where the hearty semolina flour that is needed for its production is so plentiful. This sturdy dough is used to create an impressive array of pasta shapes, from the familiar spaghetti to the more whimsical *farfalle* ("butterfly"-shaped pasta). The tubular shapes of dried pasta, such as penne, can hold substantial meat and vegetable sauces and are often served with them.

Italians are not known for their compromising nature, and although dried pasta is heartily enjoyed throughout Italy, there are times when only *pasta fatta in casa* (homemade pasta) will do. For Sunday afternoon *pranzo*, holidays, and feast days, out come the flour, fresh eggs, and trusty pasta-making equipment. To the average Italian, who consumes more than fifty pounds of pasta a year, the creation of supreme pasta is an art that is perfected over years of experience. But don't let this intimidate you! With a few tips and a little practice, you too can make delectable fresh pasta.

Before you start, here is some equipment that would be helpful: *A large wooden surface* (marble is cold and makes the dough less elastic); *a sharp metal scraper* (known as a dough blade) for cleaning the work surface and scraping up excess dough bits and flour while you are working; *a large wooden spoon* for mixing; *a large pastry brush* to remove excess flour from the dough; and *a spindle rack* (or laundry rack) to dry the dough and keep the noodles well separated.

Your shopping list for pasta is simple—flour and eggs. But to achieve Italian results you should buy ingredients that are closest to those found in Italy. *Doppio zero*, or "00" flour, is commonly used in Italy for *pasta fresca*. It is a soft wheat flour, low in gluten, that is easier to roll out than others, and the best American counterpart is unbleached, all-purpose flour. Eggs provide pasta with a binding substance, rich color, and flavor. The best American equivalent to Italian 70-gram eggs are "Grade A Large" eggs, preferably "farm fresh."

Pasta dough can be made by hand or with the help of a food processor, and our recipe below gives you instructions for both. To knead the dough by hand, follow these basic instructions: Lift up the part of the dough that is farthest from you and fold it over toward you and onto itself. Press the dough down and away with the heel and the palm of your hand, rocking your body forward as you press down, and back as you release. Turn the dough one quarter turn, and repeat the process until you have a smooth, elastic ball. If the dough is too sticky, open the ball, add some flour directly into it, close it, and continue kneading. This method will ensure that the dough is properly worked throughout and smooth.

Rolling out the dough may be intimidating to beginners, but it is actually a lot of fun once you've tried it a few times. Pasta-makers from the old school insist that hand-rolled pasta tastes noticeably better than machine-rolled, but this is debatable. Pasta machines produce an excellent result, even for novices, and take a fraction of the time. It's a good idea to work on the largest surface available, since the length of the strips of dough will increase each time you put them through the rollers. Before you put your dough through the machine make sure that it has a leathery, pliable consistency that is neither sticky nor dry. When you start rolling each strip of dough, crank the machine continuously until the strip has gone completely through the rollers. Before you roll the dough through the machine again, run your hand across the dough strip to check for sticky spots (sticky dough may get stuck in the machine). Dust the sticky areas and the work surface with flour and remove any excess flour with a pastry brush. After you've rolled out all your dough, clean the machine with a stiff dry brush, such as a toothbrush; never wet the machine to clean it.

Ideally, fresh pasta should be consumed immediately, but if you want to make it ahead it can be chilled overnight, *if* you dry the cut pasta for 30 minutes beforehand. The dried noodles should be coiled in a nest and stored in plastic bags so they will not tangle. Two hours before you're ready to use the pasta, remove it from the bags and let it sit at room temperature to dry out the humidity that it has accumulated in the refrigerator.

When it's time to cook your pasta, these simple steps will help you capture that genuine Italian texture and taste. Pasta, whether fresh or dried, should be cooked in a very large thin metal pot filled with lots of water so it can swim freely rather than stick together (the ratio should be 6 quarts of water to 1 pound of pasta). Cover the pot and let the water reach a slow, rolling boil. Then add salt (1 teaspoon of salt per 1 quart of water) right *before* you add the pasta. This may seem like a lot of salt, but don't worry—most of it will be drained away, and unsalted water will lead to bland pasta. Once the pasta has been added, stir it, and cover the pot again to shorten the time that the pasta sits in the water waiting to boil. When the water boils, partially remove the lid to prevent the water from boiling over, and stir the pasta occasionally as it cooks. Pasta should usually be *al dente* ("to the tooth"), which means tender but firm, and the cooking time will vary, depending on pasta shape, dough, and altitude. In true Italian fashion, the only way to be sure if pasta is done is to taste it.

Pasta should *never* be rinsed after cooking. The flavor of the salted pasta is distinctive and should be preserved. Serve your *pasta fresca* immediately on hot plates. Now add some of your favorite sauce, perhaps a dash of Parmesan, or fresh *pesto*, and *buon appetito!*

Pasta Dough

4 cups unbleached flour
6 large eggs, beaten lightly
3 to 4 tablespoons water

In a food processor blend the flour, the eggs, and 3 tablespoons of the water until the mixture just begins to form a ball, adding more water drop by drop if the dough is too dry. (The dough should be firm and not sticky.) Blend the dough for 15 seconds more to knead it. Let the dough stand, covered with an inverted bowl, at room temperature for 1 hour. *The dough may be made 4 hours in advance and kept covered and chilled.*

(Alternatively, on a wooden work surface mound the flour, make a well in the center, and add the eggs and 3 tablespoons of the water. With a fork beat the eggs and the water gently until the mixture is combined. Gradually beat in enough of the flour to form a paste, pulling in the flour that is closest to the egg mixture, being careful not to make an opening in the outer wall of the well. With your hands combine the remaining flour into the mixture to form a dough, adding more water drop by drop if the dough is too dry. (The dough should be firm and not sticky.) Knead the dough for 8 to 10 minutes, or until it is smooth and elastic, and let it stand, covered with an inverted bowl, at room temperature for 1 hour.)

Makes about 1¾ pounds pasta dough, yielding 1½ pounds cut pasta.

To Roll and Cut Fettuccine

To roll out the pasta dough: Set the smooth rollers of a pasta machine at the highest number. (The rollers will be wide apart.) Divide the dough into 8 pieces, flatten each piece into a rough rectangle, and cover the rectangles with an inverted bowl.

Working with 1 rectangle at a time, dust the rectangle with flour and feed it through the rollers. Fold the rectangle in half and feed it through the rollers 8 or 9 more times, folding it in half each time and dusting it with flour, if necessary, to prevent it from sticking. Turn the dial down one notch and feed the dough through the rollers without folding. Continue to feed the dough through the rollers without folding, turning the dial one notch lower each time, until the lowest notch is reached. The pasta dough should be a smooth long sheet about 40 inches long and about 4 inches wide. Cut the sheet in half so each piece is about 20 inches long. Roll the remaining pieces of pasta dough in the same manner. Let the sheets of dough dry on lightly floured jelly-roll pans or lightly dust them with flour and let them dry, hung over the tops of straight-backed chairs, for 15 minutes or until leathery but still pliable.

To cut the pasta into fettuccine: Use the blades of a pasta machine that will cut ¼-inch-wide strips. Feed one end of a sheet of pasta dough through the blades, holding the other end straight up from the machine. Catch the strips from underneath the machine before the sheet goes completely through the rollers and gently place the cut strips across floured jelly-roll pans or lightly flour them and let them hang over the tops of straight-backed chairs. Let the pastra dry for 5 minutes if cooking it immediately. *Alternatively, the pasta may be dried for 40 to 50 minutes, or until it is leathery but still pliable, and kept chilled overnight in plastic bags.*

POLENTA

To the Alpine Italian there is no other dish that is quite as loved as polenta. In fact, it is as much a part of life in northern Italy as dried pasta is throughout the south. If you have been fortunate enough to visit this glorious part of the world and have tasted this specialty, you will understand its popularity. Now we invite you to make polenta yourself and enjoy it at home.

The yellow cornmeal dish that we know as polenta has been prevalent in Italian cuisine for centuries, but in its original form it was not made from corn at all! The dish was a mush called *puls* (*pulentum* in Latin), made from spelt (a form of wheat) and other cereals. *Puls*, the forerunner of bread, was an inexpensive, filling food that fed the poor as well as the Roman Legions. Throughout the ages this early porridge took on many different tastes as various types of flour were discovered. In the Middle Ages, a millet-chestnut-and-acorn flour was used; in the fourteenth century buckwheat flour from central Asia was introduced by the Saracens; and it was only after Columbus brought back corn from the New World that Europeans were finally introduced to cornmeal.

Eventually, cornmeal was shipped from Spain to the Rialto market in Venice, and luckily the northern Italians knew a good thing when they saw it. They incorrectly christened this golden cornmeal *granoturco*, which means Turkish grain. Explanations for this strange name vary from the fanciful story that corncob silk reminded the Italians of a Turkish beard, to the more plausible theory that this yellow grain was thought to be yet another import from Turkey. Soon the Italians were making their polenta with cornmeal and cultivating their own *granoturco* in the Polesine, an area outside of Venice that offered the ideal conditions for growing corn. In 1556 a gift of corn seed was given to the Medici family in Florence, and thereafter the upper classes also began to enjoy this flavorful dish. Today polenta is served in households throughout Italy, although it is primarily found north of Rome.

Polenta is one of Italy's most versatile dishes. It can be served on its own with a little butter and Parmesan; it can be coupled with rich stews and hearty *ragus*; it can appear in a *pasticciata*, a layered dish; or, as in our recipe (page 272), it can be cooled, then grilled (or fried) as a base for various meats and game. A specialty of Lombardy, *polenta nera* (black polenta) is made with buckwheat flour and is somewhat heartier than the corn-meal variety.

Recipes for polenta vary slightly, but in its most basic form cornmeal is boiled with water and a little fat (either butter or oil) until the desired consistency is reached. Opinions differ about the type of cornmeal to be used (either coarse-grain, fine-grain, or pulverized), the amount of water to be used, and the cooking time that is required. Not to worry! These variations reflect personal preferences, which you, too, will have after experimenting with different polentas. Also, many traditionalists insist on cooking the polenta in a *paiolo* (an unlined round copper pan) that produces a half-moon shape when the cooled dish is inverted. They also prefer to slice the cooked dish with a string. We find that a stainless steel saucepan and a knife work just fine.

Before you begin, you should know that polenta spatters as it cooks, so it's important to protect your hand and lower arm with an oven mitt or a tea towel. To keep the polenta from getting lumpy, the cornmeal should be added in a steady stream to the boiling water as the mixture is constantly stirred with a long-handled wooden or stainless steel spoon. To produce a steady stream of cornmeal, simply hold it in your fist and let it sift through your fingers. When the cooking time is up, remove the pan from the heat and give it a good shake. This prevents the polenta from sticking to the sides and bottom of the pan.

No one would ever confuse polenta with a fast food (it takes a good half hour of attended stirring time), but it is worth the extra effort. And since the polenta for our veal dish should be chilled before it is grilled, you have the option of making it the day before.

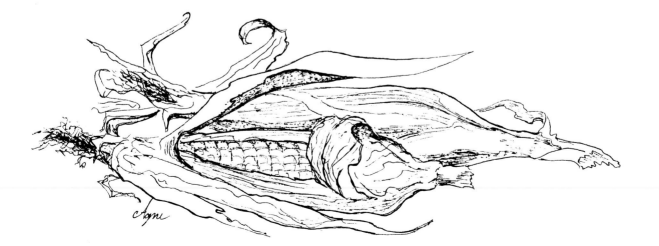

OLIVE OIL

Although many countries produce olive oil, Italy usually comes to mind first when its role in cooking is being discussed. After all, the Italians have always been passionate about this delicious oil and use it liberally, not only as a flavorful cooking fat but also as a distinctive condiment. Simple antipasti, pastas, soups, and salads all are splashed with a bit of this golden-green liquid and show it off to its best advantage. And as our market shelves attest, Italy is one of the largest olive oil exporters to the United States.

The origins of the domesticated olive tree, *Olea europaea*, can be traced back to both Syria and Crete, from where it spread throughout the Mediterranean basin. While the tree cannot tolerate extremes in temperature or dampness, it happily grows in arid climates and in poor soil. The Romans are credited with promoting the cultivation of this evergreen as they conquered, demanding olive oil as a tax payment. Egyptian, Greek, and Roman histories tell us that this esteemed oil was used in religious ceremonies, as an illuminant, as a medicine for common ailments, as a beauty aid, and, in later centuries, in cooking.

The twisted and gnarled trunks and silvery green leaves of the olive tree are a common sight throughout Italy, especially on the hills, where the temperatures are ideal for olive-growing. These noble trees can reach a height of 50 feet, although they are usually pruned to half this size to facilitate picking of their fruit. Late every spring the trees are filled with clusters of self-pollinating white flowers. Fruit begins to form in June, and throughout the growing season it changes from green to violet to red and finally to black. Harvesttime depends on the weather and the desired ripeness of the olive, and in some areas olives are not gathered until December.

Italy's olives come in over 60 varieties, and several wonderful oils are made by mixing the pressed oils of different types. The Tuscan oil made from Frantoio olives, with their peppery aftertaste, is often considered the best. In any given year, however, the oils of Calabria, Sicily, or Liguria may hold that distinction, since variations in weather, soil, cultivation, harvesting methods, handling, and pressing all determine the quality of the oil. And, as with wines, there are good years and bad years for the fruit and its product.

Several different methods are used to harvest olives, and these vary according to the ripeness of the fruit. Green olives are still firmly attached to the tree and must be hand-plucked, whereas the riper red olives are sometimes beaten or shaken from the tree into awaiting nylon nets. Some olive farmers actually choose to wait for the ripest olives to drop into nets or onto the ground. Naturally, olives that hit the ground are more likely to be bruised, and, although opinions vary, it is generally agreed that bruised fruit causes acidic, inferior oil. Some oils are made from a single variety of olive at different stages of ripeness; this kind of oil requires the olive pickers to return to the same tree two or more times to harvest the fruit.

The finest oils come from the best blemish-free fruit that has been cold-pressed. This is a mechanical processing method that uses no artificial substances or means (chemicals or heat) to extract the oil from the olives. After the olives are gathered, they are allowed to rest for a short time so that some of the water in their flesh can evaporate. Then they are brought to the local mill, where they are crushed into a pulp, as they were hundreds of years ago, by enormous granite stones. This mash is layered on straw or nylon mats, stacked atop one another, and then pressed in a screw-type or hydraulic press to release the oil. The remaining water from the flesh of the pressed olives is allowed to settle out from the oil, or it is separated out by centrifuge, and the result is cold-pressed extra-virgin olive oil, the finest oil money can buy! The same olive pulp is then pressed several more times, but second and third pressings result in a more acidic oil. Processed oils use chemicals to extract even more oil from this pulp or to neutralize the acidity of inferior olive oils, and they are not as flavorful as the cold-pressed oils.

When buying olive oil you should remember that there are basically only two types:

• natural *cold-pressed* virgin olive oil, either "extra-virgin oil" (with less than 1% oleic acid) or "virgin olive oil" (with less than 2% oleic acid)

• processed "*pure*" olive oil, which is made with the use of chemicals

You will want to use the more expensive cold-pressed extra-virgin oil when its full flavor will stand alone, as in a salad dressing or a final embellishment to a dish. The flavor of olive oil changes at 140° F., however, so when cooking at high temperatures use a less costly processed "pure" olive oil instead.

The distinctive taste of cold-pressed extra-virgin olive oils is impossible to imitate, but it is easy to be confused by the elaborate labels of foreign imports. Beware! While United States regulations state that our domestic extra-virgin oil must come from the first cold-pressed olives, this requirement does not apply to the myriad imports that fill our market shelves. Italy, France, and Spain classify as "extra-virgin" *any* oil that has an oleic acid content that does not exceed 1%, *and this includes some chemically processed oils to which a bit of first cold-pressed oil has been added for greenish color and some flavor*. The oils from Greece and Portugal are also loosely regulated. Their "extra-extra-virgin olive oil," for example, is arbitrarily labeled and undoubtedly inferior. Also, do not be fooled by high price tags—paying more does not mean that you are buying the best. Find a shopkeeper who knows his suppliers and put your trust in him. If you are buying an extra-virgin oil at a supermarket, however, look for the words "cold-pressed" on the label.

Olive oil should be stored in a cool, dark place (not in the refrigerator), because heat and light will oxidize it and turn it a copper color. If you decide to buy a large tin of oil you will want to decant it, as it is needed, into a smaller, easy-to-use container—glass, glazed clay, stainless steel, or very clean tin are preferable; avoid plastic, copper, or iron. And remember that olive oil does not improve with age. Although it may be stored for up to two years, it is best if it is used within the first year, and for maximum flavor within the first two months.

When you compare the full flavor of olive oil with the bland corn, cottonseed, and vegetable oils that we have become so accustomed to, there really is no contest. As our recipes prove, this luscious oil makes a remarkable difference.

CHEESE

In the fabled world of Boccaccio's *Decameron*, pasta-makers lived atop a tall mountain of Parmesan. They tossed their fresh macaroni in butter and then rolled it down the salty cheese slopes to the fortunate people below. Access to an unlimited supply of pasta and cheese is, to this day, any true Italian's fantasy. But the winning combination of these two beloved foods is just one example of the important part cheese plays in the peninsula's cuisine.

Sicilian cheeses date as far back as the sixth century B.C., when they are mentioned in Homer's *Odyssey*. Centuries later they became known throughout the Roman Empire and were a major part of the everyday diet of the Romans. During the Renaissance cheese graced the tables of the nobility. Today, with more than 450 varieties to choose from, Italians enjoy their cheese on its own, after dinner with fruit and wine, and as *formaggio da cucina* (cooking cheese) to enhance soups, dress up pasta and polenta, and enrich desserts.

The three menus that follow showcase many of the most loved Italian cheeses. Below we offer helpful information about these cheeses, as well as a few other favorites we thought you should try. Be sure to ask your local cheese shop owner for "Italian imports," and, if possible, taste cheese before you make a purchase. Also, store it tightly sealed in plastic wrap and refrigerated, unless otherwise indicated. But remember, cheese should always be served at room temperature.

• *Mascarpone*: Until recently, this double-cream cow's-milk cheese was not available outside of Piedmont and Lombardy because of its limited production, which was restricted to the cold months. Today, modern technology allows this very rich cheese to be made year-round. Its spreadable consistency is a cross between that of cream cheese and that of sour cream. The cheese is very white in color and slightly sweet and buttery in flavor. Italians eat it with sugar and fruit, or by itself, simply sprinkled with cocoa powder or drizzled with honey. If its container is unopened, mascarpone will keep, refrigerated, for three weeks. Once opened, however, this fresh cheese should be consumed within one week.

• *Mozzarella di Bufalo*: The original mozzarella comes from the milk of the Indian water buffalo that were brought to Italy from Asia in the sixteenth century. It is made in Campania and Apulia and plays a major role in Neapolitan cuisine. The fresh cheese has a nutty flavor, more fragrant and intense than that of the more common cow's-milk mozzarella (it also melts differently, liquefying as it cooks, unlike its slightly stringy cousin). Stored in its own brine, buffalo mozzarella squeaks when it is cut, and oozes milky whey. It comes in many shapes but usually is found in the form of a squashed ball. This white cheese should be absolutely fresh and moist, and is best if eaten within two to three days after purchase.

• *Ricotta*: Technically a by-product of cheesemaking, this moist dairy product is not a cheese. "Ricotta" ("re-cooked") is made from whey that is heated twice (the curd is used to make other cheeses). Traditional ricotta comes from Rome and is made from sheep's milk, but today's ricotta is also made from cow's or goat's milk. The fresh cheese has a smoother, more satiny texture than the supermarket variety and a sweeter flavor. In Italy it is used in both savory and sweet dishes. As ricotta ages it becomes dry, so it should be consumed soon after purchase. It can be kept for up to one week if it is stored in a container and refrigerated.

• *Stracchino*: This fresh cheese is named for the tired ("*stracca*" in Lombard dialect) cows that rested in villages on their way home from grazing in the Alpine mountains. It is a very white, rindless cheese with a soft but dense consistency that is moist, creamy, and spreadable. Stracchino at its best has a slightly sour flavor but is not sharp-tasting. It keeps for a long time, but it will become looser and more tart with age. In Italy it is often used instead of butter.

• *Fontina d'Aosta*: There is only one true Fontina and it comes from the valley of Aosta near the Swiss border. By law the cheese can be produced only in that region, so look for a cheese that carries the official "Fontina d'Aosta" name. This semi-soft cow's-milk cheese has a thin brownish rind and a pale-yellow interior with tiny round holes. Unlike other firm cheeses, once cut Fontina can get overly strong, so purchase only what you will consume within one week. Its buttery taste and elastic consistency make Fontina wonderful for creamy sauces, and it can also be eaten on its own.

• *Taleggio*: This soft cow's-milk cheese takes its name from the small town in Lombardy where it originated. It is mild but rich in flavor, and it sharpens with age. The cheese is ripened in caves for one to two months but is usually much older by the time it reaches the United States. Authentic Taleggio is branded with the official stamp of circles surrounding the letters "CTT." A plump and springy cheese, it comes in 8-inch squares and has a pale terra-cotta-colored rind and a white interior. This cheese should have a mild yet inviting aroma that is not as strong as that of a ripe Brie.

• *Gorgonzola*: Named for a village outside of Milan, this cow's-milk cheese from Lombardy has been made since the ninth century. The use of the name is protected by the Gorgonzola Consortium, and each wheel is stamped with a number identifying the farm or factory of origin. Thin metal needles inserted in the cheese create tiny holes that encourage the formation of mold during the aging period. The cheese is cream-colored with blue veins and has a thin, edible brown rind. Gorgonzola is available in two varieties: "sweet" and "*piccante*." "Sweet" Gorgonzola is not literally sweet-tasting, but has a milder, less sharp taste than "*piccante*," and it is far less veined. Both varieties of Gorgonzola should be creamier than Stilton or Roquefort, soft but not runny. As the cheese ages it gets cakey and dry; it is best if eaten within one week to ten days.

• *Parmesan*: The best-known and arguably the best of all Italian cheeses, this hard cow's-milk cheese is classified under the generic name *grana*, referring to its fine grain. True Parmesan is produced from April 1 to November 11 strictly in Reggio Emilia, Parma, Modena, Bologna, and Mantua, and "*Parmigiano-Reggiano*" is clearly stamped on its smooth, oily, pale brown rind. The handmade cheese is best when it is *stravecchio* ("very old"), aged for over two years. Its interior should be pale yellow, moist, and somewhat granular. This slightly salty, sharp cheese is usually used for grating, but it is also often eaten on its own. Parmesan should always be grated fresh, as it quickly loses its flavor after grating. It keeps for months, wrapped in foil, at the bottom of the refrigerator, and gets stronger with age.

• *Pecorino Romano*: This hard grating cheese made from the milk of *pecore* (sheep) is probably one of Italy's oldest cheeses. It originally came from a shepherds' village outside of Rome but is now produced mainly in Sardinia. The piquant, salty taste of this cheese increases with age. It has a white to yellow interior and a strong aroma. The cheese is widely used in southern Italy, where it is often sprinkled on robust sauces as a substitute for Parmesan, but it is rarely found above Rome. Grate this cheese as needed. Pecorino Romano will keep for months, wrapped in foil in the bottom of your refrigerator.

A NORTHERN BUFFET
ALLA RUSTICA

Antipasti

Fritto di Calamari con Salsa Piccante di Pomodori
(Fried Squid with Spicy Tomato Sauce)

Insalata di Fagioli Bianchi e Tonno
(White Bean and Tuna Salad)

Crostini di Fegato di Pollo   *Arneis di Roero '90,*
(Chicken Liver Crostini)   *Cantina Vietti*

Prosciutto, Taleggio, e Melone
(Prosciutto, Taleggio Cheese, and Melon)

Focaccia alla Salvia e Gorgonzola
(Gorgonzola-and-Sage Focaccia)

———————

Spezzato di Vitello, Funghi, e Olive Verdi
con Polenta alla Griglia   *Gattinara,*
(Veal and Sausage Stew with Mushrooms and Green Olives *Vigneto Molsino '85,*
on Grilled Polenta)   *Nervi*

Insalata di Carote, Finocchio, e Radicchio
(Carrot and Fennel Salad with Radicchio)

———————

Tiramisù

✑

From Left to Right: Fritto di Calamari con Salsa Piccante di Pomodori; Crostini di Fegato di Pollo; Insalata di Fagioli Bianchi e Tonno; Prosciutto, Taleggio, e Melone; Focaccia alla Salvia e Gorgonzola

Fritto di Calamari con Salsa Piccante di Pomodori
(Fried Squid with Spicy Tomato Sauce)

olive oil for deep-frying
2 pounds cleaned squid, the bodies cut
    into ½-inch rings, the tentacles halved,
    and the squid rinsed and
    drained well
1 cup all-purpose flour, seasoned with
    salt and pepper
lemon wedges as an accompaniment
spicy tomato sauce for dipping
    (recipe follows)

In a kettle heat 1½ inches of the olive oil until it reaches 390° F. on a deep-fat thermometer. In a bowl dredge the squid, in batches, in the seasoned flour. Transfer the squid, in batches, to a sieve to shake off the excess flour and immediately fry it, in batches, in the oil, turning it occasionally for 2 minutes, or until it is crisp. With a slotted spoon transfer the squid to paper towels to drain and sprinkle it with salt to taste. Serve the squid immediately with the lemon wedges and the spicy tomato sauce. Serves 10 to 12, as part of an antipasto assortment.

Salsa Piccante di Pomodori
(Spicy Tomato Sauce)

½ cup chopped onion
2 large garlic cloves, minced
2 tablespoons olive oil
a 28 to 32-ounce can ''Italian-style''
    plum tomatoes, chopped,
    including the purée
1 teaspoon granulated sugar
¼ teaspoon dried hot red pepper flakes,
    or to taste
1 tablespoon finely chopped fresh basil leaves
    or ¾ teaspoon dried, crumbled

In a heavy saucepan cook the onion and the garlic in the oil over moderate heat, stirring, until they are golden, add the tomatoes with the purée, the sugar, the pepper flakes, and salt and black pepper to taste, and simmer the sauce, stirring occasionally for 25 minutes. Stir in the basil, and simmer the sauce for 5 minutes more, or until it is thickened. *The tomato sauce may be made 1 day in advance and kept covered and chilled.* Makes about 2 cups.

Insalata di Fagioli Bianchi e Tonno
(White Bean and Tuna Salad)

1½ cups dried small white beans,
    picked over
8 cups water
2 tablespoons olive oil
two 6½-ounce cans light tuna packed in
    olive oil, drained and flaked
1 cup chopped tomato
1 large yellow bell pepper, chopped
½ cup finely chopped onion
¾ cup finely chopped fresh parsley leaves
    (preferably flat-leafed)
3 small garlic cloves, minced
½ cup extra-virgin olive oil
½ cup fresh lemon juice

In a kettle combine the white beans, the water, and the 2 tablespoons olive oil, bring the mixture to a boil, and simmer the beans, covered, for 1 hour to 1 hour and 20 minutes, or until they are just tender. Drain the beans, rinse them under cold water, and transfer them, well-drained, to a bowl. *The beans may be cooked 1 day in advance and kept covered and chilled.* To the beans add the tuna, the tomato, the bell pepper, the onion, the parsley, the garlic, the extra-virgin olive oil, the lemon juice, and salt and pepper to taste and toss the salad well. Let the salad stand at room temperature for 1 hour. Serves 10 to 12, as part of an antipasto assortment.

Crostini di Fegato di Pollo
(Chicken Liver Crostini)

½ cup chopped onion
1 tablespoon unsalted butter
1 pound chicken livers, separated and
    trimmed
1 tablespoon balsamic vinegar or to taste
1 teaspoon fresh lemon juice
2 teaspoons minced fresh orégano leaves or
    sage leaves
2 tablespoons drained capers, chopped
3 tablespoons finely chopped fresh parsley
    leaves, plus additional for garnish
    (preferably flat-leafed)
about 24 ½-inch slices Italian bread,
    brushed lightly with olive oil and
    toasted lightly

In a skillet cook the onion in the butter over moderately low heat, stirring, for 5 minutes, add the chicken livers, and cook the mixture over moderate heat, covered, stirring occasionally, for 5 minutes or until the chicken livers are just cooked through. In a blender or food processor purée the liver mixture with the vinegar and the lemon juice until the mixture is smooth. Transfer the liver mixture to a bowl and stir in the orégano, the capers, 3 tablespoons of the parsley, and salt and pepper to taste. *The liver mixture may be made 1 day in advance and kept chilled, its surface covered with plastic wrap.* Spread the liver mixture on the toasted bread and garnish the *crostini* with the additional parsley. Makes about 24 *crostini*, serving 10 to 12 as part of an antipasto assortment.

Prosciutto, Taleggio, e Melone
(Prosciutto, Taleggio Cheese, and Melon)

1 honeydew or other green-fleshed
    melon (about 2½ pounds), the rind
    discarded and the flesh cut into
    ½- by 2-inch sticks
⅓ pound *Taleggio*, the rind discarded
    and the cheese cut into
    ¼- by 2-inch strips
¼ pound thinly sliced Parma prosciutto, cut
    and/or folded into 1- by 4-inch strips

Hold a piece of melon and a piece of *Taleggio* together and wrap a strip of prosciutto around them to form a bundle. Continue to make bundles in the same manner with the remaining melon, *Taleggio*, and prosciutto. *The bundles may be prepared up to 3 hours in advance and kept covered.* Makes about 32 bundles.

Focaccia alla Salvia e Gorgonzola
(Gorgonzola-and-Sage Focaccia)

a ¼-ounce package (2½ teaspoons) active
    dry yeast
½ teaspoon granulated sugar
1 cup luke warm water
5 tablespoons olive oil
1 teaspoon salt
2½ to 2¾ cups all-purpose flour
2 teaspoons minced fresh sage or 1 teaspoon
    dried, crumbled
¼ pound Gorgonzola, grated coarse

In a large bowl proof the yeast with the sugar in the water for 5 minutes, or until the mixture is foamy, add 3 tablespoons of the oil, the salt, and 2½ cups of the flour, and combine the dough well (alternatively, an electric mixer fitted with the paddle attachment may be used). Knead the dough on a lightly floured surface, adding the additional ¼ cup flour if necessary, a little at a time, to achieve a soft, slightly sticky dough (alternatively, the dough may be kneaded with the mixer on low speed). On a lightly floured surface knead the dough for 2 minutes more, form it into a ball, and transfer it to an oiled bowl, turning it to coat it with the oil. Let the dough rise, covered with plastic wrap, in a warm place for 1½ hours, or until it is double in bulk. Press the dough into an oiled 15½- by 10½- by 1-inch jelly-roll pan and let it rise, covered, for 1 hour or until it is almost double in bulk. "Dimple" the dough by making indentations all over the dough with the fingertips, sprinkle the top of the dough with the sage, the Gorgonzola, and the remaining 2 tablespoons olive oil, and let the dough rest for 15 minutes. Sprinkle the *focaccia* lightly with water and bake it in the middle of a preheated 400° F. oven for 25 to 30 minutes or until it is golden. Let the *focaccia* cool on a rack and serve it warm or at room temperature. Makes 1 *focaccia*, serving 10 to 12 as part of an antipasto assortment.

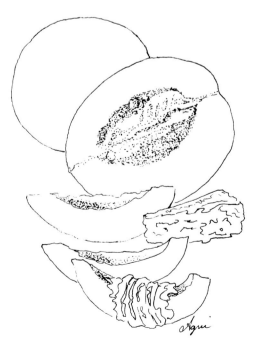

Spezzato di Vitello, Funghi, e Olive Verdi
con Polenta alla Griglia
(Veal and Sausage Stew with Mushrooms and
Green Olives on Grilled Polenta)

1½ pounds sweet Italian sausage, cut into
    1-inch lengths
3½ pounds well-trimmed veal stew meat,
    such as shoulder, cut into
    1- to 2-inch pieces
5 tablespoons all-purpose flour
3½ cups chopped onion
5 garlic cloves, minced
3½ cups thinly sliced fresh mushrooms,
    such as *porcini* or *shiitake*
¾ cup dry white wine
3½ cups water
1 tablespoon minced fresh thyme or
    1 teaspoon dried, crumbled
1¼ cups Italian green olives, pitted
    if desired
polenta (recipe follows)
olive oil for brushing the polenta

In a large heavy kettle brown the sausage over moderately high heat, and with a slotted spoon transfer it to a bowl, reserving the fat in the kettle. In another bowl toss the veal, patted dry, with the flour, coating it thoroughly and shaking off the excess flour. Brown the veal, in batches, over moderately high heat in the fat remaining in the kettle and with the slotted spoon transfer it to the bowl with the sausage. Reduce the heat to moderate and in the kettle cook the onion, the garlic, and the mushrooms, stirring, for 5 minutes. Add the wine and simmer the mixture, scraping up the brown bits, until the wine is almost evaporated. Add the sausage and the veal, the water, the thyme, and salt and pepper to taste and braise the mixture at a bare simmer, covered, for 1 hour or until the veal is tender. *The stew may be prepared up to this point 1 day in advance, if first cooled, uncovered, and then kept chilled, covered.* Stir in the olives, simmer the stew, stirring, for 1 minute, and keep the stew warm.

Cut the polenta into 12 squares. Brush the squares on both sides with the oil and grill them on an oiled rack set 5 to 6 inches over glowing coals or in batches in a well-seasoned ridged grill pan over moderately high heat for 3 to 4 minutes on each side, or until they are golden. Arrange each polenta square on a heated plate, halve it diagonally, and top it with the stew. Serves 10 to 12.

Polenta

12 cups water
½ cup olive oil
1½ tablespoons salt
3 cups yellow cornmeal
1 cup freshly grated Parmesan

In a kettle bring the water to a boil with the oil and the salt. Add the cornmeal in a slow stream, whisking vigorously to avoid forming lumps, and simmer the polenta, stirring constantly with a long-handled wooden spoon, for 30 minutes. (The polenta may spatter.) Remove the kettle from the heat, stir in the Parmesan, and immediately pour the polenta into a 15½- by 10½- by 1-inch jelly-roll pan, smoothing the top. Let the polenta cool, and chill it, covered, for 2 hours. *The polenta may be made 1 day in advance and kept covered and chilled.* Serves 12.

Insalata di Carote, Finocchio, e Radicchio
(Carrot and Fennel Salad with Radicchio)

3 large fennel bulbs (sometimes called anise,
  available in most supermarkets), sliced thin
  crosswise, reserving some of the green
  fronds for garnish
3 cups coarsely shredded carrots
½ cup extra-virgin olive oil
3 tablespoons red-wine vinegar
radicchio leaves for lining the plates

In a large bowl toss the fennel bulbs and the shredded
carrot with the extra-virgin olive oil, the red-wine vinegar, and salt and pepper to taste. Line salad plates with
the *radicchio* leaves and divide the salad among them.
Garnish the salads with the reserved fennel greens.
Serves 10 to 12.

Tiramisù

2 pound cakes (about 1¾ pounds total), cut
  into 2- by ¼-inch sticks
1½ cups well-chilled heavy cream
3 tablespoons granulated sugar

12 ounces *mascarpone* (available at cheese
  shops), at room temperature
1½ cups strong coffee or espresso
¼ cup rum
8 ounces fine-quality bittersweet chocolate
  (not unsweetened), chopped fine

Arrange the cake sticks on baking sheets, toast them
in a preheated 350° F. oven for about 15 minutes, turning them occasionally until they are golden, and let
them cool. In a bowl beat the cream with the sugar until
it just holds stiff peaks, and whisk in the *mascarpone*,
whisking until the mixture is combined well. In a small
bowl stir together the coffee and the rum. In a 13- x 9-
inch dish arrange half the cake sticks in a single layer,
brush them with half the coffee mixture, and spread half
the cream mixture over the cake sticks. Sprinkle the
cream mixture with half the chopped chocolate. Make
another layer with the remaining cake sticks, coffee
mixture, and cream mixture, sprinkling the remaining
chocolate on top. Chill the *tiramisù*, covered, for 2
hours. *The* tiramisù *may be made 1 day in advance and
kept covered and chilled.* Serve the *tiramisù*, cut into
squares. Serves 10 to 12.

DINNER ALLA ROMANA

Carciofi alla Romana
(Braised Artichokes with Parsley and Mint)

———————

Fettuccine al Burro
(Fettuccine with Butter and Parmesan)

Frascati,
Vigneto Villa Morena '90,
Fontana Candida

———————

Pollo alla Diavola
(Grilled Chicken Marinated in Pepper and Lemon)

Peperoni alla Griglia
(Grilled Red and Yellow Bell Peppers)

Broccoli all'Aglio
(Broccoli with Garlic)

Rosso di Montepulciano '89,
Poliziano

Pane di Campagna
(Hearty Country Loaf)

———————

Gelato al Limone
(Lemon Ice Cream)

Biscotti
(Almond Cookies)

🦢

Pollo alla Diavola;
Broccoli all'Aglio;
Peperoni alla Griglia

Carciofi alla Romana

Fettuccine al Burro

Carciofi alla Romana
(Braised Artichokes with Parsley and Mint)

8 large artichokes, trimmed
(procedure follows)
½ cup plus 2 tablespoons finely chopped
parsley leaves
3 garlic cloves, minced
2 tablespoons finely chopped fresh
mint leaves
1 teaspoon salt
⅔ cup olive oil

Drain the artichokes and in a large kettle arrange them stems up. Add ½ cup of the parsley, the garlic, the mint, the salt, the oil and enough cold water to reach the base of the artichoke stems, bring the water to a boil, and simmer the artichokes, covered, for 25 to 30 minutes, or until they are tender. Transfer the artichokes, stems up, to a platter, reserving 1 cup cooking liquid. *The artichokes may be prepared 2 hours in advance and kept covered at room temperature.* Spoon the cooking liquid over the artichokes and sprinkle them with the remaining 2 tablespoons parsley. Serves 8.

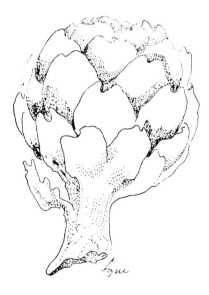

To Trim Artichokes
large artichokes with the stems
1 lemon, halved

Leaving the stems intact, bend the outer leaves back until they snap off close to the base and remove more layers of leaves in the same manner until the pale inner leaves are reached. With a stainless steel knife cut through each artichoke 1½ inches above the base and using a spoon scrape out the chokes from the artichoke bottoms. With the knife trim the stems and sides of the artichokes to reveal the pale white parts. Rub the cut surfaces with one of the lemon halves and drop the artichokes as they are trimmed into a bowl of cold water acidulated with the juice of the remaining lemon half.

Fettuccine al Burro
(Fettuccine with Butter and Parmesan)

1½ sticks (¾ cup) unsalted butter, softened
2 cups freshly grated Parmesan, plus
additional for sprinkling the pasta
¼ cup minced fresh sage leaves
1½ pounds fresh fettuccine (pasta dough
recipe on page 259 and to roll and cut
fettuccine procedure on page 259),
or dried

In a large bowl cream together the butter, 2 cups of the Parmesan, the sage, and salt and pepper to taste. In a kettle of boiling salted water cook the fettuccine until it is *al dente*, drain it well, and in the bowl toss it with the butter mixture until it is coated. Sprinkle the pasta with the additional Parmesan. Serves 8.

Pollo alla Diavola
(Grilled Chicken Marinated in Pepper and Lemon)

eight 1- to 1¼-pound baby chickens, such as
poussins or, alternatively, Cornish hens
¼ cup fresh coarsely ground black pepper
1 cup fresh lemon juice
⅔ cup olive oil
2 tablespoons coarse salt

With a knife split open a chicken along the backbone, crack the breastbone from the inside, and with the breast facing you flatten out the chicken on a work surface. Repeat the procedure with the remaining chickens.

In a bowl whisk together the pepper, the lemon juice, the oil, and the salt. Arrange the chickens in shallow baking dishes large enough to fit them in one layer, pour the marinade over them, and turn them to coat them with the marinade. Let the chickens marinate, covered and chilled, turning them several times, for at least 6 hours or overnight.

Drain the chickens and reserve the marinade. Grill the chickens on a rack set 5 to 6 inches over glowing coals, skin sides down, basting them with the reserved marinade and turning them, for 20 minutes. Discard any remaining marinade and grill the chickens for 5 to 10 minutes more, or until the juices of the thigh run clear when pricked with a skewer. Alternatively, the chickens may be broiled in batches on a lightly oiled rack under a preheated broiler about 4 inches from the heat. Begin with the skin sides down and broil each side for 10 to 12 minutes, or until the juices of the thigh run clear when pricked with a skewer. Serves 8.

Peperoni alla Griglia
(Grilled Red and Yellow Bell Peppers)

3 red bell peppers
3 yellow bell peppers
¼ cup extra-virgin olive oil

Grill the bell peppers on a well-oiled rack set 5 to 6 inches over glowing coals, turning them every 5 minutes, for 20 to 25 minutes, or until the skins are blistered and charred. Transfer them to a bowl, and let them steam, covered, until they are cool enough to handle. (Alternatively, the peppers may be broiled on a lightly oiled rack under a preheated broiler about 4 inches from the heat, turning them every 5 minutes, for 20 to 25 minutes, or until the skins are blistered and charred.)

Peel the peppers, cut off the tops, and discard the seeds and ribs. Quarter the peppers and put them in a serving bowl. Toss them with the oil and salt and pepper to taste. Serves 8.

Broccoli all'Aglio
(Broccoli with Garlic)

2 bunches of broccoli
2 garlic cloves, chopped fine
3 tablespoons olive oil
½ cup water

Trim the broccoli stems and cut them into ¼-inch slices. Cut the broccoli flowerets into 1½-inch pieces. In a kettle of boiling salted water blanch the broccoli for 2 minutes, drain it, and refresh it under cold water. Drain the broccoli well. *The broccoli may be prepared up to this point 6 hours in advance and kept covered and chilled.*

In a large heavy skillet cook the garlic in the oil over moderately low heat, stirring, until it is golden, add the broccoli, the water, and salt and pepper to taste, and cook the broccoli over moderate heat, stirring occasionally, for 5 minutes, or until it is tender. Serves 8.

(Alternatively, the dough may be made in a food processor. In a small bowl proof the yeast in the ⅓ cup warm water with the sugar for 5 minutes, or until it is foamy. In the bowl of a food processor combine the yeast mixture, the remaining 1⅓ cups water, the flour, ¼ cup of the bran, and the salt, pulse the motor several times until a dough is formed, and with the motor running knead the dough for 45 seconds.)

The dough will be soft and slightly sticky. Add the dough to a lightly oiled bowl, turn it to coat it with the oil, and let it rise in a warm place, covered with plastic wrap, for 3 hours, or until it is triple in volume.

In a blender grind the remaining bran until it is fine. Oil a 10-inch pie plate and coat the bottom and side with half the bran. On a well-floured surface shape the dough into a 10-inch round, transfer it to the pie plate, and sprinkle it with the remaining bran. Let the dough rise at room temperature, loosely covered with a tea towel, for 2 hours, or until it is double in volume. Bake the loaf in the middle of a preheated 425° F. oven for 30 to 35 minutes, or until it sounds hollow when the bottom is tapped. Makes one 10-inch loaf.

Gelato al Limone
(Lemon Ice Cream)

4 lemons
1½ cups water
1 cup sugar
¾ cup fresh lemon juice
¾ cup heavy cream
¾ cup milk

With a vegetable peeler remove the zest of the lemons, making sure no white pith is included, and cut it into julienne strips. In a heavy saucepan combine the zest, the water, the sugar, and the lemon juice, bring the mixture to a boil, stirring until the sugar is dissolved, and boil the syrup gently for 5 minutes. Let the syrup cool completely, chill it, and strain it through a sieve into a bowl, reserving the lemon zest. Chop half the zest, reserving the remaining zest for garnish. Stir the chopped zest, the cream, and the milk into the lemon syrup. Freeze the mixture in an ice cream freezer according to the manufacturers' instructions. Transfer the ice cream to a metal bowl and freeze it until it is frozen solid. Scoop the *gelato* into goblets and garnish it with the reserved lemon zest. Makes about 1 quart, serving 8.

Pane di Campagna
(Hearty Country Loaf)

1 teaspoon active dry yeast
⅓ cup warm water plus 1⅓ cups water at
    room temperature
a pinch of sugar
3¼ cups unbleached flour
¾ cup miller's bran
2 teaspoons salt

In the large bowl of a mixer fitted with the paddle attachment proof the yeast in the ⅓ cup warm water with the sugar for 5 minutes, or until it is foamy. Add the remaining 1⅓ cups water, the flour, ¼ cup of the bran, and the salt and beat the mixture until it is combined well. Fit the mixer with the dough hook and knead the dough at medium speed for 6 minutes.

Biscotti
(Almond Cookies)

1½ cups natural unpeeled almonds
1 cup sugar
2 cups unbleached flour
½ teaspoon double-acting baking powder
½ teaspoon baking soda
¼ teaspoon almond extract
1 teaspoon freshly grated orange zest
3 large eggs

In a food processor grind ¾ cup of the almonds with the sugar until the mixture is fine and in a large bowl combine well the almond mixture with the remaining whole almonds, the flour, the baking powder, and the baking soda. In a bowl beat together the almond extract, the orange zest, and the eggs, add the mixture to the almond mixture, and combine the ingredients well. Turn the mixture out onto a work surface and knead it with the heel of the hand until it forms a dough. Divide the dough in half and roll each half into a 15-inch log on a lightly floured surface.

Arrange the logs on a large, buttered, wax paper-lined baking sheet and bake them in the middle of a pre-heated 350° F. oven for 25 minutes, or until the logs are pale golden. Transfer the baking sheet to a rack to cool the logs for 5 minutes. Transfer the logs with metal spatulas to a cutting board, and with a serrated knife, cut the logs diagonally into ½-inch-thick *biscotti*. On the wax paper-lined baking sheet arrange the *biscotti* on their sides, and bake them in the 350° F. oven for 15 minutes. Transfer the baking sheet to a rack to cool the *biscotti* completely. *The* biscotti *keep in an airtight container for 1 week*. Makes 40 *biscotti*.

SOUTHERN SUNDAY LUNCH
IN FAMIGLIA

Ziti al Forno con Melanzane, Pomodori, e Formaggi
(Baked Ziti with Eggplant, Tomato, and Three Cheeses)

Selici Salentino Rosato '89,
Cosimo Taurino

———

Pesce Spada Arrosto al Finocchio
(Roasted Swordfish Steaks with Fennel and Herbs)

Zucchini Fritti Marinati
(Marinated Sautéed Zucchini with Herbs)

Pane
(Crusty Bread)

———

Insalata Verde con Arance e Cipolle
(Arugula and Lettuce Salad with Orange and Red Onion)

———

Cassata
(Layered Cake with Ricotta and Chocolate Filling)

Fichi Freschi
(Fresh Figs)

🦢

Cassata

Ziti al Forno con Melanzane, Pomodori, e Formaggi
(Baked Ziti with Eggplant, Tomato, and
Three Cheeses)

2 large eggplants (about 2¼ pounds), peeled
  lengthwise in alternating strips and cut into
  ½-inch dice (about 10 cups)
1 tablespoon salt
6 tablespoons olive oil
1 onion, minced
2 garlic cloves, minced
2 canned anchovy fillets, minced and mashed
  to a paste, or 1 teaspoon anchovy paste
⅓ cup sliced pitted brine-cured olives
½ teaspoon crushed dried red pepper flakes
1 red bell pepper, roasted (procedure on
  page 196), chopped
1 yellow bell pepper, roasted (procedure on
  page 196), chopped
about 3½ cups basic tomato sauce (recipe
  follows)
8 ounces whole-milk ricotta
8 ounces whole-milk mozzarella, preferably
  buffalo mozzarella (available at specialty
  cheese shops and some specialty foods
  shops), grated
¾ cup freshly grated Pecorino Romano
1 pound dried *ziti* or *penne*

In a colander layer the eggplant, sprinkling the salt between the layers, put a weighted plate on top of the eggplant, and let it stand for 1 hour. Rinse the eggplant and pat it dry.

In a large skillet heat 2 tablespoons of the oil over moderately high heat until it is hot but not smoking and in it fry the eggplant, in batches, stirring, adding an additional 2 tablespoons of the oil as necessary, for 5 minutes, or until the eggplant is just tender and browned lightly. Transfer the eggplant with a slotted spoon to paper towels to drain and sprinkle it with salt to taste.

In a kettle cook the onion in the remaining 2 tablespoons oil, stirring, over moderate heat until it is lightly golden, add the garlic, and cook the mixture, stirring, for 3 minutes. Add the anchovy paste, the olives, the red pepper flakes, the roasted peppers, 1 cup of the tomato sauce, the eggplant, and salt and pepper to taste, and cook the mixture, stirring, for 2 minutes. In a bowl whisk together the ricotta, the mozzarella, and half of the Pecorino Romano. Add half of the cheese mixture to the eggplant mixture and combine the mixture well.

In a kettle of boiling salted water cook the pasta for 7 minutes, or until it is just *al dente*. Drain the pasta well and add it to the eggplant and cheese mixture, combining the mixture well. Transfer the mixture to an oiled 13 x 9 x 2-inch (3-quart) baking pan, spreading it evenly. Spoon dollops of the remaining cheese mixture on top, drizzle the remaining tomato sauce evenly on top of the cheese, and sprinkle it with the remaining Pecorino Romano. Bake the pasta in the middle of a preheated 375° F. oven for 30 minutes, or until it is heated through and the pasta is crisp around the edges. *The baked pasta may be made up to 1 day in advance, kept covered with foil, and chilled. Reheat the baked pasta, covered with foil, in a preheated 250° F. oven.* Serves 8 as a first course.

Salsa di Pomodori
(Basic Tomato Sauce)

1 cup finely chopped onion
3 tablespoons olive oil
1 large garlic clove, minced
a 28 to 32-ounce can whole peeled tomatoes
2 tablespoons canned tomato paste
½ teaspoon dried orégano, crumbled
¼ cup fresh basil leaves, chopped fine

In a large saucepan cook the onion in the olive oil over moderately low heat, stirring, until it is softened. Add the garlic, and cook the mixture, stirring, for 3 minutes. Add the tomatoes, the tomato paste, the orégano, and salt and pepper to taste. Bring the mixture to a boil, breaking up the tomatoes with a wooden spoon, and simmer the sauce, covered, for 20 minutes. Simmer the sauce, uncovered, for 10 minutes, stir in the basil, and boil it for 5 minutes, stirring occasionally to prevent scorching, or until the sauce is thickened. *The tomato sauce may be made up to 1 day in advance and kept covered and chilled.* Makes about 3½ cups.

Pesce Spada Arrosto al Finocchio
(Roasted Swordfish Steaks with Fennel and Herbs)

two 1¼ pound fennel bulbs (sometimes called
  anise, available in most supermarkets),
  trimmed and cut into ½-inch dice
  (about 5 cups)
2 cups finely chopped onion
1 cup finely chopped celery

¼ cup plus 2 tablespoons olive oil
2 garlic cloves, minced
⅓ cup finely chopped fresh parsley leaves
   (preferably flat-leafed)
3 tablespoons bottled capers, drained
¼ cup fresh lemon juice
½ cup dry white wine
1 teaspoon dried orégano, crumbled
½ teaspoon salt
eight 6-ounce swordfish steaks (about
   3 pounds total), seasoned with salt and
   pepper to taste
⅓ cup shredded fresh basil leaves

In a kettle cook the fennel, the onion, and the celery in ¼ cup of the olive oil over moderate heat, stirring occasionally, until the vegetables are softened and lightly golden. Add the garlic and cook the mixture, stirring, for 3 minutes. Stir in the parsley, the capers, the lemon juice, the white wine, the orégano, the salt, and pepper to taste, and cook the mixture, stirring, for 1 minute. Remove the mixture from the heat.

Arrange the swordfish steaks in 1 layer in a large oiled roasting pan or large baking pan, drizzle the remaining 2 tablespoons olive oil over the steaks, and roast the steaks in the middle of a preheated 400° F. oven for 5 minutes. Spoon the fennel mixture over the steaks, reduce the oven to 375° F., and bake the fish for 12 to 15 minutes more or until the fish just flakes when tested with a fork. Sprinkle the fish with the basil during the last 5 minutes of baking. Serves 8.

Zucchini Fritti Marinati
(Marinated Sautéed Zucchini with Mint)

½ cup olive oil
5 zucchini (2 pounds), scrubbed and cut
   crosswise into ¼-inch-thick slices (6 cups)
2 garlic cloves, minced
1 tablespoon granulated sugar
⅓ cup white-wine vinegar
⅓ cup shredded fresh basil
¼ cup finely chopped fresh mint leaves
1 teaspoon dried orégano, crumbled

In a large skillet heat ¼ cup of the oil over moderately high heat until it is hot but not smoking and in it sauté the zucchini, in batches, stirring and turning the slices carefully, for 6 to 8 minutes, or until the zucchini

is softened, but not limp, and lightly golden. With a slotted spoon transfer the zucchini to paper towels to drain well.

In a saucepan combine the garlic, the sugar, and the vinegar, bring the mixture to a boil, and simmer it for 1 minute. Stir in the remaining ¼ cup oil. In a serving bowl layer the zucchini, sprinkling the basil, the mint, the orégano, and salt and pepper to taste between the layers, and pour the hot liquid over the mixture. Let the mixture stand until it reaches room temperature. Cover and chill it, stirring gently occasionally, for at least 8 hours, or overnight. Serve at room temperature. Serves 8.

Insalata Verde con Arance e Cipolle
(Arugula and Lettuce Salad with Orange and Red Onion)

1 bunch *arugula*, washed well, spun dry, and
   torn into large pieces
2 heads Boston lettuce, washed well, spun
   dry, and torn into pieces (about 10 cups)
3 tablespoons extra-virgin olive oil
1 teaspoon white-wine vinegar
3 navel oranges, preferably blood oranges if
   seasonally available, peeled, pith
   discarded, membranes discarded,
   and sliced thin
½ red onion, sliced thin, soaked in ice water
   for ½ hour, and drained well

In a large bowl toss together the *arugula*, the Boston lettuce, the olive oil, the vinegar, the oranges, the onion, and salt and pepper to taste. Serves 8.

287

Cassata
(Layered Cake with Ricotta and Chocolate Filling)

For the cake
6 large eggs
¾ cup granulated sugar
1 teaspoon vanilla
1¼ cups sifted all-purpose flour
1 stick (½ cup) unsalted butter, melted and
    cooled
For the filling
1 pound whole-milk ricotta
3 tablespoons heavy cream
¼ cup sifted confectioners' sugar
½ teaspoon vanilla
3 ounces fine-quality bittersweet chocolate,
    chopped fine
2 tablespoons finely chopped candied orange
    zest or glacéed orange slices (available at
    specialty foods shops and some
    supermarkets)
For the icing
8 ounces fine-quality bittersweet chocolate,
    chopped
½ cup granulated sugar
¼ cup water
1 large egg
1¾ sticks (14 tablespoons) unsalted butter, cut
    into bits and softened
4 teaspoons instant espresso powder dissolved
    in 1 tablespoon water

¼ cup orange-flavored liqueur, such as
    Cointreau
½ cup slivered almonds, lightly toasted
coarsely grated fine-quality bittersweet
    chocolate for garnish
finely chopped candied orange zest or glacéed
    orange slices for garnish

Make the cake: Butter and flour a parchment-lined, 15½-by 10½-inch jelly-roll pan. In a bowl of an electric mixer beat the eggs until they are foamy. Add the sugar, a little at a time, beating, add the vanilla, and beat the mixture for 8 minutes, or until the mixture is pale and has increased about 3 times in volume. Using a rubber spatula, fold in the flour in 3 batches. Add the butter in a stream, folding it in gently but thoroughly. Working quickly, pour the batter into the pan, smoothing the top. Bake the cake in the middle of a preheated 350° F. oven for 20 to 25 minutes, or until the cake is lightly golden and a cake tester inserted in the center comes out clean. Let the cake cool in the pan on a rack for 10 minutes, turn the cake out onto the rack, and let it cool completely. Discard the parchment. *The cake may be made up to 2 days in advance and kept, covered tightly in plastic wrap, at room temperature.*

Make the filling: Using a wooden spoon, force the ricotta through a sieve set over the bowl of the electric mixer. With the electric mixer beat together the sieved ricotta, the heavy cream, the confectioners' sugar, the vanilla, and a pinch of salt until the mixture is smooth, and stir in the chocolate and the candied orange.

Make the icing: In a bowl set over a saucepan of simmering water melt the chocolate until it is smooth and let it cool. In a saucepan combine the sugar and the water, and bring the mixture to a boil, covered, until the sugar is dissolved. Boil the mixture, uncovered, until it registers 230° F. on a candy thermometer. In the bowl of the electric mixer beat the egg until it is pale, add the sugar syrup in a stream, beating constantly, and beat the mixture until it is cool. Beat in the butter, a few pieces at a time, beating until the mixture is light and creamy. Beat in the cooled chocolate mixture and the espresso powder mixture. *The icing may be made up to 2 days in advance and kept covered and chilled.*

On a work surface trim the edges of the cake and cut it crosswise into 4 equal pieces, each about 3¾ inches by 10½ inches. On a baking sheet lined with wax paper or parchment paper arrange 1 of the cake layers, sprinkle it with ⅓ of the liqueur, and spread it with ⅓ of the filling. Top the filling with 1 of the remaining cake layers, sprinkle it with ½ of the remaining liqueur, and spread the layer with ½ of the remaining filling. Top the filling with 1 of the remaining cake layers, sprinkle it with the remaining liqueur, and spread it with the remaining filling. Top the filling with the remaining cake layer, pressing the loaf lightly to weight it. (The layered cake will become more firm as it chills.) Chill the cake, covered loosely, for at least 2 hours, or until the filling is firm.

Reserving about ¾ cup of the icing to make rosettes, frost the sides and top of the cake generously with the remaining icing. Using a pastry bag fitted with a decorative tip, decorate the top of the cake with rosettes and swirls on the sides. Carefully press the slivered almonds into the icing around the base of the cake's sides and sprinkle the cake with the grated chocolate and the candied orange. Chill the cake for at least 8 hours or overnight before serving. Makes 1 cake.

PART FOUR

A GOURMET ADDENDUM

DINNER PARTY DISHES FROM THE FREEZER

Lauren Jarrett

ost people have ambivalent feelings about the freezer. And who can blame them? While freezers hold all those marvelous ice creams, bombes, and sorbets, they often also store foods that are flat and tasteless when reheated. But this is *not* the way it has to be. Wonderful homemade dishes that are properly wrapped and stored in the freezer allow you to enjoy flavorful, nutritious food that's ready when you are. Armed with just a little know-how and a variety of test-proven recipes, you will discover that frozen fare can be absolutely delicious. We promise, our recipes will even be exciting enough to serve to your guests.

In recent years, our Addendum has emphasized the importance of capturing the bounty of each season's harvest, along with the nutritional goodness and flavor-enhancing powers of fresh herbs and spices. While freezing may seem contrary to these ideals, the amazing truth is that it can retain the freshness, nutrition, and flavor of a dish that has just been prepared with newly harvested produce and fresh-from-the-market meat, poultry, and fish.

And the benefits of freezing are many. The freezer allows you to buy up seasonal produce in quantity so it can be enjoyed even when it is impossible to find in the marketplace. Let's take blueberries, for example. What could be more of a treat than blueberry pancakes in the middle of January? On a more practical note, the freezer becomes indispensable when time is scarce. After all, who has the leisure to grocery-shop more than once a week? At the end of a long day at the office or a hectic one with the children, it is important to be able to depend on the "freshness" of readily available frozen foods. By freezing fresh dishes yourself you can avoid the additives and extra sodium often found in supermarket frozen foods.

The time factor also causes many people to shy away from entertaining at home. There is no doubt about it, a dinner party for six to eight people requires several hours of menu planning and shopping, then more time in the kitchen. Well . . . what if you could do all of this over a period of four weeks? Wouldn't that make it more palatable? This Addendum provides 24 enticing recipes to make ahead and freeze. Whether you are looking for a special starter, an exceptional entrée, a simple side dish, or a fabulous dessert to have on hand for your dinner party, or you'd like to prepare an entire make-ahead-and-freeze meal, it's all here waiting for you. Our selection of recipes includes dishes that can be easily mixed and matched to create complete menus.

As you probably already know, some foods freeze better than others, and some foods should not be frozen at all. But which ones are they? Rest assured, we have eliminated the guesswork by choosing only those that freeze extremely well. To produce a dish that is just as delicious after it is frozen as it was before, however, you will also need to know some important information about freezing. The way you prepare, package, store, and defrost frozen foods will make a big difference in the quality of the reheated dish.

The first rule of freezing is to cook with only the freshest ingredients; one cannot expect anything to be better when it comes out of the freezer than it was when it went in! On the other hand, we guarantee that if fresh ingredients are used in the following recipes (and you follow our other tips), you will taste a fresh product when the dish is defrosted and reheated.

It is also essential to completely cool food that is to be frozen before putting it into the freezer. If you attempt to freeze anything that is still warm, condensation will occur and this excess moisture will turn to ice crystals, which render food soggy and tasteless when it is defrosted. Michael Roberts, a renowned chef, suggests that food be chilled before freezing to diminish the size of the frozen crystals that will inevitably form. Smaller crystals result in less damage to the food during defrosting.

Of course, it is also necessary to package cooked food properly before storing it in the freezer. This means buying storage products that are specifically designed to be used in the freezer: plastic containers with tight-fitting lids; freezer plastic wrap or microwave plastic wrap that is heavier than the normal variety; heavy-duty resealable plastic freezer bags; heavy-duty aluminum foil (*extra*-heavy-duty aluminum foil is expensive and unnecessary); and freezer wrap. These are all non-porous coverings that will lock in flavor by protecting your frozen goods from the atmosphere of the freezer. If the food packages are not wrapped properly, the air in the freezer will cause freezer burn, resulting in damaged items that are off-tasting. Also, the food will pick up flavors and odors from other items in the freezer. Many of our recipes call for two layers of protection—the food is wrapped first in freezer plastic wrap and then in foil, to ensure a well-protected dish.

The type of freezer you use also makes a difference in the length of time you can store certain dishes. At a constant 0° F., food decay is drastically slowed down; the large chest freezers hold this optimal temperature best. Fluctuating warmer temperatures cause foods to deteriorate more quickly. Refrigerator freezers, with their varying temperatures, fall into this category. The freezer door area, for example, sometimes reaches a temperature of 10° F. Consequently, it is wise to store foods in a refrigerator freezer for a shorter period of time than you would in a large chest freezer. *Because our recipes were developed with refrigerator freezer storage in mind, our freezing period suggestions never exceed one month.*

There are some simple measures you can take to keep your refrigerator freezer at 0° F. If you do not have automatic defrosting, be sure to defrost your freezer when the ice inside is ½ inch thick. Also, keep your freezer about 80 percent full at all times: This provides a thermal mass that keeps the temperature down while leaving enough space for the cold air to circulate freely. There are also a few "do not" rules. Do not keep the freezer door open, allowing warm air to rush into it, for longer than necessary. Also, do not attempt to freeze too many unfrozen things at the same time. Whenever an unfrozen container is added to the freezer it raises the overall temperature of the unit. (Keep this in mind when freezing several trays of ice cubes at a time.)

The method you use to defrost frozen foods is as important as all our other tips. As you will see, our recipes call for defrosting dishes in the refrigerator. This allows them to come back slowly to 37° F., a temperature that will defrost the dish but still protect it from rapid decay. Often there is a temptation to defrost food in a warmer atmosphere, usually on the counter, where it is left for hours. This is not a wise practice! As mentioned above, frozen food has a tendency to lose water as it defrosts, and if allowed to defrost too quickly the result is a watery, limp dish. Also, when foods reach a temperature exceeding 40° F. decay can quickly set in. All defrosted goods should be slowly defrosted in the refrigerator and promptly consumed. (The exception to this rule is microwave defrosting. This quick method is ideal if defrosted foods are immediately reheated.)

Usually, reheating defrosted foods simply involves warming them on the stovetop or in the oven. You will note, however, that several of our recipes instruct you to correct the seasonings as dishes are reheated. Spices have a tendency to go flat during the freezing process, and the flavor of the dish needs to be revived. As all good cooks know, the proof is in the tasting, so be sure to taste as you go and add more spice if needed.

Finally, a word about freezer organization: It's worth it! If you lose track of what you have in your freezer, you will no doubt pass by the freezer life of a special dish. Labeling a container takes only seconds and will allow you to keep a freezer inventory. It is important, especially with a refrigerator freezer, to keep frozen dishes moving out of the freezer before they lose their flavor and nutritional value.

We think you will be surprised at just how delicious these frozen dishes really are. And when you plan and actually prepare a dinner over several weeks, you can relax and enjoy your guests on the day of the party. Now *that's* the way to entertain!

FROZEN STARTERS

Below you will find a variety of hors d'oeuvres and starters that would make a lovely addition to any dinner party. But don't just think of them as dinner foods — some of them, such as the soups and the Spinach and Porcini Won Ton Ravioli, for example, will also serve as light luncheon dishes, and the Cheddar, Ham, and Chutney Bites certainly would be nice to have on hand in the freezer for a special late-afternoon snack.

When freezing the soups (and any purée or stew), remember that liquid expands about 10 percent when frozen. To allow for this, leave at least a 1-inch space at the top of your plastic containers. After the soup has cooled, place a piece of plastic wrap directly on the surface before putting on the tight-fitting lid.

The freezing method used in the ravioli recipe below is called ''open freezing.'' Here ravioli are placed separately on a jelly-roll pan and frozen for a half hour before being transferred to a freezer bag. This allows you to freeze many small items at once without having them stick together. Remember to follow this method, using ice cube trays, to freeze purées and sauce bases.

Keep the following recipe in mind for those plentiful summer bushels of bright red tomatoes, but don't be afraid to try it with off-season tomatoes as well. The soup can be served warm or chilled. However, if you freeze it, be sure to reheat it as directed even if you plan to serve it chilled.

Fresh Tomato Soup with Pesto

2 tablespoons olive oil
1 cup finely chopped well-rinsed leek
⅔ cup diced fennel bulb (sometimes called
    anise, available in most supermarkets) or celery
½ cup diced carrot
2 pounds firm-ripe tomatoes, peeled, seeded,
    and chopped
4 cups chicken broth
2 tablespoons tomato paste
2 tablespoons minced fresh basil leaves or
    1 teaspoon crumbled dried
1½ teaspoons minced fresh thyme leaves or
    ½ teaspoon crumbled dried
1 bay leaf
For the pesto
2 cups packed fresh basil leaves
¼ cup pine nuts
¼ cup freshly grated Parmesan
2 cloves garlic, minced
⅓ cup olive oil

In a large saucepan heat the oil over moderate heat until it is hot, add the leek, the fennel, the carrot, and salt and pepper to taste, and cook the vegetables, stirring occasionally, for 5 minutes. Add the tomatoes, the broth, the tomato paste, the basil, the thyme, the bay leaf, and salt and pepper to taste, bring the liquid to a boil, and simmer the soup, covered, for 30 minutes. Discard the bay leaf.

In a food processor purée the soup in batches, transfer the soup to a bowl, and let it cool to room temperature. Transfer the soup to a large freezer container and freeze it, covered with plastic wrap directly on the surface and a tight-fitting lid, for up to 1 month.

Make the *pesto*: In a food processor combine the basil leaves, the pine nuts, the Parmesan, and the garlic. With the motor running add the oil in a stream and purée the *pesto* until it is combined well. Transfer the *pesto* to a small freezer container with a tight-fitting lid or to a freezer bag and freeze it for up to 1 month.

To reheat: Defrost the soup and the *pesto* in the refrigerator overnight. Transfer the soup to a saucepan and heat it over moderate heat, covered, stirring occasionally, for 15 minutes, or until it is hot. Correct the seasoning, adding salt and pepper to taste. Ladle the soup into bowls and add 1 tablespoon of *pesto* at room temperature to each bowl. Serve the remaining *pesto* separately. Makes about 8 cups, serving 6.

Corn Chowder

2 cups finely chopped onion
2 tablespoons unsalted butter
2 boiling potatoes (about ¾ pound),
    peeled and cut into
    1-inch pieces
4 cups chicken broth
1½ teaspoons minced fresh thyme leaves or
    ½ teaspoon crumbled dried
1 bay leaf
1½ cups milk combined with ½ cup heavy
    cream, scalded
3 cups fresh or frozen corn, thawed and
    drained
¼ cup minced fresh parsley leaves
sour cream and crackers as accompaniments,
    if desired

In a large saucepan cook the onion in the butter over moderate heat, stirring occasionally, for 5 minutes. Add the potatoes, the broth, the thyme, the bay leaf, and salt and pepper to taste and simmer the soup, covered, for 20 minutes. Add the milk mixture and the corn to the saucepan and simmer the soup, covered, stirring occasionally, for 5 minutes, or until the corn is tender. Remove the pan from the heat and discard the bay leaf.

In a food processor purée 4 cups of the soup and return the purée to the saucepan. Let the soup cool, transfer the soup to a large freezer container, and freeze it, covered with plastic wrap directly on the surface and a tight-fitting lid, for up to 1 month.

To reheat: Defrost the soup in the refrigerator overnight, transfer it to a large saucepan, and simmer it, covered, stirring occasionally, for 15 to 20 minutes, or until it is heated through. Stir in the parsley and correct the seasoning, adding salt and pepper to taste. If desired, serve the soup garnished with a dollop of sour cream and accompany it with crackers. Makes 8 to 9 cups, serving 6.

Veal and Pork Country Pâté

¾ pound lean veal shoulder, cut
    into 1-inch cubes
¾ pound lean pork shoulder, cut
    into 1-inch cubes
½ pound fresh pork fat, cut into 1-inch cubes
½ pound chicken livers, trimmed
⅓ cup Tawny Port or Sercial Madeira
1 large onion, minced
2 tablespoons unsalted butter
3 garlic cloves, minced, or to taste
2 large eggs, beaten lightly
½ pound smoked ham, cut into ½-inch dice
1 tablespoon minced fresh thyme leaves or
    1½ teaspoons crumbled dried
1 teaspoon salt
½ teaspoon freshly ground black pepper
1 teaspoon ground allspice
1 bay leaf
cornichons, pickled onions, and assorted
    breads and crackers as accompaniments

In a large bowl combine the veal, the pork, the pork fat, the chicken livers, and the Port and let the mixture marinate, covered and chilled, for 2 hours.

In a food processor process the veal mixture, in batches, until coarsely ground and transfer it to a large bowl. In a skillet cook the onion in the butter over moderate heat, stirring occasionally, for 5 minutes. Cool the onion mixture slightly and add it to the veal mixture along with the garlic, the eggs, the ham, the thyme, the salt, the pepper, and the allspice and combine the mixture well. (Test the seasoning by cooking a small amount of the mixture.)

Transfer the mixture to an oiled 9¼ x 5¼ x 3-inch loaf pan, smoothing the top and rapping the pan on a hard surface to compact it. Top the mixture with the bay leaf and cover the pan with a triple thickness of foil. Put the loaf pan in a baking pan, add enough hot water to the baking pan to come two-thirds of the way up the sides of the loaf pan, and bake the pâté in a preheated 350° F. oven for 1½ hours, or until a meat thermometer registers 150° F. Remove the pâté from the baking pan, discard the water, and return the pâté to the baking pan. Let the pâté stand for 15 minutes, and weight it evenly with a 2-pound weight. Let the pâté cool to room temperature and chill it, weighted, in the loaf pan overnight. Remove the weight and the foil and unmold the pâté. Wrap the pâté in freezer plastic wrap and in foil and freeze it for up to 1 month.

Defrost the pâté in the refrigerator overnight. Remove the foil and bring the pâté to room temperature before serving. Serve the pâté with the desired accompaniments. Makes one loaf.

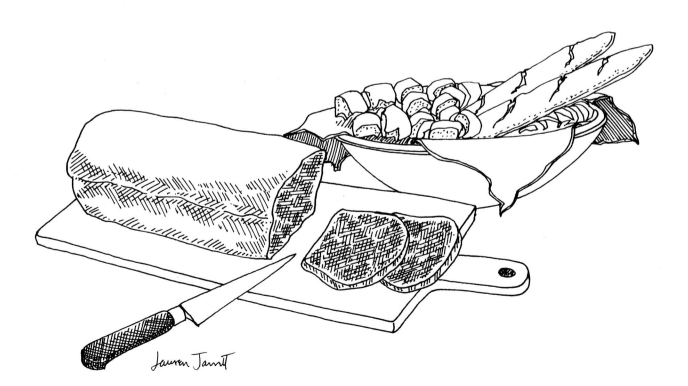

Lauren Jarrett

The following ravioli are made with Chinese won ton wrappers, a new and exciting way to create this favorite stuffed-pasta dish. The paper-thin wrappers thaw quickly for ready use and eliminate the need to make pasta, a time-consuming affair. Our ravioli are simply tossed in melted butter and sprinkled with Parmesan before serving. This simple embellishment allows the richness of the *porcini* mushrooms to stand alone. If you are a *pesto* lover, however, you may want to try it as an alternative, especially during the summer months when basil is so plentiful.

Spinach and Porcini Won Ton Ravioli

1 ounce dried *porcini* mushrooms
1 cup hot water
½ pound cleaned and trimmed fresh spinach
    leaves
2 tablespoons minced shallot
2 tablespoons olive oil
¼ pound (½ cup) ricotta
¼ cup freshly grated Parmesan
1 large egg
48 won ton wrappers (available at Oriental markets, specialty foods shops, and some supermarkets), thawed if frozen
6 to 8 tablespoons melted unsalted butter, or to taste
additional freshly grated Parmesan to taste for sprinkling over the ravioli

In a heatproof bowl combine the mushrooms with the water and let them stand for 30 minutes. Drain the mushrooms, squeeze them dry, and chop them.

In a kettle cook the spinach in the water clinging to the leaves, covered, over moderate heat, stirring occasionally, for 3 minutes, or until it is wilted. Drain the spinach, press out the excess liquid, and chop the leaves. In a skillet set over moderate heat cook the shallot in the oil, stirring, for 3 minutes. Add the spinach and the mushrooms and cook the mixture, stirring, until it is dry. Transfer the mixture to a food processor and grind it fine.

In a bowl combine the spinach mixture with the ricotta, the Parmesan, the egg, and salt and pepper to taste.

Put one won ton wrapper on a lightly floured surface, mound about 1½ teaspoons of the filling in the center of the wrapper, and brush the edges of the wrapper with water. Fold one corner of the won ton over the filling to form a triangle, pressing down around the filling carefully to force out any air, and press the edges to seal them well. Make more ravioli in the same manner with the remaining wrappers and filling.

Making sure they do not touch one another, transfer the ravioli as they are formed to a jelly-roll pan. Freeze the ravioli for 30 minutes, or until they are firm, and transfer them to a resealable freezer bag. Seal the bag, pressing out the air, and freeze the ravioli for up to one month.

To serve: Bring a kettle of salted water to a gentle boil and in it cook the ravioli in 2 batches for 4 to 6 minutes, or until the ravioli are tender and heated through. Transfer the ravioli with a slotted spoon as they are cooked to a dry kitchen towel to drain and keep them warm.

In a heated bowl gently toss the ravioli with the butter and transfer them to serving plates. Sprinkle the ravioli with the cheese and freshly ground black pepper to taste. Serves 6 as a first course.

Cheddar, Ham, and Chutney Bites

18 slices homemade-style white bread
4 tablespoons unsalted butter, melted
For the filling
2 tablespoons unsalted butter
2 tablespoons all-purpose flour
1 cup half-and-half
½ cup grated sharp Cheddar
½ cup finely diced smoked ham
2 teaspoons Dijon-style mustard
cayenne to taste
¼ to ⅓ cup chopped drained mango chutney, or to taste

additional grated Cheddar for garnish

With a rolling pin flatten each slice of bread and with a 2¼-inch round cookie cutter stamp out two rounds from each slice. With the rolling pin flatten the rounds and fit them into 36 buttered ⅛-cup gem tins. Brush the bread with the melted butter and bake the shells in a preheated 375° F. oven for 6 minutes, or until they are pale golden. Cool the shells in the tins on cooling racks for 5 minutes, then remove the shells from the tins, and let them cool completely on the racks.

Make the filling: In a saucepan melt the butter over moderate heat, add the flour, and cook the mixture over moderately low heat, whisking, for 2 minutes. Add the half-and-half in a stream, bring the mixture to a boil, whisking, and simmer the mixture over moderately low heat, whisking, for 3 minutes. Remove the pan from the heat, add the Cheddar, the ham, the mustard, the cayenne, and salt to taste and stir the mixture until it is combined well.

Spoon ¼ teaspoon of the chutney into each shell and top the chutney with a rounded teaspoon of the cheese mixture, smoothing the top into a mound. Arrange the filled shells on a jelly-roll pan and freeze them for about 30 minutes or until the filling is just firm to the touch. Transfer the shells to resealable freezer bags, arranging them in one layer. Seal the bags, pressing out the air, and freeze the bites for up to one month.

To reheat: Arrange the shells on a baking sheet and sprinkle them with the additional Cheddar. Bake the bites in a preheated 375° F. oven for 15 to 20 minutes, or until the filling is heated through. Run the bites under a preheated broiler about 4 inches from the heat for 30 seconds to 1 minute, or until the tops are golden. Makes 36 hors d'oeuvres.

Salmon in Puff Pastry

1 pound skinless salmon fillet, cut into
    four 4-ounce pieces, each measuring
    about 4 x 3 x ¾ inches
1 pound puff pastry, thawed,
    if frozen
an egg wash made by beating 1 large egg
    with 1 teaspoon water
For the sauce
⅔ cup sour cream, or plain yogurt that has
    been drained in a sieve lined with
    dampened cheesecloth for about 20 minutes
¼ cup minced fresh parsley leaves
1 shallot, minced fine

1 small garlic clove, minced fine
1 to 2 tablespoons white wine vinegar
2 teaspoons Dijon-style mustard
2 tablespoons minced fresh chives or dill
1 tablespoon minced fresh tarragon leaves

Pat the salmon pieces dry and sprinkle them on both sides with salt and pepper. Divide the puff pastry into four pieces. Working with one piece at a time, on a lightly floured surface roll out the puff pastry into a rectangle 7 x 8 inches. Arrange one piece of the salmon in the center of the pastry, brush the left and right sides of the pastry with water, and fold them over the salmon. Brush the remaining sides of the pastry with water and fold them over the salmon, pinching the seams together to secure the pastry. Make the remaining salmon packets in the same manner. Arrange the salmon packets, making sure they do not touch one another, on a large plate or jelly-roll pan and freeze them for about 30 minutes or until the pastry is firm. Transfer the salmon packets to a resealable freezer bag, arranging them in one layer. Seal the bag, pressing out the air. Alternatively, wrap the packets in freezer plastic wrap and foil. Freeze the salmon packets for up to one month.

To bake: Arrange the frozen salmon packets seam side down on a dampened baking sheet and brush the top and sides of the pastry with the egg wash. Bake the packets in the middle of a preheated 400° F. oven for 35 to 40 minutes, or until the pastry is golden and the salmon is cooked. If the bottom of the pastry begins to overbrown, slip another baking sheet under the one in the oven.

Meanwhile, make the sauce: In a bowl whisk together all the ingredients with salt and pepper to taste and transfer the sauce to a serving dish. Serve the salmon with the sauce. Serves 4 as an hors d'oeuvre or a first course.

FROZEN ENTRÉES

You will notice that many of our entrées are slow cooking, braise-type dishes. The reason for this is, quite simply, that these preparations freeze extremely well. Everyone knows that a braised meat dish is always better the second time around, but we wonder how many of you know that a frozen braise is even better! There is something about the freezing and defrosting process that actually aids in the blending of flavors.

Occasionally, a sauce such as the white wine sauce that accompanies our Braised Loin of Pork Stuffed with Prunes is frozen separately from the meat. Some sauces, like this one, tend to separate as they defrost and need to be whisked back together as they are reheated.

Sausage and Fennel Lasagne

For the béchamel sauce:
6 tablespoons unsalted butter
6 tablespoons all-purpose flour
3½ cups milk
freshly grated nutmeg to taste

For the tomato sauce:
⅓ cup olive oil
2 cups chopped onion
3 garlic cloves, minced
a 28-ounce can tomatoes, drained and
    chopped, reserving 1 cup of the liquid
1 tablespoon minced fresh basil leaves or
    ½ teaspoon crumbled dried
1 tablespoon minced fresh thyme leaves or
    ½ teaspoon crumbled dried

1 pound sweet Italian sausage, casings
    discarded, if necessary
1 large onion, minced
2 tablespoons olive oil
½ cup minced fennel bulb (sometimes called
    anise, available in most supermarkets)
½ pound mushrooms, sliced
3 garlic cloves, minced
½ teaspoon fennel seed, crushed
½ pound lasagne noodles
1 pound mozzarella, grated
1½ cups freshly grated Parmesan

Make the béchamel sauce: In a saucepan melt the butter over moderately low heat, add the flour, and cook the mixture, whisking, for 3 minutes. Add the milk, the nutmeg, and salt and pepper to taste and bring the sauce to a boil, whisking. Simmer the sauce, whisking occasionally, for 20 minutes. Remove the saucepan from the heat and cover the sauce with a buttered round of wax paper.

Make the tomato sauce: In a saucepan heat the olive oil over moderately high heat until it is hot. Add the onion and cook it over moderate heat, stirring occasionally, for 5 minutes. Add the garlic, the tomatoes and 1 cup tomato liquid, the basil, the thyme, and salt and pepper to taste and simmer the sauce, stirring occasionally, for 30 minutes. In a food processor purée the sauce until it is smooth and transfer it to a bowl.

Heat a large skillet over moderate heat until it is hot. Add the sausage meat and cook it, stirring occasionally, until it is browned. Transfer the sausage to a large bowl and pour off any fat in the skillet. In the skillet cook the onion in the oil over moderate heat, stirring occasionally, for 3 minutes. Add the fennel, the mushrooms, the garlic, the fennel seed, and salt and pepper to taste and cook the mixture over moderate heat, stirring occasionally, for 5 to 7 minutes, or until most of the liquid the mushrooms give off is evaporated. Transfer the fennel mixture to the sausage, add all but 1 cup of the béchamel sauce, and stir to combine.

In a kettle of boiling salted water cook the lasagne noodles for 6 minutes, or until slightly firmer than *al dente*, and transfer them with a skimmer to paper towels to drain, patting them dry.

Pour the reserved béchamel sauce into a greased 3-quart shallow baking dish, 13 x 9 x 2 inches, cover it with one-third of the pasta, and spread one-third of the sausage mixture over the noodles. Sprinkle the sausage mixture with one-third of the mozzarella and Parmesan. Continue to layer the remaining ingredients in the same manner, beginning with the lasagne noodles and reserving the final layer of mozzarella and Parmesan. Spoon the tomato sauce evenly over the final sausage mixture layer and sprinkle the sauce with the reserved mozzarella and Parmesan. Bake the lasagne in a preheated 400° F. oven for 30 minutes, or until it is bubbling. Let the lasagne cool to room temperature, cover it with freezer plastic wrap and aluminum foil, and freeze it for up to 1 month.

To reheat: Defrost the lasagne in the refrigerator. Remove the foil and plastic wrap and re-cover the lasagne with the foil. Bake the lasagne in a preheated 400° F. oven for 30 minutes. Remove the foil and continue to bake the lasagne, uncovered, for 15 to 30 minutes more, or until it is bubbling and completely heated through. Serves 6 to 8.

Curried Lamb

4 tablespoons vegetable oil
2½ pounds boneless lamb shoulder, cut into
    1½-inch pieces and patted dry
1 large onion, minced
3 garlic cloves, minced, or to taste
1 tablespoon curry powder, or to taste
1 teaspoon ground coriander
1 teaspoon ground cumin
½ teaspoon ground ginger
¼ teaspoon cayenne, or to taste
3 tablespoons all-purpose flour
a 1-pound can tomatoes, chopped, including
    the liquid
1½ cups beef broth
½ cup golden raisins
the juice and grated zest of 1 small lemon
1 Granny Smith apple, peeled, cored, and cubed
cooked rice as an accompaniment
roasted nuts, toasted coconut, and assorted
    chutneys as accompaniments, if desired

In a heavy kettle heat 2 tablespoons of the oil over moderately high heat, add the meat in batches and salt and pepper to taste, and sauté the meat until it is browned on all sides. Transfer the meat to a plate. To the pan add the remaining oil and the onion and cook the onion, stirring occasionally, over moderate heat for 5 minutes. Add the garlic, the curry powder, the coriander, the cumin, the ginger, and the cayenne and cook the mixture over moderately low heat, stirring, for 1 minute. Add the flour and cook the mixture, stirring, for 2 minutes. Return the lamb to the pan, add the tomatoes and their liquid, the beef broth, the raisins, the lemon juice and zest, and salt and pepper to taste, bring the liquid to a boil, stirring, and simmer the curry, covered, for 1½ hours. Add the apple and simmer the curry, covered, for 30 minutes more, or until the meat is tender. Let the curry cool to room temperature, transfer it to a freezer container with a tight-fitting lid or to a resealable freezer bag, and freeze it for up to 1 month.

To reheat: Defrost the curry in the refrigerator. Transfer the curry to a kettle and simmer it over moderate heat, covered, stirring occasionally, for 15 minutes, or until it is heated through. Correct the seasoning, adding salt, pepper, and fresh lemon juice to taste. Serve the curry over rice and, if desired, accompany it with small bowls of roasted nuts, toasted coconut, and assorted chutneys. Serves 4 to 6.

We think you will enjoy the flavorful herbed prune stuffing in the following pork recipe. Eventually, you may want to experiment with this stuffing by substituting other dried fruits for the prunes. Dried apricots would be a good choice; perhaps add a little bit more of them than the prunes.

Braised Loin of Pork Stuffed with Prunes

a 4-pound boneless loin of pork
For the stuffing:
1 clove garlic, minced fine
1 teaspoon minced fresh rosemary leaves or
    ½ teaspoon crumbled dried
1 teaspoon minced fresh thyme leaves or
    ½ teaspoon crumbled dried
1 cup (about 18) pitted prunes

2 tablespoons vegetable oil
1 large onion, chopped
1 rib of celery, chopped
3 cloves garlic, chopped
¼ cup all-purpose flour
1 cup dry white wine
4 cups beef broth
2 teaspoons minced fresh thyme leaves or
    1 teaspoon crumbled dried
2 teaspoons minced fresh rosemary leaves or
    1 teaspoon crumbled dried
1 bay leaf
1 tablespoon tomato paste
4 whole cloves

With a sharp knife make a slit along the boned side of the pork 1 inch deep. Pat the pork dry and sprinkle the slit in the pork loin with the garlic, the rosemary, the thyme, and salt and pepper. Arrange enough of the prunes to fit in one row end to end down the center of the slit. Reserve any remaining prunes. Reform the pork, enclosing the stuffing, and tie it at 1-inch intervals with kitchen string. Season the outside of the pork with salt and pepper to taste.

In a heavy kettle heat the oil over moderately high heat until it is hot. Add the pork and brown it on all sides. Transfer the pork to a platter. Add the onion, the celery, and the garlic to the pan and cook the vegetables over moderate heat, stirring occasionally, for 7 to 8 minutes, or until the onion is golden. Add the flour and cook the mixture over low heat, stirring, for 2 minutes.

Add the wine, the broth, the thyme, the rosemary, the bay leaf, the tomato paste, the cloves, the reserved prunes, and salt and pepper to taste. Bring the mixture to a boil, stirring, and return the pork to the pan. Braise the pork in a preheated 350° F. oven, covered, for 1½ hours, or until it is tender. Transfer the pork to the platter and let it cool to room temperature. Skim the fat from the surface of the cooking liquid and discard it. Strain the cooking liquid through a sieve into a saucepan, pressing hard on the solids. Over moderately high heat boil the liquid until it is reduced to 3 cups and let it cool, uncovered, to room temperature. Wrap the pork in freezer plastic wrap and foil. Transfer the sauce to a freezer container with a tight-fitting lid. Freeze the pork and sauce separately for up to 1 month.

To reheat: Defrost the pork and sauce separately in the refrigerator. Transfer the sauce to a heavy kettle and bring it to a boil, whisking. Add the pork and simmer the mixture, covered, turning the pork occasionally, for 20 minutes or until the pork is heated through. Transfer the pork to a cutting board, remove the strings, and cut it into slices. Arrange the slices on a platter and spoon some of the sauce over the pork. Serve the remaining sauce separately. Serves 6.

Lauren Jarrett

Baked Halibut Provençale

2 tablespoons olive oil
1 onion, sliced thin
1½ cups peeled, seeded, and chopped tomato
    or a 28-ounce can tomatoes, drained and
    chopped
2 cloves garlic, minced
2 tablespoons minced fresh basil leaves or
    ½ teaspoon crumbled dried
1½ teaspoons minced fresh thyme leaves
4 halibut steaks (6 ounces each), cut about
    1-inch thick, or similar firm-fleshed fish
    such as cod or haddock
½ cup chicken broth combined with
    2 teaspoons cornstarch or arrowroot
2 teaspoons tomato paste
¼ cup minced fresh parsley leaves

In a skillet heat the oil over moderate heat until it is hot, add the onion and salt and pepper to taste, and cook the onion, stirring occasionally, for 5 to 7 minutes, or until it is golden. Add the tomato, the garlic, the basil, and the thyme and simmer the mixture, stirring occasionally, for 3 to 5 minutes more, or until the mixture is thick. Spoon half the tomato mixture into an oiled shallow flameproof baking dish just large enough to hold the fish in one layer, arrange the fish steaks on top of the tomato mixture, and sprinkle them with salt and pepper to taste. Spoon the remaining tomato mixture over the fish, bring the mixture to a simmer on top of the stove, and bake it in a preheated 350° F. oven, covered with foil, for 15 minutes, or until the fish just flakes.

With a spatula carefully transfer the fish to a large plate. Bring the tomato mixture in the baking dish to a simmer over moderate heat, add the broth and cornstarch mixture and the tomato paste, and simmer the sauce, stirring, until it is thickened. Let it cool. Return the fish to the baking dish, spoon some of the sauce over it, and let the fish cool completely. Carefully transfer the fish and its sauce to a flat freezer container with a tight-fitting lid, arranging the fish in a single layer. Freeze the fish for up to one month.

To reheat: Defrost the fish, covered, in the refrigerator. Transfer the fish to a baking dish and bake the fish, covered with foil, in a preheated 350° F. oven for 20 minutes, or until it is heated through. Correct the seasoning, adding salt and pepper to taste, and sprinkle the baked halibut with the minced parsley before serving. Serves 4.

Chicken and Wild Mushroom Fricassee

a 3½-pound chicken, cut into serving pieces
flour for dredging the chicken
2 tablespoons vegetable oil
1 tablespoon unsalted butter
1 large onion, minced
1 carrot, sliced
1 rib of celery, minced
3 cups chicken broth
½ cup dry white wine
1½ teaspoons minced fresh thyme leaves or
    ½ teaspoon crumbled dried
1½ teaspoons minced fresh tarragon leaves or
    ½ teaspoon crumbled dried
1 bay leaf
½ pound oyster or *shiitake* mushrooms,
    trimmed, rinsed, and sliced
½ cup heavy cream
2 tablespoons arrowroot or cornstarch
fresh lemon juice to taste
minced fresh tarragon leaves or parsley leaves
    for garnish

Pat the chicken dry, dredge it in the flour, shaking off the excess, and season it with salt and pepper. In a large heavy skillet heat the oil and the butter over moderate heat until it is hot, add the chicken, and cook it for 3 minutes on each side, or until it is lightly colored. Transfer the chicken to a large plate and add the onion, the carrot, and the celery to the pan. Cook the vegetables, stirring occasionally, for 5 minutes. Return the chicken to the pan. Add the broth, the wine, the thyme, the tarragon, the bay leaf, and salt and pepper to taste and bring the liquid to a boil. Simmer the chicken, covered, stirring and skimming the froth occasionally, for 20 to 25 minutes, or until the chicken is just tender. Add the mushrooms to the pan and simmer the mixture for 10 minutes more, or until the chicken is very tender. Transfer the chicken, the mushrooms, and the vegetables with a slotted spoon to a large dish and discard the bay leaf. Skim the froth from the cooking liquid and strain the liquid into a saucepan.

In a small bowl combine the cream and the arrowroot. Bring the cooking liquid to a boil, add the arrowroot mixture, and simmer the sauce, stirring, until it is lightly thickened. Add the lemon juice and salt and pepper to taste and strain the sauce over the chicken and the vegetables. Let the fricassee cool, transfer it to a freezer container with a lid, and freeze it for up to one month.

To reheat: Defrost the fricassee in the refrigerator overnight and transfer it to a large heavy skillet. Bring the mixture to a simmer over moderate heat and continue to simmer the mixture, covered, stirring occasionally, for 20 to 30 minutes, or until the chicken is heated through. Correct the seasoning, adding additional lemon juice, salt, and pepper to taste. Garnish the fricassee with the fresh tarragon or parsley. Serves 4.

Ossobuco

8 pieces of veal shank (about 4 pounds),
  cut 2 inches thick and tied with string
flour for dredging the veal
4 tablespoons olive oil
2 cups finely chopped onion
1 rib of celery, finely chopped
1 carrot, finely chopped
3 cloves garlic, minced
1 cup dry white wine
2 cups beef broth
1½ cups peeled, seeded, and chopped tomato
  or a 28-ounce can tomatoes, drained and
  chopped
1 tablespoon tomato paste
1½ teaspoons minced fresh thyme or
  ½ teaspoon crumbled dried
1½ teaspoons minced fresh rosemary leaves or
  ½ teaspoon crumbled dried
1 bay leaf
2 tablespoons arrrowroot or cornstarch
  combined with 4 tablespoons water
For the gremolata
2 tablespoons freshly grated lemon zest
¼ cup minced fresh parsley leaves
1 teaspoon finely minced garlic

Pat the veal dry, dredge it in the flour, shaking off the excess, and season it with salt and pepper to taste. In a heavy kettle heat 3 tablespoons of the oil over moderate-ly high heat until it is hot, add the veal, and brown it on all sides. Transfer the veal to a plate. Pour off the fat from the kettle, add the remaining 1 tablespoon oil, and cook the onion, the celery, the carrot, and the garlic over moderate heat, stirring occasionally, until the onion is golden. Add the wine and boil the mixture for 1 minute, scraping up the brown bits. Add the beef broth, the tomato, the tomato paste, the thyme, the rosemary, the bay leaf, and salt and pepper to taste, return the veal to the kettle, and bring the liquid to a boil. Simmer the veal, covered, stirring occasionally, over moderately low heat for 1½ hours, or until it is tender.

Transfer the veal to a large plate and remove the string. Remove the bay leaf and skim the fat from the cooking liquid. Bring the liquid to a boil, add the arrow-root mixture, stirring, and simmer the sauce, stirring, until it is lightly thickened. Let the veal and the sauce cool to room temperature, combine the veal and the sauce, and transfer the *ossobuco* to a freezer container with a tight-fitting lid or to a large resealable freezer bag, pressing out the air when sealing the bag. Freeze the *ossobuco* for up to one month.

To reheat: Defrost the *ossobuco* in the refrigerator, transfer it to a heavy kettle, and reheat it over moderate-ly low heat, covered, stirring occasionally, for 20 to 30 minutes or until it is heated through. Correct the season-ing, adding salt and pepper to taste.

Make the *gremolata:* In a bowl combine the lemon zest, the parsley, and the garlic. Before serving, sprin-kle the veal with the *gremolata*. Serves 4 to 6.

FROZEN SIDE DISHES

We tried to keep these dishes straightforward and simple while offering as much variety as possible. Here you will find an excuse to buy up extra fresh pea pods and green beans when you see them in the market. Both are simply boiled, refreshed, drained, and bagged for the freezer. And don't let anyone tell you otherwise—there is a huge difference between frozen ''fresh'' market produce and the frozen vegetables in your supermarket.

You will also find a few grain dishes below. Polenta lovers will be delighted to see that it freezes beautifully. The advantages to freezing this dish are worth talking about: the 15-minute whisking time is behind you, and reheating requires minimal supervision.

And, since there is never a substitute for homemade bread, we've decided to offer a recipe for an Italian Bread Loaf with Sesame Seeds that will be a treat when company is coming. When entertaining we tend not to make bread because it is so time-consuming. The freezing option, however, allows you to make the bread on a day when you do have the time.

Rice Pilaf

1 onion, minced
3 tablespoons unsalted butter
2 cups long-grain rice
3 cups chicken broth
1½ teaspoons minced fresh thyme leaves or
   ½ teaspoon crumbled dried
1 bay leaf

In an ovenproof saucepan cook the onion in the butter over moderate heat, stirring occasionally, for 3 minutes. Add the rice and toss it to coat it with the butter. Add the broth, the thyme, the bay leaf, and salt and white pepper to taste, bring the liquid to a boil, stirring, and cook the rice in a preheated 350° F. oven, covered with a buttered round of wax paper and the lid, for 20 minutes. Remove the saucepan from the oven and let the rice stand, covered, for 5 minutes. Remove the casserole lid and let the rice cool to room temperature. Transfer the rice to a freezer container with a tight-fitting lid or to a resealable freezer bag and freeze the rice for up to 1 month.

To reheat: Defrost the rice in the refrigerator, transfer it to a buttered saucepan, and sprinkle it with 3 tablespoons of water. Heat the rice, covered, over moderately low heat, stirring occasionally, for 10 minutes, or until it is heated through. Correct the seasoning, adding salt and white pepper to taste. Serves 4 to 6.

Green Beans with Dilled Lemon Butter

3 quarts water
1 pound green beans, trimmed
3 tablespoons unsalted butter
1 teaspoon freshly grated lemon zest
1 tablespoon fresh lemon juice, or to taste
2 tablespoons minced fresh dill

In a large saucepan bring the water to a boil and then add salt to taste. Add the beans and cook them for 3 minutes. Drain the beans and refresh them under cold water. Drain the beans again, transfer them to a resealable freezer bag, and seal the bag, pressing out the air. Freeze the beans for up to one month.

To reheat: In a skillet set over moderate heat melt the butter, add the lemon zest, and cook the mixture, stirring, for 1 minute. Add the green beans and salt and pepper to taste and cook the beans, covered, over moderately low heat for 5 to 6 minutes, or until they are tender. Add the lemon juice and the dill and toss the mixture to combine it well. Serves 4.

Puréed vegetables are often favorite side dishes. The only deterrent can be the required cooking time and the food processor clean-up. Freezing the following recipe eliminates both of these drawbacks on the day you serve it. (Please note: These vegetables will give off quite a bit of liquid as they defrost. Do not be concerned, simply pour off this liquid. As the purée reheats it is magically transformed to its original color and texture and tastes wonderful!)

Rutabaga and Potato Purée

a 2½-pound rutabaga, peeled and cut into
   2-inch pieces
1½ pounds russet potatoes, peeled and cubed
1 teaspoon sugar
2 tablespoons unsalted butter

In a large saucepan combine the rutabaga, the potatoes, the sugar, and salt and pepper to taste with enough water to cover the vegetables by 2 inches. Bring the water to a boil and simmer the mixture, covered, for 30 minutes, or until tender. Drain the vegetables. In a food processor purée the vegetables, in batches, and transfer the purée to a bowl. Add the butter and salt and pepper to taste and let the purée cool to room temperature. Transfer the purée to a freezer container with a tight-fitting lid or to a resealable freezer bag and freeze the purée for up to 1 month.

To reheat: Defrost the purée in the refrigerator. Pour off the liquid that has separated from the purée and discard it. Transfer the purée to a buttered saucepan and simmer it over moderately low heat, stirring occasionally, for 10 minutes, or until it is heated through. Serves 4 to 6.

Fresh Peas with Mint

3 quarts water
2 cups shelled fresh peas (2 pounds unshelled)
2 tablespoons unsalted butter
2 tablespoons minced fresh mint leaves

In a large saucepan bring the water to a boil, add salt to taste and the peas, and cook the peas for 2 minutes. Drain the peas and refresh them under cold water. Drain the peas again, and transfer them to a resealable freezer bag. Seal the bag, pressing out the air, and freeze the peas for up to one month.

To reheat: Melt the butter in a saucepan over moderately low heat, add the peas and salt and pepper to taste, and simmer the peas, covered, for 4 to 6 minutes, or until tender and heated through. Add the mint and toss the mixture to combine. Serves 4.

Polenta with Parmesan

4 cups water
1 teaspoon salt
1 cup yellow cornmeal (not stone-ground)
½ cup freshly grated Parmesan, plus an
    additional 3 tablespoons for sprinkling
    the polenta
4 tablespoons unsalted butter

In a heavy saucepan bring the water to a boil, add the salt and the cornmeal in a very slow stream, whisking constantly, and cook the mixture over moderately low heat, stirring, for 15 minutes, or until it is very thick. Stir in ½ cup of the Parmesan, 3 tablespoons of the butter, and pepper to taste, spoon the polenta into a buttered 8-inch square baking pan, and smooth the top. Let the polenta cool. Invert the polenta onto freezer plastic wrap and wrap it up. Wrap the polenta again in foil and freeze it for up to one month.

To reheat: Defrost the polenta in the refrigerator. Remove the foil and plastic wrap, transfer the polenta to a buttered 8-inch square baking pan, and bake it in a preheated 350° F. oven for 20 minutes. Sprinkle the polenta with the remaining 3 tablespoons Parmesan and dot it with the remaining 1 tablespoon butter. Continue to bake the polenta for 5 to 10 minutes more, or until it is

heated through. Run the polenta under a preheated broiler about 4 inches from the heat for 1 minute, or until the top is golden. Serves 4.

Italian Bread Loaf with Sesame Seeds

1¼-ounce package (about 2½ teaspoons)
    active dry yeast
1 cup lukewarm water
a pinch of sugar
3 cups bread flour (high-gluten flour) or
    unbleached all-purpose flour
2 tablespoons olive oil
2 teaspoons salt
an egg wash made by beating 1 egg with
    1 teaspoon water
2 tablespoons sesame seeds

In a bowl proof the yeast in ½ cup of the water with the sugar for 15 minutes, or until it is foamy. Add 1 cup of the flour and combine the mixture well. Let the sponge rise, covered loosely, in a warm place for 45 minutes, or until it is double in bulk.

In another bowl combine the remaining 2 cups flour, the remaining ½ cup water, the olive oil, and the salt. Transfer the mixture to a floured surface, knead in the sponge mixture, and knead the dough for 8 minutes, or until it is smooth and elastic. Form the dough into a loaf about 18 inches long, put it on a floured baking sheet, and let it rise, covered loosely, in a warm place for 1 to 1½ hours, or until it is double in bulk. Make three slashes, 3 inches long and ½ inch deep, on the top of the loaf with a razor blade or sharp knife, brush it with some of the egg wash, and sprinkle it with the sesame seeds. Bake the loaf in a 400° F. oven for 45 to 50 minutes, or until it sounds hollow when the bottom is tapped. Let the loaf cool on a rack until it reaches room temperature. Wrap the loaf in freezer plastic wrap and aluminum foil and freeze it for up to 1 month.

To reheat: Unwrap the loaf, remove the foil and the plastic wrap, and rewrap the loaf in the foil. Heat the loaf in a preheated 400° F. oven for 10 minutes, or until it is heated through. Remove the foil and return the bread to the oven for 5 minutes more, or until it is crisp. Makes 1 loaf.

FROZEN DESSERTS

Perhaps the nicest dish to have completed before a dinner party is a lovely dessert. It must be extra special—after all, you don't have guests every day—and it must be simple to reheat and prepare for serving. You certainly do not want to be away from the dinner table for long while your friends are having fun. Be assured that all of the desserts below meet these demands. In fact, most of them simply defrost in the refrigerator and are ready to serve. (*And* one needs no defrosting at all!)

Our desserts are appropriate for a variety of occasions. If you are looking for a modest yet delicious cake, try our Banana Chocolate Chip Loaf Cake, or if your guests are *real* chocolate lovers, our Espresso Brownies with Hazelnuts will make their day. But perhaps the greatest surprise of the lot is our Cinnamon Apple Pie. It is absolutely delicious and no one will ever guess that you made it weeks ago!

An iced soufflé is always sure to please, and unlike its savory cousin that must be baked to puff up, the iced dessert is guaranteed to always reach impressive heights! Please note that you should make the soufflé within one week of serving time: If it is stored longer, its texture will change.

Iced Raspberry Soufflé with Raspberry Sauce

2 cups fresh raspberries or 12 ounces frozen
   raspberries, yielding 1¼ cups strained
   raspberry purée
fresh lemon juice to taste
1 teaspoon freshly grated lemon zest
1 tablespoon framboise or kirsch, if desired
⅔ cup granulated sugar
¼ cup water
3 large egg whites
1 cup heavy cream
For the sauce
¼ cup granulated sugar, or to taste
fresh lemon juice to taste
¼ cup water
1 tablespoon framboise or kirsch, if desired

Make a collar for a 1-quart soufflé dish with a 6-inch-wide doubled band of wax paper or foil that is long enough to fit around the dish. Brush the collar with flavorless vegetable oil and fit the dish with the collar extending 3 inches above the rim. Secure it with string or tape.

In a food processor or blender purée the raspberries, strain the purée through a fine sieve into a bowl, pressing down hard on the solids, and reserve ¾ cup of the purée for the sauce. To the remaining ½ cup purée add the lemon juice, the lemon zest, and the framboise.

In a small heavy saucepan combine the sugar with the water, bring the mixture to a boil, gently swirling the pan and washing down any sugar crystals clinging to the sides of the pan with a brush dipped in cold water, and boil the syrup until it reaches the soft-ball stage, or a candy thermometer reaches 240° F. In a bowl with an electric mixer beat the egg whites until they hold stiff peaks. With the mixer running, add the sugar syrup in a stream and beat the egg whites until they are completely cool.

In a chilled bowl beat the cream until it holds soft peaks. Fold the egg whites into the raspberry purée mixture gently but thoroughly and fold in the whipped cream. Spoon the mixture into the prepared soufflé dish, smooth the top, and freeze the soufflé until it is firm. Cover the soufflé, enclosing the dish completely with freezer plastic wrap and foil, and freeze it for up to one week.

Make the sauce: Into the reserved ¾ cup raspberry purée stir the sugar, the lemon juice, and the water. Transfer the sauce to a freezer container with a tight-fitting lid and freeze it for up to one week.

To serve: Defrost the raspberry sauce in the refrigerator overnight. Transfer the sauce to a serving dish and stir in the framboise. Before serving the soufflé remove the collar and let the soufflé stand in the refrigerator for 10 minutes, or until it is slightly softened. Serve the soufflé with the sauce. Serves 6.

As with our raspberry soufflé, the bombe that follows should be made no more than one week before it is served. Otherwise, you will notice a change in texture and flavor.

Orange and Toasted Almond Bombe

2 cups softened orange sherbet
¼ cup diced candied orange peel
2 tablespoons orange-flavored liqueur
3 egg yolks
½ cup sugar
¼ cup water
½ cup sliced almonds, toasted
2 teaspoons freshly grated orange zest
1 cup heavy cream
fresh mint leaves for garnish, if desired

Spread the sherbet in a lightly oiled 1-quart bombe mold or other mold to form a 1-inch lining and freeze the mold for 30 minutes, or until the sherbet is solid. In a small bowl combine the candied orange peel and the orange-flavored liqueur and let the mixture stand for 10 minutes.

In a bowl with a mixer beat the egg yolks until they are light in color. In a very small saucepan combine the sugar and the water and bring the mixture to a boil, stirring, until the sugar is dissolved. Boil the syrup, brushing down the sides of the pan with a brush dipped in cold water, until the syrup reaches the soft-ball stage, or a candy thermometer registers 240° F. With the mixer running, drizzle the syrup into the beaten egg yolks and beat the mixture until it is cool. Stir in the candied orange peel mixture, the toasted almonds, and the grated orange zest.

In a chilled bowl whip the cream until it holds stiff peaks. Fold the cream into the orange mixture and fill the orange sherbet-lined mold with it. Cover the mold with freezer plastic wrap and the lid or foil and freeze it for up to 1 week.

To serve: Unmold the bombe onto a serving plate and garnish it with fresh mint leaves, if desired. Serves 6.

Rum Raisin Figgy Pudding

¾ cup golden raisins
¾ cup dark raisins
⅓ cup dark rum or brandy
¾ cup dried figs, stemmed and chopped
½ cup milk
¾ cup all-purpose flour
1½ teaspoons double-acting baking powder
½ teaspoon cinnamon
½ teaspoon freshly grated nutmeg
¼ teaspoon ground cloves
¼ teaspoon ground ginger
½ teaspoon salt
1 stick (½ cup) unsalted butter, softened
½ cup sugar
2 large eggs, beaten lightly
¾ cup fresh bread crumbs
1 tablespoon freshly grated orange zest
lightly whipped cream or ice cream as an
    accompaniment

Butter well a 1-quart steamed pudding mold.

In a bowl combine the golden and dark raisins with the rum and let the fruit macerate for 2 hours.

In a small saucepan combine the figs and the milk and simmer the mixture over low heat, stirring occasionally, for 15 minutes.

Into a bowl sift the flour, the baking powder, the spices, and the salt.

In a bowl with an electric mixer cream the butter, add the sugar, and beat the mixture until it is light. Add the eggs, a little at a time, and beat the mixture until it is fluffy. Add the raisin and fig mixtures (including the liquids) to the egg mixture, stirring to combine.

Add the egg and fruit mixture to the flour, stirring to combine, and stir in the bread crumbs and the orange zest. Spoon the batter into the prepared mold, a little at a time, rapping the mold on a hard surface as it is filled to eliminate any air bubbles. Cover the mold tightly with the lid.

Set a low rack in the bottom of a kettle and add enough water to reach 3 inches up the sides of the mold. (The mold may be set in the water to measure the depth of the water, but then it should be removed.) Bring the water to a boil and keep it at a brisk but not rolling boil, covered with the lid of the kettle.

Place the mold on the rack and cover the kettle. Steam the pudding for 2 hours, checking occasionally to make certain the water is at a brisk but not rolling boil and adding more water if necessary. Transfer the mold to a rack to cool for 10 minutes and invert it onto the rack to cool completely. Wrap the mold in freezer plastic wrap and foil and freeze it for up to 1 month.

To reheat: Defrost the pudding in the refrigerator. Remove the foil and the plastic wrap from the pudding and rewrap the pudding in the foil. Heat the pudding in a preheated 350° F. oven on a baking sheet for 45 minutes to 1 hour, or until it is heated through. Serve the pudding with lightly whipped cream or ice cream. Makes 1 pudding, serving 6.

Lauren Jarrett

This apple pie may quickly become an old favorite, but you'll be happy to know that it is not the only type of fruit pie that freezes well. Blueberries, raspberries, or strawberries are excellent substitutions, as long as you change the pie filling as follows:

> 2 pints blueberries, raspberries, or
>   strawberries
> ⅓ to ½ cup granulated sugar, or to taste
> ½ teaspoon cinnamon, if desired
>   (delete the cloves and lemon juice)
> 1 teaspoon freshly grated lemon zest
>   (butter measurement stays the same)
> 2 to 3 tablespoons all-purpose flour
>   (depending on the ripeness of the fruit)

Cinnamon Apple Pie

For the pie dough
2¼ cups all-purpose flour
½ teaspoon salt
1 stick (½ cup) unsalted butter, cut into bits
4 tablespoons cold vegetable shortening, cut
    into bits
about 6 tablespoons ice water
For the filling
2½ pounds (about 6) McIntosh or similar
    apples, peeled, cored, and sliced
⅔ cup granulated sugar
1 teaspoon cinnamon
⅛ teaspoon ground cloves
1 tablespoon fresh lemon juice
½ teaspoon freshly grated lemon zest
3 tablespoons unsalted butter, cut into bits
3 tablespoons all-purpose flour

an egg wash made by beating 1 egg with
    1 teaspoon water

Make the pie dough: In a bowl stir together the flour and the salt. Add the butter and the vegetable shortening and blend it into the mixture until it resembles coarse meal. Gradually add the ice water, tossing the mixture with a fork, until a soft but not sticky dough is formed. Form the dough into a ball. Flatten the ball slightly, dust it lightly with flour, and chill it, wrapped in wax paper, for 30 minutes.

Make the filling: In a bowl combine the apples, the sugar, the cinnamon, the cloves, the lemon juice and zest, the butter, and the flour and let the mixture stand for 10 minutes.

Divide the dough into 2 pieces, one slightly larger than the other, and chill the larger piece, wrapped in wax paper. Roll out the smaller piece ⅛ inch thick on a floured surface, fit it into a 9-inch pie plate, and trim the edge, leaving a ½-inch overhang.

Mound the apple mixture in the shell.

Roll out the larger piece of dough into a 13- to 14-inch round on a floured surface and drape it over the filling. Trim the top crust, leaving a 1-inch overhang, fold the overhang under the bottom crust, pressing the edge to seal it, and crimp the edge decoratively with the tines of a fork. Brush the crust with the egg wash and make slits in the top for steam vents.

Bake the pie in a preheated 375° F. oven for 1 hour. Cool the pie on a rack to room temperature. Wrap the pie in freezer plastic wrap and foil, enclosing it completely, and freeze it for up to 1 month.

To reheat: Remove the plastic wrap and foil and defrost the pie in the refrigerator. Reheat the pie in a preheated 400° F. oven for 20 minutes, or until the pastry is crisp and the filling is heated through. Makes 1 pie.

If you like nuts, feel free to substitute them for part or all of the chocolate chips called for in the following recipe. One-third cup pecans and ⅓ cup chocolate chips, for example, offer a bit of crunch and chocolate flavor in this moist cake.

Banana Chocolate Chip Loaf Cake

2¼ cups sifted cake flour (not self-rising)
2 teaspoons double-acting baking powder
⅛ teaspoon salt
1½ sticks (¾ cup) softened unsalted butter
⅔ cup granulated sugar
2 large eggs, beaten lightly
1½ teaspoons vanilla extract
1 cup mashed ripe banana (about 3 medium)
⅔ cup semisweet chocolate chips
ice cream and chocolate sauce as
    accompaniments, if desired

Into a bowl sift the cake flour, the baking powder, and the salt. In a bowl with an electric mixer cream the butter, add the sugar, a little at a time, and beat the mixture until it is light. Add the eggs, a little at a time, and beat the mixture until it is fluffy. Beat in the vanilla.

Beat one-third of the mashed banana into the butter mixture and then beat in one-third of the flour mixture. Continue to alternately add the banana and the flour mixture to the butter mixture in the same manner. Stir the chocolate chips into the batter. Pour the batter into a well-buttered 9 x 5 x 3-inch loaf pan and bake the cake in the middle of a preheated 350° F. oven for 1 hour, or until a cake tester inserted in the center comes out clean. If the cake begins to overbrown, cover it loosely with a piece of foil. Let the cake cool in the pan for 10 minutes, invert it onto a rack, and let it cool completely. Wrap the cake in freezer plastic wrap and foil and freeze it for up to one month.

To serve: Defrost the cake in the refrigerator and serve it with ice cream and chocolate sauce, if desired.

Espresso Brownies with Hazelnuts

6 ounces fine-quality bittersweet chocolate
6 tablespoons unsalted butter, cut into
    tablespoons
1 tablespoon espresso powder
    blended with 1 tablespoon
    hot water
1 teaspoon vanilla
½ cup granulated sugar
½ cup all-purpose flour
½ teaspoon double-acting baking powder
pinch of salt
2 large eggs,
    beaten lightly
1 cup chopped toasted hazelnuts

In the top of a double boiler set over simmering water combine the chocolate and the butter and cook the mixture, stirring, until the chocolate is just melted. Remove the pan from the heat and stir in the espresso mixture, the vanilla, and the sugar. Let the mixture cool.

Into a small bowl sift the flour, the baking powder, and the salt.

Whisk the eggs into the chocolate mixture and stir in the flour mixture and the hazelnuts. Transfer the batter to a buttered 8-inch square pan and bake the brownies in a preheated 350° F. oven for 20 minutes, or until a cake tester inserted 1½ inches from the edge of the pan comes out clean. Let the brownies cool in the pan for 5 minutes, invert the entire brownie cake onto a rack, and let it cool completely. Wrap the cake in freezer plastic wrap and foil and freeze it for up to 1 month.

Defrost the brownie cake in the refrigerator and cut it into squares before serving. Makes 16 squares.

GUIDES TO THE TEXT

GENERAL INDEX

Page numbers in *italics* indicate color photographs
(M) indicates a microwave recipe

INDEX OF 45-MINUTE RECIPES

* Starred entries can be prepared in 45 minutes or less
but require additional unattended time

Page numbers in *italics* indicate color photographs

(M) indicates a microwave recipe

INDEX OF RECIPE TITLES

Page numbers in *italics* indicate color photographs

(M) indicates a microwave recipe

TABLE SETTING ACKNOWLEDGMENTS

To avoid duplication below of table setting information within the same menu, the editors have listed all such credits for silverware, plates, linen, and the like in its most complete form under "Table Setting."

Any items in the photographs not credited are privately owned.

All addresses are in New York City unless otherwise indicated.

Front Jacket

Chocolate Raspberry Cake: Linen damask fabric (available through decorator)—Brunschwig & Fils, Inc., 979 Third Avenue. English 19th century porcelain dessert plate and mug (vase)—Bardith, 901 Madison Avenue.

Frontispiece

Marinated Lobster Salad with Corn and Tomatoes (page 2): St. Louis "Firmament Gold" crystal bowl—Bergdorf Goodman, 754 Fifth Avenue.

Table of Contents

The Menu Collection (page 6): See Table Setting credits for Lunch on the Lawn below.
A Recipe Compendium—Apricot Berry Trifle (page 7): American sterling footed dish, 1862; sterling salver, circa 1835; sterling serving spoon, circa 1750—F. Gorevic & Son, 635 Madison Avenue.

The Menu Collection

Table Setting (page 10): See Table Setting credits for Easter Luncheon below.

A Quincentennial Celebration

Table Setting (pages 12 and 13): "Magellan" faience dinner plates by Gien—Baccarat, Inc., 625 Madison Avenue. "Iron Age" stainless-steel flatware designed by Michael Aram—Platypus, 126 Spring Street. "Europe" crystal water goblets, wineglasses, and decanter by Saint-Louis Cristal, (212) 838-3880. Linen napkins designed by Bebe Winkler—Shaxted, 940 North Michigan Avenue, Chicago, IL. "Broken Column" Italian terra-cotta candlesticks and obelisk—Frank McIntosh Shop at Henri Bendel, 712 Fifth Avenue. Flower arrangement—Castle & Pierpont, 1441 York Avenue. English burled ash and coromandel wood table, circa 1810; English nineteenth-century table globe on mahogany stand (one of a pair)—Florian Papp, Inc., 962 Madison Avenue. Five English William IV–style mahogany chairs (from a set of eight); oak revolving pedestal, circa 1870; chinoiserie side table, circa 1920 (available through decorator)—Yale R. Burge Antiques, 305 East 63rd Street. English nineteenth-century hand-painted leather screen—courtesy of The Oxford on Seventy Second Condominium, 422 East 72nd Street. "Siena" wallpaper (available through decorator)—Brunschwig & Fils, Inc., 979 Third Avenue.
Chocolate-Frosted Devil's Food Cake with Pecan and Coconut Filling (page 15): "Italian Fruit" porcelain cake stand by Ginori—Cardel, Ltd., 621 Madison Avenue.

Hearty One-Pot Dinners

Cassoulet, Mixed Green Salad, French Bread (pages 16 and 17): French faience dinner plates by Cassis & Co.— Platypus, 126 Spring Street. "Bourbon" stainless-steel flatware and serving spoon by Jean Couzon—Faience, 104 Mason Street, Greenwich, CT. Portuguese crystal wineglasses—Frank McIntosh Shop at Henri Bendel, 712 Fifth Avenue. Wood tray with iron handles—Conran's Habitat, (800)-3-CONRAN. Cotton napkins—Pottery Barn, 117 East 59th Street. French 7-quart hammered-copper casserole (lid not shown)—Bridge Kitchenware Corporation, 214 East 52nd Street. English nineteenth-century copper and brass candlesticks (on table); English nineteenth-century copper molds; English brass candlesticks, circa 1775—Bob Pryor Antiques, 1023 Lexington Avenue. "Ispahan" cotton fabric—Pierre Deux, 870 Madison Avenue. Wall finish by Richard Pellicci, Tel. (212) 988-4365 (by appointment only).

Valentine's Day Dinner for Two

Table Setting (pages 18 and 19): "Au Bain Marie" ceramic dinner plates; French faience salad plates (from a set of 4 plates and a compote), circa 1900; Nason & Moretti hand-blown pink Murano crystal goblets—Barneys New York, Seventh Avenue and 17th Street. Scottish nineteenth-century sterling flatware—F. Gorevic & Son, Inc., 635 Madison Avenue. Peill "Atlantis" crystal wineglasses—Cardel, Ltd., 621 Madison Avenue. Majolica pitcher, circa 1870—Kentshire Antiques, Bergdorf Goodman, 754 Fifth Avenue. Sterling heart-shaped picture frames,

1904 (the larger one) and 1911 (both on dining table); brass-mounted glass candlesticks, circa 1880 (on dining table); porcelain hat, circa 1910, and English silver-mounted tortoiseshell picture frame, circa 1930 (both on table in background); glass candlestick (one of a pair), circa 1860, and decorative mirror picture (one of a pair) circa 1865 (both on mantel)—James II Galleries, Ltd., 15 East 57th Street. English nineteenth-century beechwood folding tea table—Howard Kaplan Antiques, 827 Broadway. Roses—Castle & Pierpont, 1441 York Avenue. Miniature nineteenth-century cast-iron love seat (on dining table); leather sewing box, circa 1820, and reproduction bronze urn lamp and parchment lampshade (both on table in background), hand-painted tole cachepot (on mantel); English-style ottoman and pillow covered with "Patchwork" needlepoint; blue floral needlepoint pillows—Charlotte Moss & Co., 1027 Lexington Avenue. "Louis XV Fauteuil" armchair upholstered in "Minton" cotton fabric designed by Pierre Frey (available through decorator)—Brunschwig & Fils, Inc., 979 Third Avenue. *Cupid's Almanac* and *The Loves of Florizel* (on chair)—Stubbs Books & Prints, 835 Madison Avenue.

Waffled Sweet-Potato Chips (page 20): European nineteenth-century silver basket—F. Gorevic & Son, Inc., 635 Madison Avenue. Nason & Moretti hand-blown pink Murano crystal Champagne flutes—Barneys New York, Seventh Avenue and 17th Street. Silver-plate wine cooler—S. Wyler, Inc., 941 Lexington Avenue.

An Hors d'Oeuvre Buffet for the Olympics

Asian Spring Rolls; Chicken Wings Africana; Pirozhki; South American–Style Jícama and Orange Salad; Pissaladière (pages 22 and 23): "Victoria" porcelain dinner plates, trays, chop plate, sauce bowls, and footed bowl designed by Oscar Tusquets; stainless-steel and mesh basket designed by Enzo Mari for Zani & Zani; "Sol" Murano glass fruit bowl designed by Marco Zanini; "Cugino" glass-topped table on iron base designed by Enzo Mari; "Air" hand-tufted wool rug designed by

Christine van der Hurd—Driade New York Inc., 212 East 57th Street. Georg Jensen "Prism" stainless-steel flatware; Holmegaard "Princess" wineglasses and beer glasses—Royal Copenhagen Porcelain/Georg Jensen Silversmiths, 683 Madison Avenue. Green cotton napkins designed by Junko Koshina—The MoMA Design Store, 44 West 53rd Street.

Enchanted Forest Birthday Parties

For the Adults (pages 24 and 25): Fioriware "Grape Garland" ceramic dinner plates—Fioriware, Tel. (614) 454-7400. "Twig" handmade bronze and metal flatware—The Pottery Barn, 117 East 59th Street. Crystal goblets; Italian iron black birds (with glass bud vases, not shown) used as candleholders; Jule des Pres cinnamon/nutmeg bunches—Bergdorf Goodman, 754 Fifth Avenue. Linen napkins designed by Bette Blau—Bette Blau, Tel. (212) 243-4640. "Forest" handmade twig dining chairs with rush or Shaker-style webbing seats—Daniel Mack Rustic Furnishings, Tel. (212) 926-3880.

Chutney-Glazed Cornish Hens with Hazelnut and Dried-Fruit Stuffing, Potato Nests with Sautéed Shiitake Mushrooms, Lemon-Buttered Broccoli Spears (page 26): Italian iron black birds with glass bud vases—Bergdorf Goodman, 754 Fifth Avenue.

For the Children—Basket of Crudités, Individual Cheese and Pepperoni Pizzas, Trail Mix, Enchanted Forest Cake (page 27): "Maple Leaf" handmade ceramic plates—Eigen Arts, 150 Bay Street, Jersey City, NJ 07302. "Birch Tree" hand-painted tablecloth—Aimee Reed, Puttin' on the Ritz, Tel. (203) 325-9505. Steiff stuffed toy animals—FAO Schwarz, 767 Fifth Avenue. Handmade twig children's chairs; spalted maple tree stump—Daniel Mack Rustic Furnishings, Tel. (212) 926-3880.

A New England Fireside Dinner

Corned Beef with Horseradish Mustard Sauce; Steamed Root Vegetables and Cabbage with Dill; Boiled Yukon Gold Potatoes; Beet Flowers and Beet Greens Vinaigrette (pages 28 and 29): "Rambouillet" faience dinner plates by

Gien—Baccarat, Inc., 625 Madison Avenue. American coin silver flatware, circa 1830; and cotton napkins—Gail Lettick's Pantry & Hearth Antiques, 121 East 35th Street. Flower arrangement—Zezé, 398 East 52nd Street. Painted metal candlesticks—The Pottery Barn, 117 East 59th Street.

Beet Flowers and Beet Greens Vinaigrette (page 29): "Rambouillet" faience salad plates by Gien—Baccarat, Inc., 625 Madison Avenue.

Easter Luncheon

Table Setting (pages 30 and 31): Italian hand-painted ceramic plates—Barneys New York, Seventh Avenue and 17th Street. Nineteenth-century English ceramic leaf plates; English cut-glass wineglasses, circa 1800; French silver-plate salt and pepper baskets with opaline liners, circa 1870—Bardith Ltd., 901 Madison Avenue. "Lauzun" sterling flatware—Puiforcat, Tel. (212) 684-6760. "Barsac" crystal water goblets and wineglasses—Lalique, Tel. (212) 684-6760. Hand-embroidered linen and organdy place mats and napkins—Léron, Inc., 750 Madison Avenue. Staffordshire cottages, Sunderland lustre mugs, pink lustre cabbage-rose pitchers, all circa 1840—Ages Past Antiques, 1030 Lexington Avenue. Flowers—Zezé, 398 East 52nd Street. Topiary rabbits—O'Farrior Topiary, Tel. (800) 433-1191.

Boneless Leg of Lamb Stuffed with Swiss Chard and Feta; Spiced Quinoa Timbales; Honey-Glazed Baby Carrots (page 32): Silver-plate tray by Reed & Barton; sterling carving knife and fork; sterling sauceboat—F. Gorevic & Son, Inc., 635 Madison Avenue.

Frozen Strawberry Lemon Meringue Torte (page 33): Ceramic dessert plates—Keesal & Mathews, 1244 Madison Avenue. French cut-glass Champagne flutes, circa 1860—Bardith Ltd., 901 Madison Avenue. American silver tray, Boston, circa 1850—F. Gorevic & Son, Inc., 635 Madison Avenue.

A Spring Brunch

Aquavit Bloody Marys, Lemon Gem Muffins, Papaya in Cinnamon Syrup, Ham and Egg Biscuit Pizzas (pages 34 and 35): "Balloon" faience plates, mugs, and open-weave basket; French cotton napkins—Ségriès à Solanée, 866 Lexington Avenue. "Folio" stainless-steel flatware—Pavillons Christofle, New York, Chicago, Beverly Hills, and San Francisco. English silver-plate café au lait set, circa 1910—James II Galleries, Ltd., 15 East 57th Street. Hand-painted "Pilaster" cabinets by Smallbone—Smallbone Inc., 150 East 58th Street.

Lunch on the Lawn

Table Setting (pages 36 and 37): "Spiral" ceramic dinner and salad plates by Fioriware—Fioriware, 26 N. Third Street, Zanesville, OH 43710, Tel. (614) 454-7400. Hammered-bronze flatware—Zona, 97 Greene Street. Wineglasses, ironstone pitcher (used as vase), and cotton tablecloth—Wolfman • Gold & Good Company, 116 Greene Street. "Weather Master" rattan loveseat and armchair from Lane's Venture Collection—Tel. (800) 447-4700. Handmade cast-iron screen by Hecho a Mano—Domain, Inc., 51 Morgan Drive, Norwood, MA 02062, Tel. (617) 769-9130.
Grilled Porterhouse Steaks with Olive and Caper Spread, Arborio Rice Salad with Cucumber and Mint, Mixed Grilled Vegetables (pages 38 and 39): White ceramic platters, antique watering can—Wolfman • Gold & Good Company, 116 Greene Street. "Spiral" ceramic bowls by Fioriware—Fioriware, 26 N. Third Street, Zanesville, OH 43710, Tel. (614) 454-7400. Stainless-steel carving knife and fork by Lamson & Goodnow—Tel. (800)-872-6564.

A Spring Dinner

Chicken Breasts with Scallions, Shiitake Mushrooms, and Tomatoes; Herbed Farfalle; Pea and Watercress Purée (pages 40 and 41): Raynaud/Céralene "Ramage" porcelain dinner plates and butter plates; Raynaud/Céralene porcelain duck and rooster reproduced from the Carven-Grog Collection in the Musée Guimet—Baccarat, Inc., 625 Madison Avenue. Sasaki "Eclipse" wineglasses and water glasses; Chambly silver-plate flatware—Barneys New York, Seventh Avenue and 17th

Street. Linen napkins—Frank McIntosh at Henri Bendel, 712 Fifth Avenue. Mahogany double-pedestal Sheraton-style table with hand-painted border; Adam-style painted shield-back chairs (from a set of six); French eighteenth century five-panel screen—Howard Kaplan Antiques, 827 Broadway.

A Bridal Luncheon

Table Setting (pages 42 and 43): "Reflets d'Été" porcelain dinner and salad plates by Céralène—Baccarat, Inc., 625 Madison Avenue. Glass bowls with glass inserts by Sasaki—Barneys New York, Seventh Avenue and 17th Street. "Corinthian" sterling flatware, circa 1900—F. Gorevic & Son, Inc., 635 Madison Avenue. "Herend Bird" etched wineglasses—Keesal & Mathews, 1244 Madison Avenue. "Townsend" cotton damask napkins by Brook Hill—Bergdorf Goodman, 754 Fifth Avenue. Silver-plate epergnes—William-Wayne & Co., 324 East 9th Street. "Edisto" (overcloths) and "Orleans" glazed cotton chintz fabric (available through decorator)—Brunschwig & Fils, Inc., 979 Third Avenue. Silver-plate punch bowl and ladle—Wolfman • Gold & Good Company, 116 Greene Street.
Curried Smoked Chicken and Wild Rice Salad, Mixed Vegetables Vinaigrette (pages 44 and 45): China bowl and silver-plate servers—Wolfman • Gold & Good Company, 116 Greene Street. Silver-plate tray and bowl by Swid Powell—Fortunoff, 681 Fifth Avenue.

A Graduation Dinner

Roasted Loin of Veal with Garlic, Shallots, and Mustard Gravy; Paprika Potato Rosettes; Sugar Snap Peas with Lemon Butter (pages 46 and 47): "Tosca" china dinner plates from the Grand Tier Collection for Lenox China & Crystal, Tel. (800) 635-3669. "Devonshire" sterling flatware by International Silver; silver-plate tray by Reed & Barton; sterling leaf dish by Black Starr & Gorham; eighteenth-century sterling serving spoon—F. Gorevic & Son, Inc., 635 Madison Avenue. Wineglasses; "Renaissance" cotton throw (on table)—Wolfman • Gold & Good

Company, 116 Greene Street. Flowers—Zezé, 398 East 52nd Street.

Fourth of July Picnic by the Sea

Table Setting (pages 48 and 49): Schott-Zwiesel "Crystal Boutique" bowls—Cardel, Ltd., 621 Madison Avenue. "Chinon" silver-plate flatware—Pavillon Christofle, 680 Madison Avenue.
Summer Berry Mint Cream Tart (page 51): Mottahedeh "Torquay" ironstone plates—The Winterthur Museum Store on Clenny Run, (800) 448-3883.

A Bastille Day Cocktail Party

Cornmeal and Shallot Madeleines with Crème Fraîche and Caviar; Lillet au Citron; Quail Eggs with Olive Paste; Savory Cheese Galette; "Two-Dollar Cocktail"; Pernod and Water; Crab Salad with Hearts of Palm (pages 52 and 53): Pewter platter; "Lafayette" ceramic platter and plates; "Bastille" cotton fabric (for tablecloth)—Pierre Deux, 870 Madison Avenue. Martini glasses; "Pluton" highball glass; "Neptune" Old Fashioned glass—Baccarat, Inc., 625 Madison Avenue.

Dinner by the Bay

Table Setting (pages 54 and 55): Platinum luster porcelain dinner plates; "Cordova" sterling flatware by Elsa Peretti; "Optic" crystal wineglasses—Tiffany & Co., 727 Fifth Avenue. Blue glass water goblets; mosaic column candlesticks—Barneys New York, Seventh Avenue and 17th Street. Hand-painted linen napkins by Liz Wain (special order)—Gibraltar, 154 King Street, Charleston, SC 29401.
Key Lime Cheesecake (page 57): Hand-painted ceramic cake stand—Fast Forward, 580 Fifth Avenue.

Dinner from a Cool Kitchen

Tomato, Arugula, and Ricotta Salata Salad (page 58): Porcelain salad plate by Laure Japy—ABC Carpet & Home, Inc., 888 Broadway.
Cold Poached Chicken Breasts with Tuna Basil Sauce; Minted Green Beans with Red Onion; Assorted Breads (pages 58 and 59): Hand-painted porce-

lain dinner plates by Maryse Boxer—Barneys New York, Seventh Avenue and 17th Street. Wood-handled flatware, circa 1900; cotton napkins; painted wood ladder, circa 1900—Wolfman • Gold & Good Company, 116 Greene Street. Wineglasses and water glasses; painted wood table—ABC Carpet & Home, Inc., 888 Broadway. Vintage Adirondack chairs; wire planter and basket; painted tole cachepot—Treillage, Ltd., 418 East 75th Street.

Dinner on the Veranda

Table Setting (pages 60 and 61): "Nazare" Portuguese hand-painted earthenware dinner and salad plates; hand-painted hurricane lamp and glass decanter (on side table)—Casafina, Fields Lane, Brewster, NY 10509, (914) 277-5700. Glass soup bowls—Keesal & Mathews, 1244 Madison Avenue. English "Feather" silver-plate flatware—Wolfman • Gold & Good Company, 116 Greene Street. "American Originals" pressed-glass wineglasses—Pfaltzgraff, (800) 999-2811. "Grape Leaf" silk-screened cotton napkins—Liz Lauter Designs, (212) 239-9719. Hobnail glasses (with flowers)—The Pottery Barn, 117 East 59th Street.

A Labor Day Picnic Rain or Shine

"Damn the Weather" Cocktails; Tequila Sunrises; Cumin Tortilla Crisps; Picadillo Empanadas with Cornmeal Crust; Oven-Fried Chipotle Chili Chicken; Cucumber, Radish, and Tomato Salad with Citrus Dressing (pages 64 and 65): Enameled steel dinner plates and mug—The Pottery Barn, 117 East 59th Street. "Beechwood" wood and stainless-steel flatware—Conran's • Habitat, 160 East 54th Street. Cotton napkins—Dean & DeLuca Inc., 560 Broadway. Cassis & Co. hand-painted ceramic pitcher and bowl; wooden garden seat, circa 1940; "Beans" card game—Zona, 97 Greene Street. "Wild West" cotton throw—The Rug Barn, (803) 446-3561.

An Elegant Fall Dinner

Table Setting (pages 66 and 67): "Bacchanale" porcelain dinner plates—Bernardaud, 777 Madison Avenue.

"Trianon" sterling flatware—Tuttle La Préference, Tel. (617) 561-2200. "Moisson" crystal wineglasses—Hermès, Tel. (800) 441-4488. Embroidered linen napkins, circa 1930—Heritage Linens, Tel. (212) 371-4226 (by appointment only). Silver-plate goblets; nineteenth-century ebony and ivory candlesticks; Biedermeier satin birch side chairs, circa 1830; plaid obelisks; majolica urns, circa 1850—Yale R. Burge Antiques, 305 East 63rd Street. "Craquele Ottoman" cotton and viscose fabric (on table); "Sologne" cotton fabric (on sofa), both available through decorator—Clarence House, 211 East 58th Street. Flowers—Castle & Pierpont, 1441 York Avenue. *Fauxbois* walls and *faux-marbre* and *faux-lapis* mantelpiece by Richard Pellicci, Tel. (212) 988-4365 (by appointment only).

Pistachio Praline Dacquoise (page 69): Sterling tray—F. Gorevic & Son, Inc., 635 Madison Avenue. Fringed linen cloth with cutwork, circa 1900—Heritage Linens, Tel. (212) 371-4226 (by appointment only).

A Sunday Bistro Supper

Braised Lamb Shanks with Tomatoes and Rosemary; White Bean and Watercress Gratin (pages 70 and 71): "Bistro" porcelain plates by Pillivuyt—Barneys New York, Seventh Avenue and 17th Street. Taitu "Rotondo" acrylic flatware; Biot "Bellini" wineglasses—Mayhew, 507 Park Avenue. Cotton napkins—Frank McIntosh Shop at Henri Bendel, 712 Fifth Avenue. French porcelain match strikers, circa 1900; brass Champagne bucket, circa 1900; nineteenth-century milk bottles in wire carrier; brass chalkboard, circa 1900; iron chairs, circa 1880; iron and terrazzo console, circa 1890—Howard Kaplan Antiques, 827 Broadway. "McCheck" red and white cotton fabric—Waverly, (800) 423-5881.

Thanksgiving Dinner

Table Setting (pages 72 and 73): Thomas Booth porcelain dinner plates, 1868—James II Galleries, Ltd., 15 East 57th Street. "Repoussé" sterling flatware—Kirk Stieff, Tel. (410) 338-6000. "Les Jets d'Eau" crystal water

goblets and wineglasses; "Perfection" crystal Rhine wineglasses—Baccarat, Inc., 625 Madison Avenue. Vintage damask napkins; French linen tablecloth with needlepoint lace and filet lace border, circa 1830—Françoise Nunnallé, Tel. (212) 246-4281 (by appointment only). Cut-glass decanters, circa 1810; papier-mâché coasters, circa 1860; cut-glass salts, circa 1770; silver-plate and etched glass epergne, circa 1810—James II Galleries, Ltd., 15 East 57th Street. Sterling sweetmeat basket, London, 1769—F. Gorevic & Son, Inc., 635 Madison Avenue. Flower arrangement by Timothy C. Hargus—Ballastone Inn Flower Shop, 14 East Oglethorpe Avenue, Savannah, GA 31401, Tel. (912) 236-1484.

Roast Turkey with Herbed Oyster Stuffing and Giblet Gravy; Jellied Apple Cranberry Sauce; Diced Carrots and Turnips; Lemon Rosemary Green Beans; Potato, Chestnut, and Celery Root Purée (pages 74 and 75): Sterling platter by Durgin, circa 1910; sterling vegetable dish; Black, Starr & Frost sterling entrée dishes (lids not shown), circa 1915; Asprey decanter (one of a pair); Tiffany & Co. sterling coaster; Howard & Co. sterling sauceboat (lid not shown), circa 1910; sterling ladle and serving spoons—Fortunoff, 681 Fifth Avenue. Minton porcelain plates (from a dessert service), circa 1855; mahogany washstand, circa 1800; nineteenth-century three-panel painted canvas screen—Yale R. Burge Antiques, 305 East 63rd Street.

Election Night Potluck Supper

Layered Vegetable Salad with Caper and Thyme Dressing; Pork Fricassee with Mushrooms and Carrots; Paprika Rice (pages 76 and 77): "Pont aux Choux" faience dinner plates by Gien—Baccarat, Inc., 625 Madison Avenue. Wood-handled flatware by Alain St. Jonas—Barneys New York, Seventh Avenue and 17th Street. "Arlington" wineglasses—Keesal & Mathews, 1244 Madison Avenue. Cotton napkins by Tag—Wolfman • Gold & Good Company, 116 Greene Street. "Balmoral Plaid" linen and cotton fabric (available through decorator)—Clarence House, 211 East 58th Street. "4-Arm Rope" iron candelabrum by

Michael Aram—Neiman Marcus stores nationwide. Nineteenth-century Staffordshire political figures (from a collection); Wedgwood "American Bicentennial" china commemorative mug—Ages Past Antiques, 1030 Lexington Avenue. "Go with the Grain" wallpaper and "Jigsaw" wallpaper border (available through decorator)—Brunschwig & Fils, 979 Third Avenue.

Christmas Dinner

Table Setting (pages 78 and 79): Frank Lloyd Wright "Imperial" porcelain dinner plates—Tiffany & Co., 727 Fifth Avenue. Georg Jensen "Beaded" sterling flatware; silver-plate and glass candlesticks; Georg Jensen sterling compote—Royal Copenhagen Porcelain/Georg Jensen Silversmiths, 683 Madison Avenue. Lalique "Clos Vougeot" crystal water goblets, wineglasses, and decanter—Lalique, 680 Madison Avenue. Cotton napkins by Liz Wain—Liz Wain Designs, Inc., Tel. (212) 675-7953. "March Balloons" rayon, cotton, and polyester fabric (tablecloth); "Prairie Fern" wool fabric (window swag); "Prairie Mirage" cotton fabric (on armchair); "Coonley Weave" cotton fabric (child's rocking chair), all by Frank Lloyd Wright (available through decorator)—F. Schumacher and Company, 939 Third Avenue. Reproduction Greene & Greene mahogany table—The Vulpiani Workshop, 11 Field Court, Kingston, NY 12401, Tel. (914) 339-6146. Cherry barrel chairs by Frank Lloyd Wright (available through decorator)—Atelier International, Ltd., 30-20 Thomson Avenue, Long Island City, NY 11101, Tel. (718) 392-0300. Flowers—Castle & Pierpont, 1441 York Avenue.

Roast Prime Ribs of Beef with Shiitake Pan Gravy; Dried-Corn Puddings; Broccoli with Lemon and Red Pepper Flakes (page 80): Derby porcelain platter, circa 1825; English silver-plate carving set, circa 1880; English silver-plate sauceboat (one of a pair), circa 1875; English silver-plate ladle and tray, Sheffield, circa 1880—S. Wyler, Inc., 941 Lexington Avenue.

Walnut Spice Cake with Lemon Glaze; Frozen Cranberry Soufflé with Spun Sugar Cranberry Wreath (page 81): Cake plate—Tiffany & Co., 727 Fifth Avenue. Georg Jensen sterling goblets—Royal Copenhagen Porcelain/Georg Jensen Silversmiths, 683 Madison Avenue.

Brunch on Christmas Day

Scalloped Potato, Cheddar, and Chive Pie; Baked Irish Bacon with Kumquat Glaze; Red and Green Endive and Walnut Salad; Cranberry Apple Cocktails (pages 82 and 83): "Napoleon Ivy" dinner plates and platter by Wedgwood; "Alana" crystal wineglasses by Waterford—The Waterford/Wedgwood Store, 713 Madison Avenue. Cherry napkin rings; iron pie rack—Wolfman • Gold & Good Company, 116 Greene Street. Topiary—Zezé, 398 East 52nd Street. "Oatlands Tapestry" cotton fabric (on table) and "Cerise Woven Texture" cotton and viscose fabric (curtains), both available through decorator—Brunschwig & Fils, Inc., 979 Third Avenue. Paper-white narcissus in planter—Zona, 97 Greene Street.

A Recipe Compendium

Lemon Gem Muffins; Ham and Egg Biscuit Pizzas; Aquavit Bloody Marys; Papaya in Cinnamon Syrup (page 84): See credits for A Spring Brunch above. Lavender; wheat in flowerpot—Ségriès à Solanée, 866 Lexington Avenue.

A Northern Buffet alla Rustica

Fritto di Calamari con Salsa Piccante di Pomodori; Crostini di Fegato di Pollo; Insalata di Fagioli Bianchi e Tonno; Prosciutto, Taleggio, e Melone; Focaccia alla Salvia e Gorgonzola (pages 268 and 269): Square plates; pitcher; straw baskets; tablecloth—Bergdorf Goodman, 745 Fifth Avenue. Glasses; napkins—Pottery Barn, 117 E. 59th Street. Round bowls—Dean & DeLuca, 560 Broadway. Wine bottle—Zona, 97 Greene Street.

Dinner alla Romana

Carciofi alla Romana (page 276): Site Corot salad plate by Bill Goldsmith—Avventura, 463 Amsterdam Avenue. "Legend" sterling flatware—Fortunoff, 681 Fifth Avenue.

Fettuccine al Burro: (page 276): Pasta platter—Barneys New York, Seventh Avenue and 17th Street.

Pollo alla Diavola; Broccoli all'Aglio; Peperoni alla Griglia (page 277): Fornasetti screen and chair (available through decorators)—Norton Blumenthal, 979 Third Avenue. Site Corot dinner plates by Bill Goldsmith; Smyers glasses; glass urn—Avventura, 463 Amsterdam Avenue. "Legend" sterling flatware—Fortunoff, 681 Fifth Avenue. Napkins by Anichini—(800) 553-5309. Candlesticks—Barneys New York, Seventh Avenue and 17th Street. Hand-painted background by Richard Pellicci, Tel. (212) 988-4365 (by appointment only).

Southern Sunday Lunch in Famiglia

Ziti al Forno con Melanzane, Pomodori, e Formaggi (page 284): Rede Guzzini oval baker—Marel Gift Shop, Great Neck, New York. Deruta salad plates and cachepot—Avventura, 463 Amsterdam Avenue. "Verona" sterling flatware—Fortunoff, 681 Fifth Avenue. Italian wine glasses by Bill Goldsmith—Goldsmith Corot Inc., (212) 779-3254.

Cassata (page 285): Sterling tray—S. Wyler, 941 Lexington Avenue.

Back Jacket

Lunch on the Lawn: See credits for Lunch on the Lawn above.

If you are not already a subscriber to *Gourmet* Magazine and would be interested in subscribing, please call *Gourmet*'s toll-free number, 1-800-365-2454.